ARCHITECTURE HISTORY AND THEORY IN REVERSE

This book looks at architecture history in reverse, in order to follow chains of precedents back through time to see how ideas alter the course of civilization in general and the discipline of architecture in particular. Part I begins with present-day attitudes about architecture and traces them back to seminal ideas from the beginning of the twentieth century. Part II examines how pre-twentieth-century societies designed and understood architecture, how they strove to create communal physical languages, and how their disagreements set the stage for our information age practices. *Architecture History and Theory in Reverse* includes 45 black-and-white images and will be useful to students of architecture and literature.

Jassen Callender is an Associate Professor of Architecture and the Director of Mississippi State University's Jackson Center, in Jackson, Mississippi, USA.

"In an uneasy age, where holding the 'centre' seems frighteningly unlikely, this carefully reasoned book argues that our most salient architectural problem is the estrangement of modern buildings from those who see and occupy them. A challenging read, it both sprawls out over and mines deep into difficult writings. Yet it remains accessible due to lucid prose, the construction of chapters to both cogently stand alone and operate serially, and its convincing intertwining of architectural examples with philosophical arguments."

Michael Fazio, Emeritus Professor of Architecture,
Mississippi State University, USA

ARCHITECTURE HISTORY AND THEORY IN REVERSE

From an Information Age to Eras of Meaning

Jassen Callender

NEW YORK AND LONDON

First published 2018
by Routledge
711 Third Avenue, New York, NY 10017

and by Routledge
2 Park Square, Milton Park, Abingdon, Oxon OX14 4RN

Routledge is an imprint of the Taylor & Francis Group, an informa business

© 2018 Taylor & Francis

The right of Jassen Callender to be identified as author of this work has been asserted by him in accordance with sections 77 and 78 of the Copyright, Designs and Patents Act 1988.

All rights reserved. No part of this book may be reprinted or reproduced or utilised in any form or by any electronic, mechanical, or other means, now known or hereafter invented, including photocopying and recording, or in any information storage or retrieval system, without permission in writing from the publishers.

Trademark notice: Product or corporate names may be trademarks or registered trademarks, and are used only for identification and explanation without intent to infringe.

Library of Congress Cataloguing in Publication Data
Names: Callender, Jassen, author.
Title: Architecture history and theory in reverse : from an information age to eras of meaning / Jassen Callender.
Description: New York : Routledge, 2017. | Includes bibliographical references and index.
Identifiers: LCCN 2016055461 | ISBN 9781138958173 (hb : alk. paper) | ISBN 9781138958197 (pb : alk. paper) | ISBN 9781315661315 (ebook)
Subjects: LCSH: Architecture--Philosophy. | Architecture--History.
Classification: LCC NA2500 .C3127 2017 | DDC 720.1--dc23
LC record available at https://lccn.loc.gov/2016055461

ISBN: 978-1-138-95817-3 (hbk)
ISBN: 978-1-138-95819-7 (pbk)
ISBN: 978-1-315-66131-5 (ebk)

Typeset in Bembo
by Saxon Graphics Ltd, Derby

 Printed in the United Kingdom by Henry Ling Limited

CONTENTS

List of Figures	*vii*
Preface	*ix*
Acknowledgments	*xi*
Introduction	xiii
Epilogue: Today, in the Beginning …	1

PART I
Architecture in an Information Age — **5**

1	Twenty-First-Century Trajectories	7
2	Modernity's Legacy in a New Millennium	19
3	A Postmodern Profession, Circa 1991	31
4	Formal or Phenomenological: A Feud over Information	39
5	Deconstruction, Irony, the Pompidou, and the *São Pedro*	52
6	Mies van der Rohe in Chicago	67
7	Language Games	80
8	Loos and the Ascension of Space in the Marketplace	90

vi Contents

Interlude: The Information Reformation, or This Killed That   101

PART II
Architecture in Eras of Meaning   **109**

9 16 June 1904: *Ulysses* and *The Uncanny*   111

10 Marx, Meaning, and Matter   122

11 Exchange and Evolution   134

12 In What Style? Epistemes and Monsters   146

13 The *Précis* and the Paternity of Perception   161

14 De Sade versus Descartes: Competing Conceptions of Language   175

15 The Tense of Abstract Nouns   187

16 Vitruvian Cycles 1: Representations Against Space   202

17 Vitruvian Cycles 2: Physical Language and Shared Experience   211

Prologue: Babel…   223

Further Reading   *234*
Image Credits   *239*
Index   *241*

FIGURES

0.1	The fourfold structure of language	xix
1.0	Markthal, Rotterdam, ceiling	5
1.1	Markthal, Rotterdam, MVRDV Architects	8
1.2	Markthal, Rotterdam, MVRDV Architects	9
2.1	Public Library, Seattle, OMA Architects	22
2.2	Public Library, Seattle, OMA Architects	23
2.3	The structure of communication	28
4.1	Museo di Castelvecchio (exterior), Verona, Carlo Scarpa architect	40
4.2	Museo di Castelvecchio (detail), Verona, Carlo Scarpa architect	40
4.3	Memorial to the Murdered Jews of Europe, Berlin, Peter Eisenman architect	46
4.4	Therme Vals, Graubünden, Peter Zumthor architect	48
5.1	Parc de la Villette, Paris, Bernard Tschumi architect	54
5.2	Pompidou Centre (façade), Paris, Renzo Piano and Richard Rogers architects	60
5.3	Pompidou Centre (corner), Paris, Renzo Piano and Richard Rogers architects	61
6.1	Chicago Federal Center, Chicago, Ludwig Mies van der Rohe architect	69
6.2	Chicago Federal Center, Chicago, Ludwig Mies van der Rohe architect	71
6.3	Shannon's diagram of communication	75
7.1	Casa Batlló, Barcelona, Antoni Gaudí architect	86
8.1	(a) Section of Loos' Lido villa; (b) Theo van Doesburg's 1923 composition of horizontal and vertical planes	92
9.0	Pantheon Dome	109

viii Figures

9.1	Saint John's Abbey Church, Collegeville, MN, Marcel Breuer architect	117
9.2	Het Schip, Amsterdam, Michel de Klerk architect	118
9.3	Het Schip, Amsterdam, Michel de Klerk architect	119
9.4	Het Schip (detail), Amsterdam, Michel de Klerk architect	120
10.1	Strata of physical language (based on Foucault)	125
10.2	Piazza d'Italia, New Orleans, Charles Moore architect	127
10.3	Lincoln's Inn Fields home and museum, London, Sir John Soane architect	127
10.4	Gucci	128
11.1	Value Transmission, taking translation into account	140
11.2	Value Transmission, maker's perspective	142
11.3	Value Transmission, perceiver's perspective	143
12.1	Zwinger, Dresden, Matthaeus Daniel Pöppelmann architect	154
12.2	Zwinger (detail), Dresden, Matthaeus Daniel Pöppelmann architect	155
12.3	Flying buttress	157
13.1	St. Mark's Basilica, Venice, Domenico I Contarini architect	168
13.2	The Birth of Perception, version 1	171
13.3	The Birth of Perception, version 2	171
15.1	Seeing versus knowing	188
15.2	Naming	189
15.3	The time of language	194
15.4	Santa Maria Novella, Florence, Leon Battista Alberti architect	195
15.5	Field of all possible grammars	197
16.1	Pantheon (interior), Rome	208
17.1	Mosque-Cathedral of Córdoba	219
18.1	Margaret's Grocery, Vicksburg, Mississippi, Reverend H.D. Dennis	232

PREFACE

People and disciplines are remade by technology. Industrialization, to paraphrase Marx, creates not only objects, but subjects for those objects. Technology, at its best, assists humanity in attaining civilization's promise; at its worst, outpacing human evolution, it is cited as the cause of feelings of alienation, depression, and fright. Those who resist technology are said to exhibit peculiar anxieties or to experience the uncanny. They are celebrated as noble humanists fighting to protect culture from ill-advised change or derided as backward luddites who give up claims to modernity and its promise.

These tropes of western civilization are so often repeated in so many contexts that their validity is more or less assumed. Accepted as true, the tropes of technology function as baseline premises in arguments to explain a host of cultural shifts: guns radically altered notions of politics and power; printing presses homogenized cultures by making previously isolated or foreign points of view ubiquitous; steam engines redefined our sense of distance and time; artificial light diminished our reliance on the cycles of nature; and computers, civilization's late twentieth-century savior and oppressor, promise instant connectivity and threaten the dissolution of place, of roots, of meaning.

Similar tropes are active in the disciplines of architecture, architectural history, and its theory. Attitudes toward these broadly range from positive or utopian to dystopian pessimism. And, as with the examples cited above, their validity appears self-evident. Improvements in steel and elevators are cited to explain the rise of skyscrapers – and skyscrapers the rise of world cities – just as the emergence of digital parametric design and building information modeling (BIM) systems are used to justify the new shapes and construction techniques of much contemporary architecture. Negatively conceived, changes in architectural technologies are freighted with the blame for consumerism and modern existential crises. This line of critique was given prominence by Victor Hugo, developed as a challenge to authentic

x Preface

dwelling by Martin Heidegger, and extended to contemporary architecture most notably by Manfredo Tafuri, Dalibor Vesely, and Alberto Pérez-Gómez, among many others. From the initial charge of "this will kill that" to more recent diagnoses of "the malaise from which architecture suffers,"[1] the tropes of technological change serve as the usual suspects for every perceived threat to meaning.

The discipline does seem adrift, unappreciated and without aspiration. And yet, technology serves merely as a scapegoat. That is not to say that changes in technology have not had a profound impact on our lives; we undoubtedly appear as new subjects in the light of new objects, as Marx suggested. But the source of the discipline's perceived change does not lie in specific technologies and it lies deeper than the processes of production and commodification of the well-worn myths. Contrary to popular premises and conclusions, the "crisis" of modern architecture arises not from technology or the malaise of technological alienation, but from the divergence of information from meaning and the frantic search for information that might substitute for meaning. This process was, no doubt, accelerated by the Industrial Revolution but its roots are at least as old as the story of Babel.

Note

1   The context of the quote below illuminates explicitly the blame laid at the feet of technology and, more broadly, scientific progress:

> In fact, the malaise from which architecture suffers today can be traced to the collusion between architecture and its use of geometry and number as it developed in the early modern period. An analysis of the architectural intentions of the seventeenth and eighteenth centuries in relation to the changing world view ushered in by Galilean science and Newton's natural philosophy is necessary before we can understand the dilemmas still confronted by architects. Such an analysis becomes particularly significant in light of the prevalent obsession with mathematical certainty in its various forms: design methodologies, typologies, linguistic rules of formalism, any sort of explicit or disguised functionalism. Contemporary architects, who encounter a proliferation of these forms whenever they make design decisions, find it difficult to reconcile mathematics' demands for invariance (the *mathemata*) with their conception of architecture as an art rather than a science.
>
> (Alberto Pérez-Gómez, *Architecture and the Crisis of Modern Science*, Cambridge, MA: MIT Press, 1985, 3–4)

ACKNOWLEDGMENTS

My willingness to challenge received wisdom and seek alternatives has been nourished by many remarkable people. While it is customary to distinguish teachers from colleagues, separate co-workers from friends, and to categorize mentors by specific area of influence, it would be a betrayal of the rich interdisciplinary attitude these people have fostered to do so. A history of interactions with friends, teachers, mentors, colleagues, and students coalesce in the book that follows. My deepest appreciation to: Zulaikha Ayub, Chuck Barlow, David Buege, Annie Coggan, Caleb Crawford, Joseph Dickey, Burak Erdim, Mark Farlow, Michael Fazio, David Feinberg, Seema Goel, Whitney Grant, Juan Heredia, Rita Hinton, Diane Katsiaficas, Mukesh Kumar, Rachel McCann, Susan Melsop, Chris Monson, Clarence Morgan, David M. Morris, Behzad Nakhjavan, Bryan Norwood, Scott Penman, John Poros, Chris Risher, Thomas Rose, Mark Vaughan, and Kayce Williford. It is an understatement, but nevertheless true and heartfelt, to note that I have received more in these interactions than I could ever hope to return.

Despite the fact that my outlook on architecture as a practice, as a discipline subject to history, and as a topic worthy of theorization has been shaped by many, a few people deserve to be singled out relative to the work that follows. David C. Lewis, a teacher who became a close friend and colleague, read at least one draft of every chapter. His careful readings and extensive comments, his occasional doubts and frequent encouragements improved the resulting work immeasurably and kept the author's self-doubts below the threshold of paralysis. My thanks to the administrators of Mississippi State University's College of Architecture, Art, and Design. Jim West, Dean, and Michael Berk, Director of the School of Architecture, provided much-needed release time in the final semester of writing, without which the combination of teaching and administrative responsibilities would have jeopardized the completion of the text. I also want to thank the staff at Routledge, particularly editors Wendy Fuller and Trudy Varcianna, for guiding

xii Acknowledgments

the book and its author so gently through a process previously unknown to him. No doubt some readers will discover stylistic shortcomings and errors of fact. For these I bear sole responsibility.

Finally, I must acknowledge Stacy Callender for her support and loving encouragement. Beyond information, she helped me find meaning.

INTRODUCTION

Over the course of months and days culminating in the chapters that follow, I frequently was asked just what the book was about. A rote reply evolved along the lines of "it addresses the impact of the emergence of information theory on architecture theory and practice." I knew then, as now, this was not accurate. It serves, at best, as shorthand for a much broader and more significant set of concerns. The pages that follow are about architectural language. About a discipline witnessing the popular success of novels and films and wishing that it too could communicate something, anything, quite so easily.

While Victor Hugo's eloquent formulation of this dilemma dates to 1831, this set of concerns has operated in the background of architecture for centuries and, yet, are reemerging. The June 2016 edition of the *Journal of the Society of Architectural Historians* leads with an essay entitled "Architectural History: the turn from culture to media." The essay addresses "mediality" and the notion that "as a medium – that is, *a channel of transmission* – architecture can make visible an intermedial dynamic of material, technical, and social consequence."[1] In other words, architecture functions as an information infrastructure. A year earlier, an essay in the *Journal of Architectural Education (JAE)* began with the claim: "The disciplinary definition of architecture over the last half-millennium has run parallel to the history of its print culture." Noting the legacy of canonical books such as *Vers une Architecture, Œuvre Complète, Complexity and Contradiction, Learning from Las Vegas, Delirious New York* and *S, M, L, XL,* the author examines ways in which publishing and building have co-evolved and considered as alternate modes of architectural practice.[2] That issue of *JAE* and its bold assertion is dedicated to Koolhaas' *S, M, L, XL.* Throughout the issue, architecture's language function and the architect's "author-function" are assumed and presented as essential aspects of the discipline.

Such assumptions are not confined to journals. They are active in every studio critique, implied in every statement concerning architectural meaning, and evidenced

xiv Introduction

in every question of the type: "How will someone understand this building?" Considered this way, architectural language is central to the teaching, practice, and experience of this discipline. These assumptions, however, beg significant questions. Why do we conceive architecture as a language? Because numerous theorists have studied it as one? Does conceiving architecture as a language make it more accessible? Less? What is an architectural language? Does it have the same purpose as a written language? Should it function like one? These are complex, perhaps unanswerable, questions but the failure to ask and at least ponder the conclusions leaves much of contemporary architecture's critical apparatus resting on an underdeveloped foundation.

Approached stylistically, architectural elements are treated analogically as parts of speech and its systems of organizations as grammars. Classical western architecture, for example, is almost always rendered in these terms. While there is some utility in approaching architecture in this way, the evolution of language, as analyzed by Leibniz, Humboldt, Cassirer, among others, is driven by two complexly interrelated dualisms: first, of purpose, and, second, of value. Both elude stylistic analogies, or at least any that have so far been proposed. Purpose marks the temporal difference between transmission and storage, wherein language serves as either an active mechanism of transmission or as inactive mechanism of storage. This division is absolute, however, a given object's or statement's status is not fixed. Stored information becomes active the moment it is accessed. Transmitted information joins the detritus of inactive stored content when it is no longer deemed relevant.

Values form a second dualism: the distinction between information and meaning. This is not a gradated difference in degree or a continuum from meaningless to meaningful information. The categories are distinct. Information may be useful and even necessary for the propagation of life without being deemed meaningful by any person. Meaning is what is at stake to the recipient of the information, independent of that information's actionable utility. Stated differently, information may be meaningful or meaningless, and meaning may be informative or not, but it is best not to confuse the two.

These purposes and values are often muddled in everyday usage – the number of factoids we 'like' on social media is truly astounding. However, from the writings of the earliest theologians onward, this double or four-fold dualism has plagued linguists and philosophers who have, in varying ways, worked to distinguish these functions. This process made its greatest advance in the first half of the twentieth century. Claude Shannon's groundbreaking *The Mathematical Theory of Communication* treated information transmission, clarity, and entropy as discrete variables independent of content or meaning and, in the process, severed the bond of information and meaning.[3] And if it can be claimed that our information age has had an impact on our making and understanding of architecture, that impact derives from the information/meaning split.

Rudiments of Communication

In classic information theory, communication is diagramed as five essential elements. These are: (1) the source possessing content to convey; (2) the transmitter;

(3) the channel or space through which the signal moves; (4) the receiver; and (5) the destination to whom or which content is conveyed. These classic components – in addition to noise, which is an element ubiquitous but external to communication proper – constitute the totality of information transmission and hold true whether the topic is talk radio, print journalism, or architecture.

Successful communication demands capacity for translation between the levels of transmission and reception. In talk radio, this entails digital processes of encoding and decoding at each end of the signal. In print journalism, this involves writers and readers sharing a common language. What is shared between the ordering systems embedded in a building and the sensory apparatus of the users or occupants of that building, however, is not as easy to identify nor as easily understood. This difficulty is due, in part, to the two levels of proximity through which architectural communication is enacted. At the level of direct engagement, there are functions, conflicts, and meanings; lurking behind this level of immediacy, there are norms, rules, and systems.

To understand both levels of proximity and how each applies to the practices and discourses of architecture, it is useful to observe how the terms of each mirror the other. First, the domain of concerns encapsulated by physics and technology grants to architecture the impression that it is a discipline of *functions* (direct, physical engagement) given to categorization through *norms* (indirect, conceptual engagement). Second, the domain of societal concerns grounds architecture in human wants and emotions; *conflicts* (direct) arise between those concerns and the practicalities of budgets and base survival; and these conflicts find resolution only in a body of *rules* (indirect). Third, the domain of aesthetics converts physical constructions into markers or *media* (direct); and these media cohere into *systems* of signs (indirect) legible to and sharable by the initiated.

Contemporary architectural discourse has diminished the value of the indirect term in each of these pairs (norms, rules, and systems). The indirect concerns are conceptualized as reductions of or limits to possibilities, branded as aspects of an outdated, outmoded metaphysical project that imposes hierarchies and asserts a particular power structure to the detriment of humanity at large. Norms, rules, and systems of indirect engagement are seen by late information age readers as vestiges of old bureaucracies or dead myth traditions. In late media, freedom – or at least the image of freedom from norms, rules, and systems – is marketed above all else. As a result, functions, conflicts, and media are privileged. This privileging has resulted, not surprisingly, in architectures of floating, semblances of freedom and, in doing so, created the strange disjunction between transmitter and receiver.

In this acknowledgment, the consequences of abandoning myths and metaphors of indirect concerns become evident: functions, conflicts, and meanings are all forms of representation referring to and reliant upon existing norms, rules, and systems.[4] This abandonment, in turn, produces three far more profound consequences:

1. Architectural discourse is oblivious to its existence – and, more importantly, architecture's existence – as representation. As a result, functions, conflicts,

xvi Introduction

and meanings are treated as self-sufficient ends-in-themselves – as truths. Projects that address functions deemed necessary, resolve conflicts deemed important, and reference local meanings deemed significant are acknowledged for these efforts; and, in all fairness, without acknowledging that other levels of concern are both possible and necessary to ground shared experience, there is no other way to evaluate works of architecture. This consequence, written as a formula becomes:

$$\text{Architecture} = \text{what you see}$$

2.   Architectural discourse, not fully aware of its own internal connection to architectural norms/rules/systems, studies representation as additive and representation's content as exterior to architecture. As a result, architecture is deprived of those representations that allow functions, conflicts, and meanings to expand beyond the bounds of a discrete project brief, a given site, and a particular subculture – as inherent aspects of architecture itself. Written as a formula:

$$\text{Architecture} \neq \text{critical inquiry of architectural metaphor or myth}$$

3.   When attempts are made to connect architectural discourse to other bodies of knowledge – or, simply to the body – the middle terms of architectural norms, rules, and systems are excluded in the belief that this abridgement provides architecture with a more direct relation to issues that (presumably) matter. That is:

$$\text{Architecture} = x,$$

where x is defined by religion, politics, philosophy, cultural studies, physiology, "the body in space," among others. It is assumed that this excluded middle of norms, rules, and systems is simply a gratuitous link in a more essential transition. Although a link, it is necessary one. Without this middle ground of architectural tradition, architecture is either independent of all other bodies of knowledge and bodies *per se* (therefore, free-floating and incommunicative) or merely a derivative subset of some other body of knowledge (religion, politics, philosophy, cultural studies, physiology, "the body in space," etc.) with no communicative potential or cultural role of its own. Neither position is tenable.

History and Vision

What really explains the disconnect between the direct and indirect levels of engagement? So much information age theory remains biblical. Unconsciously, of course, given the ostensibly secular tenor of our overt discourse, Judeo-Christian influence is there in the very structure of our most entrenched epistemes. The Hebraic Scripture's prohibitions on uttering the name of God and making graven images, famously inscribed in the Ten Commandments, are rooted in the separation of God-as-Voice and man-as-body. One interpretation of these prohibitions is theological and disciplinary in the sense of protecting the authority of a discipline (Divine Right in the case of religions): by uttering God's name for personal use or attempting to emulate Him in physical form or both, humans infringe God's position as Creator, as Giver of meaning. It is an act of heresy: deemed wrong for eschatological reasons and punishable in ultimate terms. Another interpretation is pragmatic. These laws are understood to preserve our future reward within a discipline (Heaven in Christianity): to trespass is to forfeit an inheritance.

This prohibition remains in force, though unstated, in architectural discourse as it does in most facets of western culture. Both interpretations linger, reiterated in architectural phenomenology's rejection of shared ideational or linguistic content (such content is not the right of Gods but reserved for the Husserlian experiencing subject and extraordinary architects) and in postmodernism's attacks on the hegemony of vision (of vision as an imposition of divine-like authority by an architect which infringe rewards promised to the lay public). The tone remains Scriptural. But there is an information age shift in whose authority is being protected: the mystical aura of divine authorship, authority, and voice attributed in the Bible solely to God is, in architectural phenomenology and postmodernism-at-large, conferred upon the freedom and majesty of the individual. In other words, the prohibition on giving name through physical language has shifted from the duty to protect the sovereignty of one deity to protecting the private fantasies of billions.

All of this has implications for how we understand experience. The commonsense view is that experience is just a peculiar form of naming; it is the self-narration of events through which *time* and even *seeing* emerge. The difference between mere sensing of photons, the physiological process called *vision*, and *seeing* lies in a conceptual act which organizes the former into useful or beautiful or disturbing packets of information by which we navigate, plan, think, speculate – dare I say 'enjoy' – the world. Even profound moments of awe emerge through this narrativization in time. Against the more commonsensical view, the notion that language impedes sensory experience and perception took root – particularly in architectural phenomenology circles. This counter-belief assumes the existence of a non-temporal transaction between observer and observed or, in phenomenology's preferred terms, self and Other. As a result, a peculiar blend emerges of adoration for incommunicative experience and belief that it is the architect's responsibility to coordinate and even dictate feelings to a building's inhabitants. It is a powerful one-two combination, as if God is still meting out his Babel punishment for the pursuit of vision and knowledge. While the latter blow is no doubt troubling, deeply so, I call attention to the anti-authoritarian prohibition on making things for the eye and, through the eye, for the mind.

The disavowed commonsensical notion of experience has profound though hidden implications for the making and experience of architecture. To the extent that nomination (the act of naming) creates the visible world (seeing), then the reading of architectural language precedes its own perception in the world, or emerges with it and frames the sense of sight. Ideational structures, thus understood,

xviii Introduction

prod language and ground meaningful perception, which is to say, ideational structures ground perception.

This sheds some light on problems of information age architectural history. An anti-authoritarian agenda works in the direction of uncertainty; it is hostile to shared meaning and particularly the accumulation of meaning over time. The world, in this view, is raw information left for each to decipher according to his or her leanings. Individual stakes over those of a society or culture.

But myths matter. The greatest works of the phenomenological tradition acknowledge and borrow liberally from the accumulated history of known and knowable forms: Steven Holl's St. Ignatius in Seattle or Zumthor's Therme Vals (which harkens back to Roman baths in plan if not in section). No doubt these buildings operate at an immediate, visceral level. Self and Other. But, arguably, the power of these and most other buildings that come to be part of the perpetually accumulating myth of architectural history operate first and foremost through the eye and mind; through allusion and participation; through vision mixed with history in the form of names. This is not only necessary, given the commonsense view of experience, but ultimately a good.

Grounds for Discourse

The four-fold nature of language remains unexplored in architectural circles. Only surface faults of this deeper structure have been studied and described as if causal in their own right: formalism vs. phenomenology, conceptualism vs. sensuality, instrumentalities vs. poetics, science vs. art, productivity vs. creativity, etc. Mistaking such descriptions as causes is, at best, a distraction; at worst, it thwarts understanding of what is often conceived – perhaps as a result of the misattribution – as a crisis.

This book addresses the four-fold structure of language by returning to a commonsense view of experience (Figure 0.1). In lieu of styles or geographies, in lieu of manifestos and monographs, it analyzes language by following history backward. It is an attempt to do for architectural discourse what Hannah Arendt accomplished in *The Human Condition* and Foucault did for scientific discourse and the emergence of "man" in *The Order of Things*: to trace the linkages and faults of information, the bridges and ruptures in meaning, that are glossed by the action of time into a smooth evolution of architectural thought and language.[5] In *Architecture History and Theory in Reverse* I attempt to answer two broad disciplinary questions regarding the evolution of architectural language.

The first is the broadest and perhaps most important: given the discipline's development of more – and ever more sophisticated – theoretical frameworks, what explains the anecdotal but deepening consensus that architecture no longer serves its traditional role as a datum for communal meaning? There is no short answer to this question. To gain a foothold, this book revisits the transition from Classicism through Romanticism and Modernism to postmodernism and reveals the latter's ironies and post-critical stances as merely the most recent in a long series of evasions of norms, rules, and systems.

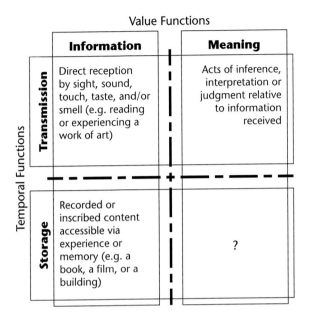

FIGURE 0.1 The four-fold structure of language

The second broad question examines the widely held belief that linguistic and sensual forms of engagement are separate and distinct in kind. Why do formalists and phenomenologists alike believe that "seeing is forgetting the name of the thing one sees"? This is a question that reappears throughout the history of architecture in various guises. The assumption that seeing precedes saying is a new form of the old belief that psychology is the foundation of sociology or, to say the same thing a little differently, that the nature of individuals explains culture; it presumes a naïve flow of time in which meaning, historical traditions, and other forms of social content are appliqués in relation to the 'real' lived experiences of individuals. At its most extreme, this belief castigates language as an enemy of experience. Even in more reserved form, it promotes the idea that sensual content is acquired first and is therefore more natural, or more essential to humanity. It is deeply problematic. But it explains, as I will demonstrate, why information has gained prominence over meaning.

Structure of the Book

This book is presented in two sections. Part I, "Architecture in an Information Age," begins with media, the present-day cynicism regarding architecture as a physical analog for meaning, and the institutionalization of the profession. It traces this cynicism back to growing fascination with both language games and "space" in the first decades of the twentieth century. Part II, "Architecture in Eras of Meaning," probes earlier formulations of language, attempts to recoup communally held aspects of architectural language and experience, and traces the techniques by

xx Introduction

which such architecture was understood. An epilogue, interlude, and prologue frame the two parts of the book. These are written as first-person accounts, each more fictional as time recedes, to immerse the reader in the historical narrative.

Why begin in the present? The history of any discipline can be analyzed in numerous ways. In chronological terms, these can be lumped into three general approaches. The traditional format is linear. It begins with the earliest people, ideas, and events in the period of interest and proceeds through ebbs and flows to the most recent people, ideas, and events – demonstrating, invariably, that some teleological aim lurks in the successive links of time or, in the hands of a less strident researcher, that there is a relationship between early and late ideas that deserves further study or, most often, some composite of these two. The second most popular and least chronological approach is topical. People, ideas, and events of various periods and places are linked, compared, and contrasted to highlight similarities and differences in societies, cultures, and geographies that are hidden by normalizing reference to a given context of time. The third, and perhaps least utilized, is reverse chronology or backward history; this approach begins with existing conditions and seeks antecedents in earlier people, ideas, and events. Following chains of precedents back through time allows discovery of sideways shifts and unbridgeable gaps that signify major ruptures in the standard story of civilization.

While each approach poses serious limitations and fosters unique opportunities, reverse chronology has two marked advantages. First, it highlights the natural perspective from which the past is viewed: history is always read in the present or, as Benedetto Croce famously said, "all history is contemporary history."[6] Second, by working backward from more or less known, or at least knowable, information, the conclusions sought are *out there*, unpredictable, in the obscure and relatively unknown territory at the far end of human time in the emergence of languages. History is discovered, not presupposed.

Part I, "Architecture in an Information Age," traces the most recent and influential branches of western architectural language to common roots. Despite the fact that these branches are varied and entwined, it is possible to track their co-evolution backward from twenty-first-century trajectories (Chapters 1 and 2), through a period of contested identities in the last decades of the twentieth century (Chapters 3–5), to their formation in the early years of the century in a rather straightforward sequence (Chapters 6–8). The intellectual movements that preceded twentieth-century Modernism are less clearly bounded by periods or dates. Part II, "Architecture in Eras of Meaning," therefore outlines the motives and essential theorists that fostered Modernity (Chapters 9–11), traces these motives to sources in the Romantic diversification of languages (Chapters 12–14), and attempts to uncover the roots of these migrations in Classical theories (Chapters 15–17). While the analysis provided here follows these broad ideological shifts along an arc that remains true to their place in the evolution of language and architecture, each ideology overlaps with the others, inflects them, and persists into the present. As a result, while each idea is introduced in an order that roughly approximates its proper location, Part II is less strictly chronological and more

Introduction **xxi**

topical than Part I. As a further result of this more topical focus, Part II draws upon literary, cinematic, and architectural sources ranging from classical to contemporary. In telling the story in this way, it is my hope that the communicative disorders of architecture across time are made visible, nameable, and known.

Admittedly, this is but one possible re-telling of architecture's history in reverse. The lineage cannot be traced with certainty or reconstructed in great detail. Too much is lost to time or obscured by the transfigurations of earlier commentaries. Yet, even were this not the case, this genealogy aims less to explain the seemingly random appearances of meaning strewn across history than to expose the disciplinary results that a focus on information begets.

Notes

1 Mary Louise Lobsinger, "Architectural History: the turn from culture to media," *Journal of the Society of Architectural Historians* 75(2) (2016): 135–139. Quoted text is from p. 136. Italics added.
2 Michael Kubo, "Architecture's Print Culture," *Journal of Architectural Education* 69(2) (2015): 207–211.
3 Claude E. Shannon, *The Mathematical Theory of Communication*, Introduction by Warren Weaver (Urbana, IL: University of Illinois Press, 1949).
4 Norms, rules, and systems, in turn, are also representations but at a different level and in reference to another series of representations or ground. Written in the form of a diagram, discourse is:

> Level 1 (function, conflict or meaning) $\rightarrow$ level 2 (norm, rule or system) $\rightarrow x$

Unfortunately, no one likes this formulation. Late media's cynicism regarding the existence of grounds (x) is one of the reasons that indirect engagement (level 2) has fallen out of critical favor – simply, why pursue an objective when the existence of that objective has been denied as mythological or retrograde in advance?
5 Hannah Arendt, *The Human Condition*, 2nd edn, Introduction by Margaret Canovan (Chicago: University of Chicago Press, [1958] 1998); Michel Foucault, *The Order of Things: an archaeology of the human sciences* (New York: Vintage Books, 1994).
6 George Allan, "Croce and Whitehead on Concrescence," *Process Studies* 2(2) (1972): 95–111.

To see is to forget the name of the thing one sees.

(Attributed to Paul Valéry)

To share is to give names to the things we sense.

EPILOGUE

Today, in the Beginning ...

Each of us a multitude, we stand, sit, eat, and think in a world that appears fully formed; the result of a slow accumulation of culture in a single-minded push from anemic beginnings to the relatively complete present. Ours is history replete with momentary disruptions and small fissures but without break. The stage set of this production is stunning in its totality and thus all the more convincing. In my own experience, on this day, I stare forward at a white plaster wall on which hang two framed color photographs documenting, on the left, my home state's progress to mechanized agriculture, and, on the right, an abandoned rural building in the process of returning to nature as if an offering of human abundance. With a turn of my head I look out windows of this second floor office and see an urban intersection complete with cars and asphalt; lights, signs, landscaping, and sidewalks; people and multi-storied buildings, both recent and vintage. Filtered through a myth of human progress, the visual complexity of this scene suggests a long continuous co-evolution of people and artifacts: all this, in proud but unquestioning eyes, the inevitable outcome of the people we are and the nobility of our inherited intentions.

As is true of backdrops in a theatrical production, it is not difficult to discern the artificiality of the scene. Most of the objects just described are not very old. The plaster wall, color prints, and frames have existed fewer than fifteen years; the cars, in most cases, less than five; the asphalt, only as old as the last election; the landscaping varies but, aside from a few mature oaks, there are no deep roots under the vegetation and no ancient foundations beneath the street furniture; the people are primarily business age – mid-twenties to early sixties; and the buildings, despite great varieties in style and allusions to older traditions, were built no earlier than 1904. It would be fair to counter that the practices embodied by these things, their histories as forms, are much older. City planning predates the Bible, buildings predate cities, and, obviously, people predate buildings. But the issue of interest here is not the factual unspooling of things in time but the imagined lineage of

2 Epilogue: Today in the Beginning ...

ideas and intentions – specifically those surrounding the practice, or practices, of western architecture.

When I turn my head away from the windows and toward the bookshelf on the opposite wall, my eyes alight on titles equally suggestive of a unified tradition. There are works anthologizing architectural theory by historical period – these include A. Krista Sykes' *Constructing a New Agenda: architectural theory, 1993–2009* (2010), Kate Nesbitt's *Theorizing a New Agenda for Architecture: an anthology of architectural theory, 1965–1995* (1996), and Ulrich Conrads' *Programs and Manifestoes on 20th-Century Architecture* (1964). Then there are the ubiquitous historical surveys – Sir Banister Fletcher's *A History of Architecture* (1896; 20th edition, 1996), Nikolaus Pevsner's *An Outline of European Architecture* (1942), and, more recently, Michael Fazio, Marian Moffett, and Lawrence Wodehouse's *A World History of Architecture* (2008) – texts that presume a tradition or lineage of which there can be a history or histories.

The existence of an architectural tradition and the appropriateness of its analysis and dissemination by written language are simply assumed. Architecture is not unique in this regard. As a discipline, it participates in the illusory totalizing project common to other aspects of culture. Music and sculpture, science and medicine, politics and religion are all represented in contemporary society as legitimate descendants of earlier human practices. Architecture differs primarily in its success: the general public assumes that architects of ten centuries ago, this past century, and those of today are engaged in essentially the same activities for similar ends, little round glasses and black garb not withstanding. Despite the fact that its practices appear to be as old as ruins discovered by archaeologists and writing fragments found in ancient myths and fables, architects' attitudes, beliefs, and roles (both self-appointed and those assigned by the discipline, the profession, and the community) are of recent origin and, if not altogether free of deep history, exist in a form with few traits in common with those of architects' supposed historical predecessors – the master builders.

When differences between present and past are noted, they are explained away. Today architecture is often described as pluralistic: a loose collection of varied solitary aims resulting in a series of minor architectures built for their own expression.[1] This description conceals as much as it reveals. It implies that changes in the built environment over the past few decades signify an evolution in design freedom marching in lockstep with hard-won progress in individual freedoms. In other words, it explains the differences between buildings of the present and those of the past by appeal to a moral teleology that stands outside architecture proper. I argue instead that there has been an inherent shift in architecture's recent past – one so thorough as to constitute two architectures, perhaps – which lies between architecture conceived primarily as a form of social communication in pre-modern times and architecture imagined as meaning-neutral vessels for the appending of private thoughts and wish fulfillment in Modernism and after. From this perspective, the apparent comprehensiveness of the scene within this office, inside the invented histories in the books on my shelf, and inscribed in artifacts outside the windows, masks a rift between the history of forms and the history of intentions – between made and maker – and the potential for communication of meaning is both laid open and diminished.

It is reasonable to ask why this rift matters. The problem is not with the loss of tradition or changes in style. That the making subject, "the architect," and the made object, "architecture," do not share a single history or, arguably, a common trajectory but nevertheless appear to us today coalesced in a single discipline is, in most regards, unproblematic. To suspect that the designers of tables, walls, streets, and buildings in earlier civilizations held very different attitudes toward their work or its use does not hamper appropriation of this table or diminish the utility of that wall or negatively impact the lives of the drivers and pedestrians and bench-sitters outside. That we occupy and make use of the things that come down to us through history is not in doubt. And there is no shortage of architectural theorists who see only the potential of new and expanding freedoms in the rift between historical and contemporary practices.[2] All of this is true and arguably valuable. However, it is worth asking if the object "architecture" once provided something to non-architects, served some societal or cultural purposes, that are antithetical to the definition of this new and newly freed professional, the architect. More importantly, was there something in earlier variants of architectural practice that might reveal our civilization to be less "fully formed" than it seems? While not intended to serve as a comprehensive history of architecture, neither of its forms nor of its practices, this work attempts to answer those questions by following architecture backward, from the present to one of its best-known early stories, and, in the process, illuminating shifts in the relationships of language and form so that even the seemingly complete but often banal scenes that comprise our contemporary landscape might be understood in the depths of its content and richness of its potential.

Notes

1   Use of the phrase "minor architectures" herein is derived from the work of Gilles Deleuze and Félix Guattari, particularly as explored in their seminal *Kafka: toward a minor literature*, translated by Dana Polan (Minneapolis, MN: University of Minnesota Press, 1986). Minor architectures emerge through the same conditions that spawn minor literatures: as "expression that precedes contents," p. 85.

2   The most ready-at-hand because so recently anthologized is John McMorrough's "Ru(m)ination: the haunts of contemporary architecture," published in *Perspecta* 40 (2008) and reprinted in A. Krista Sykes (ed.), *Constructing a New Agenda: architectural theory 1993–2009* (New York: Princeton Architectural Press, 2010), 462–471. McMorrough assumes the veracity of the 'constraint|opportunity' dichotomy – a popular view that stresses the inhibitions that constraints impose and ignores the degree to which constraints motivate the search for alternatives or, in Harold Bloom's phrase, the value of the "Anxiety of Influence."

FIGURE 1.0 Markthal ceiling
Source: Photograph by J. David Lewis.

1

TWENTY-FIRST-CENTURY TRAJECTORIES

February 5, 2016. *New York Times* headline: "In Tokyo, Brand-Name Stores by Brand-Name Architects." Hyperbole? Perhaps. Accurate reporting? Probably. Marketing ploy for the stores, the architects, and the newspaper itself? Of course. But don't for a moment think that hyping, reporting, and marketing fully describe media's role in twenty-first-century architecture.

Jean-Jacques Rousseau famously said, "The invention of theater is remarkable for inflating our pride with all the virtues in which we are entirely lacking."[1] Media is our theater. And media invents architects and architecture. Or stated with greater fidelity, architects reinvent architecture in the image of media and in pursuit of the theatricality the media can celebrate or exploit. This pursuit is responsible for contemporary architecture's indulgences, of which there are many. Blogs. Webzines. Journals. The entire city of Dubai. Strange forms. Moving parts. Wall assemblies that emit light or grow plants or decompose in extraordinary and highly prescribed ways. A deluge of spectacles coming so fast there is hardly time to do more than marvel at the accumulation. Caught in this torrent, it is useful to grasp a well-known example in order to examine the tendencies otherwise rushing past.

MVRDV is an exemplar twenty-first-century practice dealing almost exclusively in media imagery, both as source material and as product. The Stairs to Kriterion (2016) is one of the firm's most recent, and most temporary, spectacles. Rotterdam's Markthal (2014) is the firm's most award-winning and arguably best-known project (see Figures 1.1 and 1.2). In it, three theatrical impulses of late information age media are literally on display: (1) an overt presentation of technology; (2) a celebration of pragmatics or program; and (3) a hyper-saturation of imagery. The arch structure, the broad curtain walls, the interior apartment windows rotated to function as quasi-floors, and the flora pattern printed on metal panels are minor technological achievements individually, but together assert the building's newness as its primary content. The traditional schema of an open marketplace surrounded, in plan, by buildings composed of retail at lower levels and residential above is highlighted by MVRDV's rotation of the axis. Here, the context arches over instead of wrapping around the market. The floral mural is a billboard for the products that fill the building's farmers' market, grocery store, and restaurants. Finally, the intense pattern and color of the mural, punctuated by square windows along its length and drenched in light by the curtain walls at either end, form a spectacle designed as much for the camera, for viewing on the internet and in color monographs, as for pedestrians. The Markthal constitutes a media-driven shift from direct to mediated perception.

Architects, like fashion designers and lawyers, invented their necessity. By working to restructure societies and the expectations of cultures, these professions have marketed the notion of perpetual novelty – this year's dresses, new class action suits, and buildings that show up in commercials and movies. Self-promoted as understanding this whirl of the new, they make themselves doubly necessary: as inventors of novelty and arbiters of its conventions. Ironically, this invented necessity is so pervasive it seems natural to us. As recently as 1828, Heinrich Hübsch could bemoan the craze for innovative variation as something relatively new.[2] With a depth of historical perspective, one millennium, two millennia, three millennia back, the necessity of professionals fades. The services once rendered by professionals correspondingly grow entwined with the communities once served. Admittedly, this is a polemic. What I hope will be evident is the rise of professional architects and architectural media has not spawned a concomitant rise in the value of architecture to society.

FIGURE 1.1 Markthal, Rotterdam, MVRDV Architects
Source: Photograph by J. David Lewis.

FIGURE 1.2 Markthal, Rotterdam, MVRDV Architects
Source: Photograph by J. David Lewis.

In many regards, architecture is less affecting and less effective than theater or film. Film is the quintessential information age media and the best films have no equals in buildings. Consider Alexander Sokurov's (2002) film, *Russian Ark*. Filmed as a continuous 96-minute point-of-view dream sequence, a narrator wanders through thirty-three rooms of the Hermitage Museum's Winter Palace in which he witnesses scenes of Russia's pre-revolutionary history unfold. Through this journey, social, practical, and journalistic desires are engaged. Recreated scenes from history books and imagined glimpses of life behind those scenes engage our desire for sociological connection to the origins of a community. Beautifully choreographed and technically extraordinary use of a single unbroken Steadicam shot fulfills our desire to be within the film to an unprecedented degree. The harrowing ending, as hundreds of guests file out of the Palace's last ball and into the coming storm of revolution, triggers speculation on justice, class, and obligations to learn the lessons of history. This is the power of film. By comparison, much recent architecture is merely fascinating, like baubles. Arguably, Gehry's Disney Concert Hall in Los Angeles and his Guggenheim in Bilbao are functioning as intended when used as backdrops for car commercials or tourism brochures. As historian Mary N. Woods points out, "Architecture is now a chic vocation for characters in films, television series, and advertising campaigns."[3] These buildings and their makers are products of and stage sets for marketing, for the commodification

10 Architecture History and Theory in Reverse

of products or place or even people. MVRDV understands this. Their website features a question from a *Financial Times* article, "Will Rotterdam's Markthal be equivalent of Bilbao's Guggenheim?"[4] The comparison the question frames is not between two works of art or cultures or practices but whether one building will serve architecture's kaleidoscopic market effects as well as another.[5]

Indulgence in the Thrall of Media

Bright lights of discourse are few and flickering. Joan Didion does not write much criticism these days. Susan Sontag, Edward Said, and Christopher Hitchens have died. As always, Gore Vidal followed Hitch. In the narrower dialogue of architecture, Ada Louise Huxtable and Herbert Muschamp left noticeable voids. Despite the appearance of newness and engagement, most remaining late information age voices deliver narratives for which conclusions were formulated in dim instrumentalities of earlier times, behind closed doors, and change only with the movements of narrow self-interests. In other words, branding in the service of power.

There is much to lament in corporate and private interest media. The blogosphere and other forms of ostensibly 'critical' discourse assess change based on proto-religious underpinnings, whose value lies with a perceived lack of connection between future and past, destiny and history. Journalists often characterize these changes in biblical terms: a series of semi-random missteps triggered by humanity's disregard for or ignorance of the natural course of time or, worse, an intentional infidelity guiding us toward a future woefully inferior to our pre-destined promise. Such historicizing characterizations are common to the 24-hour news cycle. Moreover, the ease with which we accept classifications of a thing or an event as "natural" or "artificial," as "fulfilling our promise" or as "missteps," is evidence of just how deeply engrained these tendencies are. James Joyce's Stephen Dedalus heralded the modern age by proclaiming, "History … is a nightmare from which I am trying to awake."[6] Today, the nightmare reported in thousands of analog and digital dailies is of a different sort. It is announced in terms of loss or deviation from or irony within the present. The character of this discourse is flat: literally and intentionally shallow in its attention to spectacles. It exposes a partially excavated multitude of political, societal, cultural, economic, and aesthetic narratives and presents these as often co-existing or conflicting without exposing the in-depth, long-term causes. Read western coverage of any conflict in the Middle East – or anywhere else for that matter.

This moralizing, quasi-religious undercurrent is evidenced in various ways in much recent architectural theory. Dalibor Vesely's notion of poetics as "a way of making (*poiēsis*) in which the result preserves continuity with the conditions of its origin" is a subtle example.[7] Kenneth Frampton's closing remarks in *Studies in Tectonic Culture* are more direct: "the culture of the tectonic still persists as a testament to the spirit: the poetics of construction. All the rest … is mixed up with the lifeworld, and in this it belongs as much to society as to ourselves."[8] Peter Zumthor's impression of light as a thing that "doesn't feel as if it quite belongs in this world" and "gives me the feeling there's something beyond me, something beyond all understanding" invokes a transcendent otherworldly entity without much theorizing.[9] Arie Graafland's "On Criticality" surpasses these examples in the degree to which it attempts to justify this moralizing teleology. Borrowing from Timothy Luke's restatements of first, second, and third nature as "terrestriality," "territoriality," and "telesphere," Graafland reasserts the temptation to move from givenness (terrestriality) through personal interest (territoriality) toward detachment or newness (telesphere). While Graafland claims "all spaces are *constructs* and *real*, including our digital worlds," it is clear that he attempts this rejoinder in arrears to address a real division that he has implicitly accepted in order to build his argument.[10]

As stated at the outset, media does more than report. Amidst the bombast and despite the temporal shallowness, media plays a covert double narrative game. On the one hand, it asserts that modern societies are free-floating, synchronic, devoid of teleological trajectory. Consider the number of times a commentator has called some group "aimless" or declared some event "without precedent." On the other, media pits diachronic or disconnected past promises, such as biblical claims to the city of Jerusalem, against an imagined future, such as prophecies in Revelations, as a metric of judgment on the course of contemporary civilization. These conflicting narratives can be argued to have at least two outcomes. Positively framed, media temporalizes the a-temporal present. It invents, or reinvents, illusions of past, present, and future – illusions that are more characteristic of Classical and mythical times than our own. Negatively judged, media leverages the Industrial Age notions of 'work time' and 'leisure time' to atomize all time as times-in-conflict: 'productive time' vs. 'time wasted,' 'present' vs. 'non-present,' 'time of decline' vs. 'an age of greatness.' The resulting cultural discourse is legitimately characterized as confusing, antagonistic, or even schizophrenic depending on the level of anxiety the double narrative forces on a given individual or group.

This artificial double bind has consequences in every aspect of life. Media is not only a form of discourse; it frames and thereby limits possibilities of forms. All forms of discourse cannot help but act, react, connect and contest media streams, as times-in-conflict. This shallow presentation of spectacles underpins architecture's recent trends. It is understandable that architects, clients, builders, critics, users, and 'mere' perceivers of works of architecture are as distant from, distrustful of, and antagonistic to each other as the media streams into which they were born or to which they are stridently committed. Linguist Leo Weisgerber put it succinctly in 1950 when he wrote, "our understanding is under the spell of the language which it utilizes."[11] If you have ever listened to a true believer in architectural phenomenology and a strict adherent to East Coast formalism argue the merits of a particular project, this should be quite clear. Le Corbusier's La Tourette is much beloved by both camps but, on the one side, is framed as a work which "still proclaims the possibility of participatory, non-reductive representation in the world of electronic media and simulation,"[12] and, on the other, as one which "still remains a displacement, a subversion of the condition of the type that had formally existed."[13] Or, for another example, ask yourself if poetics, as used by Frampton

12 Architecture History and Theory in Reverse

and Vesely respectively, means one thing or many. I'll leave that determination to the reader.

Media streams proliferate. In the 1990s and 2000s, the formalists and phenomenologists and critical regionalists were joined by blob-ists, post-criticalists, object-oriented-ontologists, design/builders, greenies, and BIMsters. The ever-increasing number of categories results from and perpetuates causes for the absence of a shared language that might serve as grounds for discourse. Arguably, architecture and attempts to understand what constitutes its larger purpose suffer from this proliferation.

Media's complicity in isolating humans into solipsistic or self-aggrandizing worldviews does not suggest that the antidote lies in downgrading the importance or roles of language or even media itself. *Seeing*, in a sense that might be shared among a cohort or society, is not *forgetting the name of the thing one sees*. To see as well as to hear, touch, taste, and smell does not require a flight from cold language for the warm particulars of the body or imply virtue in grunting non-communicative isolation. Such would be a nightmarish world of profound disability. We do not first acquire language, then become social.[14] Socialization prompts communication. To be meaningful, seeing and other forms of sensing entail naming. Media then might redeem its value to communities and, in particular, the discipline of architecture by framing the potential of all discourse and thus even the potential for naming and socializing a name. To paraphrase Graafland, only media can be "critical."[15] Its potential value exists in parallel with its potential to harm. Its agency resides equally in the power to invent times and create connections across dialogues and disciplines, and peoples and places, at one extreme, and to gloss cultural contexts to the point of homogeneity, at the other. Media is the tool by which late information age actors maintain, expand, and even redefine culture. For better and for worse, its connection to architecture is anything but tenuous.[16]

It is critical to begin questioning this profession and its late information age manifestations so to allow us to once again focus on the built environment: its temperature, its weight; its affect and effect, as well as about language and meaning. In the long term, this analysis awaits its Edward Said or its Christopher Hitchens, a journalist who will unfold the complicities through which architects and architecture are connected in the highly debatable professionalization of intellectual life and demonstrate how the end of the edifice and the appearance of professional architects emanate from one and the same momentous event and yet are highly contingent. This person will point to new possibilities of design inherent in the fall of the edifice.[17] In the short term, it is worth asking: What would happen to the profession of architecture if architects were dislodged from the cycle of media and the invention of their own necessity? Is it possible that the elimination of the professional architect as he or she is now conceived might foster the formation of a new architecture, an anti-edifice of 'grounded' shared experiences among divergent peoples and places that could overcome the profession's tripartite self-aggrandizements? Perhaps. But first we should understand the terms of media's present trajectories.

Media Trends Since 1993

It has been more than two decades since Philip Bess' "Communitarianism and Emotivism: two rival views of ethics and architecture" (1993) first formalized a debate between Aristotelian virtues and Nietzschean aesthetics.[18] Bess identified these with neotraditionalism and formalism, respectively, and his analysis of aesthetics seems to hold despite the intervening years. Virtue, however, has been reframed since 1993 as a search for ethical practices and products not subject to the narrow confines of style. Given the broad acclaim of programs like *Architecture for Humanity* and Auburn's *Rural Studio* as well as the frequent announcements of competitions for the design of shelters of various sorts, it could be argued that virtue is winning the hearts and minds of the lay architectural public as the discipline's defining content. But, hearts are fickle and minds change.

Any search for beliefs held or intentions wielded requires both the broad illumination of speculative engagement and the narrowed beam of rational analysis. Cast onto present-day architectural discourse, this light allows us to see three mutually exclusive paradigms: (1) the academy; (2) practice; and (3) professional and semi-professional critics and theoreticians. Within practice, commercial architecture or the mass production of well-worn business and marketing typologies is denied consideration as serious architecture by all but a few apologists and, for that reason, I withhold discussion of it. The other two paradigms, however, have acquired adherents significant in both their numbers and fervor. Academics are concerned with ethical responsibility and social justice, while critics and theorists celebrate novelty, self-expression, or architecture as art. In the early twenty-first century, these trends have emerged as the most likely candidates for giving meaning to the notion of architectural information.

The practice of architecture can be charitable. An architect or office may donate his or her time or subsidize work. Architecture as an artifact, however, is not charitable in any meaningful sense. Ethical responsibilities are chimera incapable of being encoded in or through the act of building. Food banks provide food. Homeless shelters provide cots, blankets, and a roof. Counseling and rehabilitation centers of various sorts attempt to affect direct change in the addictions and habits of those who seek it. Architecture – buildings that are somehow more or other than mere utilitarian buildings – can house such programs but cannot be said to provide such obvious benefits. Unlike the activities of charitable organizations, architectural ambitions to solve – or at least mitigate – a societal ill operate in an illusory way akin to self-fulfilling prophecies which both require and measure success by the user's or observer's familiarity with the architects' or clients' intentions to "do good." Such substitutions of ethical intentions for meaning are ubiquitous but fall into three primary types: (1) statements of intentions to address a conflict without a rule to frame its appropriateness on behalf of a public; (2) use of signs or symbols without a system through which the signification might have meaning for a public; and (3) reliance upon an assumed functionalism without establishing a norm against which quality of service to that public is measured. For these reasons and others, it is

14 Architecture History and Theory in Reverse

doubtful that an ethical imperative – Aristotelian or otherwise – is the 'more' or 'other' that elevates buildings to the status of architecture.[19]

The other prevailing trend since 1993, emotivism, also known as Nietzschean aesthetics or the society of spectacle, largely ignores the ethical agendas just described and does not replace these with fixed intentions rooted in aspects of culture or environment. This work privileges fantastic contrivances – one-off compositions less categorized by their formal or syntactic elements than by the names or acronyms of their creators: Bjarke Ingels and BIG, Rem Koolhaas and OMA, Richard Rodgers and Renzo Piano, Herzog and de Meuron, Norman Foster and Santiago Calatrava and MVRDV. In lieu of ethics, these architects seek, quite literally, the spectacular and awe-inspiring; the making-of-show. And in a project like the Pompidou Centre, among others, a show-of-making. The dearth of information conveyed through such spectacular works will be a subject for Chapter 5. At present, it is sufficient to recall Claude Shannon's 1948 information theory revelation outlined in the Introduction. He contends that to ensure the successful transmission of information, repetition and predictability are allies in overcoming the interference of noise. Whether it is an atonal musical composition written in a new time register, a complex cipher used once and known only to two individuals, or an avant-garde work of art or architecture, as novelty increases, it becomes more difficult to distinguish message from noise and intentions from accidents. In short, complexity diminishes communicability.

Spectacles and ethics, though apparently autonomous modes of architectural practice, have two points of overlap. One we might term an ethos of spectacles as in the work of Rem Koolhaas, Frank Gehry, among others. The other is a spectacle of ethics, evident in sustainable works of Pliny Fiske at The Center for Maximum Potential Building Systems, Glenn Murcutt, and the Rural Studio. Advocates for an ethos of spectacles value novelty as a means to challenge the status quo of cultural forms and, thereby, alter the world. Theirs is change that, more often than not, is touted as "for the better" and thus virtuous. Advocates for the spectacle of ethics make a show of good intentions. Without surrendering to the instrumentality of serving a narrow program, these architects construct beautiful buildings that demonstrate ways humans might live while minimizing harm to the rest of the biosphere. Arguably, these blurred trends aspire to be, not only more than building but also, more than architecture. Samuel 'Sambo' Mockbee, founder of the Rural Studio, proclaimed this ambition: "Architecture has to be greater than just architecture. It has to address social values, as well as technical and aesthetic values." While his stance can be seen as semantic obfuscation to avoid defining the field, the blurring of ethics and spectacle very late in the information age ultimately reveals what is missing in both trends.[20]

An ethos of spectacles and a spectacle of ethics are indistinguishable in the extent to which both trade in representations. To differentiate these trends requires attention to the temporal aspects of their respective agendas. An ethos of spectacles justifies itself teleologically as an offering of emblems of a not-yet-existent future and explains its uniqueness (or difference) as progress toward not-yet-commonly-understood good. A spectacle of ethics presents symbols of widely accepted common goods, such as to house the poor or preserve biodiversity, for the express purpose of drawing attention to present-day blight and its largely non-architectural roots in the missteps of the past. Absent from both architecture as spectacle and architecture as ethics is any notion of a ground of shared meaning broader than each trend's own agenda. Trapped in their individual media streams, both trends lack those systems that provide meaning, rules that regulate appropriateness, and norms that measure effectiveness through which the non-architectural public engage and gain appreciation of the 'more' or 'other' encoded in the built environment.[21] Without signifying systems, without a ground of shared meaning, without the violent illumination of an architectural equivalent of de Sade or Nietzsche, Joyce or Foucault, Kafka or Deleuze, Hitchens or Said, today's dominant architectural trends perpetuate ethereal, substance-less, literally non-architectural buildings and practices. With a strong signifying system, with the emergence of voices capable of fulfilling architects' propensity for newness within traditions capable of being grasped by the public at large, both ethical and spectacular concerns might be revealed as parallax views of a potentially larger and more meaningful architectural project.[22]

Late information age critics lob cynicism toward notions of truths, foundations, and origins. This age admits into discourse only those traditions that come pre-restrained by an evil doppelganger or undermined by a self-deprecating twin: Left and far Left; Right and far Right; ethics and the spectacle of ethics; spectacles and the ethos of spectacles. This is how media — and thus everything that counts as contemporary criticism and the broad transmission of ideas — operate today. Media is respected and ridiculed for its opposing vectors of action; for its simultaneous and always mixed efforts for good and ill. However, it is important to note that attention to these vacillating effects — the heartwarmingly good and the sensationalized bad — distracts, as often intended from a cynic's perspective, from more fundamental and critical issues.

If the above describes enduring facts as opposed to momentary contingencies and if our late information age media's potential for framing both the positive, social, language-expanding and the negative, solipsistic, language-restricting discourses are inextricably linked, then where should grounds for physical language be sought? In 2005, Anthony Vidler suggested "four new unifying principles" in recent architectural practices: landscape, "bioform," expanded notions of "program," and diagrams.[23] However accurate his assessment, all four of these principles seem merely of-the-moment, contingent ephemera that will be as passé thirty years hence as they were three decades ago. Treatments for today's symptoms of an underlying illness we do not understand, landscape, bioform, program, and diagrams are transitory interpretations of the grounds of discourse, not aspects of the ground itself.

In *The Ethical Function of Architecture*, philosopher Karsten Harries argues that if we are to hang on to the notion of architectural language then "works of architecture must not just be meaningful in some sense but must be intended to

16 Architecture History and Theory in Reverse

communicate some meaning."[24] Given our late information age trends, it is hard to imagine what might count for meaning and by what means it might be communicable through architecture. It is certainly impossible to claim a simple definitive identity for the practice or products of architecture today. Nevertheless, people cling to the notion of architectural language. And it is clear that by 'architecture' most people mean something other, or more, than the act or artifact of building. At present, this 'other' or 'more' appears to be information itself: Architecture in the twenty-first century is the information encoded by building. But this is, at best, a provisional response. A placeholder. We must ask, what is the nature of this information? Is it a set of beliefs, intentions, typological relations, or something else? Does the information change over time and, if so, how? Is there any guarantee that today's information will have currency beyond the present? The first step beyond a provisional response requires understanding the role modernity played in fashioning this century.

Notes

1　From a footnote to Rousseau's *Essay on the Origin of Languages* quoted in Jacques Derrida's *Of Grammatology*, translated by Gayatri Chakravorty Spivak (Baltimore, MD: Johns Hopkins University Press, 1976), 239.

2　"The decline of art is hastened in no small measure by the fact that quite independently, technostatic experience is constantly growing, and daring combinations of forms, driven to extremes by the craze for variation, become progressively easier to execute." Heinrich Hübsch, "In What Style Should We Build?" in *In What Style Should We Build?: the German debates on architectural style*, introduction and translation by Wolfgang Herrmann (Santa Monica, CA: the Getty Center for the History of Art and the Humanities, 1992), 70.

3　Woods notes that, "The media are also complicit with their celebration of 'signature,' invariably male, architects like Richard Meier, Frank Gehry, Rem Koolhaas, and Bernard Tschumi in newspapers, magazines, books, television, and museum exhibitions." She also points out that this is not entirely new. "By the late nineteenth century… the architect was now a status symbol for the commercial client, just as Hunt had been for Alva Smith Vanderbilt." See Mary N. Woods, *From Craft to Profession: the practice of architecture in nineteenth-century America* (Berkeley, CA: University of California Press, 1999), 174 and 165.

4　MVRDV's official web site, "News: Markthal Wins NRW JAARPRIJS 2015, A National Award for Best Retail Building," available at: www.mvrdv.nl/en/news/markthal-wins-nrwjaarprijs (accessed October 7, 2015).

5　For more on media's role in generating kaleidoscopic content, see Manuel Castells, "Space of flows, space of places: materials for a theory of urbanism in the information age," in *The City Reader*, edited by Richard T. Gates and Frederic Stout (London: Routledge, 2011), 572–582.

6　James Joyce, *Ulysses* (New York: Vintage, 1990), 34. Hitchens would later sharpen this assessment. Christopher Hitchens, *Hitch 22: a memoir* (New York: Twelve, 2010), 420:

> It is not so much that there are ironies of history, it is that history itself is ironic. It is not that there are no certainties, it is that it is an absolute certainty that there are no certainties. It is not only true that the test of knowledge is an acute and cultivated awareness of how little one knows (as Socrates knew so well), it is true that the unbounded areas and fields of one's ignorance are now expanding in such a way, and at such a velocity, as to make contemplation of them almost fantastically beautiful.

7 Dalibor Vesely, *Architecture in the Age of Divided Representation: the question of creativity in the shadow of production* (Cambridge, MA: MIT Press, 2004), 386–387.

8 Kenneth Frampton, *Studies in Tectonic Culture: the poetics of construction in nineteenth and twentieth century architecture* (Cambridge, MA: MIT Press, 1995), 387.

9 Peter Zumthor, *Atmospheres* (Basel: Birkhäuser, 2006), 61.

10 Arie Graafland, "On Criticality," in A. Krista Sykes (ed.), *Constructing a New Agenda: architectural theory 1993–2009* (New York: Princeton Architectural Press, 2010), 396–420; quoted passage from 412–414.

11 Quoted in George Steiner, *After Babel: aspects of language and translation* (New York: Oxford University Press, 1975), 86.

12 Alberto Pérez-Gómez and Louise Pelletier, *Architectural Representation and the Perspective Hinge* (Cambridge, MA: MIT Press, 1997), 368.

13 Peter Eisenman, *Written into the Void: selected writings 1990–2004*, Introduction by Jeffrey Kipnis (New Haven, CT: Yale University Press, 2007), 48.

14 See Charles Taylor, *The Language Animal: the full shape of the human linguistic capacity* (Cambridge, MA: Belknap Press/Harvard University, 2016).

15 "'Critical' can only be used for theory, not for architecture." Graafland, "On Criticality," 411.

16 A claim made by Dalibor Vesely. See *Architecture in the Age of Divided Representation*, 33.

17 After the fall but before the power of words, forms of making that are atonal, migratory, or in exile – though not for those reasons robbed of ability to communicate. See Edward Said's "Challenging Orthodoxy and Authority," in his *Culture and Imperialism* (New York: Vintage, 1994), 303–325.

18 Philip Bess, "Communitarianism and Emotivism: two rival views of ethics and architecture," in Kate Nesbitt (ed.), *Theorizing a New Agenda for Architecture: an anthology of architectural theory 1965–1995* (New York: Princeton Architectural Press, 1996), 372–382.

19 There is nothing in the intention to provide quality buildings to the homeless or poor that is, in itself, problematic or deserving of criticism. Quite the contrary. But difficulties emerge with questions of who is being served through work that, frequently and in numerous ways, appears to address the architectural profession, the architectural press, and large charitable granting agencies more than the inhabitants of these buildings-made-architecture. Picture in your mind's eye the popular images of the work of Architecture for Humanity or Auburn University's Rural Studio; the aesthetics of these ethical structures are often foreign additions to the needs and desires of those ostensibly being served; and, to the extent those added elements are not *of*, *by* or *for* those in need, the architecture must be understood as representing a societal ill that it is not directly solving. Again, it is debatable whether or not there is any harm in these aesthetic tropes that speak *to* the architectural community *about* poverty or homelessness. Yet, as Foucault said of knowledge, any practice that resides solely within representation will produce representations that exist only as mythology. Stated differently, the more advocacy or ethical architecture relies on untethered or only loosely tethered representations for its meaning, the less it exists as an ethical architecture in reality.

20 Mockbee appears on the verge of blunting this line of criticism when he writes, "Physical poverty is not an abstraction, but we almost never think of impoverishment as evidence of a world that exists." However, his next sentence undermines the ground he has just gained. "Much less do we imagine that it's a condition from which we may draw enlightenment in a very practical way." See Samuel Mockbee, "The Rural Studio," in Sykes (ed.), *Constructing a New Agenda*, 107–15. Quoted passage is taken from p. 113.

21 By and large, the traditional and, in some sense, essential triad of system, rule, and norm – long discussed in philosophy, psychoanalysis, and religion under the rubric of Death, Desire, and Law – escapes serious contemplation in contemporary architectural education, practice, and criticism for two reasons: (1) there is a general reluctance to deal with topics that verge upon the metaphysical – a reluctance that, in America at least, originates with Pragmatism and continues to propagate itself as pragmatic; and (2) because the traditional

18 Architecture History and Theory in Reverse

triad is foundational of but invisible to direct experience, its value to the student, practitioner or critic is easy to miss and, when glimpsed in reflection, easy to dismiss. The first reason is troubling but, in broader view, nothing more than a fad, a popular impression lodged in architectural discourse for the time being in the form of critical practice. The second reason, the triad's necessity and invisibility, is a problem worthy of extended study. In fact, the triad's invisibility is so entrenched that, in literature, it has required projects with the violence of de Sade or the quotidian obscenity of James Joyce, or the brutal bureaucracy of Kafka to bring it to light; and, in philosophy, the will to power of Nietzsche, the analysis of discipline in Foucault, or the contrast of nomad and state citizen in Deleuze and Guattari.

22 Like abstract Expressionist paintings, spectacles of ethics and ethics of spectacles suffer an inability to communicate with anyone who does not already sense the world more or less as the architect or painter does; more harshly stated, late information age architectural discourse, and the architecture which is both instigator and product of this discourse, express for the sake of emitting guttural utterances to affirm its own existence and serve to deepen the cynicism that there might be more socially meaningful things to say. This rhetorical emptiness has been bemoaned by many, including architect James Stirling who complained of being "sick and tired of the boring, meaningless, non-committed, faceless flexibility and open-endedness of the present architecture;" quoted in Michael Fazio, Marian Moffett, and Lawrence Wodehouse, *A World History of Architecture*, 2nd edn (Boston: McGraw-Hill, 2008), 553.

23 Anthony Vidler, "Architecture's Expanded Field," in Sykes (ed.), *Constructing a New Agenda*, 320–331.

24 Karsten Harries, *The Ethical Function of Architecture* (Cambridge, MA: MIT Press, 1997), 86.

2

MODERNITY'S LEGACY IN A NEW MILLENNIUM

Modernity is not bookended by dates or confined to a style. Modernity springs from a questioning attitude toward existence in which humanity views itself in doubt. The earliest artists to address the uncertain place of 'Man' in the cosmos – artists as varied as Michelangelo, Shakespeare, and Cervantes – were modern before Modernism was a thing. And that underlying impulse is deeply infused in today's most postmodern of people. It is best understood as an informational bias toward authorship and identity exemplified by twentieth-century existentialism as developed more fully and far more consciously in philosophy, literature, and painting than in architecture. Jean-Paul Sartre, Samuel Beckett, and Clement Greenberg have no peers among architects and architecture's critics. Friedrich Schlegel noted that we "Moderns are fragments from [our] birth."[1] In Sartre's formulation, humans are negations, literal absences, in the otherwise solid identity of one-to-one correspondences: *we are what we are not; we are not what we are.* Several decades later, Deleuze and Guattari expressed this idea as an endless cycling between *deterritorialization* and *reterritorialization:* unnaming and renaming; decategorizing and categorizing. In Derrida, it is the *fissure.*[2] According to Harold Bloom, we suffer an anxiety of influence. We moderns are flows, lines of flight, figures of desire, unfixed identities simultaneously longing for and repulsed by the notion of fitting within a particular classification.

In anthropologist Arjun Appadurai's more recent words, this condition is a result of Information Age *media* and *migrations*: "When identities are produced in a field of classification, mass mediation, mobilization, and entitlement ... they take cultural differences as their *conscious* object."[3] This double bind at the heart of modernity, both embracing and rejecting the power of names in equal measure, directs design processes that feel natural – because they are rooted in narratives of time, place, and, to use existentialist language, Being – yet also are alien insofar as the validity of procedures and products are as much in question as the angst-ridden

20 Architecture History and Theory in Reverse

identities of designers, culture, and locality. A designer under the sway of modernity tests his or her identity through the design process, swinging back and forth between knowing and unknowing. An architect and his or her process are amalgams of identity and otherness – self and other, citizen and alien, name and anonymity, therefore both internally bifurcated and self-questioning. It is little wonder that recent works of architecture stand in the world so nameless, so style-less, so mute. Think the curvilinearity of blobs and towers composed of shards of glass as well as the prosaic repetition of contemporary public schools, big box outlets, and convenience stores. "Because meaningful life-worlds require legible and reproducible patterns of action, they are text-like and thus require one or many contexts."[4] Because modernity is always simultaneously accepting and rejecting the contexts provided by systems of classifications or known languages,[5] 'legibility' and 'reproducibility' are not only aspirations difficult to achieve; they are cultural anathemas. Legibility is unthinkable.

Modernity pushed to its limits aims to create works that are unclassifiable, irreducible or, quite literally, unthinkable. While not all contemporary architects are modern in this sense, this thought process is evident in the work of a significant number of practitioners who might be termed Modernists, Postmodernists and Post-postmodernists. They strive to create objects that communicate a Self-and-Other to other selves and other others without resorting to a ground or system of classification against which 'self' and 'other' might have communicable meaning. In Sydney Pollack's 2006 DVD *Sketches of Frank Gehry*, the elder statesman proclaims: "I have seen the future, and the future is chaos." That future is now and is a result of a Modernist rejection of classificatory tools. Restated in a language that will gain in value as this text unfolds, all of this is a result of a Modernist substitution of fragments of information (here's a bit about me; here's a symbol torn from its cultural context; here's a high tech wall assembly; here's the deformation of the form resulting from an algorithm) for older systems of information that were communicable and supportive of meaning. Old forms of design ethics – those codes and principles that seemingly allowed architects to measure, *ipso facto*, the impacts of their designs of buildings and cities, and the rules that organized the reconstructions of Chicago and San Francisco, for example – are lost or, at least, made taboo for use by contemporary practitioners. Max Weber's differentiation between an ethics of intention and an ethics of responsibility[6] has been decided in favor of intentions, for the reason that having the unthinkable as a goal, by definition, means that the resulting product – the work of architecture, cannot be measured in any frame of responsibility. As is still evident in architecture's twenty-first-century trajectories, all that is measureable in the milieu of modernity is the value accorded technological, pragmatic, and media intentions.

The privileging of an ethics of intentions over responsibility has had an extraordinary impact on the quality of architecture built in the past several decades. This relatively new ethics of architecture is modernity's legacy and is rooted in action and not in things, in intentions and not results, in agendas and not qualities. The thing, the object, the building is always, and by necessity, a bit of an

Modernity's Legacy in a New Millennium **21**

embarrassment – a failure to live up to the ideal of the unthinkable. No made thing can ever stand completely outside classification and thus all work made under the purview of such intentions, if judged in its final state as a transmitter of meaning or values, fails. The actual works of architecture that result from modernity's ethics literally stand outside the profession's judgment. As a result, the profession has proliferated systems of intentions to stand in place of and absorb the reflective energies that might be best spent in the making of architecture.

Designer and Designed

Maker and made. This pair of terms is much discussed in twentieth-century architectural thought and, like much of twentieth-century theory, its lineage is entwined with ontological and anthropomorphic rhetoric. Arguably, this rhetoric is a form of noise that complicates the perceived relation of designer and designed to a degree that ultimately degrades the encoding capacity of buildings and, therefore, their capacity to serve as architecture. Rather than dismiss it out of hand, however, it is useful to frame the problems surrounding the maker/made distinction in this language first; to identify it clearly for later pruning.

In existentialism, the Being of an architect, his or her framed and famed existence (*being-for-itself*), stands in sharp distinction from the Being of his or her creation (*being-in-itself*). The former is typified by questions, doubts, aspirations and aspersions. The latter, by its completeness – literally, it is what it is. This is as it should be. The architect is a full-fledged person with the expected menagerie of interests and obligations – some public, some private, some laudable, others not; a few architectural, and the rest ... well, it is a big world. In profound distinction, architecture is non-sentient matter without active internal interests or obligations; it passively receives its value and meaning from the interests and expectations of its users, inhabitants, and critics. Again, the phrase *as it should be* appears to fit. And this phrase would remain fitting were it not for a key aspect of the relationship between maker and made that begins in the design process. In a seemingly innocuous world of graphite or bytes, paper or chipboard or computer monitors, the relationship follows the work into the world of concrete, steel, and glass. The work of architecture is understood by critics, users, owners, and, most wholeheartedly, by the architect to be a sign for the architect's intentions.

From the education of architects through desk crits and juries where it is common to hear a critic ask, "what are your intentions?" to scholarly journals and the popular press where professional critics rhetorically demand to know, "what were the architect's goals and did he or she achieve them?" to articles, books, and documentaries that are marketed as an encapsulated version of a particular architects' worldview, intentions have become the *de facto* content and currency of architecture. Personification becomes *the* information that distinguishes architecture from mere buildings. Obviously no harm comes from dabbling in a little illusion now and then. Theater, film, magic shows, and carnivals can delight the senses; and, no doubt, enchanted words and phrases like "abracadabra" or "step right up, folks" frame experience in such a way as to maximize a sense of wonder. But, none of these things are designed to ground community – nor are they capable of doing so. The growing impetus to embody the architect's intentions in buildings results in a situation in which each project requires a borrowed Being (being-for-itself), which it does not and cannot possess, in order to have currency.[7]

Rem Koolhaas' Seattle Public Library is a striking example (see Figures 2.1 and 2.2). Notice how both the overall form and minor details are designed to resist easy naming and call into question the notion of "library" or "bench." The building is Oz-like in its otherworldliness. One expects its designer to reside behind a green curtain at its center. Short of the designer's physical presence, visitors might feel compelled to read one of Rem's books so that the initial hope that all these shifts refer to something larger than whim might be kept alive, however futilely. Overall, the building seems to refer less to the history of libraries, Seattle, or its citizens than to Mr. Koolhaas' absence. And absence is not only one of the favored forms of intentions in late twentieth-century thought. When connected to a particular architect, this intentional absence becomes a form of personification in an object (a being-for-others).

This professionalized trick of merging maker and made is not an act undertaken to rectify a recently emerged split. The Being of architecture and that of the architect have never been unified – and arguably should never be (pay no attention to that man behind the curtain). While the desire to imbue architecture with meaning is understandable, laudable even, the tether of intentions, or intentionality, is a tenuous and arguably inadequate lifeline through which social, practical, and journalistic desires might be transfused into the work. An architect's intentions and architecture's role in a community should not be conflated. In no case, should the latter require the support of the former.[8]

FIGURE 2.1 Public Library, Seattle, OMA Architects
Source: Photograph by Scott Penman.

FIGURE 2.2 Public Library, Seattle, OMA Architects
Source: Photograph by Scott Penman.

24 Architecture History and Theory in Reverse

No doubt the way we acquire and parse information has posed a significant challenge to architects and their dreams of making meaningful buildings in the last several decades. Between the invention of the printing press and the opening of the "information super highway," one read to acquire direct content. If you wanted to know about the life and times of Frank Lloyd Wright or gardening, you would pick up the most readily available books or articles and begin reading with the dual self-reassurance that: (1) someone must be vetting these publications; and (2) even if not wholly accurate, there is a limited amount of information at hand and therefore reading this is better than reading nothing. Information has evolved now into information glut and direct communication is either denigrated as banal ("oh no, another blog; another meme; another story about ...") or, in order to parse the daunting mountain of possible sources, people turn to filters and meta reading. As James Gleick writes: "When information is cheap, attention becomes expensive."[9] The problem is perplexing.

Some might argue that the elevation of intentions to the status of primary content in architecture is merely a method of moving forward in this age of information overload. Intentions, in this view, serve as anchors in a world of untethered representations. Modernist thinkers and their postmodern inheritors, however, only contribute to the overload with every new form of reference. By making things that endlessly refer back to and highlight the importance of people or ideas that are absent from the present work,[10] Modernists, to some extent, and their inheritors, to great extent, proliferate information at the cost of intelligibility and possibly meaning.[11]

Intentions as a form of architectural content take many forms. In the case of Modernism, made things are always understood as heroic offspring of the maker – author as genius. You are expected not only to see and think through the building for yourself as a form of direct reading, but you are also expected to know something of the life story or, at least, the architectural biography of its maker as a form of meta-reading. In the case of postmodernism, things are proffered as challenges to, contestations of, the notion of authorship in general and the author whose name appears on the building's plaque in particular. In reality, both forms of thought endlessly repeat the cycle of intellectual surrogacy:

Author → thing → world → thing in question → author in question (repeat)

Attempts have been made in architectural theory to sidestep this problem. Rajchman's "new pragmatism" and Speaks' "design intelligence" are examples.[12] The former is exemplary of movements that borrow theoretical underpinnings from philosophical traditions so as to avoid the charge of arbitrariness: the another-discipline's-theory-is-ground-for-my-theory theorists. The latter is exemplary of an opposing tendency: a linguistic rejection of theorization by the theory-is-dead theorists. Despite merits, these and similar efforts always appeal to extra-architectural forces which only serves to reinscribe authorial intentions at a higher level (thus adding layers of information):

Author in question (seeks) → external forces (to substitute for intentions in the making of) → thing (which is reviewed by) → world (which throws) → thing in question (which reasserts the need for) → authorship (repeat)

Why do these evasions generate the same self-referential cycle? Late information age design processes, particularly in their reliance upon the author's intentions, are understood implicitly as commandments to overcome sameness (deemed in advance to be a null result of the design process) via difference and identity (deemed a positive result). Yet, because the intention to avoid sameness inevitably falls back on a narrow set of technological, pragmatic, and critical instrumentalities, the work produced feeds the public's sense of information banality and forces a return to the well-worn paths of intellectual surrogacy in search of content.

Sameness and Difference

Renowned literary critic George Steiner wrote: "Art dies when we lose or ignore the conventions by which it can be read."[13] Thoughts about making in the pre-information age were often predicated upon a commandment to achieve sameness, continuity; to follow a hierarchy and order that produced, paradoxically, a world of differences and identities – arguably *the* world. For instance, slight modulations in the application of highly prescribed Classical elements were jarring to people in a way that we cannot assume to fully grasp (a topic for Part II, particularly Chapter 17). Assumptions of a shared ground and expectations that significant or important things would be repeated were vital when information was not easy to come by and was never taken for granted.

Here, I suggest, is the greatest difference between modern novels and architecture – say, the works of Franz Kafka compared to those of Frank Gehry. Gehry tends to produce sameness despite being engaged in the pursuit of difference, while Kafka produces differences through a willing submission to banal bureaucratic repetition.[14] If this does not make sense on the surface, imagine Gehry attempting a Kafkaesque building, perhaps a museum or monument to the great writer. Such a building would have to appear at every instant to be a purely functional and bureaucratic building while at no point being functional or efficient. It is impossible to imagine Gehry succeeding because the most profound differences, those rooted in incremental psychological changes in the reader or inhabitant from one minute to the next, are only perceptible in a noiseless and nearly informationless space. Exemplars of this strategy in arts other than architecture are easier to call to mind: in landscape architecture, there is Maya Lin's Vietnam Veterans Memorial – a black polished stone wall interrupted only by the damask of engraved names; in painting, there are the numerous installations by Robert Irwin; and in music, the ultimate ode to silence, John Cage's 4'33" – literally 4 minutes and 33 seconds of silence, anticipation, discomfort.[15] Late twentieth- and early twenty-first-century architecture possesses few parallels.[16]

'Sameness' and 'difference' operate at two different levels as design intentions and also as design outcomes. To this end, it is worth some effort to explore the rift

26 Architecture History and Theory in Reverse

between information age and mythical attitudes toward design with particular attention to unspoken attitudes about time – the relation between act and origin, verb and tense, information source and transmitter – and eventually the role time plays in perceptions of sameness and difference.

Design and Time

Some thinkers couch the categories of sameness and difference in terms of 'generic,' 'everyday,' or 'collective' grounds against 'branded,' 'unique,' or 'singular' figures. But these renamings shed little light on the issue and, in fact, move us further from the problem by turning our attention toward results – here, a nameless background building, there, a celebrated one, as if these artifacts are causes of their own differences and similarities. In information theory this is akin to mistaking the transmitter for the information source. While similarities and differences are decoded and understood by the receiver, these forms of content are conceived and encoded by the source, an architect. Therefore, it is necessary to take a step back and consider this initial translational process and its relation to time.[17]

Whether in painting or sculpture, furniture-making or film, architecture or urban design, design processes are some of the few acts in which myths of origins continue relatively unquestioned. Despite the impositions of discipline- and profession-specific rigors as well as the individuated parameters of particular projects, all of the design disciplines assume a diachronic unfolding of process that begins in a pre-project past, transitions through an initial or 'original' idea, and ends in a post-project future with the emergence of a new thing in paint or celluloid or printed master plan; digital 1s and 0s or concrete, steel, and glass. That this unfolding of time is cast in hindsight into the categories of beginning, middle, and end is, in itself, unproblematic. When this temporalization is at odds with the temporal self-image of a profession, however, a host of internal contradictions become a drag on the process of design and a barrier to the transmission of architecture's 'more' or 'other' content.

Architects' self-imagining often eschews historical weight and its determinism, perhaps more strongly than 'progenitors' of other design disciplines. This is not to suggest that architects resist the prestige afforded by appropriated history. As discussed elsewhere, the profession is founded upon an assumed lineage, with architects such as Robert A. M. Stern going so far as to claim that classicism is the "fulcrum about which architectural discourse balances."[18] Nevertheless, originality is deemed important within the profession and architects continue to measure themselves *against* a tradition. Even in the work of traditionalists like Stern, Andres Duany, and Leon Krier, one sees the influence of modern materials, modern methods of construction, and an incongruity with context that are ill-at-ease with the prescriptions of earlier times. Today's traditionalists are actors in the "now" who compare their work to a distant "then."

Most architects rest their status on the history of architecture and, simultaneously, attempt to overcome its influence to such an extent that they can claim to be

Modernity's Legacy in a New Millennium **27**

"making" history rather than simply working in or repeating it. This is a defense mechanism against the assumed evils of imitation evidenced, for example, in the exclusion of the aforementioned traditionalists – Stern, Duany, and Krier – from the otherwise encyclopedic index of the latest edition of Sir Banister Fletcher's *A History of Architecture*.[19] The profession is not bifurcated into two periods by mere accident; it actively pits history and originality against one another for its own authentication and aggrandizement.

Critical architects know, of course, that there is no such thing as pure creation, creation *ex nihilo*. They know that they are inventing in a context laden with suggestions, influences, a history of problems solved, and, often more important, problems to be avoided. Nevertheless, even the most critical professionals have difficulty escaping an image of linear time unthinkable without notions of a future, a present, a past, and eventually an origin. Every project, traced back far enough, is assumed to have had its moment of intuition, its inspiration, its breakthrough; every project is understood as original because each had its unique moment of genesis in which the architect's intention burst into brilliant existence against a dark backdrop of history conceived not as a ground but as a nothingness in which the illumination of intention is miraculous evidence of humanity's endless capacity for creation.

Architecture is thus understood as operating in one of two timescales. On the one hand, there is the archeologically long, impersonal history of designed artifacts that, while replete with monsters and fossils and composed of accidents and contingencies, is always understood as a single unified accumulation across time. This is disciplinary time. On the other hand, there is the achingly short, personal/professional time of individual design acts bracketed and labeled as discrete units, Allan Greenberg time and Frank Gehry time, for examples. The disciplinary myth of architecture's origins, described as trees and caves and primitive dwellings mimicking these forms of nature, competes with the profession's myth of contemporary genius that attempts to overcome the slow, mucky, and rutted road of history. But there is little use in claiming that one or the other is more correct, and even less use in demonstrating how one fits neatly into the other. Design processes have a very different relation to time, one that is incompatible with such macro- and micro-parsing. Design is a process through which time emerges. Design creates time.

The time that results from activities and products of design is not time as lived by an architect, and probably not that lived by the inhabitants of architecture either. To sit at a drawing board or easel or computer monitor and proceed from the intention to design to immersion in the act itself is to engage in work; and, to engage in work is to be active in the present. Although the designer may consciously reflect on precedents from the past (say, the Classical language) or imaginatively conjure design possibilities into a context of future need or use (the city of 2050 or the myriad utopias dreamed in the past), all these activities are as fully present as the pencil or brush or mouse or stylus by which they take form. Instrumentalized pasts and imagined futures never pre-exist the process, and certainly never exist of

28 Architecture History and Theory in Reverse

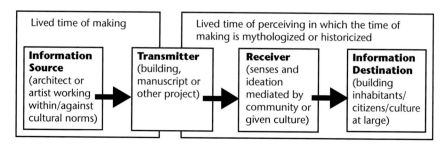

FIGURE 2.3 The structure of communication

necessity. Instead, they enter into the world contingently through the act of drawing connections out of the immediacy and givenness of the studio, its space and materiality, toward what is possible in time.[20]

Architects and other designers under the sway of professionalization are alienated from the design process and their resultant creations in direct proportion to the extent to which they believe themselves to exist in a meta-time in relation to their work. In reality, design work occurs in the normal flow of time; it is the designed object that fluctuates with and/or against the normal flow of time. Once the transmitting artifice exists independently in the world, the project or building may ground time, distribute it, foreshorten or extend it, but not in a predictable way. That we can experience Renaissance and Baroque and Modern and Postmodern artifacts and, more importantly, construct new Renaissance or Baroque or Modern or Postmodern buildings today are both results of a periodization of past lived moments into 'Renaissance' and 'Baroque' and 'Modern' and 'Postmodern' periods. Or, to extend Stern's formulation, "the history of buildings is the history of meaning in architecture [*which is the projection of time*]."[21] Yet just when all this seems understandable and ripe for manipulation by skilled or knowing hands, it is necessary to remember that architectural language is given to polysemy – each figure or trope can acquire different meanings in different times or places. All times and meanings are local. If exported, they are traded only with great effort because they are inevitably tethered to processes subject to the fluctuations of societies and cultures, and the legacies of various ideologies (Figure 2.3).

Notes

1. Friedrich Schlegel, *Athenaeum*, fragment 206, quoted in Anthony Vidler, *The Architectural Uncanny: essays in the modern unhomely* (Cambridge, MA: MIT Press, 1992), 50.
2. Derrida notes: "There is no authentic identification except in a certain non-identification … This fissure is not one among others. It is *the* fissure: the necessity of interval." See Jacques Derrida, *Of Grammatology*, translated by Gayatri Chakravorty Spivak (Baltimore, MD: Johns Hopkins University Press, 1976), 190 and 200.
3. Arjun Appadurai, *Modernity at Large: cultural dimensions of globalization* (Minneapolis, MN: University of Minnesota Press, 2005), 147.
4. Ibid., 184.

5 These are the only forms of context that can be said to exist regardless of whether classification is understood as closed or open, as a single or multi-dimensional field of names, univalent or multivalent.

6 See Leszek Kolakowski's, *Modernity on Endless Trial* (Chicago: University of Chicago Press, 1997), 156.

7 There is a vast difference between intentions and motivations. Motivations serve the architect or designer as internal checks or guides in the making of a project. Future visitors to or inhabitants of a project can be unaware of its architect's motives without adversely affecting the quality of their experience. Intentions are motivations that the architect *intends* to follow the project into the world and are expected to supplement or serve as the work's primary public content.

8 In Classical, biblical, and other now mythological periods, architecture was assumed to have an existence independent of the architect and his or her intentions. Architecture was expected to serve people directly without recourse to architectural treatises or interviews on public television. In fact, it is likely that the authorship of most buildings was (and is) anonymous to all but a few citizens.

9 James Gleick, *The Information: a history, a theory, a flood* (New York: Vintage, 2012), 410.

10 This is particularly true of postmodern architecture which always assumes a ground for architecture that is other than itself; Charles Jencks went so far as to say of deconstruction that "it works best as an exception within a strongly defined norm." See Michael Fazio, Marian Moffett, and Lawrence Wodehouse, *A World History of Architecture*, 2nd edn (Boston: McGraw-Hill, 2008), 525.

11 This problem is well represented in a classic *Sesame Street* skit. Bert and Ernie are preparing to go to sleep when Bert complains about the sound of a dripping faucet. Ernie responds, "No problem Bert," and immediately exits the bedroom. Instead of silence ensuing, a radio comes on. The cycle repeats: Bert complains about the new noise; Ernie says, "No problem"; and sounds from yet another, louder, appliance masks the radio. This skit is an apt metaphor for the tendency of architects to address noise in our built environment by proposing ever-louder solutions that serve only to render all sounds unintelligible.

12 See John Rajchman "A New Pragmatism?" and Michael Speaks "Design Intelligence (2002)" in A. Krista Sykes (ed.), *Constructing a New Agenda: architectural theory 1993–2009* (New York: Princeton Architectural Press, 2010), pp. 90–104 and 204–215, respectively. Rajchman resorts to appropriation of the Pragmatist tradition, particularly William James, as well as conceptualizations of the diagram from Foucault to Deleuze to 'ground' architecture and architectural education. Speaks turns away from theory (so far as to proclaim its end) and toward the "'chatter' of intelligence" as the content that architecture must address.

13 The line continues: "… by which its semantic statement can be carried over into our own idiom." See George Steiner, *After Babel: aspects of language and translation* (New York: Oxford University Press, 1975), 30.

14 As Deleuze and Guattari wrote of Kafka's images, with a nod to Borges, "they contain so many differences from each other because they are absolutely identical." See Gilles Deleuze and Félix Guattari, *Kafka: toward a minor literature*, translated by Dana Polan (Minneapolis, MN: University of Minnesota Press, 1986), 61.

15 Inspired in part by his study of Zen Buddhism, it is said that Cage found inspiration in an anechoic chamber. When he exited the chamber, he reportedly asked an engineer about the hum or buzzing sound he heard while inside. The engineer replied that the sound was Cage's nervous system.

16 The tendency of architects and architectural critics to claim the first two examples listed here – Lin's Wall and Irwin's installations – as forms of architecture only serves to illustrate the fact that architecture is bereft of examples of its own.

17 Steiner, *After Babel*, 28. Steiner notes that the barrier in translation is that

> an interpretative transfer … described as encoding and decoding, must occur so that the message "gets through." Exactly the same model … is operative within a single language. But here the barrier or distance between source and receptor is time.

18 Quoted in Fazio, et al., 524.
19 As Derrida writes, commenting on Rousseau's attitude toward mimesis, "But already within imitation, the gap between the thing and its double, that is to say between the sense and its image, assures a lodging for falsehood, falsification, and vice." See *Of Grammatology*, 205.
20 Deleuze and Guattari, *Kafka*, 60.
21 Robert A.M. Stern, "New Directions in Modern American Architecture: postscript at the edge of the millennium," in Kate Nesbitt (ed.), *Theorizing a New Agenda for Architecture: an anthology of architectural theory 1965–1995* (New York: Princeton Architectural Press, 1996), 100–108. Original quote, which excludes the italicized portion, is taken from p. 103.

3

A POSTMODERN PROFESSION, CIRCA 1991

The edifice is old. It is thought and the history of thought embodied in stone. Cold. Heavy. Architecture is more recent. As a profession it is little more than a few decades old and as a discipline perhaps a few centuries.[1] It is lukewarm and light, in every sense. Architecture emerged to fill a void created, as Victor Hugo suggested, by the advent of the printing press – "How can one be surprised," he asked, "that human intelligence should have quitted [the edifice] for printing?"[2] When buildings lost their primary functions as conveyors of cultural meaning and were reduced to providing shelter or symbolizing excess wealth, a new purpose had to be invented to prop up a tradition losing energy. After a few hundred years, the enormity of this project of justification and the burden of its impossibility led to the founding of our postmodern profession. This new profession's tripartite schema of self-aggrandizing technology, pragmatics, and media (introduced in Chapter 1) serves as a temporary content to fill the void of purpose and masks the discipline's edificial DNA of social, practical, and communicative desires.

Architecture is not unique in its attempts for a new start in the aftermath of tragic revelation. Many professions emerge in this way. When a human activity is depleted of its traditional function, humans institutionalize some aspect of that activity to shore up its place in society. This process fosters continuance by invented necessity in the form of artificial instrumentalities that suggest a slight change in focus and an upgrade in service. This process is healthiest when enacted by individuals consciously – by those cynically motivated, perhaps, but who are aware that they are engaging a defense mechanism for their own protection. Unfortunately, self-awareness is not always evident. Often narratives of progress, evolution, or improvement are imbibed by architects who – due to youth or lack of introspection – believe their profession and themselves to be advanced inheritors of traditions running back to the birth of civilization. As haute couture replaces clothing, as the fashion designer silently denigrates the tailor or seamstress' limitations as mere

32 Architecture History and Theory in Reverse

skilled labor, as law replaces the council of elders and the attorney arrogantly usurps the wise man and reframes his knowledge as mere common sense or provincial wisdom, architecture replaces the edifice. Oblivious to the rupture that runs through the history of new disciplines-pretending-to-be-disciplines-of-old, the architect imagines he is still the master builder, only better, more complete. He or she now offers a wider array of billable services. Such examples can be multiplied at will. But don't; it is a depressing list.

Setting aside the question of lineage for a moment, it is necessary to look at the professional as he or she exists today and explore the relationship that this existence has with the practice of making architecture, that is to say, with design. This too is new. Recent theory offers little more than a series of evasions: loose fits, emergent figures, "an architecture that admits change, accident, and improvisation" and "the production of difference at the local scale, even while maintaining a relative indifference to the form of the whole" as Stan Allen put it.[3] Evasions, by definition, do nothing to overcome the problems to which they are reactions. And, to be fair, it is unlikely that any response to our postmodern profession will result in a new ground for the shared experience of architecture. But neither the fact that the yawning void is primarily institutional and historically recent in its origin, nor the possibility that finding new ways of thinking about the built environment lies outside the current configuration of the profession diminishes the importance of returning to and explicating the relation between maker and made, between information source and transmitter.

It is critical, in short, to understand the recentness of architecture as well as to examine the implications of that recentness. One less than obvious but compelling conclusion is that the discipline of architecture is really a series of disciplines. There were arguably disciplines of societal forms in ancient Greece; of spectacles in ancient Rome; of edifices in mediaeval Europe; of public works in WPA and Progressivist-era America.[4] My intention, here, is less ambitious in scope but more radical in import than a listing of architecture's historical forms: Contemporary and highly professionalized architecture, the making of buildings in more familiar times, only apparently exists in, and as an extension of, a civilization-spanning continuum. Today's architecture – its scientific, social, and academic concerns – emerged as other such disciplines have: not through a long, slow process of evolution but as a series of radical responses to new conditions and challenges. Fits and starts. The apparent unity of architectural history is an invention akin to early archaeology: an arrangement of monsters and fossils, one-offs and common remnants, into a logical sequence that conforms to and confirms a pre-determined narrative of continuous but relatively minor change. Or to use a different metaphor, the discipline of architecture today and the discipline of architecture in the Classical age are as different as *Homo Sapiens* and *Cro-Magnons*; visually similar; genetically distinct. It takes effort, liberal use of imagination, and a willing disregard for facts to link them in a simple chain of paternity.

Nevertheless, most accept this fabricated history without question. It is part and parcel of standard myths of progress toward increasing civilization – that is, a transcendence of the isolated body toward communication with others that ultimately returns and fulfills the body's base needs.[5] If the commonly accepted trajectory of architectural disciplines truly worked in this direction, then the literal truthfulness of this tale of architectural evolution would matter very little. We would, in that situation, find ourselves embedded in meaningful communities, connected to the past and speculating on the future in ways that maximize our existence in the present. Unfortunately, this is not the case in the late West – the United States, Canada, and Australia – or, arguably, anywhere.[6] Instead recent practices have fostered a duller and colder form of making perceived by the general public as exhibiting a yawn of meaning, lacking rootedness. In the late information age, these practices force viewers to cast about for an immediate ground that is found, if at all, in bodily fetishes (amusement parks and casinos) and filmic spectacles (CGI, HD3D, and the latest summer blockbuster), which have simultaneously denigrated the last vestiges of physical language, as witnessed in the average person's inability to decipher the built environment. This absence of systems of meaning from earlier disciplines combined with a simultaneous but reactionary desire for bodily or filmic placed-ness and pleasure has led to the emergence of a new discipline of architecture, rather late in history. One consumed with generating libertine feeling despite its air of environmental and social justice. "Farewell to mystery, myth, law. Fancy and caprice, welcome."[7] Hugo was prescient.

Late Capitalism and Professionalism

1991 witnessed the publication of Fredric Jameson's seminal *Postmodernism, Or, the Cultural Logic of Late Capitalism*. In Chapter 4, "Spatial Equivalents in the World System," he addressed architecture directly. Jameson, building on Guy Debord, documented the rise of importance accorded the image, the use of "historicism as a substitute for history"[8] in his analysis of Frank Gehry's original Santa Monica home, and other issues central to the emergence of professional practice in the 1970s and 1980s. While the idea of professional architects in America started with Latrobe in the early nineteenth century, evolved with McKim, Mead and White at the turn of the twentieth century, and grew into corporate culture with SOM in the 1950s, 1960s, and 1970s,[9] the form of practice that rose to dominance in the 1970s and 1980s – now regarded as the profession's mainstream – is thoroughly postmodern, in Jameson's sense. In it, "repetition rather than radical innovation ... is henceforth at stake."[10] This postmodern profession, concerned as much with marketing and theatricality as with materials and function, constitutes a radical break from preceding practices. This is not a condition that is now past. Our recent forms of architectural endeavor – BIG's bigness, MVDVR's ethos of spectacle, Vidler's "unifying principles," the Rural Studio's spectacles of ethics, OMA's Oz-like constructions – are extensions of, alterations to, or reactions against this postmodern profession, which is to say, still postmodern. And still beholden to capital.

The fact that the contemporary discipline(s) of architecture is (or 'are') not biological offspring of earlier forms of architectural discipline is not particularly

34 Architecture History and Theory in Reverse

problematic. Nor is the possibility that it is many instead of one. Such is the nature of evolution. Its cooption by and for other forces in society, however, deserves questioning. As previously noted, this new discipline pretending to be an old discipline in shiny new clothes has been appropriated by film producers and advertisers, businesses in need of an identity and cities in need of tourism. Do these external elements add diversity to an old, ailing field, or simply play the role of noise rendering the message difficult to decipher or even impossible to hear? Two contributing factors make this question difficult to answer. First is the contradictory nature of the tales: the evolution of the profession versus that evolution's retelling in architectural discourse. Both tales undermine rational evaluation in journalistic discourses that either privilege the present or treat all times as equally fictional. Both attitudes toward the past act to remove any stable ground upon which the competing claims of continuous and episodic change might be measured.

Second, and probably the more direct contributor to the difficulty, is the profession's marketing of itself as an intersection of and response to three aspects of culture: (1) physical and technological; (2) social and pragmatic; and (3) marketing and advertising medias. It instructs us on the environment and the latest technologies available to builders in the age of climate change; it informs us about issues of social justice and the capabilities of buildings to address these; and it celebrates itself as an art form capable of rendering other things more beautiful. It presents itself as a meta-cultural agent. It is, in other words, everything to everyone. This professionalized model, popular on architecture school websites and television, can be so misleading as to misdirect inquiry away from a disciplinary representation of the structure of contemporary architecture found in the intersection of social, practical, and communicative concerns. The difference between these two sets of concerns is belied by the terms used to describe them: the profession's marketing model is based on media instrumentalities; whereas the disciplinary model described in the previous section is composed of expressions of desires, concerns, meaning.

Professional architecture possesses no such aspirations; it merely proffers their marketable facsimile. The professional model is thin. It is reduced in breadth to the zones of intersection among its instrumentalities. Social, practical, and communicative concerns, on the contrary, constitute a discipline not easily reduced to professionalization without destroying the originating desire to communicate through a built environment.

Roots of a New Discipline: 1871–2001

Despite a long entanglement with engineering problems as well as the more recent hype of a proliferation of new technologies, the field of knowledge known as architecture is not a science primarily concerned with physics and technology. Architecture, instead, exists at the intersection of multiple discourses or fields of knowledge that might reasonably be categorized as human or social sciences. Moreover, architecture is not merely an intersection of several social sciences with the domains of physics and technology. Architecture is other than its physical means. At first blush, this statement flouts convention. Yet, to apprehend its veracity, it is necessary only to understand that the emergence of architecture as a discipline and the subsequent rise of the professional architect coincided with a diminution of physics, mechanics, and technology as primary concerns.

The professional architect is an auteur of recent origin working in a field of rapidly increasing complexity. Compared to the body of knowledge necessary to effectively design buildings just a century ago – primarily centered around load-bearing masonry, simple spans, rudimentary heating, plumbing and wiring – the knowledge necessary to design contemporary structures is vast and accumulating faster than changes in styles. In addition to needing a working knowledge of static structures, mechanical, plumbing, electrical, and conveyance systems as in years past, now architects must possess a general understanding of non-static structures, biomimetic materials and skin assemblies, or alternative power generation systems as well as parametric design tools and integrated project delivery techniques. No doubt these areas of knowledge are critical to the practice of architecture in the twenty-first century and probably more difficult to master than the technologies of earlier master builder practices. Yet the rapid increase in the number and types of these bodies of knowledge has been purchased at the price of a steep decline in the expected depth of knowledge and ultimate responsibility of the architect to be able to directly answer any specific technical problem. In part, this is due to nothing more than a shift that is commonplace to every discipline and civilized life in general. With an increase in the total knowledge available, there is a concomitant decrease in the percentage of that total that each individual is expected to acquire. But, again, this overabundance of information, verging on information overload, and the need to pare it down to what is essential are not the sole reason for the demotion of mastery of physics and technology in importance in the field of architecture. Instead, what diverts the discipline's technical trajectory in the late twentieth and early twenty-first centuries is the combination of an increasing need to filter information with a rise in self-aggrandizing technologies (evidenced in both technical imagery and very real attempts at social engineering), pragmatics (budgets and techniques of construction management), and media or journalistic concerns (particularly issues of justice filtered through the sieves of ecology or poverty).

A seismic shift took place moving the field from a simple pairing of "art" and "science," both broadly conceived in the master builder tradition, to a complex tripartite consideration of concerns in the hands of a new discipline. Significant shifts in attitudes tend to follow on the heels of major wars or other traumatic events. As Derrida remarked: "The passage from one structure to the other … cannot be explained by any structural analysis: an external, irrational, catastrophic factum must burst in."[11] These brutal negations of previously collected meanings trigger our desire for reassurance in the form of mimicry of even older narratives or, conversely, inspire calls for something ostensibly new that distances us from our past, or hybridize the two.[12] Examples from American architecture include: the Chicago World's Columbian Exposition, 1950s suburbia and the notion of the 'private' home, corporate green spaces, 'modern' and 'glistening' office parks, the 1776 feet of

36 Architecture History and Theory in Reverse

Libeskind's and Childs' Freedom Tower, and the Niagara-like expanse of the falls of the Ground Zero Memorial. Architecture after the Civil War and Vietnam looked to Europe's past for precedents. Between World War I and II and through the aftermath of Korea, the built environment turned profoundly modern. The pattern, however, is not one of simple cause and effect. The relation is indirect.[13]

To a significant degree, the discipline of architecture, at least in a form with a strong family resemblance to practice today, emerged in the aftermath of a specific event: the Chicago Fire of October, 1871. Although architectural historians glorified the development of elevators, steel and fireproofing, and the subsequent verticalization of cities in the wake of the tragedy, questions of how people should re-build were (and are) broader in scope – and more profound. All three knowledge areas that triangulate today's architectural discipline emerged as topics of concern and were intensely debated in the months and years that followed, including the socio-technical complexities of cities, the pragmatics of codes and land use regulation, and media interests in wealth, poverty, living conditions, and blame.[14] The self-aggrandizing socio-technical, the pragmatic, and the journalistic are loci of both professional and academic architectural discourse because these areas of knowledge came to prominence with historical shifts that brought contemporary forms of mediated desire into being. And this process continues.[15]

Shifting desires change the terms. Architecture today is disconnected from the meaning behind the traditional rhetoric of merging art with science even if this linguistic trope persists. However, the shifts in our late information age make an additional judgment possible: Architecture is no longer, if it ever was, simply a science of human inhabitation. While the aftermath of tragic events brings about a host of technological innovations – improvements of steel, fireproofing, seismic resistance, mass production, pre-fabrication, bombproof construction – attention is drawn, by and large, more and more, to the human condition. People learn how they *should live* alone and among their neighbors. Attention shifts from what they can afford to what is safe or productive; from what is beautiful and good to what is just or right. Tracing the individual histories of these functions, conflicts, and meanings would be interesting. The implications of this divergent formulation as a totality, however, are profound for understanding both the widely intuited sense of professionals and public alike that architecture is no longer any one thing as well as the quiet fear of academics that architecture no longer communicates to anyone other than devotees.

These observations are markers of the entropy of western architectural language. In an age of information overload, our postmodern profession is, in many ways, a predictable outcome of warring factions. Many voices have and continue to speak against this narrowing grain but louder iconoclasts have marginalized them. The preceding generation of iconoclasts, in particular. Ironists, deconstructivists, formalists, and phenomenologists divvied up the last remnants of meaning in the twentieth century and, for better and worse, defined the field to the present day. As a result of their success (one might say "their market share"), the next two chapters attempt to elucidate these factions, lay bare their theoretical biases, and make plain how they packaged their differences into identifiable and marketable forms of information.

A Postmodern Profession, Circa 1991 **37**

Notes

1 "Historically ... the terms 'architect' and 'professional' have not been synonymous." See Mary N. Woods, *From Craft to Profession: the practice of architecture in nineteenth-century America* (Berkeley, CA: University of California Press, 1999), 5.
2 The translation uses the word "architecture" but the reference is clearly to the edifice. Victor Hugo, *The Hunchback of Notre-Dame* (Ann Arbor, MI: Ann Arbor Media Group, 2006), 191. All references made to Hugo and the demise of the edifice herein refer to Book V, Chapter 2, "This Will Kill That," 183–196.
3 These phrases are borrowed from Stan Allen's "Field Conditions," in A. Krista Sykes (ed.), *Constructing a New Agenda* (New York: Princeton Architectural Press, 2010), 118–133. I refer to this text again as it is a seminal text in the shift from orthodox modern practices to new potentialities. Unfortunately, it plays a game of implied rebukes. For instance: "Nonhierarchical compositions cannot guarantee an open society or equality in politics," (p. 131) suggests, wrongly I think, that hierarchical compositions always serve closed societies and inequality. Allen also fails to acknowledge the implications of his own argument; namely, a "loose fit" can be symmetrical or asymmetrical, hierarchical or non-hierarchical; the same is true of "an architecture that admits change."
4 Although we might haggle over names, periods, and even chief characteristics, this list could be expanded beyond the limits of this text.
5 According to Scarry:

> Every act of civilization is an act of transcending the body in a way consonant with the body's needs ... Higher moments of civilization, more elaborate forms of self-extension, occur at a greater distance from the body: the telephone or the airplane is a more emphatic instance of overcoming the limitation of the human body than is the cart.
>
> (Elaine Scarry, *The Body in Pain: the making and unmaking of the world*, New York: Oxford University Press, 1987, 57)

6 Even in places with extraordinarily rich architectural traditions – Greece, Italy, Egypt, China, and Japan, for examples – there is an ongoing debate of how to build in this time.
7 Hugo, *The Hunchback of Notre-Dame*, 187.
8 Fredric Jameson, *Postmodernism, Or, the Cultural Logic of Late Capitalism* (Durham, NC: Duke University Press, 1999), 119.
9 Woods, *From Craft to Profession*, 7. Also, see Woods for discussions of the rise of large firms from McKim, Mead and White to Skidmore, Owings and Merrill, pp. 138–147 and 167–171.
10 Jameson, *Postmodernism*, 104.
11 Derrida, *Of Grammatology*, 258.
12 As Derrida has written:

> The passage was in fact extremely slow, uncertain, and precarious, but since nothing in the previous state contained the structural ingredient to produce the subsequent one, the genealogy must describe a rupture or a reversal, a revolution or a catastrophe.
>
> (*Of Grammatology*, 255)

13 Diagrammatically, the process can be written as follows:

> Major upheaval → shifts in desires → alterations to/reformations of disciplines

14 It is unnecessary to put a fine point on the location, date or cause of the emergence of contemporary practice. There can be little doubt, for instance, that World War II and even the 1906 San Francisco earthquake significantly contributed to a profound

38 Architecture History and Theory in Reverse

evolution of, if not rupture in, the discipline in America. The intended point is more general.

15 A pragmatic narrowing of concerns witnessed in projective practices, for instance, is a direct result of the rejection of utopian or modernist thought by contemporary minds caught in the thrall of consumerism under the cultural logic of late capitalism. For more on this line of thought, see Roemer van Toorn, "No More Dreams? The passion for reality in recent Dutch architecture ... and its limitations," *Harvard Design Magazine* 21 (Fall 2004/Winter 2005): 22–31.

4

FORMAL OR PHENOMENOLOGICAL

A Feud over Information

In Verona, and well outside of its proper place in our reverse chronology, stands a castle built in 1354. Thick masonry walls that long protected the citizens and its leaders eventually became a storehouse for artistic treasures from the fourteenth to the eighteenth century. The twentieth-century insertions that provide these artifacts a home were designed to be incongruous with both the original structure and, at times, with the art. Bridges and catwalks cut diagonally across a void without reference to anything in the edifice. A massive cast concrete diving platform projects an ancient equestrian statue into that same void. Everywhere tiny, almost fragile-looking interventions of reveals and bolted connections and sheets of glass are cut into, placed between, or otherwise juxtapose heavy stone masses. Light pierces the interior through inverted corners. It is a strange and wonderful building.

Carlo Scarpa designed the Museo di Castelvecchio in the late 1950s and early 1960s (see Figures 4.1 and 4.2). The building is modern and ancient, illogical and highly organized, sensuous and cold, heavy and gravity-defying. It fosters extraordinary experiences because it does not confine itself to narrow categories. Castelvecchio is a building rooted in both/and constructions and strange juxtapositions. It is simultaneously difficult to understand and easy to enjoy. Every generation experiences many such moments of bewildering clarity. Despite all we 'know,' our information systems do not match reality's complexity. In response, each generation invents new names and postulates new ways of being in the world. Sometimes these new ways of being coalesce around a major language against which a host of minor languages vie for legitimacy. Arguably, western architectural language split into two dominant camps within a decade of Scarpa's unclassifiable stronghold.

1968 is touted as a watershed year for shifting roles of identity across western culture. The precision of such a date, however, belies the enormity of transformation of which the student actions and mass protests of 1968 were merely a part. A Babel-like profusion of social, cultural, economic, sexual, gendered, class and racial

FIGURE 4.1 Museo di Castelvecchio (exterior), Verona, Carlo Scarpa architect
Source: Photograph by David C. Lewis.

FIGURE 4.2 Museo di Castelvecchio (detail), Verona, Carlo Scarpa architect
Source: Photograph by David C. Lewis.

Formal or Phenomenological **41**

identities gradually gained expression throughout the 1960s and sprawled with ferocity well into the 1970s. Pruitt-Igo would be imploded in 1972, a physical manifestation of a societal implosion decades in the making. Across western culture, these identities and intentions are too numerous to presume to catalog. This exponential growth was mirrored in the professions of the time, particularly philosophy, psychology, literary criticism, and, more recently, biology, geography, and political science. Each underwent a similar proliferation of classifications and theories in an attempt to create enough forms of information to encompass the breadth of experience. In this rich soil grew an abundance of professional self-indulgences and competing marketing claims, postmodern professions and the thrall of media.

Disciplines, as opposed to professions, produce surprisingly few families or classes of intentions. Most fit comfortably into public/private or mind/body forms of classification; and late twentieth-century architecture was no exception. Arguably, two forms of architectural information vied for supremacy throughout the second half of the twentieth century and, while in vogue, held in abeyance premonitions of the profession's twenty-first-century difficulties with talking about and judging built form.[1] Increasing with each generation of Modernism and persisting in the variants that followed, most work of the past century is aligned with, and suffers the limitations of, one of the following identity/intention pairs:

1. *Architectural phenomenologists and architectural phenomenology*. The writings of Alberto Pérez-Gómez, Juhani Pallasmaa, Steven Holl, and Peter Zumthor come to mind. Often appropriating the pioneering work of Edmund Husserl via the derivative writings of Heidegger, Merleau-Ponty and others, architectural phenomenology is a stance toward design intended to privilege the body over the mind or, less abstractly, to produce work that promotes bodily experience as more fundamental to human life than linguistic or conceptual understanding. While the writing and architecture produced under the banner of architectural phenomenology exhibit vast erudition (Pérez-Gómez's *Architecture and the Crisis of Modern Science*) and dedication to sumptuous materiality (Zumthor's Therme Vals), its implicit dangers are those exposed earlier in relation to the mantra "seeing is forgetting the name of the thing one sees." These are explicit in the words of Pérez-Gómez: "We *recognize* the meaning as new and yet we cannot *name* it; we are invited to silence … What the work has to say can be found only within itself, grounded in language, and yet beyond it."[2] It is fair to restate these words rather harshly: if phenomenologically-inspired works possess meaning, it is "meaning" at a level common to hermits and noble savages; it is private, non-communicative, and ultimately solipsistic. Yet, within this theoretical stance, the alternative to solipsism can be worse. To address the communicative void, some phenomenologists resort to narrativizing or "scripting" human experience within their projects. Evidence for this can be found in myriad lectures in which an architect states, unabashedly, "I want the inhabitant to feel _____."

Architecture is reduced to a theater of feelings. It is reasonable to assume that twenty-first-century theatricality derived, at least in part, from phenomenology's privileging of feelings. And it is appropriate to question the ethical justification for such sensual puppeteering.

2. *Architectural formalists and architectural formalism.* The theoretical and built works of Luigi Moretti, Giuseppe Terragni, John Hejduk, and Peter Eisenman are central components of phenomenology's equal and opposite other. Works falling into this classification are identified by the privilege accorded the mind and logical processes of coding and decipherment over the sensual or bodily. Admittedly, as with analyses of phenomenologically-driven architecture, one has to be careful to avoid easy reductions. The best works of Luigi Moretti – Casa del Balilla and Il Girasole, both in Rome – are viscerally evocative even in their poorly maintained condition. Nevertheless, formalism's intentions are narrow and disturbing in equal measure to those of architectural phenomenology. Moretti's writings, for example, are constructed quilt-like from pieces of asocial and non-communicative aspirations. A quick glance at some of his constitutive phrases is revealing: "a fact of technical and functional order," "a work is architecture when one of the possible n structures …," "in a form that, in its figurations, has a complex of relations A (relations of rhythm, of rapport, etc.), a certain presence of this order A must be within the structure, as pure constructive value," "in its characteristic concreteness architecture is structure of density and of energies," "inevitable, intransgressible flashes of reality," "structure binds together and disciplines the different components," "each relationship between the elements of one structure must correspond to an identical relationship within the others; they are isomorphous," "…'parametric architecture' will be born [,] Its ineluctable geometric character, its rigorous concatenation of forms, the absolute freedom of fantasy that will spring up in places where equations cannot fix their own roots, will give it a crystalline splendor."[3] Here, as with phenomenological approaches, scripting substitutes for and, at times, appears intended to compensate for the absence of meaning. With formalism, as opposed to phenomenology, the script is not written to be experienced in the built work by the lay architectural public but instead to be followed by the architect, him- or herself (though almost always 'him'), in the process of making. With formalism, the script is not a path the puppets will ultimately follow but the instructions for the puppeteers to follow in order to construct their marionettes. The results of this process are works of architecture to which the terms of ethics and responsibility do not apply. It is easy, however, to locate the origins of twenty-first-century's ethos of spectacles in the assertive, context-independent constructs of formalism.

For all these obvious differences, it is phenomenology and formalism's two similarities that contribute most to recent disorders of architectural language. First, both ideologies share one attitude about the relationship between experience and Names. Eisenman and Jeff Kipnis and other formalists are as likely to say, "once you can assign a name to a work, you are no longer experiencing it" as any phenomenologist. This shared attitude is essentially a Buddhist perspective and, in an individual's search for peace and quiet, it has much to recommend it. Yet this assumption denies to architecture everything that is communal or public, social or cultural. The idea that ignorance-is-bliss or that aesthetic experience is most properly conducted passively with a blank-cow-like-stare tacitly asserts that architecture is best when it engages nothing more in us than the sensible and intellectual capacities of cats or dogs – for what exactly distinguishes the experiences of humans from other animals if not our assent to language?[4]

Second, both ideologies assume a Classical bifurcation of thought and action, conception and sensation, mind and body. Each stands firmly to one side while entertaining only tertiary excursions into the realm of the other as evidenced by Holl's allusions to poetics in his writing about architecture (linguistic expression) and Eisenman's use of a visually and tactilely rich stone in his "City of Culture" (sensual engagement). This tendency to univalent processes maintains two separate forms of truth, two methods of working, perceiving, and critiquing. If edifices are architectural exemplars rewarding to both private encounters yet also imbued with public or communal meaning, then it is clear why the two competing forms of architectural intentions produced few, if any, edifices in the past century. Given this deep rift, it is unfortunate that the perceivers and inhabitants of architecture in the late twentieth and early twenty-first centuries were and are modern people[5] who do not experience the world in either-or dichotomies – here bodily, there conceptually, in easy isolation. We are thoroughly both/and people who daily experience a sensual and intelligible world that offers a profound critique of both theories of architecture. Even a cursory glance at some of the twentieth-century's most iconic and multivalent work – the buildings of Alvar Aalto and Louis Kahn as well as Carlo Scarpa, for example – reveals the utter inadequacy of either phenomenology or formalism to predict or explain the breadth of human experience such work is capable of delivering. In light of both theories resting their foundations on the mind/body split, it is relatively easy to understand why both have failed to provide the 'other' or 'more' that might constitute meaningful architecture.

Between the two dominant late twentieth-century ideological stances of formalism and phenomenology, architecture was positioned to be both objective and subjective; both conceptually and sensually fulfilling insofar as these two identities anchored opposing corners of a domain across which consensus might have been sought. In architecture as in politics, however, consensus was rejected in favor of partisanship. The interpersonal rejected in favor of the personal. Interrelationships of people across a ground of meaningful things rejected in favor of the relationship of individual subjects to particular objects in non-communicative and, thus, non-communal pairings. Despite their methodological differences, formalism and phenomenologically-driven architecture produce the same results: private enjoyments that differ only along trajectories of solipsistic inclination; the former, like that of the classicist who derives pleasure from solving mathematical problems or assigning birds or insects to their proper biological classification; the latter, like that of the romanticist who contemplates the beauty of a sunset or scent of a flower or the sound of a babbling brook. From both perspectives, architecture is approached as the relationship of a libertine to his momentary and ultimately private object.

Despite the fact that architects such as Aalto, Kahn, and Scarpa might be said to have pointed to a middle way, phenomenology and formalism did not coalesce to form a third and broadly conceived theory. This is because the intended audience of each theory never numbered more than one. Kindly stated, perception and conception – attitudes of subject primacy and object primacy, respectively – are targeted more to the mind of an imagined inhabitant than to a community or world at large. But even that statement gives the executors of the estates of formalism and phenomenology too much credit. When the assumed independence of both perception and ideation is revealed to be, at the very least, greatly exaggerated (as sciences are doing rapidly[6]), when we recognize that sensory and conceptual processes are deeply subjective constructions of and tethers to a world, then it is clear that the architecture that results from privileging one or the other of these theories can be a response only to the mind of an architect and not the community ostensibly served.

Formalism and phenomenology's continued existence in architectural discourse both requires for sustenance and excretes as by-product a belief that individual works of architecture are finite and possess little or no meaning but provide, instead, just enough structure of information to expand in the consciousness of an inhabitant to become *Architecture*. In formalism, this expansion takes the form of the inhabitant's 'decipherment' or 'decoding' of the work and of her 'adding' the architect's previously coded ideas to her own understanding (even if those codes are labeled 'arbitrary,' 'non-representational,' 'artificial,' or 'meaningless' in advance); in phenomenology, it is the inhabitant's 'becoming' through 'discovery' of poetic linkages between the work as mimetic trigger and his or her own physiological, environmental and cultural awareness which 'fleshes out' the experience and serves as architecture's 'other' or 'more'. With the ultimate limit of architecture's potential thus bequeathed to and entombed within individual perceivers or conceivers, the value of architecture itself shrinks to the measure of the minimum effort necessary to evoke these responses. In this reduction unto death, architecture joins other disciplines – notably philosophy and painting – for which twentieth-century obituaries were numerous.

Eisenman and the End of Architecture

"We have always read architecture." Peter Eisenman says this in a note almost at the end of "The End of the Classical." The note continues:

> Traditionally it did not induce reading but responded to it. The use of arbitrariness here is an idea to stimulate or induce the reading of traces witout [*sic*] references to meaning but rather to other conditions of process – that is, to stimulate pure reading without value or prejudice, as opposed to interpretation.[7]

Formal or Phenomenological **45**

The notion that "we have always read architecture" is valid. However, the latter suggestion of a "pure reading without value or prejudice" appears so farcical, so fanciful, as to render Eisenman's conclusions, at best, "fictional." As George Steiner wrote in *After Babel:* "The concept of a normal or standard idiom is a statistically-based fiction," and "languages have been, throughout human history, zones of silence to other men and razor-edges of division."[8] But it is important to note that Eisenman wrote "The End of the Classical" in 1984, near the end of the period of popularized endings, and at a time when meaning had been eulogized by numerous others.

Relying heavily on the classificatory structure of Foucault's *The Order of Things*, Eisenman engages in a game of subtle mis-reading or, in his own words, a substitution of reading as "*indication*" for reading as "meaning or expression."[9] This linguistic play carries profound consequences for subsequent developments within the profession. When Foucault argues that the appearance of man has, as one negative result, brought an end to metaphysics,[10] we should understand that the end of metaphysics was, simultaneously, the end of a specific architectural discipline as it had been practiced for a few centuries – at least since Gutenberg's paradigm-shifting invention. Works of architecture once served as specific figures of desire within the larger field of Desire that encapsulates humanity and its societal concerns. So far, this interpretation conforms to Eisenman's use of *The Order of Things*. And yet, with the rise of the individual and individualistic 'man,' of the subjective inhabitant male or female, to the position not of reader of meaningful or expressive architecture but now a post-Classical imaginative interpreter through which lifeless or impotent, merely *indicative*, buildings gain a foothold on infinity, the work of architecture itself shrinks, ever smaller, until it is merely the representation of a stimulus, however timeless or arbitrary, grand or meek. Through such a conceptual substitution, desire is individualized and its unitary fabric parceled out; and, if pursued to its ultimate conclusion, what Eisenman describes as "the end of the Classical" becomes the end of architecture in general.

This text marks one of the last moments in the history of architecture when some concern is demonstrated that meaning has become detached from information *per se*. Twenty years later, Eisenman would memorialize the end of architecture as well as the Holocaust in his Memorial to the Murdered Jews of Europe in Berlin (see Figure 4.3). It is a work of silence approaching that of the Vietnam Veterans Memorial. The difference between Eisenman's Memorial and those of Maya Lin or the monuments of a typical cemetery is the degree to which the former is designed to look like, or *indicate*, architecture – boxes large enough to walk between or inhabit. If sculpture can memorialize a person, these boxes mark the passing of a discipline.

Given the "deaths" of other disciplines, it seems to have been accepted that this is just the way things are. In the physical work produced by Eisenman's inheritors, architecture's communicative and grounding power is abdicated to the mind of an imaginative individual who has little time or patience or concern for things outside him- or herself. The world once divided into formalists and phenomenologists is

FIGURE 4.3 Memorial to the Murdered Jews of Europe, Berlin, Eisenman Architects
Source: Photograph by Dennis Daniels.

now evermore frequently a world of mere self-expressionists. Perhaps that is just how inheritances play out. Perhaps it is reactionary to pine for lost potential and missed opportunities. And yet, while it may seem like a reasonable line of secession to transition from "architecture as conveyor of cultural meaning" to "architecture as individual expression of the architect" to "*Architecture* as an effect in the mind of isolated inhabitants," the result of this disunion is that physical works are demoted in their communal power to a level equivalent to dreams or family scrapbooks; Architecture is rendered as *mine, yours,* or nothing at all.[11]

Mine, Yours, Eyes and Skin: the Pallasmaa Identity

After Babel, and increasingly across the information age, there is a danger of humanity retreating into isolated subjectivity of me and mine, of becoming trapped in our own skins, so to speak. A zombie apocalypse anti-culture. In his stated intentions, there are few if any architectural theorists in recent time that would appear to be as interested in avoiding this trap as Juhani Pallasmaa. "From the viewpoint of cultural philosophy our entire hedonistic materialism seems to be losing the mental dimension that might in general be worthy of perpetuation in stone"[12] is an acknowledgment of the value of thought – the province of the formalists. Claiming that the "timeless task of architecture is to create embodied existential metaphors that concretize and structure man's being in the world,"[13] that the "phenomenology of architecture seeks the inner language of building,"[14] and that the "encounter of any work of art implies a bodily interaction [and] functions as another person, with whom we converse,"[15] there is cause to believe that the task of the builders at Babel has been rejoined in words if not yet in actions. In such phrases, architecture aspires to be humanity's most communicative art. An equal 'other' or 'more' alongside literature.

Unfortunately, the bulk of the words constituting Pallasmaa's oeuvre undermine the clarity and potency of this position. More common are refrains regarding language and products of ideation that are simple copies or inheritances from a long philosophical tradition skeptical of language. Rousseau was one ("that false wisdom which removes us from our place and never brings us to any other") as was his self-proclaimed disciple, Claude Lévi-Strauss ("It [language] seems to favor rather the exploitation than the enlightenment of mankind").[16] Pallasmaa is not alone in imbibing deeply from this anti-language tradition. This skepticism has taken root to the point of ubiquity; and with ubiquity, it has achieved a kind of conceptual invisibility that allows it to incriminate biological activities, such as seeing, as language's partner-in-crime. For instance, the trend in postcolonial discourses to target "hegemony of vision" as a source of discriminatory practices – accused of spawning nationalisms, racisms, sexisms, class divisions, etc. – is an indictment against language as the communicative corollary of the evil of the gaze. This philosophical double indictment has been well documented by Martin Jay, Jonathan Crary, and others. It is no wonder that architecture imbibed this trend. The evolution of Modernism into many architectural postmodernisms adopted the illicit complicity of these two powerful tools, language and vision, as established in other disciplines and, through guilt by association, proceeded to cast doubt upon various formalisms, aesthetic theories, notions of beauty, and archetypes despite Pallasmaa's occasional claims to the contrary.

In some sense, owing to the advent of mechanical reproduction, the degradation of architecture as a discipline of communicative art was well underway before these suspicions about language and vision were formalized or became widespread. As already noted, Victor Hugo presaged this crisis. In "This Will Kill That," Hugo argued that architecture had ceded its legitimacy as conveyor of meaning to the printing press by the early 1800s.[17] With the gradual loss of its prime societal role in the years that followed, architects attempted to replace narrative, history, and typology with something else. Some privileged technology or environmental performance. In the work of Pallasmaa and other architectural phenomenologists, the body was brought forward – reduced in its capacity for thought; muted in its linguistic power – as the impetus, the trajectory, and the ultimate measure of architecture.

It is difficult to find hope in this ideology. Luce Irigaray calls it a form of nostalgia which "blocks the threshold of the ethical world."[18] Conjoined with blatantly nonsensical phrases sprinkled throughout Pallasmaa's writing (for example, "phenomenologically authentic feelings true to architecture," and "[t]he senses do not only mediate information for the judgment of the intellect; they are also a means of articulating sensory thought"),[19] the result is an architectural identity, or grouping of theories which have found wide adherence bordering on a religious following, that I would call "an affirmative action of the senses". His architectural phenomenology is an attempt to "rectify" the "injustices" suffered by the other senses due to the world's collective adoration of sight and language. But this is an affirmative action utterly lacking the strong ethics of social obligation that one expects from the political variant of that term. Very few built works actually follow this ideological line. But those that do, such as Zumthor's Therme Vals, are visually mute, stripped of an architectural language one might read (see Figure 4.4). Despite an abundance of riches for the four other senses, phenomenology's denigration of vision represents a loss compared to the work of late Modernism – the mature works of Scarpa or Le Corbusier, for example, that were visual and haptic, sensual and formal, material and ideational.

On the surface, architectural phenomenology would seem to call for a continuation of the best aspects of the pursuit of full, material and ideational, presence. However, its constituent texts undermine aspirations to social discourse and to shared/sharable meaning in at least three ways: (1) relying upon individual contingent experiences as universal foundations; (2) authorizing intentional

FIGURE 4.4 Therme Vals, Graubünden, Peter Zumthor architect
Source: Photograph by Sully Clemmer.

Formal or Phenomenological **49**

manipulation of inhabitants by architects; and (3) directly promoting asocial and solipsistic experience as the purpose of making architecture. Each of these anti-discursive methodologies is found in abundance in Pallasmaa's texts. The following are not exemplars but rather typical statements for which dozens of similar comments can be substituted:

1. "Surely the fact that certain early memories retain their personal identifiability and emotional force throughout our lives provides convincing proof of the importance and authenticity of these experiences, just as our dreams and daydreams reveal the most real and spontaneous contents of our minds."[20] Granting that the things and events remembered and which occupy most the conscious and subconscious mind tend to be those things that matter to an individual, it is unclear how this truism provides a foundation on which an architect might design for people (plural) as opposed to an individual or, more precisely, for anyone other than the architect (singular).
2. "As architects we do not primarily design buildings as physical objects, but the images and feelings of the people who live in them."[21] In Pallasmaa's variant of phenomenology, architects are challenged, not to design objects that people might use and enjoy according to their will or varying needs while imbibing a larger cultural milieu of context and place but, instead, to design the experience inside the minds of the building's inhabitants. As previously stated, the practice of architecture as perceptual or conceptual mind control is ethically untenable. Its intent is manipulative. The design of "feelings" is best left to the makers of movies and writers of novels as these are things that people enjoin by choice and only for very brief passages of time. Arguably, this advocacy for sensual puppeteering is a logical outcome of a much larger agenda foisted on the discipline by its professionalization: that is, the need for architecture to be marketable, active, always struggling for greater conscious awareness in the minds of inhabitants, users, and most importantly potential clients.
3. "A strong architectural experience always produces a sense of loneliness and silence irrespective of the actual number of people there or the noise. Experiencing art is a private dialogue between the work and the person experiencing it which excludes all other interaction." "Architecture presents the drama of construction silenced into matter and space; architecture is the art of petrified silence."[22] If he were to adopt and adapt Valéry's words, Pallasmaa might say that *seeing, hearing, touching, tasting, and smelling is forgetting the name of the thing one sees, hears, touches, tastes, and smells.* Experience, in this view, resists speech as well as writing; it is here presented as wholly non-communicative and the social, the ideational, the forms of meaning larger than an individual are cast aside in favor of pure libertine embodiment as if such individualistic purity were possible – or, indeed, pure.

I rehearse these arguments against architectural phenomenology only to highlight a discrepancy. The stated intentions of Pallasmaa and other architectural

50 Architecture History and Theory in Reverse

phenomenologists appear to align with those who seek to backdrop community against a meaningful built environment and mimic the drives that fueled the actions of the people in the story of Babel. Yet those stated intentions give way, over the course of various essays (and a scant collection of built phenomenologically-driven works), to an attitude regarding language, vision, and ideation in general that has, as its biblical corollary, more in common with God's action at Babel than with the aspirations of its builders; that is to say, architectural phenomenology extends the existential crisis of Babel and Renaissance 'man' and Modernity by working toward the isolation and privatization of meaning as a pilgrimage in *presence* (which "*ought to be* self-sufficient") at the expense of community (which is derided, seemingly, as a *supplement*, an "*exterior*, outside the positivity to which it is super-added"). Of course, this critical line belongs to Derrida[23] and is best understood in the context of the language games of the middle and late twentieth century.

Notes

1 For an example of twenty-first-century architecture profession's continuing difficulties in talking about architecture, see Samuel Medina's essay, "Gab Fest: an Un-conference Conference probing a discipline in 'crisis' is short on solutions but high on drama," *Metropolis* (November 2015): 124.

2 Alberto Pérez-Gómez, "The Space of Architecture: meaning as presence and representation," in Steven Holl, Juhani Pallasmaa, and Alberto Pérez-Gómez, *Questions of Perception: phenomenology of architecture* (San Francisco: William Stout, 2006), 7–25. The quoted text is taken from pp. 22–23.

3 See Luigi Moretti's "Structure as Form" and "Form as Structure" in Federico Bucci and Marco Mulazzani, *Luigi Moretti: works and writings*, translated by Marina deConciliis (New York: Princeton Architectural Press, 2002), 175–177 and 182–184, respectively.

4 Teasing apart Rousseau's thoughts on pity and imagination, Derrida writes, "animals, although they are gifted with intelligence, are not perfectible. They are deprived of the imagination, of that power of anticipation that exceeds the givens of the senses and takes us toward the unperceived." On the following page, he continues, "Imagination inaugurates liberty and perfectibility because sensibility, as well as intellectual reason, filled and satiated by the presence of the perceived, is exhausted by a fixist concept." See Jacques Derrida, *Of Grammatology*, translated by Gayatri Chakravorty Spivak (Baltimore, MD: Johns Hopkins University Press, 1976), 182 and 183 respectively.

5 Modern people being very post breakdown of the bicameral mind. Outside the scope of the present analysis, Julian Jaynes' argument for the difference between pre-conscious and conscious mental processes is interesting in its own right; see Julian Jaynes, *The Origin of Consciousness in the Breakdown of the Bicameral Mind* (New York: Houghton Mifflin, 1976).

6 Cognitive scientists continue to accumulate evidence suggesting that logic and potential for rational thought derive from emotional response. One of the earliest popular texts to explore this linkage is Antonio R. Damsio's *Descartes' Error: emotion, reason, and the human brain* (New York: Avon, 1994). Even Derrida notes this general principle of the necessary linkage between ideational and emotive content when he writes, "only a being capable of symbolizing ... may let itself be affected by the other in general." See *Of Grammatology*, 165.

7 From note #23 of Eisenman's "The End of the Classical: the end of the beginning, the end of the end," in Kate Nesbitt (ed.), *Theorizing a New Agenda for Architecture* (New York: Princeton Architectural Press, 1996), 212–227. Note is taken from p. 227.

8 See George Steiner, *After Babel: aspects of language and translation* (New York: Oxford University Press, 1975), 46 and 56.

Formal or Phenomenological **51**

9 Eisenman, "The End of the Classical," 223.
10 See "The analytic of finitude," in Michel Foucault's, *The Order of Things: an archaeology of the human sciences* (New York: Vintage, 1994), 312–318.
11 If union is valued and it is claimed that architecture should be alive and active in the experience of inhabitants of a place, if physical constructions are to have the capacity to ground community and (ideally, perhaps) belong to a lineage conceived as the uninterrupted history of a discipline, then something of the infinite, something that is perceptual and conceptual along with other qualities not yet defined – something like the continuum of Desire – is necessary and must be incorporated into the work itself, I do not believe architecture is dead. Our historical vision is often, simply, too short-sighted and our willingness to cast away our inheritance often fueled less by rugged independence than by the terrible anxiety of standing in the shadow of the towering edifice of the accomplishments that came before.
12 Juhani Pallasmaa, "The Geometry of Feeling: a look at the phenomenology of architecture," in Kate Nesbitt (ed.), *Theorizing a New Agenda for Architecture*, 448–453. The quoted excerpt is taken from p. 448.
13 Juhani Pallasmaa, "An Architecture of the Seven Senses," in Steven Holl, Juhani Pallasmaa, and Alberto Pérez-Gómez, *Questions of Perception: phenomenology of architecture* (San Francisco: William Stout, 2006), 27–37. The quoted text is taken from p. 37.
14 Pallasmaa, "The Geometry of Feeling," 450.
15 Pallasmaa, "An Architecture of the Seven Senses," 36.
16 Both quoted in Derrida's *Of Grammatology*, pp. 141 and 101 respectively.
17 A good friend and architect has challenged my reading of "This Will Kill That" by pointing out that Hugo was referring to statuary or story carvings – literally named "histrionics" – and that the body of the building, the 'architecture', never carried meaning. I do not think this is correct. Hugo insists over and over that the printing press – via a usurpation of all forms of literacy that are not concerned with written language – will kill the edifice. Obviously, the biblical stories and local histories carved in the cathedrals were carved in statuary. But, as terminologies change over time, it is worth noting that the "edifice" and the "cathedral" and "architecture" in general were the composite of what we now consider the building *per se*, its statuary, inscriptions, mosaics, etc. The rending of these arts from one another is of more recent origin. In my opinion, architecture conceived in the absence of such totality does not deserve the name. Moreover, Hugo is insisting it is this conception of architecture – a building that serves to record and disseminate history and myth – that the printing press killed.
18 Luce Irigaray, "Love of the Other," in *An Ethics of Sexual Difference*, translated by C. Burke and G.C. Gill (Ithaca, NY: Cornell University Press, 1993), 142. The preceding sentence is prescient: "His nostalgia for a first and last dwelling prevents him from meeting and living with the other."
19 See Pallasmaa, "The Geometry of Feeling," 449 and "An Architecture of the Seven Senses," 30, respectively.
20 Pallasmaa, "The Geometry of Feeling," 450.
21 Ibid., 450.
22 See "The Geometry of Feeling," 452 and "An Architecture of the Seven Senses," 31, respectively.
23 Both quotes are taken from Derrida's *Of Grammatology*, p. 145. The core of the argument can be found in Part II, Chapter 2 "…That Dangerous Supplement…", pp. 141–164.

5

DECONSTRUCTION, IRONY, THE POMPIDOU, AND THE *SÃO PEDRO*

Formalism and phenomenology did not emerge from or blossom within a unified field. Architecture's late twentieth-century division took place in a context of increasing skepticism toward languages' connection to reality. This skepticism took various forms outside and within the discipline of architecture and methods emerged appropriate to each. Arguably, three such practices are at play in the evolution of architecture's recent trends: deconstruction, irony, and technological determinism. Deconstructivists studied the work of philosophers' and literary critics' who analyzed texts without recourse to a stable datum of meaning and developed methodologies for pitting the terms in each work against one another to both expose inherent biases and construct new readings. Ironists appropriated techniques of playful juxtapositions from literature and theater to overcome the rhetorical emptiness of novel forms and to either subvert or reinforce the commonly accepted readings of known forms. Technological determinists eschewed such language games and language-as-meaning altogether. These architects made buildings that exposed and celebrated building technologies as a (perhaps, *the*) form of information appropriate to the discipline.

A number of significant architects and theorists worked within each strategy. Rather than rehearse a litany of contributors and buildings, I will focus each movement through the lens of its most notable proponent or exemplary product: (1) Derrida's deconstruction; (2) the irony of Venturi Scott Brown; and (3) Piano and Rogers' technological marvel, the Pompidou Centre.

Derrida

No non-architect is as closely identified with twentieth-century architectural thought as French philosopher Jacques Derrida. Nor did any other twentieth-century thinker create or question as many identities.[1] The work is difficult to sum

Deconstruction, Irony, the Pompidou **53**

up or paraphrase. Derrida's philosophical oeuvre gains in complexity with every word written, and read, because Derrida himself asserted the importance of putting every word and phrase into question – of replacing each with its opposite, at the very least, if not with myriad other readings. With that in mind, the following remarks are limited to readings of three essays – "Architecture Where Desire Can Live," "The Hinge [La Brisure]," and "Edmond Jabès and the Question of the Book." Even within this narrow selection, only issues pertinent to the proliferation of information in architecture will be plumbed.[2]

Ontology thrived in the writings of the ancient Greeks, was borrowed and corrupted by Neo-Platonists and Christian apologists, and fell into disrepute with the flowering of Romanticism. It re-emerged as a topic of study in philosophy and related disciplines only in the late nineteenth century with the awakening of modernity and nationalistic tendencies. It was perhaps inevitable that doubt regarding its veracity would also re-emerge. These doubts sparked shifts in speculative philosophy and spawned myriad offshoots. For the most part, these shifts took the form of simple adaptations of traditional ontology to modern life – for example, in the work of the existentialists (see Chapter 2, "Modernity's Legacy in a New Millennium"). This is not true of Derrida. Through his work, historical references, the power of the noun, the Name, order and codification, and legibility replaced the tropes of existentialism and other forms of adaptive ontology[3] as primary terms of engagement. Derrida re-centered traditional ontology itself as a cultural artifact to be excavated, incised, and literally deconstructed.

Architecture mirrored the development of western philosophy over the past two centuries: it moved toward a synthesis of architectural Modernism and Existentialism then disintegrated almost as soon as a viable framework was established. The path from cultification to rejection of Heidegger and Sartre in philosophy or Le Corbusier and Mies van der Rohe in architecture was rapid. There are at least four significant factors that led to this reversal:

1. Rapid but conflicting advances in science and technology (and the resulting increase in the violence of war), the rise of linguistics, and the challenges to foundations by Nietzsche and others necessitated a philosophical re-engagement with the problem of grounds or foundations. Many thinkers chose to pursue this urge toward its source in Being or, to those who found this line of thinking untenable, toward its fulfillment in a substitute in the form of History, Culture, Language or Place – that is, toward something that appears as given or natural. Derrida countered. "It is not at all natural. The setting up of a habitable place is an event."[4] Architecture and notions of place are ephemeral constructions that do not provide a tether to a universal ground. "Encounter *is* separation,"[5] Derrida notes. "*Spacing* (notice that this word speaks the articulation of space and time, the becoming-space of time and the becoming-time of space) is always the unperceived, the nonpresent, and the nonconscious."[6] To the extent that human experience might be said to have a ground, it exists only in the real but unconscious and non-locatable

separations between every person, act, and event: a literal non-presence; a perceived absence. Architectural phenomenology's reliance on a metaphysic of presence is incapable of acknowledging this profound absence. Architectural formalism and its attempts to physically construct rhetorical figures, "spacing," and "events" through imagistic "traces" miss the mark. And while Bernard Tschumi's descriptions of "event spaces" draw heavily upon Derrida's language, the built works, by and large, appear to do no more than allude to these ideas as physical diagrams – his Parc de la Villette, perhaps, being a notable exception (see Figure 5.1).

2. With renewed efforts to establish political, social, and moral foundations after World War I, ontology was once again seen as a legitimate area of research. This seriousness resulted in increasing numbers of academically trained philosophers, the invention of sub-specialties, and an expansion of

FIGURE 5.1 Parc de la Villette, Paris, Tschumi Architects
Source: Photograph by Amber Ellett Penman.

Deconstruction, Irony, the Pompidou **55**

philosophical publishing. This in turn led to a baroque complexity in the study of Being that had not existed since the alchemists. *Being-in-of-for-with-* etc. dominated early twentieth-century theory. As might have been anticipated, by mid-century there was a revolt against academic complexity. This is evidenced most clearly in structuralism, a philosophical variant of architecture's *less is more*. Derrida sees this reductionist tendency as driven by a profound double misidentification of human culture with nature and nature with simplicity (or, culture ← nature = simplicity).

Both equivalences are, in Derrida's view, fatuous. "One emerges from the book only within the book, because… the book is not in the world, but the world is in the book."[7] Understanding that "book" here implicates "text" and text, by extension, "culture," Derrida inverts the terms of the previous formula: *culture*, in its intricacies and complexities, gives to humans their conception of *nature* and *world* among other assumed "givens." *One emerges from culture only within culture, because… culture is not in nature, but nature is in culture.* "Only infinite being can reduce the difference in presence,"[8] he argues in an anti-reductionist grain that swept the hard sciences as well as the humanities in the 1970s. What is 'more' is also 'different' and becomes increasingly difficult to explain with simple laws wielded by simple animals.[9] Derrida applied this view directly to architecture.

> Perhaps there is no architectural thinking. But should there be such thinking, then it could only be conveyed by the dimension of the High, the Supreme, the Sublime. Viewed as such, architecture is not a matter of space but an experience of the Supreme which is not higher but in a sense more ancient than space and therefore is a spatialisation of time.[10]

Arguably, then, *Chora* is a more useful term than space and the striving for foundations to architectural discourse is revealed as always already a striving for something outside everyday human discourse, beyond the solipsistic body, and more than contingent personal history. Architectural experience is, at the very least, broader than the brackets of phenomenology can contain or the algorithms of formalism can construct without significantly diminishing what we mean by experience.

3. Modernization in technologies and literature simultaneously created a sense of dislocation and a desire for a return that could overcome the perceived depth and pace of change. The ontological turn, in other words, was an appeal to slowness if not stasis. Heidegger responded by promoting the (invariably positive) lived experience of *dwelling*. Derrida responds to Heidegger with the *caesura* – the interruption or pause – that is not so much the opposite of dwelling as its neutral (non-valued) but necessary spacing. "Within the horizontality of spacing…it is not even necessary to say that spacing cuts, drops, and causes to drop within the unconscious: the unconscious is nothing without this cadence and before this caesura."[11] It is in this spacing in the form

of a pause or interruption that meaning is made distinguishable. "But, primarily, the caesura makes meaning emerge ... without interruption – between letters, words, sentences, books – no signification could be awakened."[12] It is this opening for meaning that marks Derrida's importance and what is most often missed by his architectural inheritors.[13]

4. Ripe with internal inconsistencies of which many early twentieth-century philosophers slowly became aware,[14] the concepts of dwelling, foundations, Being itself were thrown open to analysis and, by mid-century, full-fledged skepticism. In orthodox histories, this outcome is recorded as the end of metaphysics and, by extension, all research into universal foundations in the humanities. Derrida, on the contrary (and against the stereotype in which his work is often framed), sees in this an affirmation of intellectual endeavor.

> If words and concepts receive meaning only in sequences of differences, one can justify one's language, and one's choice of terms, only within a topic [an orientation in space] and an historical strategy. The justification can therefore never be absolute and definitive.[15]

The lack of absolutes and definitive justifications are forms of opportunities, openings to potential meaning: "A poem [and by extension all culture productions, philosophy and architecture included] always runs the risk of being meaningless, and would be nothing without this risk."[16] With these last sentences, Derrida does something that architectural phenomenology, formalism, Eisenman, Pallasmaa, and other contemporary architectural identities have proven incapable of doing. He explains why simply continuing to build the archetypal and vernacular forms of the past does not satisfy the urge to meaning in an information age culture. To continue to build in that way is to appropriate a historical contingency in hopes of finding absolute and definitive justification. It is indicative of an aversion to risk that, unfortunately, can ground only meaninglessness. But if Derrida dismisses the easy trope of copying history to gain legitimacy, his discourse cuts in the opposite direction with equal lethality. A poem would be nothing without the risk of meaninglessness; in other words, a poem that would demur the unattainable aspiration to objective meaning and chose instead to wallow in the limited certainties of subjectivity would not deserve the name 'poem.' These words apply to architecture in equal measure: architecture *always runs the risk of being meaningless, and would be nothing without this risk.*

Risqué Irony: Venturi Scott Brown

A diverse body of research, ranging from anthropology to linguistics and philosophy, emerged by the end of the 1960s and focused attention on the role that language plays in how we understand and, more significantly, what we experience as our world. The writings of Claude Lévi-Strauss, Benjamin Lee Whorf, and Michel

Foucault found wide readership. Whorf, for example, argued that unconscious "intricate systematizations of [our] own language" control our thoughts.[17] Drawing on this body of research, an architectural theory of the middle way – neither a narrow formalism of algorithms nor a phenomenology verging on sensual puppeteering – was in circulation by the 1970s. In that decade before Derrida's rise to prominence in English-speaking design programs, theorists such as George Baird, Charles Jencks, and Alan Colquhoun were opening the terrain of symbolism and reference to an architectural community loathe to abandon the fictions of modernism's purity and its myth of architect as savant who has no need for history. Christopher Alexander would publish his great manifestos for a pattern language by decade's end.

Within this middle path, and perhaps among all works of architectural theory composed in the twentieth century, no text so exposed both the general lack of awareness of and critical need for communicative physical form as Robert Venturi, Denise Scott Brown, and (in later editions) Steven Izenour's *Learning from Las Vegas*. This slim volume offers firm rebukes to formalism and phenomenology's shared "language is the enemy of experience" mythos by acknowledging the necessity for language and knowledge of historical forms to achieve conditions favorable to societal interaction. It is a seminal text insofar as it is the first to attempt to recoup significant society-grounding qualities of myth-era constructs for an information age audience:

> Meeting the architectural implications and the critical social issues of our era will require that we drop our involuted, architectural expressionism and our mistaken claim to be building outside a formal language and find formal languages suited to our times. These languages will incorporate symbolism and rhetorical appliqué … When Modern architects righteously abandoned ornament on buildings, they unconsciously designed buildings that *were* ornament. In promoting Space and Articulation over symbolism and ornament, they distorted the whole building into a duck.[18]

With the notable exception of the ongoing work of the Congress for the New Urbanism and the possible exception of Rem Koolhaas' appreciation for pop culture and kitsch, little of the import of this book survives in twenty-first-century architectural practice or education. Four implicit lessons of this remarkable book, however, are worthy of note in the spread and mutation of western architectural language. These include the importance of legibility, the power of the misquote, the hierarchy of symbols over space, and the value of complexity:

1. Physical languages or typologies differ in their practical value in the extent to which they are legible to the general populace. The conveyance of meaning differs in place and time as a result of the unique circumstances of inhabitants' and users' lives. "Architecture depends in its perception and creation on past experience and emotional association,"[19] the authors note in their analysis of the Vegas Strip. But they are fully aware that there are always two levels of

familiarity or legibility at work, which Ernst Gombrich would have termed physiognomic versus conventional meaning.[20] Physiognomic meaning is rooted in a personal history, a personal body, and extrapolated notions of a universal body (*à la* phenomenology) as a physiological result of evolution; conventional meaning draws on a broader cultural awareness including immersion in traditions and histories. Egyptian, Greek, and Roman forms – those pyramids and obelisks, columns and pediments, arches and domes that are common to the Las Vegas tableau and subsequent commercial strips everywhere – comprise the general public's vocabulary on the built environment: unspoken, perhaps unspeakable, but understood in broad strokes by almost everyone through enculturation. Architects aware and capable of manipulating both levels, the personal and the culturally inculcated, multiply their means of introducing complexity and contradiction, and thereby encoding possible meanings, into their work. "That is," as the authors write much later with a subtle shift of emphasis, "architecture that depends on association in its perception depends on association in its creation."[21]

2. A physical language exists when elements have been ordered and codified. Its authority or power to affect outside of its own time and place, however, is heightened in inverse proportion to the general public's understanding of that order and codification. This observation is the source of formalism and phenomenology's shared rejection of names as a method for extending or heightening or privileging experience ("seeing is [not quite being able to place] the name of the thing one sees"). Admittedly, to say that a language's potency is, to a significant degree, rooted in the average person's lack of fluency or inability to speak the elements' proper names is counter-intuitive. But it is rooted in psychology. In part, authority is conveyed by lack of fluency because humans seek order, order is a form of power, and power, in turn, is a form of desire. As with all figures of desire, it is precisely the gaps in knowledge or understanding that give a thing its "need-to-be-acquired" quality.[22] The greatest architectural example of this is the Classical language as recorded by Vitruvius, which is operative today as a result of a broad but general architectonic literacy and specific illiteracy of the populace. Las Vegas Strip architecture of the 1960s, 1970s, up to the present, appears laughable to architects, artists, historians or well-traveled novices with fluency in the referenced languages. To tourists with limited architectural awareness, however, it appears as grandeur, as beauty, as a clear intent to communicate in a foreign and exotic tongue. Even to indoctrinated and savvy observers, intentional misquotes or inappropriate references or incongruous juxtapositions of elements or unexpected materials drawn from discordant traditions can disarm our default (or trained) cynicism and allow for a moment of (near pure) perception. "The familiar that is a little off," in Venturi's words, "has a strange and revealing power."[23]

3. When viewed by savvy observers in a mode closer to denotative than connotative understanding, a physical language or typology is composed of nouns. Not personal pronouns nor verbs or adverbs. Proper and generic nouns.

Deconstruction, Irony, the Pompidou **59**

We stand in front of things and say 'it is _____' not 'my feeling is _____' or 'it causes _____.' In Venturi Scott Brown's words, it is "an architecture of communication over space ..." in which the "Symbol dominates space."[24] Architecture that takes communication or the grounding of cohesive communities as its 'other' or 'more' is not an architecture that directs attention to space because space in and of itself is, tautologically, non-communicative. Meaning can be embedded in matter if it can be embedded anywhere. Of course, the privileging of matter and symbols brings inherent risks, ranging from the making of neutral or banal spaces to places of sadistic domination:[25] the objects made and their proportions represent hierarchies, knowledge, and power. If done poorly, without reference to a physical language that the inhabitant has some familiarity with, it reduces subjects to awed foreigners standing outside the language. But the risk of not attempting communicative materialized architecture is greater still. According to Venturi Scott Brown,

> Our money and skill do not go into the traditional monumentality that expressed cohesion of the community through big-scale, unified, symbolic, architectural elements ... apart from theaters and ball parks, the occasional communal space that is big is a space for crowds of anonymous individuals.[26]

4. The power or authority, the grounding desires, of physical languages can be induced by juxtaposition or methods of collage. This is perhaps the most important lesson. Information age buildings can gain in communicative power by hybridizing historical references in ways that are contradictory at a conceptual level. This includes using contemporary materials to build traditional forms, traditional materials to build contemporary forms, along with a host of other permutations such as placing forms in contexts of which they are of little or no use (note, again, Tschumi's waterwheel, Figure 5.1).

In a passage of self-critique, Venturi and Scott Brown write: "We began to realize that few of our firm's buildings were complex and contradictory ... There was little in our work of inclusion, inconsistency, compromise, accommodation, adaptation, superadjacency, equivalence, multiple focus, juxtaposition, or good *and* bad space."[27] The value of this criticism of the work of Venturi Scott Brown by Venturi, Scott Brown, and Izenour is the importance they place in overcoming either-or thinking in the making of communicative (or, at least, potentially communicative) architecture. "Irony may be the tool with which to confront and combine divergent values in architecture for a pluralist society and to accommodate the differences in values that arise between architects and clients."[28]

Pompidou and the *São Pedro*

In 1941, four Brazilian fishermen, or *jangadeiros*, sailed from Fortaleza south, down the Atlantic coast of South America, to Rio de Janeiro to protest both a serfdom-like economic system and the *jangadeiros'* ineligibility for national retirement benefits. The four men weathered more than 1600 miles and 61 days at sea on their traditional six-log fishing raft (*jangada*). Upon arrival, they were greeted as national heroes and escorted directly to meet with President Vargas. Their *jangada*, the *São Pedro*, was carried on the crowd's shoulders through the streets of Rio. Though not architecture, that small raft offers several points of comparison with mid-century technologically-oriented practice, an exemplar of which is Renzo Piano and Richard Rogers' Pompidou Centre built 5700 miles away some three decades later (see Figures 5.2 and 5.3).

It has been said that repetition makes most things look better. A field of bricks in a wall or floor or street is more beautiful than the individual burnt clay block. A harbor with a dozen or more masts, riggings, and sails triggers an emotive response in seasoned sailor and landlubber alike. To look down and see underfoot a straightforward repetition of log beside log beside log is charming (if not exactly comforting). In the straightforward technology of a *jangada*, these simple repetitions allow the character of the materials, the hand, the trace of its service, that is to say, its details or characteristics of both direct presence and history to come forward. As Marco Frascari might have said, perception of the *São Pedro* is equally constructed and construed.[29]

A simple rewording of the preceding sentences to describe the Pompidou is not possible without taking significant liberties with common understanding of some

FIGURE 5.2 Pompidou Centre (façade), Paris, Piano and Rogers Architects
Source: Photograph by Amber Ellet Penman.

FIGURE 5.3 Pompidou Centre (corner), Paris, Piano and Rogers Architects
Source: Photograph by Scott Penman.

of the terms. The word "repetition," with its human bias, its connotation of intentional action, is inappropriate to machine mass-produced elements; and the common alternative, "reproduction," is linked to procreation despite Walter Benjamin's celebrated use of that term. "Frequency" is more on point in works through which architects attempt to make a demonstration of particular technologies. And frequency, as a form of oscillating repetition unaffected by hand or history, is understood as so unintentional as to dethrone character – which it no longer serves – as an old-fashioned idea tethered to romantic notions of change over time.

At the Pompidou Centre, frequency becomes the meta-meter replacing previous aesthetic or functional measures. Whereas the perception of repetitions in the *São Pedro* could be compared positively, negatively or in neutral terms to the history of *jangadas* and their necessary function, the turn to frequency as primary conveyance of content at the Pompidou bars external measures of history or function. The individual systems, and each system individuated as a frequency of constituent parts, supersede history and are displayed for appreciation outside their function. In fact, it is possible to argue that the myriad elements of structural, mechanical, and conveyance systems are moved to the exterior by Piano and Rogers simply to decorate the shed; in other words, functional elements are converted to ornament and the frequency of their

62 Architecture History and Theory in Reverse

appearance on the skin of the building serves no purpose other than to ironically garner attention:

> Parts = visibility. More parts = more visibility.

A key distinction between the *São Pedro* and the Pompidou, both nearly pure manifestations of two sets of technology (one very old and the other more recent), lies less in the types of technology exhibited than in the direction of reference.[30] This is a difference that matters. The Pompidou is less like other buildings than the *São Pedro* is like other rafts. In Paris, ornament expected at the center or core of buildings is committed to the periphery; the normally occluded or inaccessible is made apparent in an attempt to radicalize difference. Hyper-difference is exhibited by Piano and Rogers as if it is a new being – a replacement Being – that announces its temporal displacement from the city's fabric. It is a building made to be a spectacle even in the city of lights. "'There's nothing to be wondered at there,'" as one of de Sade's characters says, "'one need but be mildly jaded, and all these infamies assume a richer meaning.'"[31] And, more or less, this is successful. Nevertheless, radical heterogeneity puts the burdens of searching for co-existences, external hierarchies, and dependencies on visitors who are made responsible both for constructing the Pompidou's proper name or unique identity out of myriad common elements of which it is composed and, working in the opposite direction, discovering the essential common names, its large-scale ordering, that links it to other Parisian buildings. While it could be argued that this radicalized difference is constructed upon the shared elements and systems common to all buildings in an attempt to provide a datum so that the building is construed (but not *seen*) as part of the histories of architecture and of Paris, it is not rooted in symbols that the general public might understand or even find vaguely familiar. It looks less like a foreign language than an alien one. It fails to meet Venturi Scott Brown's call for general legibility. While the pieces and parts of its actual construction are largely known, its composition is so intentionally unfamiliar that when tourists look for meaning or collections of meanings that might anchor the building in its context or discipline, they are likely to be frustrated. The apparent absence of relation to a known language of architecture, in either history or place, results in the architects themselves emerging as the only possible loci of reference for the Pompidou (*à la* Rem Koolhaas at the Seattle Public Library). It is more common than not for a person seeing this building for the first time to ask, "What were the architects thinking?" than "What is it?" – thus the building also fails Venturi Scott Brown's test of valuing the symbol over its empty space or, in this case, its absent makers.

This brings into focus half of the core criticism of architecture identified as "technologically-oriented" or architects as "technological determinists." Fear of the invisible is exhibited in the Pompidou; but the invisibility does not refer to the object, the work of architecture. To make so many normally hidden elements visible and mechanically frequent is to make them equal, inert and subservient in respect for its authors. Naming, of course, is at play here. But *everything* is named at

Deconstruction, Irony, the Pompidou **63**

the Pompidou and, due to that comprehensiveness, each aspect is underwhelming in a way that is analogous to the flotsam of which *Ulysses* is composed.[32] Appreciation for *Ulysses* is, to an exceptional degree, an appreciation for James Joyce and the breadth and frequency of his external references – "Joyce is so very well read; I hate his books but he is so very talented," is a type of praise not difficult to imagine. Appreciation for the Pompidou, similarly, lies not in its shared meaning nor in its audacity nor in its technical prowess but in the respect it demands for its authors and their encyclopedic virtuosi display: "Wow! Amazing! They exposed everything."

The other half of this line of criticism against seemingly technologically driven architecture is much subtler than, and yet inextricably enmeshed in, fear of the invisible. Human artifacts like the *São Pedro* are not objects designed to reference a maker but instead to act as a lever between humans and the world through which we (literally, in this case) navigate. A work like the Pompidou, on the contrary, is simply an extravagant sign for its makers' mastery of technology but contains little or no discernible meaning unto itself. In this sense, despite its allusions to technology, the building counter-intuitively mimics idyllic nature and dabbles in modernist ontology. Throughout history, Nature, first nature Being, is reified as good because innocent, empty, pure: idyllic nature serves merely as a sign of its omnipotent creator. The *São Pedro* is raft as objective fact, a real thing upon which to fish. The Pompidou is architecture as a sign for 'Truth' – Truth in the form of the existence of its makers, perhaps, and empty in itself pursued through de Sadean/Joycean proliferation of little ugly truths, no doubt, but an assertion of non-architectural, non-communal 'Truth' nonetheless. And in this sense, at least, the Pompidou is a building that occupies an identity somewhere between the playful game of names, popularized by Derrida in the 1960s and 1970s, and the serious aspirations of mid-century Modernism and the hero Architect who preceded it.

Notes

1 See, for instance, p. 572 of Jacques Derrida's "Pointe de folie – Maintenant l'architecture," in K. Michael Hays (ed.), *Architecture Theory since 1968* (Cambridge MA: MIT Press, 2000), 570–585:

> Let us never forget that there is an architecture of architecture. Down even to its archaic foundation the most fundamental concept of architecture has been *constructed*. This naturalized architecture is bequeathed to us: we inhabit it, it inhabits us, we think it is destined for habitation, and it is no longer an object for us at all. But we must recognize in it an *artifact*, a *construction*, a monument. It did not fall from the sky; it is not natural, even if it informs a specific scheme of relations to *physis*, the sky, the earth, the human and the divine. This architecture of architecture has a history, it is historical through and through. Its heritage inaugurates the intimacy of our economy, the law of our hearth (*oikos*), our familial, religious and political 'oikonomy,' all the places of birth and death, temple, school, stadium, agora, square, sepulchre. It goes right through us to the point that we forget its very historicity: we take it for nature.

2 These essays can be found in the following sources: "Architecture Where Desire Can Live: Jacques Derrida Interviewed by Eva Meyer" (originally published in *Domus* no. 671), in

64 Architecture History and Theory in Reverse

Kate Nesbitt (ed.), *Theorizing a New Agenda for Architecture* (New York: Princeton Architectural Press 1996), 144–149; "The Hinge [La Brisure]" in *Of Grammatology*, translated by Gayatri Chakravorty Spivak (Baltimore, MD: Johns Hopkins University Press, 1976), 65–73; "Edmond Jabès and the Question of the Book," in Jacques Derrida, *Writing and Difference*, translated by Alan Bass (Chicago: University of Chicago Press, 1978), 64–78. Notably absent are Derrida's collaboration with Peter Eisenman starting in the 1980s and published in 1997's much maligned *Chora L Works* as well as his challenge to Eisenman's use of philosophical terms in "A Letter to Peter Eisenman," *Assemblage*, No. 12 (August 1990), 6–13. The selection of the three texts included here as opposed to other essays by Derrida is based on pertinence to the narrative being constructed. In no sense should this be understood as an attempt to summarize his thought on architecture.

3 Such as derivation, the verb *to be*, designation, and articulation.
4 Derrida, "Architecture Where Desire Can Live," 145.
5 Derrida, "Edmond Jabès and the Question of the Book," 74.
6 Derrida, "The Hinge," 68.
7 Derrida, "Edmond Jabès and the Question of the Book," 76.
8 Derrida, "The Hinge," 71.
9 Arguably the most important anti-reductionist essay published in the twentieth century was P. W. Anderson's "More is Different: broken symmetry and the nature of the hierarchical structure of science," in which he argued that discovery of fundamental laws does not guarantee the ability to reconstruct or explain highly complex systems: "In this case we can see how the whole becomes not only more than but very different from the sum of its parts," *Science*, New Series, 177, No. 4047. (Aug. 4, 1972): 393–396.
10 Derrida, "Architecture Where Desire Can Live," 148.
11 Derrida, "The Hinge," 69.
12 Derrida, "Edmond Jabès and the Question of the Book," 71. Eisenman mimics this language when he writes: "The meaning is in the relationship; the architecture is between the signs." See Eisenman, "Architecture and the Problem of the Rhetorical Figure," 176–181 in Nesbitt (ed.), *Theorizing a New Agenda for Architecture*, 181.
13 Derrida, "Architecture Where Desire Can Live," 147:

> What emerges here can be grasped as the opening of architecture, as the beginning of a non-representative architecture … In order to talk about the impossibility of absolute objectivation, let us move from the labyrinth to the building of the Tower of Babel. There too the sky is to be conquered in an act of name-giving, which yet remains inseparably linked with the natural language. A tribe, the Semites, whose name means 'name,' a tribe therefore called 'name' want to erect a tower supposed to reach to the sky, according to the Scriptures, with the aim of making a name for itself. This conquest of the sky, this taking up of a position in the sky means giving oneself a name and from this power, from the power of the name, from the height of the meta-language, to dominate the other tribes, the other languages, to colonize them. But God descends and spoils this enterprise by uttering one word: Babel and this word is a name which resembles a noun meaning confusion. With this word he condemns mankind to the diversity of languages.

14 Heidegger spent his later years attempting to overcome these inconsistencies.
15 Derrida, "The Hinge," 70.
16 Derrida, "Edmond Jabès and the Question of the Book," 74.
17 Benjamin Lee Whorf, *Language, Thought, and Reality: selected writings of Benjamin Lee Whorf*, edited by John H. Carroll, Stephen C. Levinson, and Penny Lee (Cambridge, MA: MIT Press, 1956), 252.
18 Robert Venturi, Denise Scott Brown, and Steven Izenour, *Learning from Las Vegas: the forgotten symbolism of architectural form*, revised edition (Cambridge MA: MIT Press, 1977), 161 and 163.

Deconstruction, Irony, the Pompidou **65**

19 Ibid., 87.
20 See p. 256 of Alan Colquhoun's "Typology and Design Method," in Nesbitt (ed.), *Theorizing a New Agenda for Architecture*, 250-257.
21 Venturi, et al., 131. In this, Venturi, Scott Brown, and Izenour are echoing an earlier – if less widely distributed – position of Colquhoun (257):

> It would be impossible to conceive of constructing a language a priori. The ability to construct such a language would have to presuppose the language itself. Similarly, a plastic system of representation such as architecture has to presuppose the existence of a given system of representation. In neither case can the problem of formal representation be reduced to some preexistent essence outside the formal system itself, of which the form is merely a reflection. In both cases it is necessary to postulate a conventional system embodied in typological problem-solution complexes.

22 According to Deleuze and Guattari,

> Everything is desire.... One would be quite wrong to understand desire here as a desire *for* power, a desire to repress or be repressed, a sadistic desire and a masochistic desire.... There isn't a desire for power; it is power itself that is desire.

Gilles Deleuze and Félix Guattari, *Kafka: toward a minor literature*, translated by Dana Polan with foreword by Réda Bensmaïa (Minneapolis, MN: University of Minnesota Press, 1986), 56. If one is tempted to object that the relationship between experience, order, power, and desire presented here is circular, I would respond, "Yes, the relationship is circular."

23 Venturi, et al, 130. Again, Colquhoun is prescient:

> If, as Gombrich suggests, forms by themselves are relatively empty of meaning, it follows that the forms which we intuit will, in the unconscious mind, tend to attract to themselves certain associations of meaning. This could mean not only that we are not free from the forms of the past and from the availability of these forms as typological models but that, if we assume we are free, we have lost control over a very active sector of our imagination and of our power to communicate with others.
>
> (p. 256)

24 Venturi, et al., 8 and 13.
25 An attitude expressed by Lévi-Strauss in the *Conversations* regarding writing that architects and critics seem to believe is true of physical languages: "writing itself, in that first instance, seemed to be associated in any permanent way only with societies which were based on the exploitation of man by man." Quoted in Derrida, *Of Grammatology*, 119. Wilhelm von Humboldt made this point much earlier: "Albeit language is wholly inward, it nevertheless possesses at the same time an autonomous, external identity and being which does violence to man himself." Quoted in Steiner, *After Babel*, 82.
26 Venturi, et al., 50.
27 Ibid., 128.
28 Ibid., 161.
29 The broad definition of "detail" as well as the distinction between actual construction and mental construal is borrowed largely from Aberti by way of Marco Frascari, "The Tell-the-Tale Detail," in Nesbitt (ed.), *Theorizing a New Agenda for Architecture*, 500–514.
30 Deleuze and Guattari note that Kafka distinguished two types of technological trajectories: "those that tend to restore natural communication by triumphing over distances and bringing people together ..., and those that represent the vampirish

66 Architecture History and Theory in Reverse

revenge of the phantom where there is reintroduced 'the ghostly element between people'." See Deleuze and Guattari, *Kafka*, 30.

31 See p. 329 of the Marquis de Sade's "The 120 Days of Sodom," in *The 120 Days of Sodom & Other Writings*, compiled and translated by Austryn Wainhouse and Richard Seaver, Introductions by Simone de Beauvoir and Pierre Klossowski (New York: Grove Press, 1987), 181–674.

32 The latter, for example, although set in Ireland on June 16 1904, so nearly attempts an encyclopedic record of a single day that it includes even subtle reference to the tragic fire aboard the *General Slocum* in New York on the preceding day without mentioning it by name (see Joyce's *Ulysses*, 221). Neither the name of the vessel nor the nature of the tragedy is mentioned by Joyce until p. 239 (and, even then, the description garners fewer than one hundred words).

6

MIES VAN DER ROHE IN CHICAGO

From a historical perspective, the heady era of architectural theory and theorist's-name-as-architectural-brand was brief, fitting neatly in the last four decades of the twentieth century. *Learning from Las Vegas* (1972) and *S,M,L,XL* (1995) – arguably the first and last textual monuments of this period, respectively – were published a mere twenty-three years apart. The accumulated writings of that time vastly expanded intellectual approaches to, or lines of descent from, the discipline. The two preceding chapters are sketches of only a few – but arguably the most significant – of these themes. And yet, despite the myriad identities and turns of phrase developed in late twentieth-century theory, the Pompidou Centre's agenda of non-architectural, non-communal 'Truth' is nonsensical in the idioms of that period. It is a remnant. Its ancestry lies in a timeless questioning of fixed identities. To understand the Pompidou, it is necessary to extend the preceding line of thought back in time, before the heady decades of theorizing, toward the end of high modernity and the neo-Realism of a post-war world.

In cinema, this period is marked by Roberto Rossellini's *Rome, Open City* (1945) and his unglamorized depictions of Rome's real streets and the tragic but true-to-life fates of its people. Rossellini served as a transitional figure in Italian cinema in a literal sense. He made films in the brief clearing between the horrors of war and falsities of propaganda just ended and the symbolism-filled and sometimes absurdist avant-garde that soon followed. In architecture, Ludwig Mies van der Rohe valued similar presentations of reality, time, and architectural technologies (I-beams and bronzed plate glass) as both ornament and a unique idiom of architectural language.[1]

Mies, too, is a transitional figure, but in less obvious ways; and the analysis of 'Truth' in architecture and the eventual differentiation of this notion from architectural 'Language' does not unfold by obvious routes. While the Seagram Building in New York and 330 North Wabash in Chicago present rather

68 Architecture History and Theory in Reverse

straightforward comparisons to the Pompidou – all are foregrounded by public plazas, exhibit vague characteristics of European palazzos, and apply technology-as-ornament to the exterior side of the skin – it is not in architecture *per se* that the most significant transition of the twentieth century takes root. Instead, the path for chasing Pompidou's legacy back towards Mies' modernity lies in the winding domain of referentiality and an underlying economic model of experience. Or, as Mies said, "What matters is not 'what' but only 'how'."[2]

In a much-lauded analysis of war, Elaine Scarry says that the body killed in action exhibits "a nonreferentiality that rather than eliminating all referential activity instead gives it a frightening freedom of referential activity."[3] At the moment it loses its ability to speak, feel, act and react, organic matter is ripe for cooption by any and every need or desire, belief or propaganda. This is true of young soldiers, objectifications of women, and bloated bellies on late night infomercials. What is true of mute organic matter is doubly true of the inorganic. Standing in front of steel and glass and other inert materials, it is common to conflate values with economics, feelings with accounts, and beliefs with instructions. Modern economics, one might say, attempts to equate quantity with quality. Quantity of effort or material or sacrifice is, in this view, a correlate of value.[4] As the modern age drones on through postmodern decades into our late information age, it becomes increasingly difficult to conceive of a particular inorganic thing as having value in itself. Value now accrues with frequency and the notion of a deferred return. Stated the other way around, each individual product is a sign of its value but only through its potential for multiplication. This is a truism bequeathed by modern economics that holds true, regardless of whether the consumable in question is a building, film, food item, art object or a soldier, sex symbol or starving child.

This system appears relatively stable when framed within a single human life span. Yet it is inherently unstable. Fundamental shifts in reference are an ever-present danger to value in such an experiential economics for "when the referential direction is determined by proximity or juxtaposition," Scarry notes, "what is proximate, what is juxtaposed, can be changed."[5] Considered from this perspective, the exemplars of Mies' oeuvre arguably shift from the singularities of Barcelona and Seagram and 330 North Wabash to the twin apartment towers of 860–880 Lake Shore Drive and the tripartite Chicago Federal Center.[6] In these Chicago-based works, Mies was able to deploy multiple buildings in close proximity. The multiplication of figures under his control – both at the scale of a building (in the repetition of glass panels, mullions, granite pavers, and other details) and at the scale of the block or neighborhood (in the replication of the towers themselves) – allowed Mies to reinforce the perception of value through frequency and simultaneously fix its domain of reference. Each tower relates to its mate, which differs primarily in a 90-degree rotation of axis (see Figure 6.1). Unlike Piano and Rogers' signature collaboration, which references nothing so much as the absence of the architects, Mies remains outside the frame of public reference in Chicago but is unmissed and unsearched for because he is replaced by a physical field of reference of his own making. These two projects by Mies, in other words, form a closed loop.

FIGURE 6.1 Chicago Federal Center, Chicago, Ludwig Mies van der Rohe architect
Source: Photograph by David Buege.

While both the Lake Shore Drive apartments and the Federal Center were designed in the first half of the twentieth century, it is fair to pose the sort of question Derrida would soon be asking in the second: can there be a fixed reference in a closed loop? The question is akin to asking if there is a beginning or middle or end to a Möbius strip. The answer seems to be an obvious and emphatic "no." But stating it that way is a disservice to the referential complexities of experience.

Unlike value in the intercourse of finance, it is unclear how experiential value is acquired or exchanged. Yet a kind of economics is at work. If it is possible for an individual to imbibe or 'take in' a work of art without exchanging or sharing its content with anyone else as architectural phenomenologists suggest, then the value of that experience cannot be explained via its potential for subsequent trade. In other words, value must be acquired in the interaction of person and thing. If it is possible for a thing to have value in the absence of its author or architect as is arguably the case in Mies' best work (and, given our continuing fascination, seems to be the case with much of architecture's recorded history), then we must allow that things in themselves are capable of storing embodied value for the arrival of a recipient to come. This last point has the immediate ring of romanticism or even mysticism about it but, were it not true, deferred appreciation – i.e. the possibility of a visitor or inhabitant having a meaningful experience in a place after the architect and the architecture's apologists have left – would be impossible.

The notion of value stored in things is a difficult one, inaccessible in the mode of the phenomenological reduction of sensory experience to a pure present. If it is

70 Architecture History and Theory in Reverse

possible for a thing to possess value, it is a possibility that only makes sense given a history: a past, a present, and a future. It must be possible to record content in a thing to be retrieved or read at a later date. Architecture understood as information added to and conveyed by building is architecture understood as a continuously broadcasting transmitter; it merely awaits an appropriate receiver.[7]

This notion poses difficulties. For instance, an experiential economics rooted in stored information is, of necessity, an economics prone to entropy. Does the value of the work also, of necessity, diminish or change over time? If architecture is understood as information added to and conveyed by building, is architecture a message encoded by an architect in the past and made available across the future? And does that encoding entail the risk of indecipherability or mistranslation?

It is not possible to resolve these difficulties immediately. Nevertheless, reflection on the Federal Center towers opens territory in which a solution is possible. Mies' strategy is a neo-realist one: it is an economics of plentitude. These buildings are not open compositions or blank surfaces awaiting the projection of unintended meanings. These are not empty structures to be filled with content. What is built is intended as complete. Like the sparse narratives of fellow Modernist Samuel Beckett, Mies provided exactly the content he deemed necessary. The cycle of reference is limited to the site, the buildings (and its technologies), and the visitors. This closed-loop of reference explains the generally rapid dissipation of value one attributes to the labors of the architect or builders when one stands in the presence of these buildings. One does not go looking for Mies. Less is not more. In Mies' work, the expectation of more or curiosity about the absent author is rendered as exorbitant. Like the stripped declarative sentences of Hemingway, more is simply unnecessary.

What these buildings reveal is critical: Mies strives to surround the visitor with proofs of plentitude – hard linear and planar materials ostensibly performing straightforward tasks in defiance of gravity, wind, sun, and snow – but also, simultaneously and perhaps more importantly, he offers resistance to entropy via formality, simplicity, and durability (see Figure 6.2). These are Vitruvian traits of every language, recognizable to people from various places and times (see Chapters 16 and 17). Plentitude is not excess. A glorified and unchecked enthusiasm for excess brings forward a burden of accumulated matter and a reliance on frequency that threatens to collapse any system of meaning. Excess of information is the resultant character of much postmodern form making, of which the Pompidou Centre stands as the epitome.

Heraclitus, one of the first philosophers of plentitude, wrote: "The most beautiful order in the universe is a heap of sweepings, piled up at random."[8] Mies does not go so far in his preference of less over more but he does offer a measured reprieve, a form of restrained plentitude: "The unformed is not worse than the over-formed," is Mies' formulation.[9] This is not an oxymoron. Restrained plentitude is the perfect fit of need to want; or, in economic parlance, supply to demand. In modernist ontology, it is a measure of Being without extra or profit: *Being-In-Itself*, to use the jargon of the time. What is most important in this architectural provision of 'just enough' is the mental space and time it dares not

FIGURE 6.2 Chicago Federal Center, Chicago, Ludwig Mies van der Rohe architect
Source: Photograph by David Buege.

presuppose to close. Mies' buildings, like Beckett's novels, matter for, in a brief window of time in the windy city, he stopped short of sensual or conceptual puppeteering and allowed for the slow emergence of meaning via a thorough grasp of the economy of form.

Form, Function. Truth, Fiction. A Rejoinder

Hans Hollein declared architecture "purposeless" in 1962.[10] Mies died in 1969. In the wake of Hollein's pronouncement and Mies' death, misattributed functionalisms of varied flavors and in various guises have dominated architectural theory, to the point that the relatively recent split between form and function has come to seem natural or simply given.[11] Debate over the origin of the form-function dialectic is mired in a host of contingencies that differ with culture and discipline. The debate cannot be resolved. Moreover, it is doubtful that any one answer would contribute to a greater understanding of the evolution of architecture and architectural language over the centuries. The more important question concerns acceptance: why is there such strong belief in this dialectic among twentieth-century architects and architectural theorists?

The answer to that question begins more than two millennia ago. It begins with Aristotle. Of course, he isn't around now. He has been dead far longer than Mies. When the great philosopher was alive, however, he liked to unify things that had been cleaved by the pre-Socratics: Heraclitus' notion that change is the essential

72 Architecture History and Theory in Reverse

character of the world as opposed to Parmenides' belief in permanence and that all change is mere illusion, for example. As with old-time magicians cutting women in half, Aristotle recognized that the better part of a trick always resides in bringing the parts back together. In the elder philosopher's case, it wasn't women that interested him but wisdom. Sweeping his left arm over one half of knowledge, he announced that Wisdom is both *Sophia* and, gesturing with his right, *Phronesis*. *Sophia* appears through history in various philosophical guises such as metaphysics, rationalism, subjectivism, innateness, realism, the id/ego/superego complex. It is generally understood to be accessible through hermeneutics and phenomenological reduction, teased out via interviews and IQ tests, or deciphered by psychoanalysis. The latter, *phronesis*, plays equally diverse roles across time well into the information age – showing up as positivism, empiricism, objectivism, behaviorism, nominalism, determinism and the 'blank slate.' It is pursued best when direct observation is filtered through the prisms of hard sciences' use of norms, rules, and systems. These two portions of Wisdom also appear divided by temporal cast. Sophia is at the core of mystic traditions' divination of past events and prophecy of the future. Phronesis operates in the present and is skeptical of other tenses.

A showy flourish of his arms bringing his hands together overhead: "*Abra....*

No one seemed to notice that Aristotle never finished the trick. He walked off stage, the heady end of philosophy dangling out of one box and its worldly feet kicking impatiently from the end of another. The languages adopted by these Siamese twins of Wisdom separated in ancient Greece and kept apart all these years have, as one would expect, diverged to alien proportions in almost every facet of scientific and artistic classification over the past two plus millennia: ontologically (nature vs. nurture), epistemologically (principles vs. facts), methodologically (intuition vs. observation), and aesthetically (qualities vs. quantities). In modern academia, the cleaved siblings coexist on campuses as Humanities and Sciences where, in terms of language, the former produces Poetry, the latter, Linguistics. Sophia today dwells in *fiction*; Phronesis seeks its home in *truth*. Permanently divided.

None of this is necessarily good, or, strictly speaking, necessary. It is possible that there are no separate layers of reality and phenomena; phenomena and substances; laws and essences; regularities and beings; beings and time or beings and nothingness. It is reasonable to assume that Sophia and Phronesis are not universal givens that humans discovered and adopted when we became conscious, philosophizing beings. Perhaps both are produced by the same subjective analyses through which they are made visible.[12]

...cadabra?" Not so fast.

There is a reason Aristotle said "Abra..." and walked off, stage right. As noted, the tricky part of any illusion is reunification – its undoing. Heurism and positivism, the two research methodologies between which the pendulum of architectural discourse swung throughout the second half of the twentieth century (and arguably still swings), remain mutually exclusive and, worse, untranslatable due to the classificatory differences that have evolved during the long separation of Sophia

Mies van der Rohe in Chicago **73**

and Phronesis. The fact that modes of inquiry are multiplying in the twenty-first century, such as rubrics of sustainability and metrics of integrated project delivery, does not indicate an impending conclusion to Aristotle's trick.[13] Instead, cleaved bodies are piling up on stage.

The problem was adopted by and persists in architecture. Louis Sullivan first committed the phrase "form follows function" to writing in 1896. In his New Babylon project, Constant Nieuwenhuys deepened, and darkened, the split with phrases like: "The modern city is dead; it has fallen victim to utility."[14] The city, a living form in Nieuwenhuys' view, is Sophia. Its killer is function, Phronesis. Unfortunately, more recent architectural theory is just as far from finishing the trick of unifying the subjective and objective realms as Nieuwenhuys in 1960. Form as distinct from function has become an axiomatic fiction like three-dimensional space or Newtonian mechanics: so well worn, so comfortable, and so often useful that its absolute truth appears not to matter.

Architects, like other people, seldom question information that proves useful. While it could be argued that believing in the form–function split at least does no harm and occasionally assists us in getting things done, this is true only if we accept at least one of four possible assertions regarding architectural language: (1) throughout its long history of forms, architecture never had communicative power and thus there is no unity of form and function to recapture; or, (2) a unity of form and function once existed but is no longer necessary, therefore Victor Hugo was justified in eulogizing architecture's power to embody cultural meaning; or, (3) architecture has the capacity to convey small private meanings between initiates or members of a particular sect but only when certain forms are treated as symbols with assigned meanings but it does not have, nor does it need, a broader scope of intelligibility; or, (4) humans no longer need objects with communicative power. If one or more of the above is true, then the irreducible gap between form and function or quality and quantity is unproblematic because there is neither need nor desire to cross from one side to the other. Ideation and sensation can remain in separate boxes. If it doesn't matter, we can resolve to accept philosopher Ludwig Wittgenstein's early formulation: *Whereof one cannot speak, thereof one must be silent.*

Readers inclined to this interpretation need read no further.

It is assumed from this point forward that the reader is not prone to unquestioning acceptance of early Wittgenstein, or any other bifurcationist for that matter. That is not to say that readers are expected to disavow dualistic tendencies. Cleaving predates Aristotle, Plato, and even the pre-Socratics. It is biblical: heavens and earth; day and night; water and sky. Yet, in writing this book, I am motivated by the belief that the separation of form and function, matter and content, of quantity and quality – the inheritance of Babel formalized by Aristotle and propagated by contemporary media – introduces many forms of disorder in the evolution of architectural language.

Continued bifurcation of quantity and quality rests on a libertine bias: pleasure is only possible in the comparison of what we *have* (matter at hand in the present, judged valueless) to what we *want* (content conceived as residing in an absent, never possessed past or future matter).[15] This bias is not limited to profane, self-interested authors like de Sade. The libertine position parallels and was perhaps born of a Gnostic ecclesiastical tenet: the body is to be rejected in favor of mind or soul; the former is base, empty, a poor substitute for pleasures accessible only through the activity of the latter (*à la* the formalists). Quantity, an accumulation of matter by a libertine or Gnostic devotee, is stripped of inherent value in both systems. It is reduced to a mere field that the mind or soul has already or will soon act across in search of higher, more wondrous rewards than this ground provides. Quality is understood as rooted in acts that pre-exist specific objects of desire and is measured in the labor of acquiring satisfactions. Where quality appears to coincide with an inanimate or inorganic artifact (in the libertine's implements of sadomasochism or in religious relics, alters, and manuscripts), this coincidence is revealed as possible only insofar as that object can somehow be said to contain, or attach itself to, language as *the word*: in both cases, always as words of dominance or submission.[16]

The tendency to see meaning in things often triggers a rebuttal of "irrational" or "tender-mindedness." Marshall McLuhan's pithy phrases "the medium is the message" and "the content of a medium is always another medium,"[17] begins to explain these rebuttals. "The medium is the message" illuminates a confusion of objects and representations in the late information age. McLuhan's distinction between hot and cool media clarifies the problem further. The idea that matter is simply an empty receptacle into which ideas can be poured without possibility of matter and content merging is so pervasive, its representation so stealthy, that crosses and chairs and trees and rocks are accepted by most people as cool media in McLuhan's sense: that is, we are convinced that 'we' do all the work of meaning-generation in the presence of such things. The reverse, in fact, is probably more often true. These objects are all forms of hot media: the cross or chair or rock think for us and are so convincing in their roles as "meaningless" objects that attempts at serious contemplation are thwarted before such contemplation begins.[18]

The fact that ascribing meaning to a St. Andrews Cross or a rock or tree is seen as irrational is only part of the problem. "Irrationality" is a symptom of a more pervasive tendency to understand all unifications of matter and content as "fictional." More accurately stated, judging a thing to be "irrational" rests on the assumption that the fiction|truth split is meaningful to the conveyance and constitution of meaning. This is not the case. Perceived meaning is always and only a decipherment of an expression or representation in a shared language. Neither truth nor fiction plays a role. Every expression and representation is incomplete in terms of providing its own internal justification. Instead, expressions and representation announce the need for a foundation or undermine existing ones or call forth memories as sources or some combination of these.[19] This is true of all forms of human- and naturally-produced objects. Representation has always been a veil separating content from perception while enticing us to discover a hidden unity. To acknowledge that the St. Andrews Cross or trees and rocks or the decorative motifs of Art Deco can be and have been many things to many groups is not to acknowledge that meaning is merely ephemeral or subjective. It is to admit to a contextually-bound but profoundly real connection between form and content that can be read on the surface of meaningful objects with a little knowledge of that contextualizing language.

Experience is never true. But that is not to say it is not meaningful. Aristotle cleaved knowledge into a visible world of representation (assumed fictional) and an invisible ground of reality (assumed to be true). Given this inheritance and the depth to which it is ingrained, there is great need to overcome the separation of judgments into empirical, observational, positivistic, *a posteriori* experiences on the one hand and rational, universal, heuristic, *a priori* truths on the other. But such unity must be sought farther back in time, in eras of meaning, before form was relegated to chasing after function.

A Postscript on Mies and an Introduction to Claude Shannon

To better understand the relationship of form to function to message to meaning, it is useful to introduce Claude Shannon and his seminal paper, "A Mathematical Theory of Communication" (1948).[20] Shannon was the first to fully conceive information in abstract, mathematical terms and to distinguish it from meaning or semantic content. He was uninterested in the latter terms.[21] He focused on the form of communication because it is a communication system's form that allows a system to function. "What matters in the case of information, and produces its distinctive physical consequences," anthropologist Terrence Deacon notes, "is a relationship to something not there."[22] Once functioning, it can transmit any message content desired. Meaning is subsequent to successful transmission in Shannon's view. His classic diagram gives the basic form of every communication system ever constructed (Figure 6.3).

Shannon's diagram calls attention to an ever-present threat: noise. Some form of noise, Shannon realized, impacts the channel space of every type of communication. He agreed with his predecessors and contemporaries that

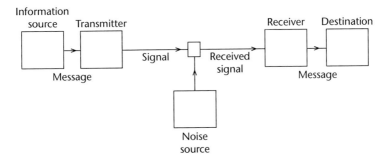

FIGURE 6.3 Shannon's diagram of communication
Source: Claude Shannon, The Mathematical Theory of Communication. Copyright 1949, 1998 by the University of Illinois Press. Used with permission of the University of Illinois Press.

76 Architecture History and Theory in Reverse

redundancy is necessary to overcome this threat and ensure that the message sent by a source and received at a destination are the same (ideally) or, at least, contain so few errors as to be comprehendible. A bad cell phone connection, for example, can be overcome by merely repeating words or key sentences multiple times. Shannon demonstrated that, with sufficient channel space and without concern for economy, any transmission could be rendered error-free in this way. He also understood the contradictory need to utilize channel space efficiently – regardless of whether the material at hands is words or building components, there is a limit to the amount of repetition one can afford. Shannon solved the problem via probability. English, for example, is highly predictable and this explains the legibility of shortened, fragmented, and even botched messages such as "cn I C U 2nit?" and "y s, di u h ve din r?" Shannon hit on the idea of reducing information to bits, 1s and 0s, and building in enough redundancy that each unit (letter, word, image, etc.) could suffer one accidental inversion without harming decipherability (the probability of multiple inversions in a single transmitted unit being very low). If every letter in the alphabet is given a 5-digit sequence of 1s and 0s, and 'A' is coded as 10101 and 'B' as 11011, for example, a received message of 11111 is most likely to be 'B' with one coding or decoding error and not 'A' with three errors.[23] Thus, the deleterious effects of noise – inverting or erasing individual bits – are overcome in a very economical way.

It is impossible to do Claude Shannon's information theory justice in a few hundred words. Nevertheless, its value to understanding the way in which Mies' mid-twentieth-century architecture functions cannot be overstated. With Mies, form is put in the service of function; the "what," in Mies' language, is reduced to "how." The transmission of information is distinct from and prior to the reception or decipherment or construction of meaning by the experiencing subject. Redundancy combined with simple coding systems make both error or noise detection as well as perception of novel conditions easy. To make comparisons between these statements and the works of Mies van der Rohe's high Modernism requires only the smallest of steps.

Evidence suggests that Mies did not construe function narrowly. His I-beam mullions are pure appliqué and the exposure of these at corners or where buildings meet the ground are, likewise, superfluous to the structure behind, as Venturi admiringly and others negatively have noted. That Mies' lack of devotion to a fundamentalist view of function would be chastened by some architects and historians is troubling. This criticism, rooted in the notion that a work of architecture is always responsible for 'telling the truth,' signals a shift in architectural thinking from the object itself, *à la* De Stijl, to its relational consequences, specifically as a bellwether of morality. Even more troubling, this can be understood as a shift from thinking of the architectural object as potential container of meaning (expressive but open and, at worst, ineffectual) to object as overt message (didactic and closed and, at worst, admonishing). What is exposed in critiques of a lack of 'pure' functionalism in Mies and 'dishonesty' in a host of other architects since, modernists and traditionalists alike, is a shift that has as its own paradoxical consequence the devaluing of inhabitants' values in favor of the values of an owner or architect or both and their *a priori* intentions for the project. Architectural intentions expected to linger beyond the initial design process are invariably destructive to the experience of others.[24]

Although the work of Mies van der Rohe offers only a proto-language, his gift was making buildings that neither perform the act of interpretation for the inhabitant, despite being simple and ordered, nor assume a moral conclusion. Mies offered form. That form's content is both complete and open – intentionally and carefully but also so subtly that most of his inheritors have failed to perpetuate his legacy.

It has been said that "[Shannon] Information is the archetypical absential concept."[25] Architecture from Mies onward strives to be just such information – its *Less is More* "presence" increasingly relying on informational self-sufficiency, via doubling and coding, instead of connections to communal rituals, myths, and typologies. Arguably architecture's success after Mies is measured by the clarity or forcefulness of its message's delivery against the background noise of society.

Notes

1 "Architecture depends on its time. It is the crystallization of its inner structure, the slow unfolding of its form. That is the reason why technology and architecture are so closely related." Excerpt from a speech given at the Illinois Institute of Technology (IIT) in Chicago in 1950. See Ludwig Mies van der Rohe, "Technology and Architecture," in Ulrich Conrads (ed.), *Programs and Manifestoes on 20th-Century Architecture*, originally published in 1964 (Cambridge, MA: MIT Press, 1975), 154.

2 Excerpt from a Deutscher Werkbund speech given in Vienna in 1930. See Ludwig Mies van der Rohe, "The New Era," in Conrads, *Programs and Manifestoes*, 123.

3 Elaine Scarry, *The Body in Pain: the making and unmaking of the world* (New York: Oxford University Press, 1987), 119.

4 Contrary to etymology, "labor" and "work" are merging: the latter slowly subsumed by the former. A brief history of the distinction between the two terms – work and labor – can be found in Hannah Arendt's *The Human Condition*, pp. 79–85. The thesis that the two terms are losing distinction over time, however, contradicts Arendt's analysis. Hannah Arendt, *The Human Condition*, 2nd edn, Introduction by Margaret Canovan (Chicago: University of Chicago Press, [1958] 1998).

5 Scarry, *The Body in Pain*, 119.

6 The latter is composed of two towers, the Dirksen and Kluczynski Federal Buildings, and US Post Office Loop Station.

7 See Figure 0.1 on p. xix, the four-fold structure of language, in the Introduction.

8 Heraclitus, *Fragments*, translated and with commentary by T. M. Robinson (Toronto: University of Toronto Press, 1991), fragment 124.

9 Excerpt from a letter published in *Die Form* in 1927. See Ludwig Mies van der Rohe, "On Form in Architecture," in Conrads (ed.), *Programs and Manifestoes*, 102.

10 Walter Pichler and Hans Hollein, "Absolute Architecture," in Conrads (ed.), *Programs and Manifestoes*, 181–182. Passage quoted from p. 182.

11 As Eisenman notes, "the dialectic form and function is culturally based." See Peter Eisenman, "Post-Functionalism," in Kate Nesbitt (ed.), *Theorizing a New Agenda for Architecture* (New York: Princeton Architectural Press, 1996), 82.

12 As myriad twentieth-century thinkers have stated, from Heisenberg to Feyerabend to Jameson, the prisonhouse of our senses modifies everything that comes in and alters everything that goes out. There is no escaping the prison of the embodied mind, the human animal, nature nurtured.

13 Such rubrics can be seen as moves to add weight to a third classification – the *techne* of architecture, but, if these achieve anything, it can be added that this tendency to increase the number of perspectives over the past century has led, without justification or compensation, to a general belief that an objective ground, if such a thing can be said to exist, is fragmented into at least as many pieces as there are theoretical frameworks. A heuristic researcher might state the dilemma this way: "Unity is progressively problematized for the positivist by his assumption of objective (factual) data in an environment mediated by the subject and his or her (according to positivists) 'fictionalizing' perceptions." For the positivist, the terms of the dilemma flip: "The failure of heuristic researchers and Husserlian phenomenologists lie in their attempts to synthesize a bifurcation – of logic versus the transcendental – the second half of which is false or perhaps provisional and, at best, only an emergent phenomenon." Who can blame Aristotle for leaving the twins in separate boxes?

14 Constant Nieuwenhuys published *New Babylon* in 1960. The quoted text is taken from p. 177 of an excerpt published in Conrads (ed.), *Programs and Manifestoes*, 177–178.

15 See Marquis de Sade's "The 120 Days of Sodom," in *The 120 Days of Sodom & Other Writings*, compiled and translated by Austryn Wainhouse and Richard Seaver, introductions by Simone de Beauvoir and Pierre Klossowski (New York: Grove Press, 1987), 361–362.

16 Experience is never pure. This can be witnessed in the words of architectural theorists such as Walter Pichler who, in 1962, wrote: "Architecture is the law of those who do not believe in the law but make it. It is a weapon." See Pichler and Hollein, "Absolute Architecture," 181. Those rare inanimate objects that appear to possess characteristics of language with metaphysical or divine connotations are useful as counterpoints to the bifurcation of matter and content that has suffused most aspects of everyday life. Examples range from rocks and trees in the minds of naturalists to the St. Andrews Cross in the minds of sadomasochists to the St. Andrews Cross in the minds of the religious. At first blush, it is tempting to dismiss such examples as irrational or purely fictional; certainly a little tender-minded; and claim that, despite the superficial unity of matter and content, each such example does as much to reinforce the bifurcation as deny it (in the sense that a disinterested viewer might say the meaning "is projected upon" or "is in relation to" the object which remains, in *reality*, "just" an object). Perhaps this impression is correct. For the moment, however, consider the following hypothesis borrowed from Foucault: Inanimate objects that appear to carry meaning "possess characters which language can scan and define because they have a structure that is, in a way, the dark, concave, inner side of their visibility" (*The Order of Things*, 237). Assuming this hypothesis is true, it is less reasonable to ask why rocks and trees and St. Andrew's crosses exhibit an ability to be both sensuous matter and linguistic content than to question, instead, why so few other material objects exhibit this affinity to human language. Michel Foucault, *The Order of Things* (New York: Vintage Books, 1994).

17 See Marshall McLuhan, *Understanding Media: the extensions of man*, introduction by Lewis H. Lapham (Cambridge MA: MIT Press, 1994). McLuhan argues that "content" and "message" are distinct in mediated experience and that changes in "content" impact individuals far less than differences in media. Compare this to Scarry's distinction between the issues decided in war and the substantiation process of war itself:

> This by no means means that the issues on the two sides are the same, for there may be… an expanse of justice that separates them; but it does mean that the substantiation process itself, the collective work of the bodies injured in the external space of conflict, is the same regardless of what it substantiates, is the same whether what it substantiates is a construct suffused with beauty and justice or one containing the very antitheses of these attributes.
>
> (Scarry, *The Body in Pain*, 138)

18 A prestigious philosophical lineage exists along these lines. "Perception is never a mere contact of the mind with the object present; it is impregnated with memory-images

which complete it as they interpret it." Henri Bergson, *Matter and Memory*, translated by N.M. Paul and W.S. Palmer (New York: Zone Books, 1999), 133. Also: "As for the concept of experience ... it belongs to the history of metaphysics." See Jacques Derrida, *Of Grammatology*, translated by Gayatri Chakravorty Spivak (Baltimore, MD: Johns Hopkins University Press, 1976), 60.

19 This is why Deleuze and Guattari claim that literature indicates the ground of collective values: "It is literature that produces an active solidarity in spite of skepticism." They continue by saying,

> and if the writer is in the margins or completely outside his or her fragile community, this situation allows the writer all the more the possibility to express another possible community and to forge the means for another consciousness and another sensibility.
> (Gilles Deleuze and Félix Guattari, *Kafka: toward a minor literature*, translated by Dana Polan, Minneapolis: University of Minnesota Press, 1986, 17)

20 Claude E. Shannon, "A Mathematical Theory of Communication," *Bell System Technical Journal*, 27, (1948): 379–423, 623–656. The paper was later republished, with an accessible introduction by Warren Weaver, as *The Mathematical Theory of Communication* (Urbana, IL: University of Illinois Press, 1949).

21 Writing on Claude Shannon's accomplishment of separating information from meaning, anthropologist Terrance Deacon notes that "this progress came at the cost of entirely ignoring the representational aspect that is its ultimate base." See Terrence W. Deacon, *Incomplete Nature: how mind emerged from matter* (New York: W. W. Norton & Company, 2013), 372.

22 Ibid., 373.

23 It is worth noting that Shannon also "found new precise theorems which placed limits upon what could be achieved." See Andrew Hodges, *Alan Turing: the enigma* (Princeton, NJ: Princeton University Press, 2014), 315.

24 One may legitimately question the need to rehearse the awful side effects of "form follows function" and "minimalist" rhetoric given that we have moved beyond these schools of thought, passed through deconstruction and architectural phenomenology, and are now many years into the green revolution and the social justice epoch. Rereading Scarry's magnificent work *The Body in Pain* while reflecting on the rise of architectural phenomenology in the wake of both "form follows function" and "minimalism" renders a prescient message: the body, she says, "is only brought forward when there is a crisis of substantiation" (Scarry, *The Body in Pain*, 127). Reread that sentence.

Architectural phenomenology did not fulfill its promise; or perhaps it is more correct to assert that architectural phenomenology did all it could for the profession given that it eschewed the intellectual and rhetorical qualities commensurate with complete human experience. Nevertheless, the movement gained such traction over the last several decades of the twentieth century because the knowledge that once accrued in the space of interaction between a knowing subject and the work of architecture is reduced – in formalism, minimalism, green architecture, and social justice-oriented practice – to predetermined outcomes and a series of expected, and sanctioned, understandings. Architectural phenomenology persists because the discipline of architecture is bereft of meaning, has been for centuries according to Hugo's prophecy, and the alternative movements are so utterly unsatisfying. The persistence of architectural phenomenology and its glorification of the experiencing body, in other words, is a mark of a deep crisis of substantiation. Eisenman might explain this as a result of mistaken attribution: the belief that architecture is a humanist practice, the *forms* of which must *function* for some imaginary universal body. See Eisenman, "Post-Functionalism." Architecture might achieve more if it believed its purpose was less.

25 Deacon, *Incomplete Nature*, 373.

7

LANGUAGE GAMES

BIG, MVRDV, OMA, Gehry, Architecture for Humanity, Stan Allen, Eisenman, Pallasmaa/Holl/Zumthor, Venturi Scott Brown, Piano & Rogers, and Mies. Emotivism, Communitarianism, Formalism, Phenomenology, Irony, Deconstructivism, and Presence (of which, less is more). If branding is creating information in the form of words or images to fill a perceived void of meaning, then the history of architecture over the past one hundred years or so is a history of branding.

On the face of it, describing contemporary architectural practice, as well as its history and theory, as the manufacture of brands may seem unfair. "Architecture has simply evolved,"[1] one might argue in the belief that the gradual transformation from Mies' *Less is More* to Venturi's *Less is a Bore* to emotivism's *More is More* to Bjarke Ingels' *Yes is More* is an understandable (if tedious) progression. But, as Wilhelm von Humboldt observed, "All understanding is at the same time a misunderstanding, all agreement in thought and feeling is also a parting of the ways."[2] And architects are parting ways at a frightening pace.

At first blush, cause and effect appear circular – each brand is created to fill an informational void between existing, uncommunicative brands; and every new brand introduces new interstitial voids between itself and existing brands. That is, branding seeks to fill as well as perpetuate ever-widening information streams. This is true as far as it goes. And yet, these divergent brandings are late information symptoms of an earlier and broader crisis in language itself: the cleaving of words from fixed objects of reference. Since Babel and at an accelerating pace in the past few centuries, the lowest common denominators of public reference and the most private levels of discourse have come to sound like alien tongues.[3] Two World Wars fought in a span of thirty years deepened burgeoning doubts as to whether communication of significant ideas between divergent groups is possible. Evidence of this doubt, and arguably the form most inhibiting to architecture's communicative potential, remains media's drive to proliferate nomenclature in order to justify newspapers followed by radio and television, and now the 24-hour cycle of cable news, blogs, and social media.[4] But such sowing of doubt is not limited to advertisers and media moguls. Many twentieth-century philosophers and linguists have contributed to skepticism. A few have argued that the relationships between language and reality are purely arbitrary and that there is no meaningful ground to discover. Most argued that some language functions are biologically innate and that tethers anchoring matter to meaning are real but misstated by earlier thinkers and, as yet, poorly understood. As a result of this skepticism, philosophers and linguists felt justified in constructing ever-larger terminological toolkits aimed at correcting earlier formulations (the way Steven Pinker follows Chomsky).

Although slow and subtle enough to be practically invisible within a typical lifespan, this continuous re-narrativizing as simultaneous expression and attempted mitigation of doubt is easily seen by taking stock of the bewildering array of words and phrases, movements and slogans strewn across almost any discipline's recent past. As evolutionary biologist Stephen Jay Gould and linguist John McWhorter note, such diversity emerges to fill niches. In biology, these niches are unexploited ecological opportunities. In language, they are the sudden perception of heretofore-unnoticed gaps in expressive potential. Similarly, in architecture the niches are perceived voids in a disciplinary lineage, and these voids are filled with all sorts of brands, regardless of whether that lineage and its voids are real or imagined.

We all know the stories. Embedded in the legends and fables near the beginning of our imagined lineage, in places like Babel, and more recently in the manifestos of functionalism, words were conceived as conveyances of direct content without need of interpretation or decipherment. The builders at Babel imagined they simply needed a tower to reach meaning. Visionaries of the functionalist era, like Buckminster Fuller and Henry van de Velde, were not information age people but naïve realists who did not see the content of the world as free-floating codes contingently and impermanently affixed to signifiers. In pre-information era Babel through the end of the nineteenth century, there was (or there was a belief in) a single communicative form transparent to meaning, place, and content. From the 1960s onward, languages have floated free of form and have meaning only in narrowly construed and highly prescribed ways. This significant transformation resulted from two linguistic tendencies: one is the privileging of private over public concerns and the other involves a revaluation of subjectivity and organic matter – along with the design metaphor of both, 'organic form' – over inorganic objects. Although these tendencies are closely related, I will introduce each separately.

Public vs. Private

A written thread stitching public understanding to the physical world extends from Thales through Aristotle, Newton and Locke to Rousseau and Marx. In the last half century, this thread has become increasingly dilated and frayed transforming 'understanding the physical world' into an esoteric and, at best, idealistic concern.

82 Architecture History and Theory in Reverse

Elaine Scarry calls the straining of this thread "the process of derealization" and warns of its consequences: "The more the process of derealization continues, the more desperately will each side work to recertify and verbally reaffirm the legitimacy and reality of its own cultural constructs."[5]

Some in disciplines connected to the study of language and classification in the second half of the twentieth century attempted to reaffirm their legitimacy by casting doubt on the language-reality thread. They derided the notion that philosophy or other disciplines offer a representation of reality or "mirror of nature." They retold the story of knowledge and harnessed it to the belief that language is a puzzle or game. Ludwig Wittgenstein's *Philosophical Investigations* (1953) and Richard Rorty's *Philosophy and the Mirror of Nature* (1979) are the early and late exemplars of this tradition. People who accept this perspective say things like: "Though we constantly 'play' at translation or de-coding, language is ultimately untranslatable because the only ground is the provisional and always shifting agreement of individuals," or "an idea's truth matters less than people's use of it." In this neo-pragmatic culture, twenty-first-century media's commerce in sectarian meanings took hold and, as its progeny, screen-printed artifice such as MVRDV's Markthal mural replaced reality.

This view's most significant adherents are often accused of deconstructive obscurantism (Jacques Derrida and Bernard Tschumi) or postmodern relativism (Richard Rorty and Robert Venturi). Reacting to the crossfire of these unappealing options, at least two camps of refugees have emerged. One, traveling along the path of Husserlian or Heideggerian phenomenology, turns to the trope of *presence* as a one-stop fix to the "language+matter connection" – *à la* Mies. The other camp, noticeable even in a cursory glance at recent literature on the subject, plays host to myriad apologists arguing for an essential connection between words and things[6] in an attempt to reweave the near end of the thread – *à la* the Congress for the New Urbanism. Both camps assert normative positions. Unfortunately, not much can be salvaged from the *presence* camp; its premises are primarily mystical; its veracity proportional to your faith. And as important as overcoming the division between language and matter is to the apologists and as serious as their efforts sometimes are, their work is too limited by nostalgia to address the deeply entrenched inheritance of Modernism's language | matter and private | public divisions.[7]

The location of the last shared knot along the thread is debatable. One candidate for this position is the mid-century publication of Wittgenstein's *Philosophical Investigations* which provided significant, perhaps 'the', impetus to present-day examinations of language for philosophers, linguists, and architects alike. Wittgenstein argued that "meaning" is bound up with use – though meaning is the wrong word and something like reference or information seems closer to the mark.[8] This is no simple functionalism. *Word* reference and even *sentence* reference differ, in his view, depending on the system of language rules (i.e. the game) in which they are employed. This is to suggest, in language more common to the study of architecture, reference or information is exclusively context dependent. In Wittgenstein's stylistic pithiness: "The kind of certainty is the kind of language-game."[9] That the reference intended by one person can be deciphered by any other is due, according to Wittgenstein, to family resemblance – in present-day language, perception of a preponderance of features existing in a network instead of reliance on a particular trait; a kind of intuitive classification agreed upon by a group. All of this is reasonable in a particular place at a particular time. But what happens to the spread of information across time and in differing locales? What about meaning? Have we no need or obligation, or even desire, to communicate beyond the xenophobic circumference of a home time and hometown?

Few philosophers and fewer architects have attempted to answer this challenge without resorting to retrograde historicism. From the philosophical side, Ian Hacking's notion of "human kinds" – those entities or types that might not exist as objective facts of nature but can still be regarded as real because recognized and capable of influencing and being acted upon by humans – is one of the conceptual lifelines offered in response to Wittgenstein. There can be little doubt that Hacking's work – particularly his *Making Up People* (1986) and *Historical Ontology* (2002) – offer both the physical and social sciences a means by which to link matter to substantive ideas. But the language game persists. To declare that human-created kinds are real, as Hacking does, while circumscribing 'reality' as limited to a given group of people operating in a particular historical-political context is not a significant advance over theories treating language as private codes or ciphers. Such connections are not only prone to naïve misunderstanding; they are often intentionally misrepresented.[10] Language treated as a game is language in which there are rare, and usually singular, winners and a field of subjugated losers. The winners constitute a Zeitgeist, a standard model; reference to other, non-conforming, models comprise a teratology confirming only the existence of inferior alternatives that the winning theory allows us to avoid. There is no shortage of examples of this in architectural history or criticism, from J-N-L. Durand's narrow selection of architectural elements through Nikolaus Pevsner and Sigfried Gideon's white male Eurocentricism to Kenneth Frampton's recasting of architecture as tectonics.[11] In fact, it could be argued that the history of architectural history and theory is nothing other than a chronological collection of such language games: a record of the winners.

There are things that Wittgenstein got right. Use matters. Roots evolve. And there are things that Wittgenstein's apologists, extenders, and critics have since got right: constancy of root evolution is marked by the slower and more uniform change of inflections, for instance. But all of this agreement suggests that the present-day preoccupation with invisible or deep structure is in fact the same impetus fueling the evolution or transformation of language from the beginning. Arguably, the impulse to language at Babel was one and the same as the impulse to language today, though today obscured behind veils of assumed depth, complexity, and indecipherable codings.[12] To look back across the information age toward meaning and myth traditions is to look at a history across which language was not at one moment a simple and naïve associationism and at another a confused tangle of empty signs, but was and remains a search for intimate connections between human consciousness and the material world. From the moment consciousness emerges in human culture, language is more than a representation of *the Word*, or a use, or a discipline-specific bracketing of experience. Words were and are to the activity of thought what bodily expressions were and are to the activity of the emotions – i.e. direct attempts to extend humanity beyond the confines of the individual. Words are our social body; our conscious occupation of the world through meaning.

In this light, it is interesting to note that Wittgenstein had little regard for the writing of St. Augustine. Augustine's conception of language was imagistic. For all of the flaws that we might identify in reading the latter's work from the perspective of the twenty-first century, he wrote about language in a way that is arguably more useful to understanding architectural language than philosophers who have walked in his long shadow. I will take this up in the following pages. For now, understand the implications of the strategy being deployed when Wittgenstein dismisses Augustine's "picture" of language in favor of "use" or actions: something more important than the privileging of verbs over nouns is being asserted. Wittgenstein's notion of language as a type of game implicitly but forcefully suggests that subjects are more important than objects and that matter ultimately doesn't matter: in other words, *It's all about me; about winning and losing.* Whether correct or not, this is a game we cannot play in ignorance … or afford to play in apathy.

In Praise of the Organic

The section title above is misleadingly truncated. It is meant to convey the totality of shift from the respect once accorded the objectivity of things to the privilege accorded to the personal and subjective. Technically, it should read: "In praise of the organic: the perceived inferiority of inorganic and non-sentient organic matter as a result of associations of matter with written (dead) as opposed to spoken (living) language," an instance of poetic license – at most, a poetic misdemeanor – but one which nevertheless belies a serious point.

Despite some Platonic, Aristotelian, Rousseauist, and Hegelian bumps which castigated writing as a betrayal of life or lived experience,[13] humanity has experienced a few thousand years of comforting and even pleasurable use of both spoken and written language. Arguably, this relative bliss came to an end with early twentieth-century Protestant guilt and ensuing Werkbund-like bifurcations separating aesthetics or pleasure from function and responsibility. Witnessed in de Saussure's demonization of writing as an ossified shell concealing real, spoken language; witnessed in the replacement of theories in which written languages were understood as natural, and inevitably visible, representations of the world (*à la* St. Augustine) with theories in which systems of writing are viewed as abstract, and invisible, classifications of use, human kinds, beliefs or ideas about language itself (*à la* Roland Barthes); the resultant shift reduces the value of all non-sentient matter to 'world as text' with 'text' understood as derogatory by most. As noted by Steven Pinker, the extreme end of this transition was written by Barthes more than forty years ago:

"Man does not exist prior to language, either as a species or as an individual."[14] Matter, in this view, does not matter as much as what you say about or feel for it.

Admittedly, the significance of this argument to either the discipline or the profession of architecture is not immediately obvious. Architecture, it might be argued, is not in danger of minimizing the value of non-sentient matter. Thinkers from Schiller to Roger Scruton have praised architecture as a material and objective art. Concrete and steel and stone provide the material reality (or "materiality" in today's idiom) through which architectural intentions are conveyed – even if those intentions claim to privilege the subject or mimic organic patterns. Furthermore, someone might point to the profession's increased focus on recycling as an indication of a rise in the importance accorded matter in the past few decades. This too is true, but only at a surface level. Deeper lies a fault line more significant than that signaled by Leonardo da Vinci's Vitruvian Man. The early twentieth-century transition from inorganic to organic values, along with the concomitant shift from public to private-oriented design approaches, cleaves architectures of today from earlier architectures of meaning or myth.

Babel's rift, extended by the Werkbund and Wittgenstein, is not comprised of matter *per se* but a change in matter's connection to meaning in physical language or formed matter. In order to perceive this rift, it is first necessary to clear the above-mentioned counterarguments from our line of sight. The first of these states that architecture values matter as much as ever because architecture must employ matter to simulate organic forms or affect the senses of a subject. Antoni Gaudí's Casa Batlló (1904) in Barcelona is a rather obvious and beautifully undulating example (see Figure 7.1); similar to Casa Milá in its ability to elicit descriptions focused on material make-up.[15] Yet, it is worth asking to what the undulations are aimed. Arguably, Gaudí does not intend to draw attention to stone and iron or even his virtuosity of composition; here emphasis is placed on organic reference and simile – stone in "wave-like rhythms" and iron "like … seaweed." Inorganic materials matter less than the organic world you are expected to conjure. The second argument points to interest in recycling and sustainable sourcing as proof that architecture values matter as much as ever. Recycling and the increased use of recyclable materials are less signs of respect for matter *per se* and more signs of the lack of value accorded to formed matter: the shorter the intended lifespan of any particular building, the greater the admission that a given disposition of matter, its form, is devoid of meaning.

Consider the following edict from Theo van Doesburg: "Form. Elimination of all *concept of form* in the sense of a *fixed type* is essential to the healthy development of architecture and art as a whole."[16] The roots of modernity's suspicion regarding direct communication[17] and the value accorded matter are clear in religious dogmas of various faiths. As loaded as they are with a spiritual as opposed to a bodily bias, it is not difficult to understand how these views became part of naturalist- or 'organic'-oriented design practices or how these ideas spread so far – from the Arts and Crafts Movement to Frank Lloyd Wright to Bruce Goff; from the Metro Station at Place de la Bastille in Paris to the Xanadu Gallery in San Francisco to the

FIGURE 7.1 Casa Batlló, Barcelona, Antoni Gaudí architect
Source: Photograph by David C. Lewis.

Price House in Bartlesville, Oklahoma. This new value system peeks through the veil even in van Doesburg's use of the phrase "healthy development" as mutually exclusive of form. All of this made sense within a given cultural milieu at the end of the nineteenth century and the explosion of potentially de-humanizing technologies. How this perspective has not only survived but, in fact, deepened its position in architecture as extended through Frank Gehry and Zaha Hadid, in a culture which has become synonymous with materialism and technological innovation, is far more perplexing. A single answer is elusive but it is reasonable to suspect that, as with the declining attention to direct meanings in literature in the information age, the rapidly decreasing lifespan of works of architecture fosters and is fostered by the largely subconscious acceptance of one or more of the four following arguments:

1. *Horizontal versus hierarchical relations of character.* While infrequently assumed in relation to sentient life, it is common to evaluate the various capacities (and the material qualities serving those capacities) of inorganic and non-sentient matter as equally necessary or unnecessary. The materials used in the construction of buildings are weighed against one another in an informal matrix of needs and wants: tensile or compressive strength or both; porosity, density, and weight; rate of thermal and moisture transmission; color and texture; resistance to fire, impact, decay, rot, rust, etc. Along with these properties, come the secondary qualities of context and image, availability and cost, client comfort and familiarity of local craftspeople with the material, etc. Typically, no single property of a given material will prompt a favorable decision because, in isolation, the properties of matter are conceived as meaningless, more or less. What is dead is assumed to be dead in all regards. What is solid and opaque, simply solid and opaque.

2. *Equality of character is evidence of the equality of functions.* Note the percentage of bridges constructed of reinforced concrete or steel as compared to the relatively scant number of bridges constructed from wood timbers. Note the frequency of various materials used as structural frames for modern high-rises: there are many in steel followed, in descending order, by concrete and (at great remove) by load-bearing masonry or pre-cast concrete panels followed (at even greater remove and only in non-industrialized countries) by mud bricks. In bridges and high-rises, function tends to dictate character. Thus, the frequency with which an unexpected material for a particular function is encountered is a measure of only the popularity of visual tropes of sentiment or prestige in human consciousness – i.e. those idyllic covered wooden bridges of New England or the 1980s granite-clad towers of New York, Los Angeles, and Houston. Matter, in this view, is mere matter; deviations in material are ascribed to individual whims ("beauty is in the eye of the beholder") or cleverness. In other words, what matters is what we might say about the work, its information, not what it is.

3. *Orientalism of matter relative to humanity.* When inorganic or non-sentient organic matter arises as a topic of theoretical contemplation, it appears as an Other to sentient organic matter. It is Orientalized. As Other, the non-sentient is assumed to be, and to remain, a relation of visible to visible; the invisible, or deeper cause, is the province solely of the sentient, the organic, of life. Matter is treated as an inactive or neutral mirror for human experience in full

positivity. Read again the words of the architectural phenomenologists in this regard. Desire is thus rendered as occurring only "in the [mind] of the beholder" … but this 'beholder' is simultaneously rendered as desiring nothing that is actually *out there* inside the matter of the world; this beholder is treated as if he or she desires only his or her own imagination. Matter does not matter.

4. *Classification and nomenclature, the order of beings and the order of words, remain linked in the inorganic, the non-sentient, the dead.* That is, while admittedly arbitrary, the relations of words, particularly written words, to matter are generally accepted as fixed in comparison to the linkages between words and humans, for example. When this difference is contemplated, the relative permanence of the horizontal linkage between concept and percept in matter is recorded as a simplification – a sign of inferiority when compared to humans' ability to endlessly remake, rename, to fictionalize and reclassify. Read again the words of the formalists. Given this perceived inferiority of inorganic or non-sentient matter, it is not surprising that architects in the first decades of the twentieth century abandoned material qualities and surface development in favor of "space" – the latter being an endlessly formable and renamable non-entity unburdened by limitations of classification because it possesses no character of its own. With Modernism began the usurpation of objective matter by subjective space. Figures gave way to the void. Space came to represent us – our surrogate selves in the world of twentieth-century architecture.

Notes

1 Architectural evolution, like evolution is biology and language, should not be considered improvement or progress. All forms of evolution are best thought of as forms of transformation. John McWhorter, *The Power of Babel: a natural history of language* (New York: Harper, 2003), 13.

2 Quoted in George Steiner, *After Babel: aspects of language and translation* (New York: Oxford University Press, 1975), 181.

3 Numerous linguists have documented this tendency of languages and dialects within languages to diverge from one another and previously common references. A good general analysis is Chapter 5, "The Thousands of Dialects of Thousands of Languages All Developed Far Beyond the Call of Duty," of McWhorter's *The Power of Babel*, pp. 177–215. Because language does not stand in fixed relation to the external world, "language change does not stop at the boundary of necessity … left to its own devices, a language will develop baubles – linguistic overgrowth that, whatever its interest, is incidental to the needs of human exchange and expression" (pp. 192, 215).

4 Words are easier to invent than new types of matter or forms of activity, and easier to invest oneself in than investigating larger ideas of grammar. It is difficult to believe Noam Chomsky's ideas of deep structure (the notion of an underlying, context-free language structure that takes on diverse "surface structures" when enacted in unique circumstances) when, for instance, Brits, Americans and citizens of other former British colonies struggle to communicate despite similar histories, pervasive international media, and shared physiologies operating under identical laws of physics.

5 Elaine Scarry, *The Body in Pain* (New York: Oxford University Press, 1987), 128.

6 See the writings of Chomsky, Lakoff and Johnson, Pinker, Bowker and Star, and Berreby.

7 These divisions are as old as the principle of separate evaluation of esthetic and manufacturing qualities espoused by the Deutscher Werkbund. See Michael Fazio,

Marian Moffett, and Lawrence Wodehouse, *A World History of Architecture*, 2nd edn (Boston: McGraw-Hill, 2008), 462–463.

8 "Seeking to grasp the force of Wittgenstein's criticism of 'private objects', one is made aware of the possibility that the obscurities, the indeterminacies in the logic of the case, stem from a refusal to distinguish between 'reference' and 'meaning'." Steiner, *After Babel*, p. 166.

9 Ludwig Wittgenstein, *Philosophical Investigations*, translated by G.E.M. Anscombe (Malden, MA: Blackwell, 1997), 224.

10 As Elaine Scarry points out, such are ruthless strategists' dreams for their opponents: through temporary alliances, codes, camouflage, bluffing, etc., they hope their enemies will be denied access to meaning. See Scarry, *The Body in Pain*, p. 133.

11 Rule #1: never open a book of architectural theory without being cognizant of the fact that you are stepping into an ongoing, and perhaps bitter, struggle. Not a word of it is disinterested or innocent.

12 The Epilogue of McWhorter's *The Power of Babel* offers a brief but elegant analysis of the lineage from the first or Ur-language to the languages of today. See "Extra, Extra! The Language of Adam and Eve!" pp. 287–303.

13 See Jacques Derrida, *Of Grammatology*, translated by Gayatri Chakravorty Spivak (Baltimore, MD: Johns Hopkins University Press, 1976), 25.

14 Roland Barthes, "To Write: An Intransitive Verb?" in Richard Macksey and Eugenio Donato (eds.), *The Language of Criticism and the Science of Man: the structuralist controversy* (Baltimore, MD: Johns Hopkins University Press, 1972), 135. Quoted in Steven Pinker, *The Blank Slate: the modern denial of human nature* (New York: Viking, 2002), 208.

15 For example: "Its façade of pitted elephantine stone rises and falls in wave-like rhythms, while the iron front of the balconies seem tossed about like galvanized seaweed," Dan Cruickshank, *Sir Bannister Fletcher's A History of Architecture* (London: Routledge, 1996) 1362.

16 See Theo van Doesburg, "Towards a Plastic Architecture," in Ulrich Conrads (ed.), *Programs and Manifestoes on 20th Century Architecture* (Cambridge, MA: MIT Press, 1975), 78–80. Passage quoted from p. 78.

17 For an excellent review of modernity's literary turn from direct writing, see George Steiner's *After Babel*, pp. 176–190.

8

LOOS AND THE ASCENSION OF SPACE IN THE MARKETPLACE

Architectural critic and historian Siegfried Giedion published *Space, Time and Architecture* in 1941. Architect and historian Bruno Zevi published *Saper Vedere l'Architecttura* [*Architecture as Space*] in 1948. Giedion develops an elaborate argument for the necessarily individual character of relationship between observer and space.[1] Zevi calls for a spatial shift in architectural thinking from the outset.[2] For insight into the emergence of information age architecture, however, one does not have to look inside either book. The titles record a paradigm shift:

architecture = space, or architecture = space and time.

It is extraordinary how banal these once bold assertions appear to late information age readers. And this seeming banality is significant for what it hides. Once we acknowledge the profundity of this shift, a series of other developments – Shannon's theory of communication as propagation of information through "channels," the privilege accorded private interest over public discourse, and architects' increasing forays into organic form – no longer appear as historical happenstance. Language and language preference in the first half of the twentieth century evolved in a cultural milieu dominated by the popularization of "space," "spacetime," and a host of "space-" metaphors. Such ambiguous generalizations of "space" are an excellent medium for various cults of the individual. "Space" serves as a proxy for our subjectivity in a material world.

The legacy of this milieu still undergirds design thinking in the early twenty-first century. A 2015 *New York Times* article celebrating the centennial of Einstein's General Theory of Relativity, "Space, the Frontier Right in Front of Us," serves as evidence. More than a third of the article praises the artistic freedom that Einstein's theory proffered. An equal portion deals exclusively with "Space in the Marketplace" – in other words, our growing sense of entitlement to personal space in public places.[3] What Einstein meant by "space" doesn't receive much space in the article.

The consequences of our growing fascination with space and space-oriented rhetoric are two-fold: (1) it distracts from and perhaps inhibits appreciation of time; as a long-term consequence, time-based aspects of Quality become incomprehensible; and (2) it leads to a diminishment of the value accorded to architecture of earlier eras. Though not readily apparent, this latter consequence spurs a loss of spatialized time, a devaluation of matter, a reduction of physical language literacy, and thus, in sum, the loss of content that might give ground to our increasingly subjective and ultimately solipsistic lived experiences. As the geographer Doreen Massey so eloquently says: "For liberal-individualist it is abstract space; for Habermasian, public space ... for communitarian, community/local space; for postmodern, corporeal/intimate space. The shift towards the local is impressive and not encouraging."[4]

Acts against Time

Einstein published his Special and General Theories of Relativity in 1905 and 1915 respectively. Of significance to artists, architects, and poets, these groundbreaking treatises set out an argument for the existence of space. No doubt "space," in the senses of literally or metaphorically empty voids existed long before Einstein. Pre-Socratics had pondered the void's size and the extent of its emptiness; geometers and physicists had tried to formalize methods for mapping it and the movement of objects through it; Dada poets and Cubist painters tried to privilege it over time through automatic writing, montage, and fragmented, non-narrative compositions.[5] But it is only in the wake of Relativity and the two theories' dissemination in popular media that space was accepted as real – as a reality to be sculpted and felt.

Not surprisingly, the popularized notion of space that would inflect poetry and film, art and architecture for the remainder of the century is a gross oversimplification. According to Einstein, "spacetime" is real insofar as it is capable of being deformed by matter and of contextualizing perception. "Spacetime" is intentionally one word; it is inappropriate to think the two terms independently. For better and more often worse, however, it was often only the "space" aspect of spacetime that architects and critics in the early decades of the twentieth century took seriously. Adolf Loos' *Raumplan* is an obvious 'for better' example of this seriousness. In his unbuilt Lido villa (see Figure 8.1 (a)), Loos anticipates the movement of occupants via stairs through a succession of rooms and, thus, implies an awareness of time as an ingredient of spatial perception. It demands imaginative inhabitation. Van Doesburg's diagram of horizontal and vertical planes is an equally influential but, arguably, 'for worse' example insofar as it is intended to be understood from a single vantage point and at an instant (see Figure 8.1 (b)). It is to be looked at as a whole. Figure 8.1 compares these two highly influential diagrams.

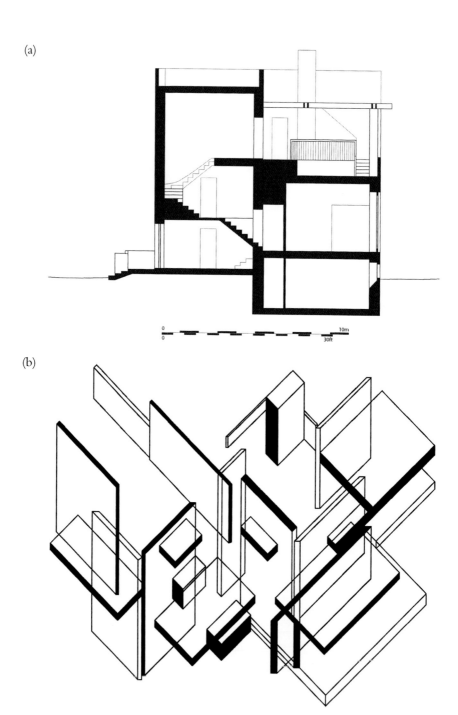

FIGURE 8.1 (a) Section of Loos' Lido villa; (b) Theo van Doesburg's 1923 composition of horizontal and vertical planes
Source: Drawings by Ryan Fierro.

This seriousness, for better and worse, spawned the majority of the "spatial exploration" rhetoric that followed in association with the work of Frank Lloyd Wright, Le Corbusier, and Paul Rudolph, their adherents, and their critics. These architects were not physicists and their legacy of privileging space over time or spacetime in the making of architecture would matter very little, were it not for the fact that both ends of the communication dyad (here, a speaker or author or architect; there, listener or reader or inhabitant) require desire for engagement. Claude Shannon, working in a space-oriented culture, missed this aspect of communication: the receiver has to want to receive information for it to be conveyed as meaningful. As Loos said, "All art is erotic;" the erotic is a state of desire; and desire is a condition of, and is enacted in, time.[6]

Modern architecture's ambition to distance itself from disciplinary history, from precedents and lineage, is well established. "Modern ornament has no parents and no offspring, no past and no future," according to Adolf Loos' *Ornament and Crime* (1910).[7] And Le Corbusier's *Toward an Architecture* (1923) is filled with so many pleas for newness and condemnations of custom that the title is often mistranslated as *Towards a New Architecture*. But architecture was not alone among late nineteenth- and early twentieth-century disciplines in this regard. Time as a rigorous subject is absent from the estates of modern metaphysics and phenomenology before Henri Bergson[8] and Edmund Husserl[9] and does not gain entrance into the main edifice of philosophical thought until Heidegger carried it through the front door in 1927. Sigmund Freud kept the majority of his ruminations on the nature of time private.[10] Because one does not get a better or more accurate view or come closer to 'Truth' the further time is chased back along the avenues of memory and side streets of recorded criticism, time is a distrusted quantity. As a result, time is almost — and "spacetime" completely — absent from twentieth-century consciousness as a malleable constituent of architectural design prior to the widespread dissemination of the ideas of the phenomenologists.

And yet, time is there, embedded in works of architecture in its arrest. Architects practicing a few centuries ago possessed one striking advantage over their present-day counterparts: architecture and artifice in general were conceived as triadic compositions of language, matter, and quality understood as interrelated, equal, and equally real concerns. Just prior to the emergence of modernity, architects were capable of addressing major questions (admittedly incapable of being articulated centuries ago) that are unanswerable (and oddly out of fashion to ask) today. These include: Does quality reside in the object of desire? In the labor of the maker? In the expended labor of perception on the part of the inhabitant or user? Prior to Guttenberg, the answer to these might have been a single "yes" or "all of the above." But today?

The information age is an altered field and the present-day relation between language, matter, and quality is not a simple one. Each is accorded different levels of scholarly and practical value. Each is relegated to a different place in various hierarchies of reality depending on the discipline and professional aspirations of the person doing the ranking (for the poet, language is perhaps most real; for the blacksmith, matter; for the diamond cutter, quality). Each is now measured in a pervasive market economy culture; at every level of human existence, teetering quantities of supply and demand destabilize meaning. As a result, it is reasonable to suggest that the total number of objects experienced which convey quality, in any given system of measure, inevitably shift the values of all other objects in that system: an increase in the number of luxury cars, for instance, reduces the value accorded to any particular car; diamonds as numerous as grains of sand would be nearly worthless. This is the domain in which architecture as a profession, and perhaps as a discipline, is now practiced.

As the total amount of information in the world has grown beyond all comprehension, many aspects of language have paradoxically atrophied. Only "experience" remains as a rubric or conceptual trope across which architectural academics and theorists merge evaluations of language, matter, and quality. Formalists and phenomenologists both employ it for this purpose. As a rubric, universalized or homogenized 'experience' is useful but its constituent elements tend to be unequally tethered; one element of the triad is usually treated as a result of the other two (when a material is fetishized in the hands of a skillful architect and rendered poetic in the language of contemporary media, for example, the project is accorded the distinction of having achieved "quality"). To be effective, this rubric must be parsed; its constituent pieces understood. It is important to note that the reason(s) for which an experience is sought and the measure(s) of that experience are not one and the same. That is, need or desire is not a standard by which we might judge an object of experience; desires are merely motivations to or toward experience. Motivations are instrumentalities. And, in the domain of recent time under the sway of information age ideology, it is irresponsible to coalesce measures of instrumentality and measures of quality in a single plane of criticism.

Acknowledging the split between instrumentality and quality makes clear that an experience or an object of experience does not exhibit quality by virtue of symbolizing a want or need. A vase or painting or sports car are not of high quality because I want them or even 'need' them. Stated in this way, this is rather obvious but it has implications largely unrecognized for spacetime. Wants and needs are understood only in relation to temporal agendas: I want or need something (present tense), I used to have (past tense) or I will have (future tense). In order to be distinct from instrumentalization and thus be accessible to perception in the present, Quality can only be a measure taken in the present against the datum of the passage of time – and humans' attempt to arrest, speed up or otherwise alter that passage. Wright's Robie House and Loos' Moller House sustain experiences of quality not because manipulations of spatial arrangements privilege the perception of space but because those manipulations arrest the perception of time. In other words, quality is a non-temporal measure against a change in, or expectation of, desire; every act of making quality, of seeking quality, and perceiving quality is an act taken in time against time.

Time in Search of Content

From the Classical to the Information Age we envision a radical shift as having occurred, particularly across the period opening with the Industrial Revolution and closing with World War II, and attribute this to varying precipitous events. As evidence of this shift, called a "break" by some and a "turn" by others, cultural anthropologists often point to the rapid dissemination of new technologies (steam engines, radios, airplanes, televisions), advances in the models of physical sciences (evolution, relativity, and quantum mechanics), and the emergence of the social sciences (psychoanalysis, psychology, sociology). While almost all commentators acknowledge that these advances are rooted in earlier ideas of sometimes clear and often obscure provenance, the results are conceived as so radical as to earn monikers such as "paradigm shifts" or "emergent phenomena" by all but the most reticent. Theorizations of architecture are no exception. Histories delineated by Pevsner, Gideon, Mumford and most of their lesser-known but more recent inheritors are written as if the works of the proto-modern period can scarcely belong to the same discipline as works by Bernini and Borromini and Michelangelo; and, at the level of disciplinary structure (perhaps) and professional organization (certainly), there is a degree of truth in this. Architects have invented cloaks of fiction about their activities and wrapped their products in media conceits that, no doubt, alter perceptions to the point of creating an entirely new professional class and thus new classes of professional objects as discussed earlier. The importance accorded this Zeitgeist shift in relation to architecture, however, is overstated, and its form, understandably, misunderstood.

Broadly considered, the modern fetishization of technology is merely an evolutionary branch of architecture's growing fascination with responsibility. Though recent architectural discourse appears to differ from the Classical and the mythical in terms of a relatively new appreciation of "function" and "technology," these terms – function and technology – are merely recent descriptors for very old notions of duty and utility. Loos chastised the Werkbund for forgetting this in designing chairs that force people to adopt new methods of sitting.[11] Just as our anatomy and desire to sit have (or should have) guided the evolution of chairs, ideas of duty have organized or guided human actions for much of recorded history.[12] Similarly, information age architectural formalisms represent incremental evolutions in the ordering of figure/ground, solid/void, axes/termini now combined with a concomitant and culturally-driven reduction in attention to surface that accords less value to matter than did the builders of the Nile valley, Jerusalem, Athens or Rome. And today's various forms of architectural phenomenology are, to some degree, philosophical and quasi-religious outgrowths of those base animal facts of perception and gestalt psychology which undergird every encounter with every built environ. In all cases, formal and phenomenal, these are aspects "of a general shift by which 'information' has been conceptualized as disembedded from materiality" as geographer Doreen Massey notes.[13]

There is merit in one aspect of the popular version of the Classical/Information Age shift for understanding architecture – less historico-physiological, more

96 Architecture History and Theory in Reverse

meta-cognitive. Call it the Absolute/Zeitgeist divide. It notes the transition from concerns with timelessness, focused on human relationships with unchanging Absolutes (be they Deities or astronomic observations), to twentieth- and twenty-first-century happenings and events lived by humans in time, a Zeitgeist. Proponents of this split acknowledge that the builders of Babel differed from us little in biology or physical abilities but argue that we are of a different species when it comes to beliefs and motivations.

This is an important tale but its merit is not in its standard telling. In the standard version, judgments of buildings in Classical eras were made against temporally fixed, objective, necessary orders of knowledge while evaluations in contemporary societies are free-floating, subjective, contingent; a transition, in other words, from spatial order to temporal flux. While it is true, perhaps, that the temples and artifacts of Classical periods were measured as "similar" and "different" according to a stratification of knowledge assumed to be permanent and timeless – and equally true that today we assume all such relations to be impermanent and subject to the whims of changing perspective – the shift is not from a timeless spatial distribution of knowledge (or architecture) in a physical past to a temporal distribution in our own event-oriented present. A spatial stratification such as Classicism glories precisely in its endurance in and through time. That is, it is only in the duration of temples and artifacts that Classical peoples perceived their ideas as timeless; they are intrinsically about time.[14] Information age temporal stratifications, histories, happenings, events and whimsical changes of opinion, on the other hand, claw for the substance of space: a place in which to happen. In other words, the standard telling has gotten the ideas mixed up. A more accurate and revealing ending for this tale is to say that mythical and Classical eras spatialize time while Romantic and modern ideologies seek to invent and glory in space in order to give meaning to temporal flux.

This could be seen as quibbling or word play. Admittedly the new phrasing does not immediately illuminate anything new about architecture, its changing discourses or its diminishing importance in contemporary societies until an additional fact is acknowledged: the lived or temporalized space that defines the late information age is not architectural space. I will refrain from highlighting, italicizing, underlining or putting that last phrase in bold; but I think it is of first-order significance. Lived space is the combination of the characteristics and temporal sequence of places in which things happen in a spatialized analog in the conscious mind. Loos' *Raumplan*, for instance. Classically understood, architectural space is a social and linguistic construct that orders and gives meaning to the seemingly transparent medium that fills vessels as well as the voids around and between discrete masses (and which, before Einstein, was not generally accepted to exist). This more stringent and discipline-specific form of space – another designation for the Classical term *Chora*, perhaps – is inextricably bound to the legibility of a physical language. Because lived space is not and cannot be conceived as existing in the world on its own, formed matter is recognized as the necessary locus of character and serves as a physical analog to mind space. The transition of architecture from pre-information spatialized time to information age lived space is a transition from time understood as subservient to space to time that is not believed to be spatial but is experienced as such.

Let me put a finer and more polemical point on this assertion. It was not in the emergence of Modernity or the upheaval of the Industrial Revolution that a real breach occurred. It occurred as a consequence of an exodus, in the loss of spatialized time, a reduction in the value accorded matter, a diminishment of physical literacy, an increase in information and decrease in shared understanding, and thus in the loss of content that might unify our increasingly subjective and ultimately solipsistic experiences.

Notes

1 "The essence of space as it is conceived today is its many-sidedness, the infinite potentiality for relations within it ... In order to grasp the true nature of space the observer must project himself into it." Siegfried Giedion, *Space, Time and Architecture: the growth of a new tradition* (Cambridge, MA: Harvard University Press, 1967), 435–436. Giedion is describing the transition from Renaissance perspective and reliance on Euclidean geometry to the new conception of space that took hold in art and architecture in the early twentieth century. See "The Research into Space: Cubism," pp. 434–443.
2 Zevi wrote:

> A satisfactory history of architecture has not yet been written, because we are still not accustomed to thinking in terms of space, and because historians of architecture have failed to apply a coherent method of studying buildings from a spatial point of view.
>
> (Bruno Zevi, *Architecture as Space: how to look at architecture*, revised edition, translated by Milton Gendel, edited by Joseph A. Barry, New York: Horizon Press, 1974, 22)

3 Natalie Angier, "Space, the Frontier Right in Front of Us," *New York Times*, November 24, 2015, available at: www.nytimes.com/2015/11/24/science/space-the-frontier-right-in-front-of-us.html (accessed November 24, 2015).
4 Doreen Massey, *For Space* (London: Sage Publications, 2006), 186.
5 According to George Steiner:

> The most penetrating record of this attempt is contained in [Hugo] Ball's memoir, *Die Flucht aus der Zeit*, issued in 1927. The "'flight from the times" could only succeed if syntax, in which time is given binding force, could be broken.
>
> (George Steiner, *After Babel: aspects of language and translation*, New York: Oxford University Press, 1975, 194)

The best one-stop source for the evolution of ideas about space is Edward S. Casey's *The Fate of Place: a philosophical history* (Berkeley, CA: University of California Press, 1998).
6 Adolf Loos, *Ornament and Crime: selected essays*, translated by Michael Mitchell (Riverside CA: Ariadne Press, 1998), 167. In more recent language: "Desire is not a form, but a procedure, a process," Gilles Deleuze and Félix Guattari, *Kafka: toward a minor literature*, translated by Dana Polan (Minneapolis: University of Minnesota Press, 1986), 8.
7 Loos, *Ornament and Crime*, 171.
8 "Duration seemed to [Bergson] to be less and less reducible to a psychological experience and became instead the variable essence of things, providing the theme of a complex ontology." Gilles Deleuze, *Bergsonism*, translated by H. Tomlinson and Barbara Habberjam (New York: Zone Books, 1988), 34.

98 Architecture History and Theory in Reverse

9 *Vorlesungen zur Phänomenologie des inneren Zeitbewusstseins* (1928) [English translation: *On the Phenomenology of Consciousness of Internal Time* (1990)] was Husserl's only sustained text on the topic published prior to the twenty-first century.

10 "[Freud's] sparse references to time are usually qualified in terms of their being 'hints' or 'suspicions'. And in a late exchange with Marie Bonaparte … Freud confirmed that he had kept his ideas about time private." See Kelly Ann Noel-Smith, "Freud on Time and Timelessness: the ancient Greek influence," PhD thesis, Birkbeck, University of London, 2014, 110.

11 According to Loos:

> Members of the Werkbund are confusing cause and effect. We do not sit in a particular way because a cabinetmaker has made a chair in this or that way, the cabinetmaker makes the chair in a particular way because that is the way we want to sit.
>
> (Loos, *Ornament and Crime*, 163)

The quoted passage is taken from "Cultural Degeneration," pp. 163–166, which is one of Loos' most cogently argued and most relevant essays against the proliferating desire for freedom of invention amongst designers. The passage begins: "No individual, nor any organization, created our cupboards for us, our cigarette cases, our jewelry. Time created them for us, and they change from year to year, from day to day, from hour to hour."

12 For instance, refer to the opening lines of Homer's *Odyssey*.

13 Massey, *For Space*, 96.

14 The archaeologist J. J. Coulton has acknowledged the role of duration, characterizing Greek temples as "monumental" because they endure longer than human life. See J. J. Coulton, *Ancient Greek Architects at Work: problems of structure and design* (Ithaca, NY: Cornell University Press, 1982).

The human race has two books, two registers, two testaments: masonry and printing; the Bible of stone and the Bible of paper.

[…]

In its printed form, thought is more imperishable than ever; it is volatile, irresistible, indestructible … how can one be surprised that human intelligence should have quitted architecture for printing?

(Victor Hugo, The Hunchback of Notre-Dame, *1831)*[1]

The idea of reading a building as we would read Milton or Dante, and getting the same kind of delight out of the stones as out of the stanzas, never enters our mind for a moment.

(John Ruskin, The Stones of Venice, *1851)*[2]

INTERLUDE

The Information Reformation, or This Killed That

At this, the mid-point in a backward recounting of disciplinary time, I pause to regain sight of a mythical plain, a tower, and the promise of shared language. At the end of my tale, which coincides with architecture's origin story, I attempt to fill the voids of intentions and actions that the nine-verse biblical account of Babel remands, along with posterity, to isolated confusion. For the time being, however, I am interested only in the story as given — without the embroidery of archaeological evidence or speculation into ancient motives — and, even with that limitation, only insofar as it illuminates practices of architecture in eras of myth and meaning that reveal points of comparison to a modern discipline that has assumed a vintage name.[3]

Babel, the Story of

Literary critic George Steiner has written:

> Our speech interposes itself between apprehension and truth like a dusty pane or warped mirror. The tongue of Eden was like a flawless glass; a light of total understanding streamed through it. Thus Babel was a second Fall, in some regards as desolate as the first.[4]

From whence then to begin? It is not possible to assert many things with certainty from the approximately two hundred words that make up the whole of the story in English translation. There are only plausibilities. Of these, most important to the history being reconstructed here is the stated intention for building the city and its tower: *so that we may make a name for ourselves* ... This is a new and singular level of ambition in the biblical text, exceeding even Adam's charge to name everything in the Garden. "We" is collective.

102 Interlude: The Information Reformation

Though we must be cognizant of the dangers inherent in projecting modern consciousness, foreign values, and our own intentions onto the actions of earlier people, on the basis of these words, it seems reasonable to assert that glory was a significant goal. But whose glory? Glory in the eyes of whom? At first glance, the use of a plural subject "we" – *so that we may make a name* – suggests that it is not a reference to a singular earthly authority; it is inconceivable that any individual could grant such praise to the whole of the people of Babel or that any one person would dare such aspiration. That presumption, combined with the absence of reference in those nine short verses to a particular authority, either by name or title, suggests that the construction of the tower at Babel was neither for the glorification of an architect nor even King Nimrod. But if not for King or country (arguably, the same thing in BCE Mesopotamia), nor architect or wealthy patron, all that remains, in terms of possible loci for the glory sought, is the artifact itself (outward/material/objective culture), the builders and inhabitants (inward/spiritual/subjective culture), or a deity larger than, but not coexistent with, either place or people. Of these three choices – Deity, Humanity, and Artifact – the middle term is no doubt most appealing to modern readers. Consider each, however, with a biblical mind.

Deity

In the realm of myth recorded in Genesis, each thing and every act is organized around, if not coordinated by, a physically absent God. While it is difficult from the perspective of recent time to conceive of a God or group of deities needing to *make a name* for himself/herself/themselves, the Judaic tradition is structured around giving name – and thereby praise – to God. The plurality of the subject also does little to discredit the idea that the construction is for the glorification of God; "we" is as easily conceived as referring to the whole of Creation – and thus to God – as to a group of individuals or tribe. The fact that the monotheistic God of Judaism is claimed to abhor the construction is not proof that the construction was not intended for him. Instead it is evidence only that the builders and inhabitants were incorrect as to the glory their work might bring. Note that when God reveals his displeasure, the work is not only destroyed but it is abandoned; the builders do not try again. This fact is the strongest suggestion that the work was intended for the glory of God.

There are only two circumstantial pieces of evidence that effectively remove God from consideration as the locus of glorification at Babel: first, God is presented as taking a positive role in the making of architecture and cities only much later in biblical tradition; second, and arguably the stronger evidence, there is the significant referent given in the quoted passage ... *for ourselves.*

Humanity

It is logical to declare humans the intended recipients of glory at Babel, given the combination of "we" and "for ourselves." Human and God are discrete entities in

Genesis stories. The common phrase, "God made (hu)man in His own image," is not a rebuttal of separation or claim to oneness but evidence of a split. Apart from the totality of creation, humans are the only entities to which "we" and "ourselves" easily refer. From our position in the information age no leap of faith is required to imagine humans acting for ourselves or mere self-aggrandizement. A need remains, however, to demonstrate the opposite: that humanity's project at Babel might not have aimed so narrowly at self-glorification.

Artifact

Arguably, in biblical times, every human action was considered an act toward, or away from, God. From the building of altars to the sacrificing of animals to the casting of idols, the physical remnant served as an artifact for or against faith: a third term inserted between God and Humanity to act as talismanic supplement. Later, in the Classical age, humans authored representations with far greater intention – perfecting their final form as paintings, mosaics, sculptures, and buildings – in order to discover real but hidden links between self and God via the mirror of mimesis.[5] Rome is largely a collection of such artifacts. This evolving urge toward the construction of ever more elaborate physical manifestations of faith – third terms: artifacts, levers, prosthetics, imitations – might be dismissed as mere hubris were it not for the second most important half-certainty embedded in the Babel story: the construction of the city and tower is intended as a direct manifestation of the one, shared language in physical form. "Architecture began like all writing," as Hugo said.[6] Our present-day conception of language as a host of diverse systems of representation obscures this aspect of the story.

Biblical language never aims to 'picture' or stand as a substitute. The *Word* is. It is Being itself. It is full presence uncorrupted by humans. It is also not identical with God. In the time of Genesis, according to Maimonides, discourse is assumed to have real transactional power.[7] The *common discourse* shared by all people in the land of Shinar, the Fertile Crescent, and beyond is the ground that spans the chasm between imperfect humanity and its perfect creator. As a result of its inbetweenness, however, this discourse – *The Word* – is no more revealing of either humanity or deity than a bridge is descriptive of the towns on either of its two banks. Its physical manifestation is not to the glory of Man or God: the building of the city and the tower, like the writing of commentaries on Scripture, is a study in links that exist between parent and child: through architecture and word. In this one sense, at least, it is possible to say (with a slight change in emphasis) that the builders of Babel sought literally to make *a Name* for their selves.

Before returning to the appropriate place in this reverse chronology, and while acknowledging that the present text is not intended as metaphor or parody of scholarly exegesis, there are profound similarities that might be drawn between the project at Babel and that of Modernism. Both Babel and Modernism evolved from disparate and, in some ways, antagonistic visions that slowly coalesced into "single-minded architectural juggernaut[s],"[8] experienced a brief moment of cohesion,

104 Interlude: The Information Reformation

and disintegrated rapidly under a barrage of challenges – some assumed to be divine, others clearly all too human. Both Babel's builders and the great twentieth-century Modernists privileged information over meaning in seeking a Name for themselves or their artifacts or both and, in both cases, succeeded. Just as the literary aftermath of every strong poet is characterized by a period of wild descent and strange new wordings by inheritors fearful of succumbing to influence, Babel's and Modernism's successes are evidenced in the rapid diffusion and struggles that followed. While speculation on the attitudes prevalent at Babel is a topic for the final pages, it will serve us well to understand some of the factors that spurred the Babel-like dispersion of Modernism into so many local and untranslatable dialects across the western world.[9]

This Will Kill That

At Princeton, in their only known meeting, Le Corbusier attempted to explain to Einstein how he, Corbu, had incorporated relativity into architecture. Einstein is reported to have suggested that Corbusier failed to grasp the theory. This anecdote is telling.

In reviewing his special theory of relativity, Einstein wrote without timidity, "we entirely shun the vague word 'space,' of which, we must honestly acknowledge, we cannot form the slightest conception, and we replace it by 'motion relative to a practically rigid body of reference.'" When Einstein does invoke "space," as he does with his later work, he is explicit about its subservient character: "According to the general theory of relativity, the geometrical properties of space are not independent, but they are determined by matter."[10] Comfortable, seemingly harmless, the quasi-mystical conceits of pen and mind perpetuated by architects and critics alike distract the profession from physical matter and issues of physical language and, one would think more important, any potential to discuss space in a way that is actionable.

Many information age architects and architectural theorists, Corbusier included, write and think about space in terms of nineteenth-century Classical Mechanics: a medium imbued with near mystical qualities of the ether and accorded, at the very least, a perceivable existence through which citizens and tourists move over time. Such naïve usages of "space" and the prerequisite naïvety of thought that fosters such usages should not have survived the shift to modern science in general or the publication of Einstein's earth-moving critique in particular. But such is the persistence of pre-modern myths.

There are serious implications that derive from the absence of what we might deem romantic material concerns – such as legibility, narrative, and desire – in favor of an architectural obsession with "space" and spatially biased thinking too loosely conceived. First, if space is not conceived in a way that acknowledges its dependence upon and infinite variability under the influence of matter, then there is no purpose to the bulk of criticism and research within the profession in the last hundred years or so.[11] Second, the evolution of built form over time obeys no external rule in the absence of "a practically rigid body of reference" that grounds space. Third, alterations or transformations of meaning attached to such an ungrounded evolution of form can only appear to emerge from principles peculiar to and limited by a given project – in other words, they are no longer transactional. These last two observations are equal and mutually amplifying manifestations of a belief in space. For a "space first" thinker, judging the appropriateness of any particular arrangement of matter is limited to asking questions of a peculiar type: "does the appearance of the form get in the way of seeing *the* space?" or "does the shape of the building support the programmatic use of spaces to which the building is intended?" Intentions are conceived as residing in the absence of, or between the elements of, formed matter. Materials are reduced to their technical or environmental functions and the material world is reduced in value to its necessity for making the spatial world visible and giving us information as to spatial purpose.

It is hard not to conceive this type of thinking as rooted in the Judeo-Christian exhortation of faith in an invisible, disembodied, but nevertheless all meaningful spirit at the expense and degradation of physical appearances and their 'mere' bodily manifestations: *Do not concern yourself with the things of this world* ... It would be less a joke than satire to suggest that the shift from meaning-in-matter to information-in-space constitutes a Protestant Reformation of Architecture.[12]

There is more to this satire than an easy comparison of spatial-devotion to religious belief (though I think that comparison is a valid one). The largely non-physical domain of information age architecture and its movements – from space-oriented design to attempts to address functionalism, the environment, and social justice – creates one impression above all others: information age architecture is forever looking for new non-architectural information to represent. This tendency aligns with the central (and, in my opinion, worst) tenet of both proselytizing religions and the emergent architecture profession alike: the belief we possess deep and hidden truths we are obliged to present to the world. For architects, at least, Einstein should be understood to have exposed the frailty of one such truth. The problem is not that each of us – architects or members of religious sects – potentially adhere to the wrong truth; the problem lies with believing that conveying truth or a personally held position is the sole or primary purpose of writing or designing or any other form of communicating. Communication has little to do with conveying truths. It is certainly not what it does best. And truths as varied as "buildings should be sustainable" or "poverty exists" or "algorithms can produce interesting shapes" or "I want people to 'feel' *this*, here" or "deconstructing the tradition is clever and necessary" or "I'm being ironic" are all hopelessly pedantic and dull when rendered as information on or in buildings. Architectural meaning is not what buildings tell us but what is at stake in the things we build.

Community is not the coming together of people who share a fixed set of beliefs. Differences in people's cultures and backgrounds foster unique intersections of representations, images, and even spaces; and these representations, images, and spaces gain in meaning as they are compared, mixed, and shared on a heterogeneous field. Community, in other words, is a layering of meaning that grows out of difference; and it is reasonable to claim that there is no particular truth or body of information that trumps the aspirations of people to communicate those differences. It is likely that a passion for physical language, the desire for communicable architecture and places, is a result of the human urge to deal with those myriad differences. Fostering such is the closest thing architecture has to an ethical mandate. The daring and sometimes capricious but always self-conscious qualities of Mannerism, for example, can be thought of as aesthetic expressions targeted at the careful balance and harmony of the High Renaissance; Mannerist expressions even can be considered sadistic insults hurled in the midst of Renaissance seriousness.[13] It is critical, however, that this mandate move beyond sloganism or proselytizing or mere poke-in-the-eye heresies in order to become operative. In order to do this, it is first necessary to tease apart the two primary forms that "fostering a place for the communication of differences" might take.

Philosophers Gilles Deleuze and Félix Guattari argue that everything incessantly moves back and forth between "progress" and "becoming." Progress occurs only in systems of language [striated space]; becoming occurs only in the absence of such systems [smooth space]. It is possible to distinguish "progress spaces" that allow existing ideas and meanings to develop, merge, hybridize, etc. from those "becoming spaces" that are non-hierarchical in order to allow invention. Architects give great lip service to the latter. It is incumbent upon architects and theorists, however, to recognize that the former, spaces of progress (spaces of language), are those that allow the meanings of the community to propagate.[14] Developing physical language is neither a project of asserting the intentions held dear by an architect nor an absenting of all existing meanings in order to establish a blank slate. Physical language grows out of existing languages. Communication is an act of progress, not one of becoming.

This last comment brings us back to space and its fairly recent Protestant architectural ascension. Spatial solidity or spatial permanence is an illusion propped up by language. This illusion is made more convincing because language appears to resist time in the sense that literature seems to 'survive' across time – and time, in everyday language, is understood to be the equal opposite of space. Arguably, the situation is quite different; transitions in language trigger perceptions of various space-times.[15]

Einstein's simple admonition is useful. In the note to the fifteenth edition of his popular exposition of *relativity* he wrote:

> Space-time is not necessarily something to which one can ascribe a separate existence, independently of the actual objects of physical reality. Physical objects are not *in space*, but these objects are *spatially extended*. In this way the concept "empty space" loses its meaning.[16]

Geographer Doreen Massey is more explicit. "Space does not exist prior to identities/entities and their relations."[17] In this light, it is legitimate to say that 'perceptions' of space are always and only conceptual. All spaces are language spaces. Or, in language only a little less terse, all spaces perceived are language spaces read and understood. Ruskin was correct in saying we do not read buildings as we do Dante or Milton, but we do read them.

What does all of that mean? It means the space | language bifurcation on which information era architecture is founded is a myth of illegitimate birth. It means slogans such as "to see is to forget the name of the thing one sees" are meaningless. It means, finally, that a search for meaning in architecture is separate from and inhibited by the noise of intentions and assertions of information deemed valuable by architects. Intentions and information are almost always means for architects to make a name for himself/herself/themselves (historically, almost always *him* unfortunately).

Acknowledging these delusory tendencies prompts a new way of understanding Hugo's famous question, "how can one be surprised that human intelligence should have quitted architecture for printing?," as well as his verdict.[18] The difficulty for architects is not that media, from the advent of the printing press forward, has taken a role away from architecture. Media has not killed architecture. Instead, it is the architectural profession's refusal to cede to media the role of delivering information – a responsibility for which media is better suited – that has led to architecture's present lifeless state. The printing press did not kill architecture. Architecture, in its ambition to be a form of media, has lost itself in information and empty space.

Notes

1 Victor Hugo, *The Hunchback of Notre-Dame* (Ann Arbor, MI: Ann Arbor Media Group, 2006), 195 and 190–191.
2 John Ruskin, *The Stones of Venice*, edited and abridged by J.G. Links (New York: Da Capo, 2003), 166.
3 I am not a theologian and the analysis offered here is not theological.
4 George Steiner, *After Babel: aspects of language and translation* (New York: Oxford University Press, 1975), 59. A comment on page 232 clarifies this one:

> There have been so many thousands of human tongues, there still are, because there have been, particularly in the archaic stages of social history, so many distinct groups intent on keeping from one another the inherited, singular springs of their identity....

5 As Demetri Porphyrios notes: "Classicist would argue, architecture is the imitative celebration of construction and shelter qualified by the myths and ideas of a given culture." See "The Relevance of Classical Architecture," in Kate Nesbitt (ed.), *Theorizing a New Agenda for Architecture* (New York: Princeton Architectural Press, 1996), 92–96. Quoted passage, p. 95.
6 Hugo, *The Hunchback of Notre-Dame*, 184.
7 See Moses Maimonides, *The Guide for the Perplexed*, 2nd edn, translated by M. Friedländer (London: Routledge, 1904).
8 Michael Fazio, Marian Moffett, and Lawrence Wodehouse, *A World History of Architecture*, 2nd edn (Boston: McGraw-Hill, 2008), commenting on Modernism. See p. 505.
9 Underlying the above is a concern with language. The notion of architectural or physical language is important to any reading of the Babel story insofar as language is necessary to grounding sharable content. It is unclear why the value of language, and particularly

physical language, has gradually diminished to the point that it could be argued we live in a post-literate world. Perhaps there is fear that widely held architectural literacy would return humanity to the vices and excesses of Sodom and Gomorrah or unduly limit the freedom of architects. Or perhaps architects' fear of a common language is as old as the mythical abandonment of Babel – and shares its psychological and sociological origins.

10 Albert Einstein, *Relativity: the special and the general theory*, translated by Robert W. Lawson (New York: Crown Publishers, 1952), 9 and 113, respectively.

11 If this is true, so be it.

12 Continuing with the satire, the activity of a "space first" designer is co-opted as a liturgy in the service of a belief. In this view, design is simply an activity through which a believer either mimics ("proselytizes") meaning or mimics ("proselytizes") appearances for pedagogical purposes. "Design of space" so naively construed can only mean the perpetuation of an exclusive tradition. Since, as a rule, systems of belief tend to resist pluralism and the formation of new meanings, it is relatively easy to understand the vehemence with which adherents of *this* or *that* space-myth defend their approach as *the* true method. It falls to the conscientious skeptic to ask if there might be a form of design that creates meaning outside the empty framework of space or if there is one that creates a rich datum for the later application of meaning by the community and against which a particular community might carry out the dialogue of the world as it appears to them.

13 Nikolaus Pevsner, *An Outline of European Architecture*, Jubilee Edition (Baltimore, MD: Penguin, 1961), 340.

14 Unfortunately, the profession of architecture has become so enamored with defending the profession's rights to creativity and invention that even well intentioned architects tend to undercut the meanings held dear by inhabitants, users, citizens and tourists, and force upon them the alien values of 'seeing,' 'feeling,' and 'becoming.'

15 As Julian Jaynes notes, "History is impossible without the spatialization of time that is characteristic of consciousness." See Julian Jaynes, *The Origins of Consciousness in the Breakdown of the Bicameral Mind* (Boston: Houghton Mifflin, 1976), 251.

16 Einstein, *Relativity*, vi.

17 Doreen Massey, *For Space* (London: Sage, 2006) 10.

18 The verdict: "Printing will kill architecture." Hugo, *The Hunchback of Notre-Dame*, 184.

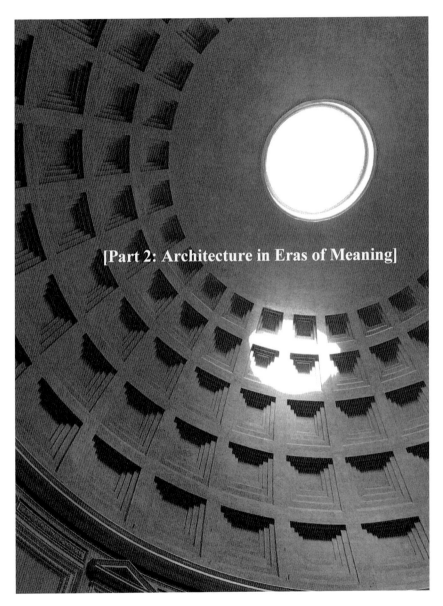

FIGURE 9.0 Pantheon Dome
Source: Photograph by author.

9

16 JUNE 1904

Ulysses and *The Uncanny*

Imagine seeing a close friend or family member but sensing that the person is not who she claims to be. She looks identical, has the same voice and mannerisms, and even possesses a level of familiarity – intimate knowledge, that only your loved one could reasonably possess; and yet, you somehow know that she is a "double" or impostor. Appearance is at odds with emotional response – the first, well known, the other, foreign. This intuition is so strong that you begin to fear this other, locking your door, calling the police, fleeing, or worse. While it sounds like science fiction, this disorder is real and its cases well documented in psychiatric literature.[1] It is called Capgras syndrome, or the Capgras delusion, in honor of French psychiatrist Joseph Capgras who, in collaboration with Jean Reboul-Lachaux, first described its symptoms in 1923.

Excerpts from case histories published in the popular press hint at the nature of experiences suffered. For instance, the story of Mrs. D:

> Her belief that her husband had been replaced by another unrelated man. She refused to sleep with the impostor, locked her bedroom door at night, asked her son for a gun, and finally fought with the police when attempts were made to hospitalize her.

The story of Fred:

> He began to see her [Wilma] as a "double" (her words). The first episode occurred one day when, after coming home, Fred asked her where Wilma was. On her surprised answer that she was right there, he firmly denied that she was his wife Wilma, whom he "knew very well as his sons' mother", and went on plainly commenting that Wilma had probably gone out and would come back later.

112 Architecture History and Theory in Reverse

Or the story of Diane: "she presented with delusions that a man was making exact copies of people – 'screens' – and that there were two screens of her, one evil and one good."[2]

Those familiar with Sigmund Freud's theory of the uncanny – either by reading *The Uncanny* (1919) or from references to it in Anthony Vidler's *The Architectural Uncanny* (1992) – will notice a strong resemblance between these case excerpts and Freud's famous descriptions:

> The "uncanny" is that class of terrifying which leads back to something long known to us, once very familiar … on the one hand, it means that which is familiar and congenial, and on the other, that which is concealed and kept out of sight … knowledge does not lessen the impression of uncanniness … These themes are all concerned with the idea of a "double" in every shape and degree, with persons, therefore, who are to be considered identical by reason of looking alike … or the foreign self is substituted for his own – in other words, by doubling, dividing and interchanging the self.[3]

The similarities between the states described by Freud's theory and those of Capgras are, well, uncanny and interesting as mere observations. If we take seriously, however, Vidler's assertion that the uncanny is "a metaphor for a fundamentally unlivable modern condition,"[4] insights into the uncanny provided by recent theories on Capgras are revealed as more than interesting; they possess diagnostic potential.

So, what causes Capgras syndrome? Philosopher William Hirstein explains it as follows:

> We represent the people we know well with hybrid representations containing two parts. One part represents them externally: how they look, sound, etc. The other part represents them internally: their personalities, beliefs, characteristic emotions, preferences, etc. Capgras syndrome occurs when the internal portion of the representation is damaged or inaccessible.[5]

Capgras is a misidentification delusion indicated by the severing of facial recognition from emotional response; of appearance from feeling; and arguably, information from meaning. The same is true of the uncanny. Experience of the uncanny is a symptom of an absence of meaning where it would normally be expected or absence of an expected emotion in lieu of another. Read these symptoms again. They are surprisingly accurate descriptions of experiences of much present-day architecture, which is lamented as being in crisis.

What Freud documented and attempted to explain in 1919 was a category of modern Industrial Age experience. Increases in documented cases of Capgras suggest that such experiences are proliferating in the Information Age. Here, at the beginning of Part II, I look at a few instances of twentieth-century works – from the realm of literature as well as architecture – that sought to subvert the uncanny's power to disassociate information from meaning. From that vantage point, a path toward eras of meaning in architecture opens.

Combatting the Uncanny in Literature (Broadly Construed)

History is replete with shifts, discontinuities, substitutions. Threads fray. Some rifts are invented out of sheer boredom. As Freud suggested "[w]e are so made that we can derive intense enjoyment only from a contrast and very little from a state of things."[6] Paradigms overlap for a time, competing until one achieves dominance and the others are relegated to the status of mysticism. The gradual victory of space over time in the first half of the twentieth century is one such example in the story of western architecture's transformation but arguably not the most significant.

While from earliest times humans have sought meaning, invented systems of it and debated the relative merit of each to the point of bloodshed, meaning became problematized in the twentieth century to an unprecedented degree. If a real cultural shift occurred with Modernity, it was and remains in the perceived durability of meaning. As we've seen, the opening of the last century of the past millennium was marked by a radical increase in attention to existential problems. Through these problems, an implicit belief emerged that representations always mask facts of existence. Every representation presumes a presence or truth or hidden reality – the latter of which is almost never available to direct perception, if it can be said to exist at all. Freud called this negation "which is the formulation of a previously repressed thought, feeling, or desire, one that enters consciousness only by being disowned … The repressed is accepted intellectually but not emotionally."[7] It became fashionable to inquire from whence "words," "beings," and "needs" arise if not from deep roots in Language, Nature, and Desire. These were the questions asked by few prior to the age of Modernity – of those Rousseau comes to mind as an exemplar of a relatively small movement. But with the dawn of the last century, these questions became a type of intellectual currency put into circulation by Freud, Heidegger, and Wittgenstein; traded by Derrida, Merleau-Ponty, and Maslow; provocatively if incompletely redeemed by George Steiner, Ernst Cassirer, and Julian Jaynes; and asked, exchanged, and provisionally answered again by a host of others. "In our attempts to communicate or to persuade or simply interest others, we are using and moving about through cultural models among whose differences we may select, but from whose totality we cannot escape," the psychologist Jaynes wrote. It is in

> [our] forms of appeal, of begetting hope or interest or appreciation or praise for ourselves or for our ideas, that our communications are shaped into these historical patterns, these grooves of persuasion which are even in the act of communication an inherent part of what is communicated.[8]

And yet, Jaynes continues, the "very notion of truth is a culturally given direction, a part of the pervasive nostalgia for an earlier certainty."[9] This response typifies

114 Architecture History and Theory in Reverse

Modernity in the sense that questions retain their intellectual currency only under the assumed legitimacy of the initial supposition of an 'original' behind every 'facsimile' and representation.

At first blush, the preceding paragraph runs counter to the tale the twentieth century tells of itself. Foucault, for instance, suggested that modern philosophic and literary endeavors were a rejection of representative discourses that dominated earlier traditions. Given the clarity of elapsed time, however, it seems that Modernity was less a rejection of representative discourse than a shift to a different level of representations as well as a shift in the value and attention accorded representation itself. From the romantically tinged "Language," "Nature," and "Desire" to the scientifically minded "words," "beings," "needs," and "drives," the modern age is one that turns to the strata of analytic discourse for substitute grounds – *as-if Truths* – and seeks unity in secondary reflections upon lived experience and the synthesis of mind and body (though, by and large, these are still assumed to be separate even in the twenty-first century). Modernity marks the historical moment at which it became possible to exchange and trade *information* independent of *meaning*. And the increase in both reported uncanny experiences and rhetoric regarding its causes are symptoms of this traumatic shift.

From the perspective of everyday twenty-first-century instrumentalities, the move from Romanticism's "Language," "Nature," and "Desire" to Modernism's "words," "beings", and "drives" or the resulting emergence of the "uncanny" is of debatable importance. The closer we cling to mere information (external representations) and the wider the berth we give to metaphysical notions (internal representations), the more user-friendly we find our world. Yet, this substitution poses tremendous difficulties for the conveyance of meaning; and it shades many aspects of our daily lives as a little off, filled with doubles and impostors, as not quite right.

No art so consistently evokes or invokes the uncanny as literature. Freud, in fact, used literary examples in order to explain his theory.[10] "Just as all neurotic symptoms, like dreams themselves, are capable of hyper-interpretation, and even require such hyper-interpretation," Freud wrote in *The Interpretation of Dreams* (1899), "so every genuine poetical creation must have proceeded from more than one impulse in the mind of the poet." As a result, creative writing "must admit of more than one interpretation."[11] According to his analysis, the uncanny is affected by writers who present what seems to be the real world only to subsequently use our comfort and familiarity with those external representations to shock us with situations that rarely if ever happen in real life.[12] That is, the literary uncanny occurs when the information appropriate to ordinary contexts are juxtaposed with meanings or emotions tied to extraordinary circumstances. Kafka was a master of this technique. But the literary uncanny is now so common as to render a list of contemporary proponents excessively long – and creates the impression that it is simply the technique by which literature is written.

It is interesting to note, however, that there was a moment in early twentieth-century literature that suggested an alternate path for Modernity. Authors such as

16 June 1904: *Ulysses* and *The Uncanny* **115**

James Joyce and Samuel Beckett, so-called modernists, did not problematize meaning so much as render a given state of things directly without asserting an instrumental narrative over and above that available to lived experience. Like Jacques Tati in his later film *Playtime* (1973), Samuel Beckett and James Joyce turned the responsibility for narrativizing events over to the reader or observer. In 1933, Joyce published this:

> Universally that person's acumen is esteemed very little perceptive concerning whatsoever matters are being held as most profitable by mortals with sapience endowed to be studied who is ignorant of that which the most in doctrine erudite and certainly by reason of that in them high mind's ornament deserving of veneration constantly maintain when by general consent they affirm that other circumstances being equal by no exterior splendour is the prosperity of a nation more efficaciously asserted than by the measure of how far forward may have progressed the tribute of its solicitude for that proliferent continuance which of evils the original if it be absent when fortunately present constitutes the certain sign of omnipollent nature's incorrupted benefaction. For who is there who anything of some significance has apprehended but is conscious that that exterior splendour may be the surface of a downwardtending lutulent reality or on the contrary anyone so is there inilluminated as not to perceive that as no nature's boon can contend against the bounty of increase so it behoves every most just citizen to become the exhortator and admonisher of his semblables and to tremble lest what had in the past been by the nation excellently commenced might be in the future not with similar excellence accomplished if an inverecund habit shall have gradually traduced the honourable by ancestors transmitted customs to that thither of profundity that that one was audacious excessively who would have the hardihood to rise affirming that no more odious offence can for anyone be than to oblivious neglect to consign that evangel simultaneously command and promise which on all mortals with prophecy of abundance or with diminution's menace that exalted of reiteratedly procreating function ever irrevocably enjoined?[13]

If meaning is not transparent here – and it almost certainly is not – it is because this and most of the subsequent passages from *Ulysses* are Joyce's attempt to transcribe with brutal directness the complexity of representations that make up the mental life of an individual or community and his/her/their struggle for meaning in the late Industrial Age. Here words are turned into a battering ram attempting to access the depth of both forms of representation – external and internal; informational and emotive; words, beings, and needs as well as Language, Nature, and Desire; that is, toward life in its full social context. What is provided is the hyper-interpretation without the prosaic, information age interpretation.

Ulysses stands as the great anti-Uncanny work of twentieth-century literature. It subverts Freud's formula by invoking an increasingly strange appearance (see above) to convey an emotionally tinged story that is all-too-familiar. This marks

116 Architecture History and Theory in Reverse

the book's importance: *Ulysses* is the near end of a romantic trajectory that begins with de Sade's *The 120 Days of Sodom,* moving from de Sade's representation of all possible desires and disfigurements to Joyce's almost exhaustive representation of a single day (June 16, 1904) in a small place. In both works the proliferation of words, including the uninhibited declaration of well-worn but normally suppressed ideas, is a method for overcoming the classifying dangers of Language, Nature, and Desire without simplifying recourse to words, being, or needs.

Unfortunately, Joyce's post-romantic alternative has seldom been followed and even when taken up by serious thinkers (Deleuze and Guattari) or filmmakers (such as Tati) the work produced is often dismissed as fringe or experimental and in no case admitted as communicative or fostering of shared meaning. Maybe the difficulty of such work helps to explain the popularity of its opposite, books and essays that project clear and concise instrumental bits of how-to or do-it-yourself information. Or perhaps, following Heidegger's totalizing tome *Being and Time* by six years, Joyce's alternative merely appeared too late in the process of transition from Romanticism to Modernity.

Combatting the Uncanny with the Fiction in Question (Architecture)

Joyce's post-Romantic alternative is a path traversed less frequently by architects than other modern makers. Why this is so is not immediately obvious. Architecture began with the first constructions that exceeded pure necessity and developed in parallel and at pace with early civilization; as a marker of identity, its evolution slowed with the invention of the printing press; it stagnated after the difficult but socially fulfilling concepts of Language, Nature, and Desire lost currency to the conceptually easier pragmatism of Progress and Productivity; and, in the information age, lost all legibility when architects attempted to overcome the populace's (and perhaps their own) boredom with Modernity by manufacturing difference for the sake of faster consumption ultimately rooted in familiar or didactic external representations and communicative of nothing. A facsimile built to replace the original without the latter's inherent purpose. It is for this reason that a project such as Barry Parker and Raymond Unwin's Letchworth (1904) can be seen as the first and the last communicative planning project. It was arguably the only garden city in which image and purpose coalesced: prior to Letchworth, the ideas and idylls of the garden city movement were too nascent to support the image; after 1904, the image became passé.

It is not my intention to suggest that no communicative architecture has been built in the past hundred years. There are numerous examples of buildings that neither succumb to the horror of the uncanny nor the doldrums of practicalities. Marcel Breuer's St. John's Abbey Church (1961) is an example of Joyce-like post-Romanticism in architecture (Figure 9.1). It uses a bewildering profusion of everyday materials (brick, concrete, stained glass, wood) and allusions to archetypal forms (arches, altars, bells, buttresses, campanile, pews) in the service of the

FIGURE 9.1 Saint John's Abbey Church, Collegeville, MN, Marcel Breuer architect
Source: Photograph by David Buege.

metaphysical tradition to which they normally refer. Breuer does not juxtapose materials and forms in shocking ways. His ambition is the opposite of the uncanny: unexpected richness of formed matter (external representation) utilized to communicate rather well known and expected emotional content (internal representation). Such ambition is not necessarily rare. It is echoed in the inspired projects of Carlos Scarpa, Álvaro Siza, and Rafael Moneo, among others. But these examples are arguably rooted in eras of meaning and become statistically rarer as late information age glut accumulates.

One example of an anti-Uncanny architecture deserves greater attention. Het Schip ("The Ship") was designed by Michel de Klerk in 1919 – the same year Freud published *The Uncanny*. The building's appearance is highly unconventional. Some parts make vague reference to the features of ships including nautical lines, portals, and a 'bridge' as well as waves or watermarks (see Figures 9.2 and 9.3). Other parts utilize brickwork common to the Amsterdam School to evoke conical forms, turrets, chimneys, etc. (see Figure 9.4). Other shapes defy allusion. This bewildering strangeness, however, stops at the threshold between exterior and interior. Inside, the building is a post office, meeting spaces, and socialist affordable housing. Inside, the building's purpose – understood in both terms of program and meaning or interpretation – is plainly legible. As with *Ulysses*, Het Schip subverts the Uncanny. There is no evidence that de Klerk was aware of Freud's theory. Instead, he was motivated by a desire to embody the values of proletariat housing in a form that reified Marxist ideas and honored the building's inhabitants.

FIGURE 9.2 Het Schip, Amsterdam, Michel de Klerk architect
Source: Photograph by J. David Lewis.

A couple of points must be made before moving further back in time. It is difficult to talk about loss or rarity without sounding like a retrograde historicist. Nevertheless, since the 1904 of Letchworth or the "1904" engraved on the oldest building visible from my office or the fictional '16 June 1904' of *Ulysses* there has been a diminishment in the average person's expectation of and ability to perceive meaning in architecture – to read physical language – due to confusions wrought by the profession's attempts to make merely novel artifices (interesting external representations) or copy bits of well-known imagery (absent the purposes to which those images responded) or compose appearances intended to instruct people as to the purpose of the building (information that has no communicative value in its own right). Information age uncanniness has become a proxy for societal meanings toward which we no longer aspire. Legibility of architectural languages lies closer to an archetypal literacy appropriate to the realm of myth and further from the domain of scientism, analytic philosophy, linguistics, psychology, etc. of the information age; the disavowal of "Language" and "Desire" in favor of the more pragmatic and less-aspiring small w "words" and smaller n "needs" comes at the price of declining literacy of architectural language, decreased communication, and, as a result of these, the general diminishment of shared meaning. The second half of this text will attempt to develop the implications of these assertions.

FIGURE 9.3 Het Schip, Amsterdam, Michel de Klerk architect
Source: Photograph by J. David Lewis.

One additional note: "Architecture in an information age" argued that the distinction between *true* and *false* is not relevant to quantitative analyses regarding the *conveyance* of information. Information is either successfully conveyed or not; its correspondence to some external reality is semantically trivial. Furthermore, when information is interpreted qualitatively, it is its usefulness, not its truth, that matters. Similarly, *true* and *false* have little impact on meaning; those things or ideas which we accord value due to their meaning to us are seldom things or ideas for which questions of truth or falsity even make sense. Moreover, judgments of *difficult* or *easy* have little place in qualitative *evaluations* of meaning. The dark, difficult, incomprehensible aspects of experience exposed by de Sade and the seemingly limitless expanse of these are revealed in Joyce to be synonymous with the experience of, the search for, meaning itself. As a result, the hypothesis that literacy in general and the legibility of architectural language in particular is diminished by the overtly practical analytic bent of Modernity will be pursued in Part II by tracing the motives and motivating beliefs active in the overlap of the last decades of the Romantic period and formative years of Modernity. But first, some of the notions of exchange, evolution, and style that we have come to accept as common sense must be excavated, understood as material history, and moved beyond.

FIGURE 9.4 Het Schip (detail), Amsterdam, Michel de Klerk architect
Source: Photograph by J. David Lewis.

Notes

1 For instance, William Hirstein and V.S. Ramachandran, "Capgras Syndrome: A Novel Probe for Understanding the Neural Representation of the Identity and Familiarity of Persons," *Proceedings of the Royal Society: Biological Sciences* 264(1380) (1997); V.S. Ramachandran and S. Blakeslee, *Phantoms in the Brain* (London: Harper Perennial, 1998); Haydyn D. Ellis and Michael B. Lewis, "Capgras Delusion: A Window on Face Recognition," *Trends in Cognitive Sciences* 5(4) (2001): 149–156.
2 Wikipedia, Capgras delusion, available at: https://en.wikipedia.org/wiki/Capgras_delusion (accessed January 20, 2016).
3 Sigmund Freud, *The Uncanny*, translated by Alix Strachey (*Imago*, Vol. V., 1919; reprinted, *Sammlung*, Fünfte Folge), available at: http://web.mit.edu/allanmc/www/freud1.pdf, 1-9.

4 Anthony Vidler, *The Architectural Uncanny* (Cambridge, MA: MIT Press, 1994), Preface, x.
5 Science Satire Serpent, Capgras Delusions Prevent Divorce – Inc. Comment from Prof. Hirstein, http://sciencedevil.wordpress.com/2012/11/16/we-all-have-capgras-delusions-they-prevent-divorce (accessed March 25, 2016).
6 Sigmund Freud, *Civilization and its Discontents*, Introduction by Louis Menand, translated and edited by James Strachey (New York: W.W. Norton & Company, 2005), 53.
7 Harold Bloom commenting on Freud's attitude toward Shakespeare. See Bloom's *The Western Canon: the books and school of the ages* (New York: Riverhead, 1995), 364.
8 Julian Jaynes, *The Origins of Consciousness in the Breakdown of the Bicameral Mind* (Boston: Houghton Mifflin, 1976), 445.
9 Ibid., 446.
10 This is true of *The Uncanny* as well as *The Interpretation of Dreams*, which draws heavily upon Shakespeare.
11 Sigmund Freud, *The Interpretation of Dreams*, translated by Dr. A. A. Brill (New York: Modern Library, 1994), 164.
12 Freud, *The Uncanny*, 18.
13 James Joyce, *Ulysses*, 1961 corrected edition (New York: Vintage, 1990), 383.

10

MARX, MEANING, AND MATTER

Three thinkers triangulate the twentieth century: Charles Darwin, Sigmund Freud, and Karl Marx. Whether invoked by name, invoked consciously or not, aligned with or written in defiance of, arguably all subsequent theorists work in a field opened by these men and are situated between them. Freud (1856–1939), introduced in the previous chapter, plumbed the depths of subjectivity: what, in essence, are the internal mechanisms that render the world strange, wonderful, fear inducing or hopeful? Darwin (1809–1882), as discussed in the next chapter, pondered the mechanisms of nature through which we, such strange subjectivities, come into being and, more importantly, challenged teleological worldviews. Then there is Marx (1818–1883).

It is commonplace to conceive the work of Karl Marx as the beginning of modern economic and political theory – a prophet of the twentieth century. This reputation is well earned. *Capital, Volume I* is the first text to demonstrate the interdependence of economic structure, technological biases, and societal form in a capitalist conception of value.[1] It exposed the tendency of capital toward 'enlarged reproduction,' particularly on the backs of workers, and anticipated both expansion of and subsequent challenges to unionized labor. Along these lines, it is possible to search Marx for forecasts of today's contemporary architecture: from the rise of repetitive construction techniques and the transformation of buildings into advertising, OMA to MVRDV to BIG, on the one hand, to the honoring of southern and southern hemisphere architects addressing societal ills, Samuel Mockbee's MacArthur Foundation "Genius Grant" in 2000 and Alejandro Aravena's 2016 Pritzker Prize, on the other.

Like Freud, Marx recorded and attempted to explain Industrial Age shifts in culture and perception. In the twentieth century, Marx's theories fueled debates in myriad academic disciplines considered social or objective just as Freud's did for disciplines focused on the individual or the subjective. Architectural theory has borrowed heavily from both. Less frequently noted, but just as true, Marx failed to anticipate the ascendency of information generally[2] and information as a commodity in particular. As a result, *Capital, Volume I* can be viewed as a final record of a form of experience now past. 'Part One: Commodities and Money', in particular, provides a pre-information age account of the basic elements of exchange: commodities, the process of exchange, and circulation. In what follows, I mine each of these elements for meaning subsequently buried under late capitalist information.

The Quarry of Social Hieroglyphics

A commodity is a bearer of value. Value under capitalism, according to Marx, is objective but immaterial. That is, it is purely social.[3] "Value ... transforms every product of labour into a social hieroglyphic ... as much men's social product as is their language."[4] This view that social kinds are different from but just as objective or real as natural kinds was not new in 1867. Marx here echoes Jean-Jacques Rousseau's 1762 formulation that, "conventions form the basis of all legitimate authority among men."[5] Rousseau and Marx, along with a host of Enlightenment thinkers in between, assert the reality of immaterial conventions and the power of those invisible forces to exert influence. The chief difference, however, between Marx and his predecessors on this point is significant: *value, as an immaterial convention conveyed hieroglyphically through commodities, renders real social relations between real people opaque.* Under the sway of capitalist value, Marx argues, we begin to see our relations with each other as a "fantastic form of a relation between things."[6]

What is true of commodities is true of other social constructs. We can think of social constructs, in fact, as commodities – language-commodities, disciplinary-commodities, knowledge-commodities – and these, like other commodities, are subject to fallacies of misplaced concreteness, which render meaning opaque. Often, for instance, historical periods are conceived metaphorically as archaeological strata (Classicism, Romanticism, Modernism, Postmodernism, to name but four) in the sense that the artifacts and debris of the past are always available to increased understanding with only a little more digging. As with its geological and archaeological analogies, historical strata are expected to accrue incrementally and more or less evenly over time resulting in parallel lines of ever more familiar forms of life stacked on the ever older and stranger. Where the results of digging subvert this expectation – where geologists and archaeologists and historians find ruptures, shifts, the old resting on the new, or seemingly diverse strata intermixed – researchers devote special effort, as these are places in which something out of the ordinary is assumed to have occurred.[7] This is often taken as more than mere metaphor. The stratification of knowledge or technology over time is conceived in similar ways as accrual through sedimentation, in its expected evenness and relative consistency from time to time and place to place, and in its susceptibility to change in character due to the application of outside force during turbulent periods. And there are times when this approach is useful to various disciplines.

124 Architecture History and Theory in Reverse

Study of the strata of various history-commodities, however, does not and cannot result in isolated study of fixed layers of sediment as is appropriate in geology or archaeology. History-commodities must be studied as always already ruptured, shifted, palimpsested or mixed; every layer is viewed through at least one other – and often many more. This is not to be bemoaned. The various strata of knowledge become lenses reordered and layered so as to reveal hidden congruities and correspondences that formulate new domains of knowledge and time. If the geological reference makes this sound like an inconvenience, perhaps the analogy is wrong; perhaps history should be conceived as woven instead of layered, perhaps a damask of knowledge. The choice of analogy is irrelevant as long as it does not render the social relation more opaque.

What is missing in the archaeological metaphor is Marx's focus on process. Estimating the value of a Classical-temple-commodity requires something far more complex than a static view of the object within the strata of Classical time. It requires, in Marx's view, an understanding of the socially necessary labor time embodied in its making – by which, "it changes into a thing which transcends sensuousness" – and a transposition of that transcendence into a universal equivalent (in economic terms, money, or in experiential terms, into the human needs and conventions of the time and culture from which it is viewed).[8] These introductory remarks and their links to architectural language are rendered a little clearer by looking into the more recent confluence of Romanticism, which arguably lingered in cultural consciousness into the early twentieth century via the Arts and Crafts Movement, and Modernism, which arguably first pulsed to life in the thinking and factories of the late eighteenth-century Industrial Revolution. This overlaying or interweaving results in an emergent domain in which physical language in general and architectural language in particular are revealed as products of two sets of constituent forces. To the side of the past, the stratum of Romanticism introduces the competing motives of *formalizing values* and *interpreting values* born of the intellectual inheritance of Language, Nature, and Desire. To the side of the present, the stratum of Modernism applies force along its dual trajectories of *formation* and *conveyance* of words, beings, and needs. Four fundamental aspects of physical languages emerge at the intersection of these two strata: joints (articulation of surfaces and forms); classification (naming and numbering of parts); origins (historical reference and prerequisite forms); and character (the material and formal aspects of things through which judgments of qualities are conveyed). Following the literary convention, I call this resultant period of mixed strata post-Romanticism – although proto-Modernism would be no less accurate.

Owing much to Foucault's general table, Figure 10.1 provides a means of staking out the potential field of architectural language conventions in the domain of recent time. As an unintended finding, it is interesting to note that the diagram is graphically sufficient to demonstrate the relationship between analysis and evaluation of architectural language-commodities without the conceptual inclusion of "space" or any of its linguistic corollaries. There are three possible

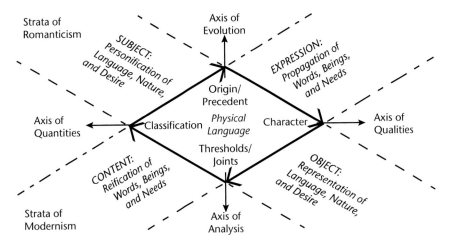

FIGURE 10.1 Strata of physical language (based on Foucault)

interpretations of this fact: (1) space can be understood as the unrepresented and undifferentiated ground across which specific bodies of knowledge are spread as the page is the neutral field supporting the ink of the diagram; or (2) space, conceived as an extant and active medium, architectural space or *Chora*, simply does not exist or, at a minimum, is irrelevant to understanding architectural language-commodities; or (3) space only comes into existence or becomes capable of being perceived (if these are not the same thing) through the establishment of a particular domain of knowledge, such as Classicism, Romanticism, Modernism, etc; that is to say, space is discourse dependent. Interpretations 1 and 2 are not mutually exclusive alternatives; space (as neutral field of opportunity) ≠ *Chora*. Interpretation 3 differs radically from the others, and is worth considerable study, but puts us too far ahead of the argument being developed.[9] I note this unintended finding in order to make this point: an arching market hall, a faceted library, social housing, a Classical temple, etc. is not recognizable as an architectural language-commodity because of its space. Nor is it a commodity, according to Marx, as a result of its materials. Specific architectural language-commodities are recognized as such only where corresponding forms of architectural language-exchange exist.

Window Shopping

In the event that Marx's language strikes one as difficult due to the intervening century and a half since its publication and the Foucault-inspired diagram of overlapping strata requires more cognitive exertion than appears justifiable, the domain of post-Romanticism survives in a variety of present-day instances of exchange – or, more accurately, preludes to exchange. Examples range from digital interactions such as texting, Skyping, and eBay negotiations to the old-fashioned analog experiences of window-shopping and haggling at the farmers' market. All of these processes of potentially unconsummated exchange move us beyond the simple direct valuing of a thing or event for itself and its ability to address a need (estimative value; use value; firmness) or the valuing of a thing for its comforting narrative of social concerns and potential future use (appreciative value; exchange value; commodity) toward a reciprocal but mediated form of valuing which can result in nothing more, but also nothing less, than pleasure (aesthetic/simulacra value; commodity fetish; delight).[10] These differing forms of value are not inherent in the thing but result from changes in perspective.[11] "From the point of view of wealth," Foucault wrote from a postmodern domain, "there is no difference between need, comfort, and pleasure."[12] A nearly identical sentence can be written for the post-Romantic alternative: From the point of view of a building, there is no difference between need, comfort, and pleasure. From the point of view of a person engaged in a post-Romantic exchange, however, the building becomes an architectural language-commodity, a symbol.[13] And at the moment a thing becomes a symbol, differences in values take on meaning.

As revealed in the diagram of the strata of history, a chief aspect of transition from Romanticism to Modernism is the shift in focus from value judgments to analyses of formation and conveyance; more simply, from valuing to analyzing; or perhaps, though less certain, from appreciating to making. The intersection of these two strata produces two possible domains or navigations of knowledge – post-Romanticism or post-Modernism – as a result of the function by which the intersection is affected. Postmodernism, for example, can be understood as a subtractive conjunction; architectural or physical language, if it is anything at all in postmodern thought, is what remains available to human experience after the biased or mythological contents of Modernism and Romanticism have been delegitimized and meaning demoted to mere fiction. Post-Romanticism, on the contrary, is a summative process in which every new creation, every visual or haptic phenomena created, whether grounded in modern or romantic or classical bias, causes a revaluation of the objects of perception, as well as the acts of perception, that have gone before. "The making of an artifact is a social act, for the object (whether an art work or instead an object of everyday use) is intended as something that will both enter into and itself elicit human responsiveness," as Scarry aptly noted.[14] From this perspective, postmodernism and post-Romanticism are not alternative anthologies of tastes but, instead, represent radically different ways of understanding the connection of present to past as well as the evolution of thought across time; the former owes much to the rhetoric of overcoming and subjective freedom, authenticity, and existentialism of Heidegger and Sartre; the latter, to the late ingenious Mr. Darwin.

It is easy to imagine Charles Moore's Piazza d'Italia in New Orleans (1978) and Sir John Soane's home and museum, in Lincoln's Inn Fields, in London (1812–1813) as representatives of post-Modernism and post-Romanticism, respectively (see Figures 10.2 and 10.3). While both architectural language-commodities borrow and blend from various historical strata without care or concern for notions

Marx, Meaning, and Matter 127

FIGURE 10.2 Piazza d'Italia, New Orleans, Charles Moore architect
Source: Photograph by Laura Smith Taylor.

FIGURE 10.3 Lincoln's Inn Fields home and museum, London, Sir John Soane architect
Source: Photograph by Acroterion. Wikimedia Commons. CC BY-SA 3.0. https://commons.wikimedia.org/wiki/File:Soane_museum_gallery.jpg Converted from color to black & white.

128 Architecture History and Theory in Reverse

such as appropriateness, Piazza d'Italia utilizes a strategy of emptying traditional forms of all possible pleasure and immediate utility so that only the appreciative values of historicized names remain. Lincoln's Inn Fields palimpsests a world history of forms into a simultaneous presence in which needs and comforts are indistinct from the pleasures derived. The former is subtractive, a shallow archaeology. The latter is additive, an exchange that blends strata. These exemplary projects, however, suffer as examples insofar as only those who are lucky enough to tour each in person can understand the deep rift in experiences elicited. In terms of contemporary building types and accessibility, the similarity and difference between these two domains is better witnessed in the most prosaic of examples – a typical retail storefront in a strip shopping center. Our banal world: plate glass layered with sales posters and vinyl lettering separates the window-shopper from the glossy colorful objects carefully organized and lit (see Figure 10.4). It is not difficult to imagine Jean Baudrillard rhapsodizing over such a spectacle. Postmodernists as well as post-Romantics tend to judge this scene according to the overlap of subject and object mediated by the window frame. That is to say, in both domains values receive a new order in relation to the perception of quality in the presence of a pleasure commodity – regardless of whether that commodity elicits visual, haptic or intellectual pleasure or some combination.

Attention to this surface similarity, however, only reinforces an essential difference. Again, the postmodern subtracts. It is likely that Baudrillard would have argued that pleasure production occurs in the simultaneously transparent and reflective surface

FIGURE 10.4 Gucci
Source: Photograph by David C. Lewis.

of the store window, in the resultant palimpsest. This image suggests that there are at least two necessary aspects to pleasure commodities: the post-Romantic immediate or aesthetic value and the post-Modern that might be called simulacra value. In the latter view, the "original" referents – the "objects" perceived as well as the perceiving "subject" – are, at best, questionable but unnecessary constructs that linger from earlier knowledge strata. The postmodern subtracts and, once an illusory and ultimately unreal site of value is established, the instantiating forms are no longer necessary; at all times, the image is detached and serves as the sole locus of value even if surrounded by a host of observers and objects. As at Moore's Piazza d'Italia, in the postmodern view of the shop window the world is commodified and it is the intellectual value accorded commodity or appreciative value that truly matters. For the post-Romantic, in full additive mode, the mediating frame of the store window is merely a device allowing the reciprocal character of the beings (subjects and objects) on either side to be conjoined. In this view, the window is thick; its environment viscous; the sidewalk shopper wants, needs, takes pleasure in contemplating objects inside; the salesperson wants, needs, takes pleasure in contemplating the wealth embodied in the human being just outside the door; another sidewalk shopper sees the interior of the store as an inviting refuge from the heat, the cold, the rain; a customer inside views the weather outside romantically and practically by turns depending upon a host of factors which, as Joyce narrativized in his magnum opus, change persistently from moment to moment in extreme ways. As Ernst Cassirer said of mythico-religious experience, the window-shopping experience

> is determined not so much by the content of the experience as by the teleological perspective from which it is viewed. Whatever appears important for our wishing and willing, our hope and anxiety, for acting and doing: that and only that receives the stamp of verbal "meaning."[15]

Born of the same geologic forces, the two domains reside on opposing sides of the information/meaning divide. Contrary to a strict postmodern perspective which strips every scene of meaning, every post-Romantic view through a display window increases and diminishes, gives and takes, orders and reorders values according to factors dispersed across a social field of objects and subjects even if, at any given moment, there is but one window shopper – a feeling akin to that experienced in Soane's Lincoln's Inn Fields house.

Solicitation, the Circulation of the Sensuous

> Commodities first enter into the process of exchange ungilded and unsweetened, retaining their original home-grown shape. Exchange, however, produces a differentiation of the commodity into two elements, commodity and money, an external opposition which expresses the opposition between use-value and value which is inherent in it.
>
> *(Karl Marx,* Capital*)[16]*

130 Architecture History and Theory in Reverse

Rebecca West once said:

> As we grow older and see the ends of stories as well as their beginnings, we realize that to the people who take part in them it is almost of greater significance that they should be stories, that they should form a recognizable pattern, than that they should be happy or tragic.[17]

Information is the province of the young. This renders meaningful exchange difficult. Architects, perhaps more than any other artists, struggle with authorship and ponder the locus of meaning to the point of paranoia. As a result, the question "How does the activity of window shopping elicit a meaningful response?" appears as a logical rejoinder to the paragraphs above. At first blush, an answer is just as obvious. While the store window designer knows that he or she is using manipulative means to form a milieu just as suggestive as the stages of Henrik Ibsen or August Strindberg, that retail designer knows as well as the great post-Romantic playwrights that the value of the work is in the successful transmission of a trigger image or interrogative narrative to an intellect standing just outside the plate glass partition who is, by and by, expected to browse his or her own dense catalogue of suggestive images and partial narratives in order to complete the tableau. Success, in other words, is measured by the degree to which the window shopper believes the objective facts of the tableau to be connected with his or her own history, feelings, and desires. The thickness of this post-Romantic storefront, its density and meaning constructed from inside and out, is lost on the average twentieth-century architectural theorist for whom everything is wholly 'either' or 'or' – *either* the complete conveyance of a set of intentions created by the architect *or* pure sensory spectacle to be defined by the inhabitant; temporally, *either* longing for the past *or* rhetoric of a pure present.[18] This rather logical response, however, is incomplete insofar as it fails to capture the potential breadth and subtlety of post-Romanticism. Simple commitment to any of these myopias may result in sales but, with greater certainty, produces a largely unsatisfying and ultimately uncommunicative professionalized world.

Part of the difficulty for twenty-first-century architects and theorists is the adoption of their predecessors' modernist attitudes toward authorship and postmodernist concerns regarding those attitudes as guiding conceptual frameworks over the past century. In an exchange of commodities, as Marx stated, "there develops a whole network of social connections of natural origin, entirely beyond the control of human agents."[19] Authoring is not the only – or even the best – means of communicating; but even those who cast doubts as to its centrality (the post-structuralists, for example) only reinforce its importance. The problem is that authoring is presented in the form of 'telling' within modern and postmodern camps. Arguably, engagement in both meaningful dialogue and extraordinary physical experiences are more often the result of solicitation – soliciting not telling, because the latter, as conventionally practiced, assumes a self-sufficiency and lack of reciprocity that undermines engagement by limiting the transmission of content to the linear temporal immediacy of mere sight or hearing. Stated more directly, authors aim at descriptions of states; solicitors attempt provocations to states. It is the difference between having and wanting; or between Being and desiring. Any sense that this is a subtle distinction or a difference merely of degree is false. "To have" or "to be" are mutually exclusive notions to those of "wanting" or "desiring." The former lies in the territory of description. All value arises with the latter.

More than telling, and a more complex form of exchange, is necessary. At first glance, in analyses of any solicitation-induced exchange – be it the store owner's organization of merchandise, the dreamscapes of the best post-Romantic dramatists, the advances of a prostitute or an online flirtation – value can be seen as the result of an exchange or as its precondition. However, both views are, in themselves, incorrect; or, at best, only partially correct. The exchange of values in experience is simultaneously the motive directing engagement and the content or meaning derived from such engagement. Like price in economic forms of exchange, value in the experience trade is "purely ideal or notional;" it is a "social pledge."[20] It is neither in the commodity nor in the eye of the beholder. It is a necessary social relation. Beginning and end; cause and effect; neither either nor or.

But where, you may ask, does this social relation come from?

"The universe," as de Sade first formulated, "would cease on the spot to subsist were there to be an exact similarity amongst all beings; 'tis of this disparity there is born the order which preserves, contains, directs everything."[21] The solicitor calls to the window shopper (the play's audience, the passing gawker, the online lurker) on the basis of differential character, real or illusory does not matter; relative to the buyer (the viewer, the lonely walker or internet denizen) the solicitor possesses an abundance of some particular character, attitude or holding. Value can only be understood as an accounting, a moving by addition and subtraction, of an apparent dissimilar distribution of Being. Things, events, ideas only have value relative to this apparent surfeit and its potential reorganization; and the act of solicitation is the impetus necessary to initiate negotiation toward a redistributed situation already forming in the buyer's mind.

Though brief, the above should be sufficient to make clear why soliciting is a more apt description of the act of design than authoring. Nevertheless, an accounting of values is very much in need of explanation. Perhaps nowhere is the above as teasingly incomplete as in the implicit suggestion that values are traded; that for every quality or value acquired, a real or imagined absence is created elsewhere. If value exchange obeys something like a law of conservation, where, in this view, are we to understand the subtraction to occur in meaningful experiences? Where is the loss felt?

In the realm of architecture at least, it is possible to hypothesize that loss occurs in the labor of construction; in the lost or expended energy and fuel and materials; or perhaps in the distance between what was sought as a design idyll and what was literally constructed in concrete and steel; or in the perceptible gap between the hopeful call to exchange attempted by the architect and the lackluster response by inhabitants. Yet these and other suggestions cannot serve a deeper understanding

132 Architecture History and Theory in Reverse

of the transmission of values via physical language or the architectural language-commodity without addressing the problem of subtraction. To answer the above question requires significant elaboration of both soliciting communication and solicited values along a host of trajectories: in domains of origins, exchange, and translation; in the relationship of materials and values, systems of power and classification, and mythic formulations of time and space; in the problem of the entropy of values over time in relation to human perception; and, ultimately, the changing role of signs between eras of myth and our information age.

What is needed to illuminate the post-Romantic period is something akin to a law of experiential economics. And this, I believe, lies further back in time, nearer to architecture's origin story.

Notes

1 Karl Marx, *Capital, Volume I* expands Adam Smith's conception of value as labor time. In Marx's formulation, value is socially necessary labor time. Karl Marx, *Capital: a critique of political economy, volume 1*, introduction by Ernest Mandel, translated by Ben Fowkes (New York: Penguin Books, 1990).
2 This observation belongs to Robert Wright, *Nonzero: the logic of human destiny* (New York: Vintage, 2000). See p. 376, note 152.
3 Marx, *Capital*, 138–139.
4 Ibid., 167.
5 Jean-Jacques Rousseau, *The Social Contract* (New York: Maestro, 2012), Book I, §4. Elsewhere, Rousseau writes, "The social order is a sacred right which is the basis of all other rights. Nevertheless, this right does not come from nature, and must therefore be founded on conventions" (ibid., Book I, §1).
6 Marx, *Capital*, 165.
7 For example, note how Nikolaus Pevsner characterizes the diversity of architectural styles in the nineteenth century in his *An Outline of European Architecture*, Jubilee Edition (Baltimore, MD: Penguin, 1961), 622.
8 Marx, *Capital*, 162–163.
9 Anyone interested in reading a parallel argument regarding the emergence of space in discourse, please see Jacques Derrida's *Of Grammatology*, translated by Gayatri Chakravorty Spivak (Baltimore, MD: Johns Hopkins University Press, 1976), 288–290.
10 Each parenthetical reference is composed of analogous terms drawn from Foucault, Marx, and Vitruvius, respectively. The sole exception is the term "aesthetic/simulacra value" which is posed by the author mindful of Baudrillard's contention that simulacra are copies for which we no longer possess the original.
11 "Only a material whose every sample possesses the same uniform quality can be an adequate form of appearance of value" as Marx notes of the money commodity. See *Capital*, 184.
12 Michel Foucault, *The Order of Things* (London: Routledge, 1989), 198.
13 Marx is adamant in this assertion: "Every commodity is a symbol, since, as a value, it is only the material shell of the human labour expended on it." *Capital*, 185.
14 Elaine Scarry, *The Body in Pain* (New York: Oxford University Press, 1987), 175.
15 Ernst Cassirer, *Language and Myth*, translated by Susan K. Langer (New York: Dover, 1953), 37.
16 Marx, *Capital*, 199.
17 Quoted by Christopher Hitchens in his 2007 introduction to Rebecca West's *Black Lamb and Grey Falcon* and reprinted as "Rebecca West: Things Worth Fighting For," pp. 191–221, in *Arguably: Essays by Christopher Hitchens* (New York: Twelve, 2011), 196.

18 As an example, consider Pevsner's critique of Romanticism: "Whatever its object, the Romantic attitude is one of longing, that is antagonism to the present," *Outline of European Architecture*, Jubilee Edition (Baltimore, MD: Penguin, 1961), 587. For Pevsner, this flatly stated *Either* is balanced implicitly against the *Or* of Modernism which pursues the present.
19 The preceding sentence is also significant in this regard. "We see here … how the exchange of commodities breaks through all the individual and local limitations of the direct exchange of products, and develops the metabolic process of human labour." Marx, *Capital*, 207.
20 Ibid., 189 and 228.
21 Marquis de Sade's "The 120 Days of Sodom," in *The 120 Days of Sodom & Other Writings*, compiled and translated by Austryn Wainhouse and Richard Seaver, Introductions by Simone de Beauvoir and Pierre Klossowski (New York: Grove Press, 1987), 426.

11

EXCHANGE AND EVOLUTION

Friedrich Engels' famous graveside eulogy for Marx reveals much. "Just as Darwin discovered the law of evolution in organic nature, so Marx discovered the law of evolution in human history."[1] Karl Marx wrote *Capital, Volume I* (1867) in a milieu already transformed by Charles Darwin's *Origin of Species* (1859) despite a mere eight years separating the publications. While Marx references Darwin only twice, and then only in footnotes, it is the latter who has had the more profound impact on thought. The theory of natural selection states the process of mutation and the process of determining the suitability of those mutations to an environment are not causally linked. Mutations in form are utterly random. Those mutations that possess an adaptive advantage tend to help its life form survive longer and reproduce more. That is to say, evolution is *not* end-oriented. Anthropologist Terrence Deacon calls it Darwin's "metaphysical rout of teleology."[2]

This conception of evolution as a non-goal-oriented process of after-the-fact value judgments has enabled much scientific progress over the past 150 years. Yet, this idea also poses problems of misappropriation. At its worst, evolution has been co-opted as a justification for "social Darwinism" in science: from the relatively benign positivism of Karl Popper, to the strict behaviorism of B. F. Skinner, the Nazism of H. L. Mencken, and the eugenics of Ernst Rüdin. Social Darwinism shows up in everyday life in our "winner-take-all" competitive spirit, our "survival-of-the-fittest" market system, and our general disregard for "big-picture" meaning in favor of "immediate-use" information. Such misappropriations have overshadowed Darwin's accomplishment.

To understand the implications of this "metaphysical rout" for architecture, greater clarity to the notion of values and how these are traded within and between cultures is needed.

From the point of view of physical language, there is no difference between need, comfort, and pleasure. Note the worldwide similarity of architecture from very early times, even – perhaps particularly – in the most profound of human-made spaces such as temples and sacred buildings: Aztec and Egyptian; Mayan and Babylonian; the Incan citadel at Machu Picchu and the Greeks' at Mycenae; the visual similarity of these to each other as well as to more mythical places (from a Western perspective, places like Ankgor Wat and the terraced landforms of Japan and China; and, though in very different materials, of Viking architecture to the shrines of Japan). These easy comparisons are not given to suggest that physical languages arose from the influences of exploration and trade leading to shared traditions. Nor is this a proto-argument for the existence of some sort of primordial physical language that all humans shared at the birth of civilization. Nor should we ignore the fact that these buildings have been singled out in the historical record by western historians and archaeologists. The point is simpler but more stable and can be found in the writings of Hübsch, Durand, Alberti, and Vitruvius: physical languages arose in the confluence of available materials, climatic considerations, physical needs (for shelter, comfort, defense, etc), and the desire for meaning. The resultant similarity of physical languages points only to the very limited range of possibilities that each of these factors, mammalian physiology and psychology included, entail.

Most of us readily accept that materials, climate, and physiological and psychological needs vary narrowly; we are a single species evolved on one and the same planet after all. It is the other factor, the desire for meaning and the range of meanings desired, that is likely to appear open to wide fluctuation. 'Meaning,' as has been stated, is what is at stake in communication. The drive to record meaning in works of art or architecture is the human impulse to shore up seemingly important issues in the absence of proof or certainty. Meaning is therefore an offshoot of belief, but not synonymous with it, that results from a mutually accepted classificatory framework of a family, tribe, or discipline, and that results in a standardized if informal cognitive imperative relative to a cohort, a place or a time in history. From this perspective, for example, gravity is meaningful to some (particularly to physicists) and not so meaningful to most (use of the term to indicate that we don't float away is so banal as to make everyday discussion of it literally meaningless). Meaning construed in this way respects the late philosophy of Ludwig Wittgenstein who argued that meaning is a measure of usefulness – although the term 'usefulness' overemphasizes utility whereas 'transportability' is closer to the mark. This view of meaning also accords with the term's usage by many canonical western thinkers across diverse bodies of knowledge. Clearly meaning is subsequent to and layered upon more basic concerns of mere survival, such as acquisition of food and shelter; and this point aligns with Maslow's hierarchy of needs, Marx's evolution of history, and the minimum standard of living necessary for the functioning of laws in Rousseau's social state.[3] But meaning's lateness does not contradict the preceding comment on physical language's emergence. Once civilizations reach the point of embodying themselves in architecture – that is, when they begin producing (literally, building) physical language – they are already beyond concerning themselves with merely the basest of individual needs.

136 Architecture History and Theory in Reverse

Civilization is synonymous with aspirations regarding the needs, comforts, and pleasures of a people. Within any given culture, physical language is always already a blend of such aspirations beyond survival and short of certainty. What is less clear is how values evolve relative to need, comfort, and pleasure so that physical languages enter the world of exchange and become capable of being shared.

It is first necessary to disentwine meaning from value.

Meaning and value are related but serve different purposes. As defined above, meanings can be internal and shared by as few as two individuals or external and social; meanings can be debated and differences of opinion can lead and have led to horrific events (the Slave Trade) as well as to noble endeavors (Amnesty International). That is to say, meanings are broad and, while not measurable in absolute terms of true or false, often taken very seriously. Values emerge from meanings but are not communicative restatements or translations so much as attempts to stabilize the admittedly relativistic character of meanings. Values are attempts to fix the exchange rate and make meanings comparable in the "marketplace of ideas."

Such economic metaphors will prove useful to understanding the transitional milieu of post-Romanticism and the underpinnings of Modernity. As straightforward (but albeit simplistic) as this formulation seems, however, it poses difficulties; and these must be addressed. Are values, for instance, a form of pledge or fiction applied to meanings and accepted by common assent? If so, does it follow that – as with currency – values are automatically exchangeable or tradable? Are values infinitely marketable? If not, how are they traded?

Consider for a moment what materially constitutes physical language. In Aristotelian terms, physical language is formed matter. Marx, in turn, might say that formed matter is memory made material: "objectified human labour."[4] If value is a pledge made for or against physical language as suggested in the preceding chapter – if it is "a self-duplicating representation, a deferred exchange"[5] made in arrears – then ultimately value is relative to the capacity of both form and material to express, hold or justify that pledge. If this is the case, formed matter must ultimately vouch in both aspects of its character for the pledge to have the power of self-duplicating representation and thereby support deferred exchange. Unfortunately, formed matter's capacity to underwrite such an oath is questionable insofar as form and material are independent variables and given to the wild abandon of whims of meaning across time or place or both. Nothing in formed matter guarantees value or the type of experience that will be had of it. There is no formula or ratio.

There have been many instances in my life when I have stood in a space consecrated to beliefs that I neither hold nor understand in which I have nevertheless felt the communication of values as directly and viscerally as I have felt the appeal to commerce in the farmers' market – each sacred space and farmers' market serving as experiential Galápagos. However, I have also stood in spaces – sometimes familiar, other times utterly foreign – and felt as little compelled to respond as I would if presented with a popular magazine in an unknown language or challenged

Exchange and Evolution   **137**

to debate the likelihood of my body floating off the surface of the planet next Thursday. The fact that the answer to any form of the question, "are values exchangeable or tradable?" is an ambiguous "sometimes" – combined with the, at best, dubious ability of any formed matter to vouch for meaning over time – reveals the pledge model of values as unsatisfactory. And yet ...

The unsatisfactory character of the pledge as typically understood is not necessarily a death knell to every possible value-as-pledge model. Consider again those spaces that, although foreign or strange, despite representing beliefs either unknown or known but reprehensible or combinations thereof, still manage to communicate across the vicissitudes of time and place – those temples in the jungles of Central America or high in the Andes in the eyes and mind of an information age tourist, for example. How is it that the sense of importance held for these buildings by the Aztecs, the Maya, and the Incas who built them is transferred to even the most uninitiated visitor hundreds of years later? Superficially, it is possible to respond by saying formed matter is more easily recognized if the variations of both form and matter are kept within known limits; and, to the extent this is achieved, recognition of the content or meaning of any particular example of formed matter spreads faster. Certainly, all of these temples share forms and materials and methods of construction among themselves and with iconic structures the world over. But such similarities do not explain the sense of communication; the as-if conveyance; the immediate sense that "this is important" because "this *means* something."

Arguably, the nature of the pledge has yet to be understood. Or, better stated, it has been understood but we must trace its lineage through Hübsch to Durand, from Durand through de Sade to Alberti, and from Alberti to Vitruvius. At present, it is enough to understand that: (1) the pledge exists only in relation to a given commodity; a pledge of value makes no sense if not connected to an artifact of some kind; and (2) every commodity entails myriad, even contradictory, pledges – those of experts and laypeople, secular and theological, those of locals and those becoming acculturated.

It is difficult to doubt that the relation of formed matter to physical language's capacity to communicate (via its quality, content or meaning) shifts in time. And, with just as little doubt, what counts as quality evolves in and is subservient to a serial system of signs which branch and either die or morph or conjoin with others in accordance with humanity's cultural evolution across time. While changes in meaning obviously occur, to assume that these variations ultimately undermine the power of the pledge is to misunderstand when and where the pledge is taken. The pledge to values was not taken in the jungles of Central America or Cambodia or on the high ground of the Andes or at Mycenae or even on the much nearer historical-cultural ground of John Wood the Younger's Royal Crescent. Temples and other such buildings of aspiration were built as direct material manifestations of belief, physical assertions of meaning, and not as second-hand representations, not as stand-ins or pledges. The pledge does not occur in the beginning; it is taken in backwards glance. Value is determined "after-the-fact." When Ruskin claimed

138 Architecture History and Theory in Reverse

that a "wall has no business to be dead,"[6] his challenge is better directed to vacationers than Venetian architects; in reality, it is a call for a post-hoc application of value by observers to a material edifice already evolved by others and, simultaneously, an acknowledgment of the firmness of the original architects' and patrons' desire to stake themselves and their beliefs in the world.

Translatability

In his very late post-Romantic novel *Canada*,[7] Richard Ford's adolescent protagonist finds himself deposited, alone in all but the basest of senses, in a desolate prairie not of his birth or upbringing. Deprived of contact with his incarcerated parents and runaway twin sister, Dell alternates between clinging to the meanings acquired in childhood and, more stultifyingly, the values attached to these, on the one hand, and taking the advice of his anti-savior Mildred Remlinger, on the other hand, to seek his grounding in the pure present without recourse to the home of his past or promise of his lost future. That these seem to Dell – and the majority of us, if we are honest – to constitute mutually exclusive and impossible options is an artifact of the mistaken belief that meanings and values are interchangeable or, at least, ultimately rooted in the same temporal or physical source.

Some meanings are capable of remaining relatively stable over millennia. Think of *Gilgamesh*. Values, on the contrary, are fluid. Some narratives, for example, are little regarded when first written, achieve great renown after decades, and later fall into disrepute. That this is so matters. Why, matters even more. To understand the why it is necessary to acknowledge that values are not created and transmitted according to pre-existing and historically stable pledges. That is to say, the perception of value in the present is not based upon a direct or linear transmission of a value asserted by designers or makers, architects or builders, in a bygone era *à la*,

Pledge (past) → material making (record) → perceived value (present)

In parallel to Wittgenstein's late notion that meaning is use, it is important to note that values are neither passive nor simply given but are measured from the vantage point of an active, and thus changing, mind – an evolved state measured after-the-fact. Instead of emerging with the act of its carrier's making, values are a perpetual reframing of the world's extant matter from the shifting prospect of the present:

Belief/imagination (past) → formed matter ← pledge of value (present)

In this revised formulation, the middle term "formed matter" receives its value anew with successive temporal and cultural presents and therefore could be said to have embodied as many values as people who have encountered that object over time. Yet even this second, more proximate, version revives earlier dilemmas. How is it that some objects more than others are commonly agreed to be "of value"? And how is it that, despite wild fluctuations in systems of belief and cultural

Exchange and Evolution **139**

norms across time and place, some objects tend to hold relatively fixed types and consistent levels of value? *Gilgamesh* is, again, a literary exemplar. And just as *Gilgamesh* turns our attention to words and the evocation of concepts like friendship, even casual reflection upon such questions refocuses analysis on formed matter and its complicity in conveying not only the rudiments of physical language but, ultimately, value itself. "The common element in these different interests," says Rousseau, "is what forms the social tie; and, were there no point of agreement between them all, no society could exist."[8]

Concerned as they are with seemingly untethered and ultimately nonmaterial rules of use as the ground of meaning, Wittgenstein's language games provide no toehold to problems of values. While it makes sense to say that the pledge is a social and linguistic lien placed on objects post-hoc, every lien nevertheless refers to and requires the stratum of a very particular extant object; and, unless we concede that values are purely arbitrary relations to the physical world, it is logical to assume that some preemptive judgment of the object is made prior to the assertion of the valuing pledge. That phrase – "of the object" – is the locus of 'a' and perhaps 'the' dilemma. In the everyday world of commerce and consumption, for example, formed matter is an instrument signifying quality; and quality, conversely, is understood to serve as the content upon which values are grounded. But even in the value-conscious world of markets and commerce, stability is difficult to find. The ordinarily assumed and seemingly straightforward linear progression from formed matter to a solid ground of value rooted in qualities is revealed as extraordinarily complicated, to say the least, when the consumer realizes that his or her "must buy" purchase of last year or last week is no longer *the* thing to own; that it has become, in two words, worth less, or, in a single and more extreme word, worthless.

In the case of objects that were once highly esteemed but quickly lost value, it might be argued that a simple mistake in attribution occurred at the moment of purchase or praise; that those objects actually lacked "quality" (whatever that is) from the beginning. This is probably true for a host of consumer objects – technological novelty is the sine qua non of this category of things. In other cases, the loss of value is a mere contingency of the backward-looking nature of the pledge. When someone says, "this is the greatest car ever produced," the statement is implicitly temporal: "this is the greatest car produced to this point in time." Obviously, subsequent automotive innovations or the discovery of a previously unseen flaw demand the issuance of revised appraisals. But in both situations, it is critical to note that all revisions to the pledge are made in relation to perceived characteristics of the thing itself. From this it is possible to suggest that, although value pledges are often made on mistaken grounds and are relativistic and infinitely revisable and subject to appropriation to myriad rule sets in myriad games, such pledges are never made independent of a referent quality or set of qualities existing in the world. Commonplace assertions that values are purely subjective ("beauty is in the eye of the beholder") are problematic. More firmly stated, the assumption that the changing needs and felt desires of a person or group of people replaces the ground of earlier beliefs and the realities of formed matter as sole determinants of value is untenable. Quality becomes circular and literally unbuildable with this slippage.

Matter Matters

Some people believe that humanity shared a single unchanging language in which meaning and values were firmly grounded in the mythic primordial time before Babel. After Babel, in the absence of shared literacy, in a time of multitudinous perspectives, untethered meanings and shifting values, formed matter is the only logical entrée of quality into the world and the best ground on which to explain how some objects hold value.[9] It is clear that a simple formula such as "Formed matter = Quality" will not suffice because it only works to the extent that both form and matter serve established symbolic systems; and it is as true as it is trite to say that sign systems are fragmented and relativistic in our information age.

A revision to the formula at the opening of this section is therefore necessary. Borrowing some language from the world of meta-mathematics, it is important to acknowledge the impossibility of proving the consistency of any theory of objects (or formal system) within that theory (or system).[10] Architectural theory is henceforth reduced to analyses of the relation between formed matter and its communication of value despite the occasional inconsistency of architectural meaning and frequent changes in architectural values across time, in different places, and between groups. The work of W.V. Quine, particularly his indeterminacy of translation thesis, challenges the veracity of this essay's second formula. As Quine argued, "What makes sense is to say not what the objects of a theory are, absolutely speaking, but how one theory of objects is interpretable or reinterpretable in another."[11]

What was rendered above as present and past both impinging on formed matter is reconceived in light of Quine as shown in Figure 11.1.

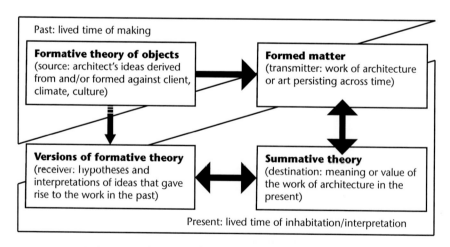

FIGURE 11.1 Value transmission, taking translation into account

A few things are revealed in this new formula. First, the originating theory of the designer or maker is inaccessible to users or inhabitants even if maker and ultimate user is one and the same person. The instantiating belief (at project conception) and the value pledge (at project perception) are discreet acts united only through the mediating object and a (perhaps poorly remembered or largely invented) version of the project's formative motives. Second, most common notions of quality are brought into a condition of translation, or translatability, only through this highly mediated, triangular relationship between extant formed matter (upper right), our own framing languages/beliefs (lower right), and the mirror we construct in the image of the 'Other' (the assumed, perhaps fictional, beliefs attributed to the original maker or, in psychoanalytic terms, collective cognitive imperatives) (lower left). All communication in physical language is limited to this triangle because it is only here – between the existing physical thing, present-day subjective judgment, and assumed or inherited understanding of cultural content – that we find both common ground and expression worthy of comparison.

Material and Values

> Shall we admit that the divine spirit descends into human bodies, there to be even defiled by passions, and nevertheless not believe it in a case where there is no attendant engendering of evil? ... for see how an image, after Art has portrayed in it a god, even passes over into the god himself! Matter though it is, it gives forth divine intelligence.
>
> *(Callistratus,* Descriptions*)*[12]

Because we are indoctrinated to narrow notions of authorship in which artists of all types tell their readers stories, we cannot help but continue to ask how it is that an artist, a sculptor or architect, transfers value from his or her own privately-held intentions to the minds of waiting observers through the currency of mute canvas, stone, steel or glass. The fallacious nature of the indoctrination thus bears repeating. For this reason, Darwin's famous line against the notion of pure perception – "How odd it is that anyone should not see that all observation must be for or against some view if it is to be of any service!" – was rejoined by paleontologist Stephen Jay Gould: "Objectivity is not an unobtainable emptying of mind, but a willingness to abandon a set of preferences – for or against some view, as Darwin said – when the world seems to work in a contrary way." Gould later shortens the formulation: "Data adjudicates theory, but theory also drives and inspires data."[13]

Quine's work on translation does more than highlight the over-simplification at work in the "belief/imagination → formed matter ← pledge" formulation. It also reveals that the diagonal linkage between the earliest and latest acts of imagination in the revised four-square diagram – beliefs of the original makers vs. the valuing pledges of the present-day perceiver – are indeterminate regardless of shortness of time span considered or abundance of records kept. That is, there is never a condition of immediacy between an original formative theory of making and resulting summative theory of experiencing. Indeterminacy of translation means that the intentions of authors, architects, and makers are always inaccessible to readers, inhabitants, and users; even if the architect and user are friends and standing beside one another talking as they walk through the building; even, arguably, if the architect and the perceiver are one and the same person. Cleaved across the implied but never realized axis connecting maker's intentions and perceiver's pledge, the four-square formulation reveals much about the possibility of communication between past and present. Thus cleaved, the diagram breaks into two constituent triangles. The least knowable node in each is the projected version of the formative theory; whether it is the one imagined, at the time of making, as the most likely future interpretation of the artifact or, from the vantage point of the present, as a historical reconstruction of the ways in which the made thing has been interpreted by other observers, the lower left node of each triangle is always a product of speculation and suffers the vicissitudes of serial subjectivities. Formed matter is the only constant, tethering, however loosely, the world of intentions to that of lived perception.

This is difficult to grasp in words. Thus, these two triangles are here redrawn twice – first from the vantage point of makers (formative node privileged) and again from the vantage point of perceivers (summative node oriented). Formation of value in the realm of making, for instance, looks something like Figure 11.2, while formation of value in the domain of perception looks quite different, as shown in Figure 11.3.

The revelatory force of the differences between these two formulations is not immediately obvious. Superficially, the differences are similar to those between the circulations of commodities for the simple satisfaction of needs under a direct barter system as against the circulation of money for its own sake under capitalism. The former is finite in duration while the latter is self-perpetuating.[14] However, the differences run deeper.

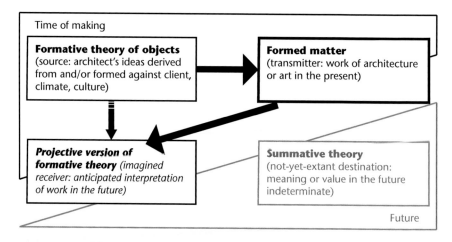

FIGURE 11.2 Value transmission, maker's perspective

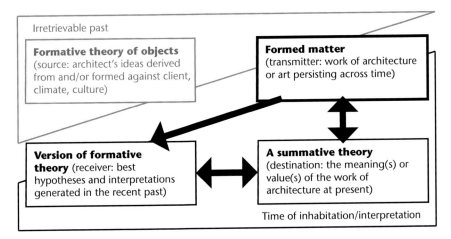

FIGURE 11.3 Value transmission, perceiver's perspective

Arguably, some of the most beautifully rendered passages in Elaine Scarry's *tour de force*, *The Body in Pain*, revolve around the separation of body and voice in Judeo-Christian scripture. Of particular relevance to the problem of narrow notions of authorship is her attention to the double necessity of the body: first, as an instantiation or physical record of an original creation; and second, as a site for all future alterations or modifications. This double necessity underscores the importance of formed matter for the authors of the early books of the Bible; "the Word is never self-substantiating: it seeks its confirmation in a visible change in the realm of matter. The body of man is self-substantiating."[15] Perplexingly, given its weight and density, architecture seems to lack this power of self-substantiation. The problem of values in architecture is essentially the problem of the interrelation of pledge to slippery concerns such as character, increasing desirability of objects, and the diminished affect resulting from the construction of numerous buildings that do not, as a whole, point to the existence of a common vocabulary. Again, this does not appear to be a necessary, or even the most likely, state of affairs. The most stable feature of both triangles above is the shared solidity of formed matter; it is there, for the maker or patron, as product and record of an original act; and it is there, for inhabitants and visitors, as the body onto which meaning accrues.

Matter matters. Whether discussing Greek or Judaic Gods, barter or capitalism, statues or buildings, matter matters. It is often assumed that architectural value judgments necessitate the establishment of a standard based, in part, on measuring the value of the materials employed as well as mitigating the distortion that exists between the surface conditions of those materials and their formal order. While more or less true, this last sentence can be rewritten to conform with the comments on modernity's many motives and, in the process, shift its focus and increase its clarity: Post-Romantic value judgments necessitate the establishment of two theories of objects – one concerning the meaning of materials employed and one concerning formal order –

144 Architecture History and Theory in Reverse

and a pledge that supports the translation of one into the other for purposes of communication or exchange. Post-Romantic values and value judgments *per se* are thus linked by the material that serves as a sign for the act of measuring quality.

This last comment serves as something like a truism for what remains. Unfortunately, and due in no small measure to our investment in late nineteenth- and early twentieth-century capitalistic thinking, a host of simplistic associations present themselves: Price ≈ value. Wealth ≈ quality. Quantity of goods ≈ surface conditions of buildings. None of these, however, are very useful in establishing a theory of objects concerning either material or form. Sir Christopher Wren's great London churches are, no doubt, worth a great deal in monetary terms, exhibit the extraordinary resources of the church at the time of construction, and are literally composed of tons of matter; but none of this explains the perception of value in the mind of a visitor – whether devout congregant or humanist sightseer. Speculations on value and quality must therefore move beyond word replacement, materials *per se*, and storytelling into larger spheres of language and communicative systems that take the measure of humanity and things against an invisible but assumed pledge. Stated the other way around, speculative domains of language and labyrinthine systems of signification which dominated scholarly thought between the end of the Classical era and beginning of Modernity – as opposed to the economic systems thinking that emerged triumphant in the twentieth century – are better suited to the perception of materials as surfaces possessing qualities. And to these ideas we next turn through the writing of Heinrich Hübsch.

Notes

1 Delivered at Highgate Cemetery, London, 17 March 1883. Available at: www.marxists. org/archive/marx/works/1883/death/dersoz1.htm (accessed November 4, 2016).
2 Terrence W. Deacon, *Incomplete Nature: how mind emerged from matter* (New York: W. W. Norton & Company, 2013), 115. See also pp. 110–114 for a discussion of evolution's after-the-fact vs. goal-oriented quality.
3 Rousseau states, "The social state is advantageous to men only when all have something and none too much." *The Social Contract* (New York: Maestro, 2012), Book I, §9. As Ernst Cassirer noted in relation to the transubstantiation that occurs under the influence of the spoken word: "In the beginning, sensual impulse is followed immediately by its gratification; but gradually more and more mediating terms intervene between the will and its object," *Language and Myth* (New York: Dover Publications, 1953), 58. Meanings are sets of mediating terms.
4 Karl Marx, *Capital: a critique of political economy, volume 1*, Introduction by Ernest Mandel, translated by Ben Fowkes (New York: Penguin Books, 1990), 188.
5 This is how Michel Foucault describes money. See *The Order of Things* (New York: Vintage, 1994), 181.
6 John Ruskin, *The Stones of Venice*, edited and abridged by J.G. Links (New York: Da Capo, 2003), 45.
7 According to Richard Ford:

> There was no feeling, once the hills disappeared behind us, of a findable middle point from which other points could draw a reference. A person could easily get lost or go crazy here, since the middle was everywhere and everything at once.
> (Richard Ford, *Canada*, New York: Ecco, 2013, 216–217)

8 *The Social Contract*, Book II, §1.
9 For an alternative reading of the Babel myth, see George Steiner, *After Babel* (New York: Oxford University Press, 1975), 286.
10 This is the result of Gödel's second incompleteness theorem. An excellent description can be found in Chapter 3 of Rebecca Goldstein's *Incompleteness: the proof and paradox of Kurt Gödel* (New York: W.W. Norton & Company, 2006), 147–205.
11 W.V. Quine, *Ontological Relativity and Other Essays* (New York: Columbia University Press, 1969), 50.
12 A passage in support of the power of idols from Callistratus' *Descriptions*, translated by A. Fairbanks (New York: Loeb Classical Library, 1902), 10.
13 Stephen Jay Gould, "Dinosaur in a Haystack," available at: www.inf.fu-berlin.de/lehre/pmo/eng/Gould-Dinosaur.pdf (accessed March 29, 2016).
14 See Marx, *Capital*, 253.
15 Elaine Scarry, *The Body in Pain* (New York: Oxford University Press, 1987), 181–243; quoted passage, p. 193. The following parenthetic remark sums up the trajectory of interest here: "it is precisely the condition of having a body that makes one susceptible to the original alteration of having been created, and that makes one then susceptible to subsequent alterations, such as multiplication and growth."

12

IN WHAT STYLE?

Epistemes and Monsters

> [N]othing within a human being is so deep, so rare or so wide-ranging that it may not pass over into language and be recognizable there.
>
> …
>
> Just as no concept is possible without language, so also there can be no object for the mind, since it is only through the concept, of course, that anything external acquires full being for consciousness.
>
> *(Wilhelm von Humboldt,* On Language)[1]

Why is a pocket knife given to me decades ago by my grandfather more highly prized in my sight and to my touch than an identical knife found at a flea market or second-hand store, especially if there are no discernible differences in material condition or quality of workmanship, age or patina? All such experiential judgments that exceed the discriminatory powers of the direct senses and concerns for utility (does it function as well as other units of its type) are linguistic in nature. Arguably, judgments of the so-called direct senses and of utility are as well.

Discernments of objects loved or hated, valued positively or negatively, are manifestations of associations which cling to the object via language: my pocket knife's rust is a record of my grandfather carrying it in his pocket when he swam in creeks and rivers as a boy; and the nicked handle an artifact of its years of use on the family farm. Assuming language is central to understanding the relationship of materials and values, it is possible to move on to the rudimentary ways in which competing interests gain importance through and are disseminated by language. How, in other words, does language both convey and create? Report and invent?

At the most fundamental level, today's languages are residue of ancient episteme. I use *episteme* in lieu of *style* as the latter implies a recognizable appearance. An episteme is a scaffold on which a particular body of knowledge is organized and judgments of its veracity are made. It is reasonable to doubt that ideas related to

In What Style? Epistemes and Monsters **147**

practical knowledge, on the one hand, and theory, on the other – or simply, observation and speculation – necessarily share one *episteme* even when focused upon the same issue or circumstance. The human body studied medically or desired sexually can be thought of as distinct bodies, even if it is the same flesh under consideration. Epistemes persist as long as some group considers it useful; and this explains, in part, why radically different points of view exist side by side in a single culture. Still today, there are Platonists and Aristotelians; puritans and libertines; Christians and Muslims and atheists; conservatives and liberals and anarchists; Classicists, Romanticists, and Modernists; not to mention hybrids of all possible sorts. Each of us a multitude, every person carries several epistemic lenses, ranging from a few for the most narrowly concerned to a multitude possessed by the intellectual gadfly. Rousseau might call these tools the "registers of our wills," a ground to our pledges that are "both free and subject to the laws."[2] As a result, each of us understands – and, feels – a very different world. And yet, we can understand each other's worlds.

This returns us to problems of value, change, and speculation versus signification in communicative experience that emerged in the previous three chapters. How is it possible to understand physical language across time and in different places if epistemes come and go with time, vary from place to place, and even compete with each other for place of privilege? Heinrich Hübsch wrote the seminal architectural essay on this topic, "In What Style Should We Build?" in 1828. While Hübsch got many things wrong and contributed significantly to the information age bias for function and against decoration (and against meaning), I turn first to the things he got right, more or less. Triangulating three aspects of linguistic agency, implicit in Hübsch and later made explicit in Foucault's writings, helps us discern the shape of an answer to the question: 'how is it possible to understand architecture across time and place?'

Aspects of Agency

1. Exchangeability of Ideas

Hübsch begins his essay with an almost unassailable assertion: "whoever starts his investigation from the point of view of practical necessity will find a secure base." He identifies practical necessity as fitness of purpose (commodity), lasting existence (solidity), climate, and building material.[3] These are far too broad, however, to constitute the elements of style. The epistemes first acquired by language learners and most common across cultures are those near the middle of taxonomic hierarchies. Philosopher Charles Taylor points out that cats and dogs are recognized before felines and canines or Siamese and Labradors; chairs and tables before furniture in general or an Eames or Wassily or Barcelona in particular.[4] Hübsch correctly identifies similar mid-range taxonomies as the essential parts of buildings: "walls, ceilings, piers or columns, doors, windows, roofs, and cornices."[5] We possess a bodily understanding of these: fixed surfaces to our sides, those overhead,

148 Architecture History and Theory in Reverse

those that move to allow passage, holes in surfaces through which we receive light and air, etc.

The power of such mid-range taxonomies and elements derives from their universality – even if not formally named within a culture or society. In *The Order of Things*, Michel Foucault wrote: "There is no life in the Classical period, nor any science of life; nor any philology either … In the same way, there is no political economy, because, in the order of knowledge, production does not exist." He was wrong.[6] The intricacies of a full-fledged debunking would require many pages, yet the kernel of rebuttal is straightforward: absence of any conceptual category or episteme ('production', for instance) from the formal logic elaborated by the thinkers or makers of any given time period (e.g. 'Classical') does not preclude the possibility of that category's existence as a general or intuitive organizing principle utilized by a significant minority (and perhaps a majority) of people living and working in that era. To acknowledge that 'production' is unlikely to have existed as an overt or self-conscious organizational principle for people working, or benefiting from work, in the Classical period does not entail that an informal knowledge of production (the idea of making for other than personal or immediate consumption) and even a nascent awareness of political economy (the sense that exchange and power are related) did not exist. It is across such silent, unrecorded but nevertheless active epistemes that physical languages communicate.[7]

Foucault's error is important because it demonstrates the dangers of assuming that the terms of formalized language ("production" in this case) precede the informal episteme (the general sense that things are produced, for example). In architecture, we might think of epistemes as systems of order by which we identify a building as belonging a style; and evidence of styles pre-existing their formalization are strewn throughout the history of architectural languages. When Pevsner praises Longleat in Wiltshire as the earliest building of Elizabethan episteme, for instance, it is important to remember that this demonstrates no prescience on the part of Longleat's designer of a coming "Elizabethan Style"; it signifies only that the designer in 1580 was immersed in a design and construction culture infatuated with "the Italian Early Renaissance, the Loire style in France, and the strapwork decoration of Flanders" as well as an English sensibility that valued restraint over exuberance.[8] The Elizabethan style is, in other words, a body of knowledge composed of pieces of several existing physical languages filtered through the specificities of place, culture, climate, etc. But, importantly, by the time the "Elizabethan" episteme acquired its name, most of its greatest examples had been built.

2. Docility toward Rank

In *Discipline and Punish*, Foucault argues for disciplinary production in the form of rank.[9] Here Foucault is incisive. Discipline, which entails the organization of people and things by rank, is one of two dominant forms of the exercise of power (the other being punishment). It is only through the framework or discipline of a discipline that values, inherently subjective and subject to myriad contingencies, emerge and spread as a hierarchy of qualities. In other words, systems of qualities or epistemes are always the result of an imposition of values on matter, living or not, from a position of authority – be it Linnaeus or Lamarck, sovereign or surveyor, master builder or design critic. Read carefully, the position being formulated here turns traditional relations on their head: here, values are individual and largely personal judgments; the coalescence of these result in qualities, which are, by turns, social and interpersonal. Qualities are law-like constructs; submitted to because these are *registers of our wills*. If the significance of this change is still hard to grasp, consider the point this way: Qualities are imposed upon formed matter as ascriptions of rank which are, by necessity, communicative; furthermore, the qualities of formed matter that might be shared, the qualities that might be said to 'matter,' are linguistic constructs through and through – rooted in the founding values of individuals, perhaps, but always under a social transubstantiation: had my grandfather been a famous or socially significant person, the nicks in the handle of what is now *my* pocket knife would be qualities that *all* could *see* ... and understand.

This last point regarding social transubstantiation is hard to accept from within the current episteme of western architectural criticism and publication. It implies that architecture of shared or sharable experiences benefits from an individual docility on the part of the architect in favor of qualities rooted in socially constructed myths or meaning. Architects today eschew both legibility and constraints on their freedom. Hübsch did not. He advocated the making of buildings that conformed to function, material properties, and climate. Like most of the architects of the pre-information period, who asserted authority through epistemes borrowed or coalesced from existing languages (and without suffering so deeply the fear of influence that retards information age practice),[10] Hübsch feared "the unprejudiced majority" would see architecture they could not understand "as something they can do without." And, once ordinary people could see the great monuments of antiquity, Hübsch claimed the poor imitations available to them could only appear as "abominations."[11]

3. The Subjectivity of Power

Not every deviation from tradition or a given episteme is an abomination. After responding to function, climate, and material properties, Hübsch says, "Let the artist's taste have free rein." He goes so far as to admit that, "Once necessity is satisfied, there is pleasure in free creation."[12] Hübsch, however, immediately backpedals on this freedom, fearful of its implications.[13] This backpedaling is not the result of uncertainty but a deep rift that runs through language and experience. "There are two meanings of the word 'subject':" Foucault writes in "The Subject and Power." It means, "[to be] subject to someone else by control and dependence, and tied to his own identity by a conscience or self-knowledge."[14] In this later and lesser known essay, Foucault goes to great length to demonstrate that the purpose for studying power is always to gain a greater understanding of what it means to be a subject – linguistically and experientially – under the influence of power relations.

150 Architecture History and Theory in Reverse

Many contemporary architectural discourses, particularly those with phenomenological, technological, sustainability or social justice agendas, refer to buildings themselves as participatory and participating subjects in an attempt to construct meaningful experience. That is to say, these architects and authors talk about our dialogic relation with buildings as communicators of (sensory, historical, ecological or ethical) content. I agree insofar as matter matters as the locus for our pledges. The authors of such discourses, however, disagree with each other, and I with them, as to the freedom or autonomy that any architectural subject (building or human) possesses. To be a subject is not to be wholly free or autonomous, as Hübsch correctly sensed. There is no inherent contradiction in saying that a work of architecture exists as a participatory subject and as a docile body. We and it, people and things, are often both. We receive rank from outside and wear badges of shame or honor as context demands: *we can be both free and subject to the laws*.[15] Things, to the extent they are subjects, do the same. My pocket knife's deviations from mint condition serves as an example here too. Yet architecture is central to culture in a way that a pocket knife cannot be. Architecture has to both assert and obey a range of epistemes, even internally conflicting ones, if it is to communicate as a subject in a society.[16]

Bifurcation: "Truth" and Speculation

Things fall apart, as Shakespeare said. Language and its constitutive epistemes are particularly prone to parting. Some are understood as rooted in observation of the world and gain stability from the slowness of anthropological, geological, or cosmological change; this is the language of science. Other epistemes are castigated as speculative, founded upon hopes, wishes and fears, human desires, and are considered stable only within a narrow cultural milieu in which they are born, propagate, and die; this is the language of literature, poetry, and mysticism. The distance between observation and speculation – like that between truth and falsity or fact and fiction – is an artifact of differences in perspectives.

Epistemes often are described as if resulting from *a priori* truths. This is not the case. In fact, we deal with few *a priori* truths on any given day; and these are limited, primarily, to tautologies, definitions, and operations of mathematics. Our relationships with cultural epistemes are fuzzier – subject to combination, change, and being forgotten in direct proportion to their *a posteriori* content.[17] This content is that which, accumulated in time, organizes experience as a field of knowledge; defines the relations of objects to objects, objects to subjects, and subjects to subjects; grounds practical endeavors; and fosters belief in a discourse held to be useful. An episteme comes to be regarded as an *a priori* truth only when its assembled nature is unified and overcome by belief.[18] Like quantum mechanics or M-theory, Judaism or Christianity, herein is found the "truth" of phenomenology, formalism, sustainability, social justice, and other epistemes of the architectural profession through which rank of goodness or beauty or correctness is awarded: each is essentially a system of belief. And a belief institutionalized, as Montesquieu warned, molds its believers as long as the institution survives.[19]

In What Style? Epistemes and Monsters   **151**

Long before Vitruvius, the Greeks differentiated the continuous from intervals. From the beginning of the sixteenth century (if not earlier), architects divided builders from decorators and the Gothic from the Renaissance. With Ruskin, the roof-ceiling assembly is separated into the "Roof Mask" and the "Roof Proper." Many of these old epistemes survive today. With Hübsch, it is the more familiar roof, ceiling, and cornice. It is the nature of language to bifurcate. To understand this compulsion, consider two common assertions that underlie the observation versus speculation split:

1. As conceived by Foucault, and grounded in the narrow linguistic formulations of Thomas Hobbes (1588–1679), John Locke (1632–1704), and Étienne Bonnot de Condillac (1714–1780), well-constructed languages – the kinds of language that lend support to *techne*, sciences and religions and the epistemes upon which professions are built – are formed from a mixture of assumed *a priori* truths and reified *a posteriori* instrumentalities. Well-constructed languages, thus form *taxonomies* that end nature as 'life' or a living and changing concern, and convert it to thingness – in part, as a result of the reification of language and, in part, for the express purpose of stabilizing and preserving the institutions language has fostered. This amount of classificatory power, and the smallness of difference it frames, requires that an extraordinary stability of difference be assumed and maintained to keep it distinct from the world at large, i.e. to keep it special.
2. If creativity is to be understood as the positing of new, as yet unclassified, works of imagination, then languages appropriate to creative making, in contrast to well-formed languages, must be open or not yet formalized into an episteme; either that, or creativity must borrow well-constructed languages; call them into question; mix them with other, contradictory discourses; or minorize them, to borrow Deleuze and Guattari's terminology.

Humboldt, one of history's most astute observers of language, framed these divisions in various terms: intellectual versus phonetic techniques; mental principles versus organic laws; etc. While there are reasonable points in each of these statements, it is difficult not to notice that between well-formed languages, *techne*, scientific classifications, mental principles, to one side, and organic, phonetic, creative writing (drawing, making, speaking) and techniques of minorization, to the other, the world of language is itself often divided into a simple either-or construct. The horrific consequences of even this most common bifurcation are difficult to miss. De Sade's Curval said, "It seems to me one never sufficiently exploits the possible."[20] One does not have to be a debauching character to understand the sentiment. All systems of classification or mores or professional episteme reduce the range of possible or acceptable or reasonable action. Bifurcations reduce the realm of possibilities by half.

And yet, this is still only half of the problem. Bifurcations throw both similarity and difference into question. If intervals and differences are understood as selections based on bias and propagated via prejudice, it is important to remember that it is

152 Architecture History and Theory in Reverse

the faculty of memory and imagined similarities that props up notions of continuity. Space and time, Being and knowledge, things and words, nature and classification – these are just four recent human bifurcations. Studied more closely, all of these splits are open internally to re-bifurcation and re-combination at will making it impossible to know where or even if such divisions exist. It seems that, with shifts in criteria, so go our bifurcations.

This is known today, if not much discussed. And obviously, the Romantic tendency to categorize the world into differences and similarities has value to architects, inhabitants, and everyone else for every conceivable purpose. It is essential, however, to note that both differences and similarities operate in relation to a whole – or, less grandly stated, in relation to a much larger sample than the world as it exists within any particular episteme. Yet, if this is true, and if quality is rooted in rank and rank in epistemes, as suggested in the previous section, how is the endurance of any physical language to be understood given the ephemeral character of all systems of classification? How, in other words, is it possible to construct things, buildings and places, that might participate in grounding a community that are meaningful to many (not just the architect or client) and for more than a few hours, days or weeks?

These are difficulties that Hübsch instantiates with his language of "truth in the fullest meaning of the word," "the first great conventional lie," and "the rightness of the arrangement."[21] In using words like truth and rightness, and in asserting, "that the factors controlling the shape of the less essential parts … become less objective the more detailed they become,"[22] Hubsch is accepting Hobbes, Locke, and Condillac's privileging of fixed systems over speculative invention. What is missing in Hübsch is an appreciation for the process of invention of a suitable opposite term (the equal other) that necessarily occurs when one term or entity is deemed a lie or is frighteningly off-putting.[23]

Markers in Time, Not Styles

Linguist Dell Hymes once said: "Most of language begins where abstract universals leave off."[24] Earlier I noted the frequent observation made by historians and anthropologists and world travelers that Mayan temples 'look like' and share some aspects of organization with Babylonian, Egyptian, Hindu, and Shang Dynasty works of architecture despite any credible evidence of comingling or influence. In addition to similarities in appearance, western visitors frequently report that the 'spiritual' presence of the former temples linger just as powerfully as in the latter examples despite a gulf of time, place, and belief. Taken together, these observations are often cited, by Jungian psychologists and pattern-language classicists alike, as evidence that an essential unconscious archetype, a proto-physical language, undergirds all human making. Perhaps. It is an interesting if untestable hypothesis. Yet, such a hypothesis is not the most compelling conclusion that might be drawn from these anecdotes. It is arguably more interesting to note what anthropologists and psychologists and architectural theorists seem to make of such similitude: the experience (imagined or real) of continuity fosters the perception (or understanding or, even, invention) of history – all histories.[25]

Why do these monuments look alike? Arguably there were a host of practical constraints that both prompted and limited the form of elevated temple complexes as much as or more than ideology or cultural content. In addition to the psychological and sociological, these are matters of practical geography (it is possible to survey larger expanses of earth and sky as well as to see more of the horizon from elevated platforms), physiology (there is a maximum angle of incline that human bodies can navigate with and without steps which does not vary much across time, gender or race), geology (some building materials are widely available, uniform in their compressive and tensile strengths, and best stacked and secured in similar ways), and astronomy (from a terrestrial perspective, the heavens appear to move; and the particular movements of the sun, moon, planets, and stars are similar for most of the elevated temple builders). Given that the powers and limitations of human bodies, availability and characteristics of materials, and the laws of physics and the cosmos are more or less the same for all people across human civilizations, there is no reason to experience 'mystery' when confronted with similarities in world architecture. What makes history and provides meaning – what, in fact, deserves the awe of mystery – is not the reoccurrence of the same but the inevitable emergence of inexplicable difference against this uniform ground of constraints. Oddities and perversions, these monsters of species are not exceptions that clarify or prove the rule. Instead, deviations are the extremes that broaden the range of species, make the same "merely" the same, and stretch the domain of "normal" to the point that "normal" and "abnormal," "similar" and "different," even "here" and "there" begin to have meaning in context.

From this point of view, it is the differences between Mayan, Babylonian, Egyptian, Hindu, and Shang Dynasty temple complexes that matter; even more important are the subtle and not so subtle variations that exist within each of these cultural milieus. And yet, the range of deviation from one Mayan temple or Egyptian pyramid to the next is so narrow, so of-the-type, that I am fearful the larger lesson will be missed. A more radical example is necessary. Consider instead Matthaeus Daniel Pöppelmann's Zwinger in Dresden (see Figures 12.1 and 12.2) and, by way of introduction, Pevsner's description:

> The gate pavilion especially is a fantasy unchecked by any consideration of use. The ground-floor archway has instead of a proper pediment two bits of a broken pediment swinging away from each other. The first-floor pediment is broken too, but nodding inward instead of outward. The whole first floor is open on all sides – a kiosk or gazebo, as it were – and above its attic, swarming with figures of putti, is a bulbous cupola with the royal and electoral emblems on top.[26]

It is difficult to name this work; perhaps this partially explains why this project and its architect are so seldom discussed in recent architectural history. In evolutionary

FIGURE 12.1 Zwinger, Dresden, Matthaeus Daniel Pöppelmann architect
Source: Photograph by David M. Morris.

FIGURE 12.2 Zwinger (detail), Dresden, Matthaeus Daniel Pöppelmann architect
Source: Photograph by David M. Morris.

terms, it is worthy of the label "monster" – this being the moniker used by Aristotle and other thinkers of antiquity to castigate Beings that fell outside an ostensibly complete but not necessarily comprehensive system of classification. But monsters are more than outliers that reify the norm. Despite facts of shared physiologies, materials, and physics, western architectural language is not a homogeneous system occasionally disrupted or forced to vary.[27] "Variations" exist only against the ground of a nomenclature – only against the urge to clarify which posits history. Before the appearance of things distinct enough to be called monsters, the non-historicized world is utterly heterogeneous: bits of matter and force bouncing to and fro. This is why the arrival of Gilgamesh, fire-breathing dragons, frenzied prophets, and the demon-possessed still matter to us today. Continuity and variation, identity and difference, emerge in time only on the heels of a monster, a great singularity, which exposes a rupture in the otherwise smooth unspooling of time in gentle undulations. Every monster is a difference that enlarges lived identity and, more importantly, creates the need for language to explain, to corral, and to protect normalcy from the perceived threat of its existence. This last point is critical for understanding the migration of architecture under the sway of Romantic languages. Missing this point, as Hübsch does, reduces works like the Zwinger gate pavilion to misguided decoration or an "abomination" of an existing, correct language. And it robs it of potential for meaning.

156 Architecture History and Theory in Reverse

To what purpose were Pöppelmann's gate pavilion and the great temples of the Maya and other cultures built? While thinking of an answer, notice that neither the practical limitations enumerated above nor those promoted by Hübsch serve a response. Nor is the answer programmatic – or, at least, not merely so. No one would go to such lengths and invest so much material and energy simply to mark an entry point or provide space for burial or sacrifice or worship of some kind. Only one reasonable response emerges: there is no need to construct an architectural language for things that never change or are readily visible (here a door; there a church). What all the symbolic entries and all the temple complexes across time and place share is their existence as physical markers of conditions and correspondences that are, at best, seldom noticed (the marking of astronomical alignments, the seasons, the summer and winter solstice, for examples) or beliefs and ideas that are, by necessity, physically absent (expressions of god, the order of heaven, symbolic or moral order). Monsters always serve the non-physical, whether demon or god or other hidden order. The speculative. They constitute the inventive aspect of language and mark time actively; changing, morphing, smoothing languages created to define and contain them.

In response to monsters, in recoiling fear, another type of architecture emerges; and it also marks time, though in a passive or reflexive way. Fossils hold a fascination equal to monsters in the Romantic mind. The conceptual opposite of living and inventive language, fossils are those buildings found in every culture which serve obvious responsibilities, meeting physically observable criteria without taking the task of fostering meaning; "they stand in the place of ideas," as Ruskin said of flying buttresses,[28] and serve at best as a comforting measure laid across the heterogeneity of culture (Figure 12.3).

Fossils. Monsters. This language is old. It is Romance terminology for a long-perceived discontinuity between an inherently homogenized worldview and one of radical heterogeneity. The former is centered on the belief that perceived divisions are no more or less real than our perceptions of similarities or continuities and that a unified ground underlies all perception of change or difference. The latter assumes that it is the unique object, being, or idea that eschews orthodoxy and provides rungs of meaning across time, through which the remainder of the world appears to persist as a stable entity. The irreducibility of these positions has a long lineage in Western thought from the diametrically opposed systems of Heraclitus and Parmenides, to Humboldt's division of the form of language into sensate intuition-feeling versus methods of incorporation-categorization,[29] to the writings of their twentieth- and twenty-first-century descendants.[30] Neither constitutes a style in isolation from the other.

Deleuze and Guattari have addressed this problem in depth. In essays like "1440: The Smooth and the Striated," the work reveals strident bifurcations such as (smooth) becoming vs. (striated) history as abstract distinctions at the ends of a single continuum.

> No sooner do we note a simple opposition between the two kinds of space than we must indicate a much more complex difference by virtue of which

the successive terms of the oppositions fail to coincide entirely. And no sooner have we done that than we must remind ourselves that the two spaces in fact exist only in mixture: smooth space is constantly being translated, transversed into a striated space; striated space is constantly being reversed, returned to a smooth space.[31]

There is no more need for an either/or choice between the felt continuity of immediate presence, on the one hand, and a hermeneutic of societal or cultural meaning, on the other, than there is need for a Kierkegaardian choice between aesthetics and ethics. Both are experienced. And experience, in the largest sense, is an amalgam of sensation and ideation – or, smooth and striated. The idea of choosing one or the other is nonsensical.

As most architectural theorists maintain the rigid distinctions of antiquity, it is worth the effort to follow this thread. Sometimes, simply thinking through the chain of connected words resolves apparent mysteries. History, as a regrouping of experiences into serialized products, consists of both smooth and striated narrativizations: the seemingly continuous fabric of spatial beings is the world of striated space constructed on the ground of existing bodies of knowledge; the seemingly discontinuous thread of events in time is the lived or felt but not-quite-conceptualized action of the human animal in smooth space. While histories are various specialized forms of language, History emerges as a discipline and becomes visible to the average citizens of an existing knowledge system, or State, only because the two types of space disguise themselves as – or play the part of – the other.

FIGURE 12.3 Flying buttress
Source: Photograph by David C. Lewis.

158 Architecture History and Theory in Reverse

This can be framed a little more architecturally. Striated space is the summative displacement of beings and things in and against an established order. Smooth space is the formative volume in which change occurs. This does not mean that the work of striating striated space is active (a kinetic ordering) while the smoothing tendency of smooth space is passive (a void of mere potential). In fact, neither the passive-active dichotomy nor its potential-kinetic equivalent quite works. Serial placements and summative displacements of ideas and objects and beings into a given or growing hierarchical system is relatively easy; towing or pushing that system of meaning across an always uneven and forever undeveloped desert terrain, however, is hard.

As with all bifurcations, and as stated at the outset, observation and speculation are less facts or truths than emergent phenomena from differing perspectives. Each is a manner of description that can be elaborated endlessly and simultaneously effaced by the next desert wind. For the purpose of understanding Romantic architectural language, it is important to acknowledge the totality from which these two narrow descriptions spring. Meaning requires both the heterogeneity of monsters in speculative language and the homogeneity of repetition in observational language. The former only appear different or similar against the uniformity of the latter. The eruption of a unique condition in language, whether written or spoken or physical, is conceivable only because so much of language is striated and fossilized and, thus, known to a community of speakers and readers. My grandfather's pocket knife arguably operates at both levels – conforming to classification and rank, on the one hand, and deforming these hierarchies via nicks, rust, wear. Information age architects tend to undervalue this process, preferring to build monsters and leaving history to provide the datum necessary to know them as such.

Notes

1 Wilhelm, Freiherr von Humboldt, *On Language: on the diversity of human language construction and its influence on the mental development of the human species*, edited by Michael Losonsky and translated by Peter Heath (Cambridge: Cambridge University Press, 1999), 81 and 59. Or as Derrida notes: "There is no social institution before language, it is not one cultural element among others, it is the element of institutions in general, it includes and constructs the entire social structure." Jacques Derrida, *Of Grammatology*, translated by Gayatri Chakravorty Spivak (Baltimore, MD: Johns Hopkins University Press, 1976), 219.
2 Jean-Jacques Rousseau, *The Social Contract* (New York: Maestro, 2012), Book II, §6.
3 Heinrich Hübsch, "In What Style Should We Build?" In *In What Style Should We Build: the German debates on architectural style*. Introduction and translation by Wolfgang Herrmann (Santa Monica, CA: the Getty Center for the History of Art and the Humanities, 1992), 63–101. Quotes from pp. 64 and 67.
4 Charles Taylor's analysis of metaphorical language in Chapter 5, "The Figuring Dimension of Language," of *The Language Animal* provides an extraordinary account of this process. See pp. 129–176. Charles Taylor, *The Language Animal: the full shape of the human linguistic capacity* (Cambridge, MA: Belknap Press/Harvard University, 2016).
5 "In What Style Should We Build?" 66.
6 It is difficult to write those words given the breadth and profundity of his scholarly output. Nevertheless, Foucault's assertion that there is no political economy in the Classical period is firmly rooted in allegiances to mono-directional time and the exclusivity of *a priori* knowledge; and, both assumptions are almost certainly wrong. At

In What Style? Epistemes and Monsters **159**

the very least, the possibilities of multivalent time, as well as an appreciation for *a posteriori* and mutually exclusive but co-existing *a priori* bodies of knowledge, challenges the veracity of his position. From the point of view of a post-Romantic interest in formed matter and the exchange of values across time, the importance of revealing the flaws in Foucault's early analysis of wealth cannot be overstated. See Michel Foucault, *The Order of Things* (New York: Vintage, 1994), 166.

7 Broch would have called these silent but active episteme the 'Logos' as opposed to the 'Archetypes' of language. See George Steiner, *After Babel: aspects of language and translation* (New York: Oxford University Press, 1975), 319.

8 Nikolaus Pevsner, *An Outline of European Architecture*, Jubilee Edition (Baltimore, MD: Penguin, 1961), 507–508.

9 According to Foucault:

> In discipline, the elements are interchangeable, since each is defined by the place it occupies in a series, and by the gap that separates it from the others. The unit is, therefore ... the rank: the place one occupies in a classification.
> (Michel Foucault, *Discipline and Punish: the birth of the prison*, translated by Alan Sheridan, New York: Vintage, 1995, 145)

Based on the world of commerce, it is reasonable to suggest that qualities – accumulated value judgments – are not necessary precursors to and will not necessarily result in a privileging of monetary political economies insofar as qualities, so understood, are too much subject to the whims of consciousness to ground an economic model of exchange. The same is true for the world of exchange in physical language. Such concepts as quality, price, and trade are united, in both commercial and physical languages, in a circular relation that is subservient to, and derived from, more basic forces: those of power, dominance, docility, and exchange.

10 Again, it is revealing to read Pevsner.

> In fact we find nowhere in [Inigo] Jones's work mere imitation. What he had learned from Palladio and the Roman architects of the early 16th century is to regard a building as a whole, organized throughout – in plan and elevation – according to rational rules.
> (Pevsner, *Outline of European Architecture*, 516)

11 "In What Style Should We Build?" 82.

12 Ibid., 65 and 70.

13 See discussion of this point in Chapter 1.

14 "Both meanings suggest a form of power that subjugates and makes subject to." From "The Subject and Power," first published in English in Dreyfus and Paul Rabinow's (eds.) *Michel Foucault: Beyond Structuralism and Hermeneutics*, 1982, and reprinted in James D. Faubion's (ed.) *Michel Foucault: power, essential works of Foucault, 1954–1984*, Volume 3, Paul Rabinow, series ed. (New York: The New Press, 2000), 326–348. The quoted passage is taken from p. 331 of the reprinted essay.

15 Humboldt eloquently wrote:

> Language belongs to me, because I bring it forth as I do; and since the ground of this lies at once in the speaking and having-spoken of every generation of men, so far as speech-communication may have prevailed unbroken among them, it is language itself which restrains me when I speak.
> (Humboldt, *On Language*, 63)

16 Pevsner quotes Inigo Jones on the relationship between interiors and exteriors. "He wrote: 'Outwardly every wyse man carrieth a graviti in Publicke Places, yet inwardly

160 Architecture History and Theory in Reverse

hath his imaginacy set on fire, and sumtimes licenciously flying out, as nature hirself doeth often times stravagantly', and demands the same attitude in a good building." This argument remains potent. Pevsner, *Outline of European Architecture*, 518.

17 As Derrida obliquely said, "Before being its object, writing is the condition of the *episteme.*" See *Of Grammatology*, 27.

18 "Belief is the act of imagining. It is what the act of imagining is called when the object created is credited with more reality (and all that is entailed in greater 'realness,' more power, more authority) than oneself." Scarry, *The Body in Pain*, 205.

19 "At the birth of societies, the rulers of Republics establish institutions, and afterwards the institutions mould the rulers." Quoted by Rousseau in *The Social Contract*, Book II, §7, this comment is better known to contemporary readers in the form given it by Winston Churchill.

20 Marquis de Sade's "The 120 Days of Sodom," in *The 120 Days of Sodom & Other Writings*, compiled and translated by Austryn Wainhouse and Richard Seaver, introductions by Simone de Beauvoir and Pierre Klossowski (New York: Grove Press, 1987), 470.

21 "In What Style Should We Build?" 77, 78, and 87.

22 Ibid., 64.

23 Writing about demon possession and the possessed|exorcist bifurcation, for instance, Julian Jaynes notes that the exorcist comes into existence subsequent to and in order to replace the 'demon' in the possessed person's need for external authority. "The cognitive imperatives of the belief system that determined the form of the illness in the first place determine the form of its cure." Julian Jaynes, *The Origins of Consciousness in the Breakdown of the Bicameral Mind* (Boston: Houghton Mifflin, 1976), 350.

24 Dell Hymes, "Speech and Language: on the origins and foundations of inequality among speakers," (*Daedalus*, issued as the *Proceedings of the American Academy of Arts and Sciences*, CII, 1973), 63.

25 "Even as the human mind can dream a future so it can reshape the past," is George Steiner's pithy summation. See *After Babel*, 338.

26 Pevsner, *Outline of European Architecture*, 473.

27 See Marco Frascari, *Monsters of Architecture* (Lanham, MD: Rowman & Littlefield, 1991).

28 See John Ruskin, *The Stones of Venice*, Edited by J.G. Links (Cambridge, MA: Da Capo Press, 2003), 90.

29 See *On Language*, § 18, 140–142.

30 Of these, Gilles Deleuze and Félix Guattari stand apart. In their provocative collaborations, both homogenizing and differentiating ideas find expression. The former finds echoes in such phrases as: "Becoming produces nothing other than itself. We fall into a false alternative if we say that you either imitate or you are. What is real is the becoming itself...becoming lacks a subject distinct from itself." Statements according value to the monster can be found in more succinct form: "History is made only by those who oppose history." (Gilles Deleuze and Félix Guattari, *A Thousand Plateaus: capitalism and schizophrenia*, translation and foreword by Brian Massumi (Minneapolis, MN: University of Minnesota Press, 1987), 238 and 295.

31 Ibid., 474.

13

THE *PRÉCIS* AND THE PATERNITY OF PERCEPTION

Heinrich Hübsch was not writing in a vacuum in 1828. Nor was he writing to fill a disciplinary void. Hübsch was writing against the ideas of episteme or style championed by Jean-Nicolas-Louis Durand in his *Précis des leçons d'architecture données à l'Ecole polytechnique* (1802–1805) and its graphic addendum (1821). At first blush, this assessment is incorrect. Hübsch is indebted to Durand and, read casually, "In What Style …?" seems to be little more than a synopsis of the *Précis*. Both works address architecture as a composition of essential elements conforming to material qualities, economy, and climate. Both consider its execution a pursuit of truth and consider decoration as a deviation from that pursuit. Both men denigrate imitation of the classical orders. Nevertheless, one difference of opinion between these two authors underlies most architectural debates since. For J-N-L. Durand, the disposition of elements is judged for how it conforms to or offends established conventions; that is to say, the relation of whole to part is socially conceived and socially judged. For Hübsch, everything that isn't narrowly functional is merely a matter of artistic whim; both the normative and expressive aspects of physical language are, in Hübsch's mind, firmly in the domain of individuals and thus have limited value to society.

The information age retains Hübsch's worldview – the only deviation being our praise for non-social, non-communicative individualism. We exhibit lesser tendencies to invent than desires to reject unities, parse cultures, and distribute the remains to individuals – as if society at large is a burdensome dowry to be dragged about and shirked as soon as possible. Imagine the questions an architect or art critic from the Byzantine period might pose: "How did this information age arise? Why has it entailed a rejection of shared physical language? Why have unifying styles been replaced with adoration for personal histories and expressionism? Whose sovereignty is being defended in this shift from social order to proliferating and isolating subjectivities: the architects' or the inhabitants'?" If we answer the latter question with "both," then it would be reasonable for the Byzantine critic to ask what aspects of the lives of architects and inhabitants are protected through this rejection of order and shared meaning.

It is impossible to imagine all possible answers to these questions but it is a safe bet that most of the answers our visitor hears would fall under the nebulous heading of "freedom" and, more specifically, "freedom from authority (someone else's meaning)" or "freedom to be new" or "creative." In the realm of relationships between people or between people and institutional apparatuses this makes some sense. But what is 'freedom' in the relationship between made things and people? And why is this type of freedom inherently, or even contingently, good?[1] J-N-L. Durand's subtly negated such freedoms by asking questions of his own:

> But, some will say, would not architects and architecture suffer if the art were thus, to some degree, popularized? We do not think so; but, even supposing this to be true, either society is made for architecture and for architects, or architecture and architects are made for society: is there any man worthy of the name architect who can hesitate for one moment in this matter?[2]

Under Romantic Signs, Part One: Impediments

One of my earliest memories of undergraduate education is a debate in a course entitled "Introduction to Architecture;" we first-semester freshmen were to argue what creativity is and what its limits are. Always a contrarian, I took the position that pure creativity – the notion that ideas or things can emerge without precedent – is a myth; that creation *ex nihilo* is a divine fantasy at best. Today, I am a bit more reticent. While it is difficult to conceive a logical argument that would disprove the old sayings "no thing emerges from nothing" or "there is nothing new under the sun," it is also an exaggeration to state that every science and history and art evolves from another in a linear or logical sequence; there must have been at least one first science or first history or first art that emerged to fill an absence. In fact, there have probably been many such firsts. Furthermore, creativity is not simply the formation of something from nothing, but an activity that might be evidenced in the unique union of two or more existing things or ideas. One has to conjure only a few names (Brunelleschi or Borromini or Bernini, Einstein or Eisenstein or Eisenman) or call to mind a few projects of Baroque Moorish juxtaposition (Toledo Cathedral by Narciso Tomé or the Sacristy of the Charterhouse, Granada, by Luis de Arévalo and F. Manuel Vasquez) to verify this notion, though a long and varied list could easily be produced.

Yet these concessions – (1) that new ideas and things occasionally seem to spontaneously appear in the absence of obvious parentage; and (2) that creativity can be evinced in a unique union of given ideas – do nothing to support an information age rejection of shared meaning and physical language for the purpose of protecting freedom. In fact, the ease with which an extraordinary list of creative thinkers and makers can be made from histories of peoples ostensibly suffering

The *Précis* and the Paternity of Perception   **163**

under the oppression of others' ideas, combined with the near total absence of people who have invented ideas or objects without the backdrop of an existing episteme, suggests that the anti-authoritarian strain of the 'freedom to be creative' argument is invalid. Incorporating an arch into the design of a building, choosing to live in a building with Greek columns or not wincing at the sight of an obelisk does not suggest that a person is unaware of new construction technologies or new styles; none of these things makes one an authoritarian any more than avoiding all tradition makes one free. Arguably, the appropriate word is not "free" but "limited" – limited and largely unable to communicate.

Furthermore, a building's perceivers, users, and inhabitants are always going to feel and think according to their own (cultural, societal, familial) dispositions and inclinations despite the architect's best efforts to mold perception – as argued by Edward Sapir, Benjamin Lee Whorf, and others. To the extent that upbringing and genetics allow, humans subjected to architecture are always already free. Free in front of a Greek temple or Byzantine palace or Greg Lynn blob alike. A building cannot make one more or less free in any sense that honors the rich potential of that word. All an architect can hope is that inhabitants "get" it, "like" it, and find it beautiful or useful or, when the stars align, both.[3]

Why then is the absence of a shared physical language so often assumed, in our time and culture, to be good? Here, the common answer relies less on notions of freedom than authenticity. That is to say, not in defense of autonomy but an appeal to a Zeitgeist. "It is impossible to be true to self and the times if one is borrowing from another time," as one variant of the argument goes. Aspects of this argument are persuasive; and there are architectural educators who believe there is a moral impetus to privilege contemporary buildings and architects over those of the past in student travel and study. This attitude requires belief in a meta-time, in Truth as a quality of an ever-changing present. There is, however, a serious problem with this view. The three modes of knowing available to us – observation, documentation, and myth (or first person, second person, and third person experience, if you prefer) – are so intertwined as to be inseparable the further one attempts to look back toward origins.[4] For a Hübschian wandering through the built environment this means there is no easily verifiable measure of the relative distance from observation, documentation, and myth (as given in history) to 'reality' or 'truth' (as a condition of the present); as a result, if one is honest, all that is possible today is action undertaken in good faith – whatever such a subjective phrase means in an information age.

It would be nice if this last sentence was believed by the profession-at-large to be a complete and accurate response to the question, "what is 'freedom' in the relationship between made things and people?" However, it is clear that action undertaken in good faith is not the measure of 'free' information age practice. This is evidenced differently in today's major professional bifurcation: on one hand, by the avant-garde's tendencies to disavow immersion in history and to dismiss the possibility of shared physical language in the present; and, on the other, by the traditionalists' tendency to copy images of the past, wholesale or in part, with

164 Architecture History and Theory in Reverse

impunity.[5] But to act in good faith is not to prefigure the answer; and neither free-for-all-art-for-art's sake nor cheap image-draped sentimentality offers much promise of securing the fruits of faith, good or bad.[6]

The foregoing comments attempt to render visible the various escape routes by which the architectural profession avoids the search for shared meaning in the present: dedication to 'creativity' or uncommunicative newness, mimicry of inert no-longer-communicative pasts, substitution of technological innovation in lieu of the design of formed matter, and displacement of ideas embodied in things in favor of non-embodied and non-architectural content (such as, but not limited to, social justice and functionalism). So much effort is dedicated to these escape routes because their implicit biases are so deeply entrenched in education, practice, and criticism that mindfulness of their resultant disruptions – that is, conscious awareness of the ongoing project of proliferating western architectural languages – is often difficult. Despite this peculiar myopia, there are significant obstacles to shared physical languages; and these are dangerous because they are so difficult to see. In addition to those already noted, there are at least five impediments to a widely-shared, language of things – all of which, Durand argued against:

1. *Proliferating agendas*: the number and diversity of types of research that do not seem to share common threads with one another or earlier architectural traditions are growing. Although useful and perhaps necessary to the perpetuation of a profession, sustainability, parametric design, and design|build practices are activities that do not lend themselves to the formation of an integrated ground of shared meaning. While the inhabitants of an eco-village might draw a considerable portion of their identify from the knowledge that they live in a sustainable community, for instance, the meaning of this identity is tethered to an impermanent and relational difference – "*my* community is meaningful because it is does not waste energy like *your* community" – and will suffer diminution in lockstep with the hoped-for decline in such difference (i.e. when sustainable communities are the norm, inhabitants will have to look to other aspects of their community for meaning). In this example, meaning – or what passes for meaning, flees as it approaches ubiquity in the built environment; similar examples leading to the same conclusion could be drawn for other forms of research. This tendency may be called the obstacle of short-term goals which, arguably, spawn short-lived languages. Durand advocated for a cohesive agenda rooted in "fitness," "economy," "solidity," "salubrity," "commodity," and "disposition" – i.e. qualities that serve all buildings in all times and all places.[7]

2. *The cult of subjectivity*: the self-interests of those involved in these diverse research areas, their self-identification, and *our* identification of *them* all work to fragment the discipline. A quick glance at proposed session topics for upcoming architectural conferences and symposia clarifies the problem: here, the sustainability-focused will gather; there, the digital form-givers; somewhat near, the educators interested in integrated project delivery meet; way over

there, the serve-the-world through not-very-good but ultimately cheap-and-quick buildings crowd; and somewhere behind us, historians gather and compare subtle variations amongst the orders and note with bemusement the relative absence of the Corinthian in American architecture. Nowhere, it seems, are people meeting to acknowledge that these are all aspects of a larger and more important concern. This is the obstacle of self-interested, and perhaps self-serving, specialization. Durand argued against this in saying, "architecture is not the art of making a certain number of designs; it is the art of making all possible designs."[8] To this end he advocated conceiving the ensemble first to establish a clear idea for the relationship of parts.[9]

3. *Smooth v. striated, synchronic versus diachronic*: in Deleuze and Guattari's terms, smooth space is the domain of an actor operating in a pure present; striated space is the domain of epistemes through which a perceiver, cognizant of the past or anticipating the future or both, moves knowingly.[10] Experientially, smooth space is synchronic observation; striated space, diachronic narrativization. Though mixable and, arguably, ideal ends of a single continuum the differences between these modes are largely ignored and thus made all the more irreducible. Romantic architectural language, in order to be meaningful in immediate experience and to communicate across distances in time and space, acknowledged the human production of both types of space or, better stated, both types of relation between human and world. Durand puts the two timescales on relatively equal footing when he claims that forms and proportions are justified by both the synchronic "nature of things" and the diachronic "respect that we owe to ... the orders of the ancients and those imitated from them."[11] Unfortunately, subsequent scattered tribes of practitioners and educators have tended to practice one relation over the other; phenomenologists promoting smooth, synchronic space; formalists, greenies, and design-builders, the striated and diachronic. This scattering is a result of the obstacle of temporal bias.

4. *Ideational incompleteness*: no system of belief, no ideology, no history beyond the most simplistic, axiomatic or tautological, can be proven consistent and complete within the confines of that system or belief. In mathematics, this is a fundamental principle for which Kurt Gödel provided two theorems in 1931. In the humanities, verifiability requires testing from multiple perspectives and yet, as argued in Part I of this work, architectural educators, students, and critics are at least as resistant to submitting their thoughts to the rigors of alien ideology as the general public. Freedom and authenticity are assumed to necessitate an absenting of external validation. As a result, architectural research tends to produce self-fulfilling prophecies – and much self-assurance – that have more in common with religions than sciences. This is the obstacle of the limits of systems that Durand argued against in his condemnation of the "exclusive preference ... accorded to geometric drawing."[12]

5. *Observer effects*: much discussed in quantum mechanics, it has been shown that assertions regarding position and momentum always bear an inverse relation of

precision. According to the Sapir-Whorf hypothesis, language and knowing, their interplay, and subsequent understanding, also obey this principle and it is one that plagues all efforts at translation: one cannot speak of or write about a set of ideas without changing it – even to the point that the result of the conscious observation might legitimately be described as the invention of an entirely new phenomenon. Analogously, the fact that the concepts we use to render or describe architecture are borrowed and cannot be applied to the search for a unified physical language without altering the course of the latter is particularly damning. This is the obstacle of observational and translational uncertainty. Durand acknowledges this difficulty when he notes that architecture is often linked to other arts, particularly drawing, and is limited by them.

Of these five information age obstacles to shared meaning – short-term goals, specialization as identity, temporal bias, ideational incompleteness, and observational uncertainty – only this last and, arguably, most damning might also serve as a fulcrum across which to leverage Romantic possibilities. "Better still, in view of architecture's importance," Durand's suggestion for getting around this impediment goes, "let it be treated in accordance with its true principles."[13]

What are these true principles? Superficially, it is reasonable to assert that uncertainty is problematic only if there is an object or event being studied to which there is a responsibility to be true or represent accurately; in simple terms, if the task for the profession is to develop a physical language where one does not currently exist, then there is no condition in danger of being 'changed' through our pursuit. But this is a statement that remains utterly reasonable only from a semantic point of view and utterly meaningless to research and practice. The real positive potential of the last obstacle begins to become clear by noting that the attendant uncertainty of relation between language and concepts and things might be overcome via indirect observation. This idea, however, is simpler to write than to grasp. Allow me an example.

Discussing the ways in which the people of the Torah indirectly caused God to proclaim his sentience by investing themselves in the making of non-sentient idols and graven images, Elaine Scarry writes: "Though the people's making of idols always fails, their remaking of God and of themselves does not fail: the material statue is a tool or lever across whose surface they reach, repair, and refashion the primary Artifact."[14] While a full elucidation of Scarry's argument would take many pages, a restatement of the essential point is rather straightforward: by making an artifact (an idol or building) that purports to contain all the qualities of a greater thing (a deity or architectural language), the difference between the former and the latter comes forward as a new, fully present content in its own right. This observation necessitates a revision to an earlier statement: "A building cannot make one more or less free in any sense that honors the rich potential of that word" is not wholly true. A building, absent an architectural language through which buildings become architecture, cannot make one more or less free; but the passion induced in inhabitants or users or interested observers who try to join a given

The *Précis* and the Paternity of Perception **167**

building to its promise of language undergirds perceptions of all freedom and meaning in architecture. He or she or they change the words and thus his or her or their own behavior. This indirect observation is the ground on which all languages are built – and on which a search for physical language begins, despite the fact that there is nothing new …

Under Romantic Signs, Part Two: Ordering Passions

Language is created and controlled, inventive and narrowing, as has been argued by Humboldt and a host of thinkers since.[15] The rapid development and flourishing of Romantic language were a response to the relative dearth of language capable of communicating the breadth of human experience and was sustained by the pleasure of having so old and so powerful a need filled. At first jolt, every pang of passion is cryptic. At that first jolt, it is a pure sensation that might be termed "desire" or "passion" only in the incomplete sense that the first musician's part played without the second can be designated as "call and response:" a passion or desire fully deserving of either of those names is the combination of immediate sensory *call* and ideational *response* even if the latter is merely an awareness of a conceptual aspect of want or need that is not yet understood, not yet fully conscious, not yet heard.[16] That is,

$$\text{stimulus (sensation)} + \text{order (ideation)} = \text{Desire}$$

This is true even if the mental component is unknown or not-yet-deciphered:

$$\text{Given stimulus} + \text{unconscious but established order} = \text{experienced Desire}$$

Anyone who has given serious thought to the relation of passion and order understands this simple equation. To use a popular Romantic metaphor, the mind is a mirror of nature. Inside its frame, it is possible to perceive and make meaning of self and the self's relation to the world. In the mirror, language and moral codes emerge as a response to the call of the sensory apparatus. Languages, in this reading, are our attempts to steady the passions. They are comprised of conscious efforts and unconscious consequences that exert order on sensation. Underneath, there is only raw undifferentiated feeling.

Architecturally, consider John Ruskin's description of his experience upon entering the depths of St. Mark's in Venice (Figure 13.1):

> [A]nd here and there a ray or two from some far-away casement wanders into the darkness, and casts a narrow phosophoric stream upon the waves of marble that heave and fall in a thousand colours along the floor…and the glories round the heads of sculptured saints flash out upon us as we pass them, and sink again into the gloom. Under foot and over head, a continual succession of crowded imagery, one picture passing into another, as in a dream; forms beautiful and terrible mixed together; dragons and serpents, and ravening

beasts of prey, and graceful birds that in the midst of them drink from running fountains and feed from vases of crystal; the passions and the pleasures of human life symbolised [sic] together, and the mystery of its redemption; for the mazes of interwoven lines and changeful pictures lead always at last to the Cross, lifted and carved in every place and upon every stone ....[17]

Old and often entertaining stories such as this are neither myths nor dismissible as romantic reverie. Ruskin's description of St. Mark's interior strikes me as a measured and truthful account of an encounter that defied simple reporting; he tells his story from the perspective of a pilgrim making his way from innocence to enlightenment. This is worthy of respect and probably deserving of the moniker of "true" as far as it goes. Notice in the formula "stimulus (sensation) + order (ideation) = Desire," however, that an implied axis of time points in opposing directions: in one reading, running from sensory presence toward conceptual ordering, as in Ruskin's account; and, in the other, running from ideation back in time toward instantiating sensation. This is not a misreading of the formula.[18]

These reveries and formulas may seem trivial before noting that the passions acquire a name at the instant in time when sensory presence meets conceptual ordering regardless of which realm of activity – sensory or ideational – one encounters first. In the traditional reading given above, one proceeds from sensual to conceptual. In this order, before law and ontology, the name is the beginning – or the *call to* discourse. Yet, the reverse also leads to a result. Laws and ontologies and narratives conjoin to form the names of missing sensual input. It is even possible

FIGURE 13.1 St. Mark's Basilica, Venice, Domenico I Contarini architect
Source: Photograph by David C. Lewis.

to suggest that a succession of such names, forming figures or tropes of desire, act as triggers to prolonged sensory *want* in the absence of that last unsolved variable. What might appear as pseudo-mathematical pedantry reveals a rather useful fact: Language is both product, as sublimated desire, and constitutive of new desires.

Various arts have utilized this relationship for centuries. The power accorded Botticelli's "The Birth of Venus" in the fifteenth and sixteenth centuries, for example, is difficult to understand outside the framework described here; the physically absent sensual character of the goddess herself (portraying to various viewers "love" or "sex" or "female form") is made clear through the physically present representation of her form in a mythical scene. Nowhere is this technique used more effectively, however, than in literature. In few and relatively non-explicit terms, scenes of Bloom's cuckolding are made an object for the mind and simultaneously denied to the body in reading *Ulysses'* dream chapter. Very differently, de Sade unleashes such a torrent of words – an oeuvre of thousands of explicit descriptions – that the horrific physical acts described seem never to actually happen but, instead, are always on the verge of possibility. In philosophical terms, Georges Bataille called attention to this better than anyone, revealing the violent suspense across which desire and language stare in mutually amplifying stillness.[19]

Still, all of this may seem trivial, still a form of pedantry, until one considers the implication for architectural language. There is a tendency to conceive an upsurge of sensory impulse as a necessary prerequisite for a subsequent and supplementary naming of offences/writing of the laws which, together, ultimately ground full experiences of desire; most moral laws and taboos arise in this order. While it is possible that many forms of language have come into being in similar fashion, it is also possible that desires and passions for a physical language might come about as the result of language itself.[20] "For any art to be practiced with success, it must be practiced with relish, with love ..." Durand notes. He follows immediately, however, with words of admonition: "You cannot love what you do not know."[21] The stories we tell ourselves organize our experiences; cause us to seek similar experiences; which is to say, language might trigger the need or desire for physical form: the ideational might call forth the sensual.

The Paternity of Perception

In *The 120 Days of Sodom*, De Sade wrote, "There is a proverb – and what splendid things proverbs are – there is one, I say, which maintains that the appetite is restored by eating."[22] Desires are cyclical. Desires to see, to hear, to touch, to taste, and to smell are fueled by giving names to things seen, heard, touched, devoured, and inhaled. In a universe without empty space or, more accurately, in a universe in which space is dragged into existence by matter and language, the old mythologies of space-as-vessel or space as place in which matter is created and arranged are null and void. Space is brought into the world by the very matter it is understood to contain and acquires its identity as a 'place' or a 'vessel' only through the ordering processes of language. As existence precedes essence, matter precedes space even

170 Architecture History and Theory in Reverse

though the latter in both cases (essence and space) appears to most of us as a necessary precondition of the former.

Analogously, and as a result of similar mental habits, there is a tendency to conceive the three parts of the linguistic process – perceiving, naming, and judging – as occurring, always and by necessity, in that order. Many of us naïvely assume that matter emerges in once empty space; subsequently we perceive it, name it, and judge it. Thus, the presumed chain of events can be described as:

$$Space \rightarrow matter \leftrightarrow perception \rightarrow nomination \rightarrow judgment$$

Not only is this scientifically dubious, but architecturally speaking, there are dire consequences for believing this to be an accurate model of the accrual of human awareness from void to values. The probability that naming precedes seeing and other forms of perception has been raised several times in this work. Nevertheless, merely exchanging the positions of the words 'perception' and 'nomination' does not correct the above formulation for that modification would reduce the act of judging to an aftereffect, to some extent a casual result of perception. This is where the danger lies: naming and judging are related activities – but not in either order that the human mind tends to conjure. It could appear that nomination and judgment emerge together, in tandem; or that nomination precedes judgment by a small margin, as if on a long tandem bike; but neither is true. Judgment occurs first and gives birth to names.

No doubt this last statement sounds false in very obvious ways. Asked to describe my own interaction with things, I would have to admit that it *seems* I first perceive things (see, touch, etc.), then learn the appropriate nomenclature (understand its name and its classification in a larger episteme composed of similar things) then judge it as better or worse, more different or more similar, than others of its type. The force of this 'seeming' is the root of the problem. It motivated Romantic forays into language from Giambattista Vico, Johann Gottfried Herder, and Humboldt onward. In fact, the common sense acceptance of this 'seeming' is so pervasive that it is as if every act is conceived as coming from the body of an ignorant but noble savage learning to navigate through an alien world via a slow but continuous outward extension of self.[23] Perceptual psychologists have remarked upon the human body's capacity to extend its sentience through or across tools: we manage to navigate cars down the center of highway lanes while sitting hard pressed to one side of the interior; musicians acquire a familiarity with their instruments that borders on the awareness of one's own body; and then there are the prosthetic commonplaces of scissors, spectacles, pencils, and walking sticks.[24] This is true. It is a mistake, however, to extrapolate from this list and find in it proof of sensation (or perception) leading to information (or ideas). Bodily sensation spawns the urge, but only the urge, to make noise, to move, to act outwardly upon the world. Noises as language, moving as traveling, and marking as writing are named activities born into the world only through a process of conceptualizing the difference between mere reflexes or mere motor acts and acts of intention. No one

The *Précis* and the Paternity of Perception   **171**

attaches "mere" to intentional acts. No one takes a drive, plays music, cuts paper or cloth, corrects vision, makes marks on paper or canvas, or adopts an aid for walking without first judging these as possible actions to be taken and, more significantly, as actions in need or want of being taken. Perception emerges only as a result of such interactions conceived as a series of acts that could have been otherwise, or not at all. That is to say, it is only in the wake of understanding the impulse (to drive or play music, to cut a pattern or correct shortcomings in vision, to write or correct deficiencies in mobility), that one can perceive the act ('driving' or 'performing,' 'cutting' or 'seeing,' 'writing' or 'walking').

Thus, the common-sense formula might be re-written as in Figure 13.2.

Notice how Durand's three categories of forms and proportions – and even the order in which he addresses them – align with this formula (Figure 13.2): (1) "those that spring from the nature of materials, and form the uses of the things they serve;" (2) "those that custom has in a sense made necessary to us;" and (3) those "that earn our preference through the ease with which we apprehend them."[25] Still, in all probability, it remains unclear where the 'danger' lies even if the revised formulation makes sense. This can be clarified but only by understanding the relationships between various kinds of history and the gradual evolution of human awareness that this formulation entails (Figure 13.3).

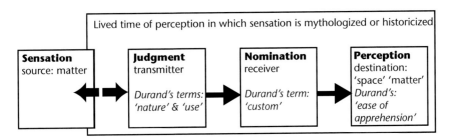

FIGURE 13.2   The birth of perception, version 1

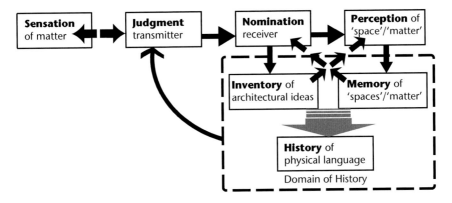

FIGURE 13.3   The birth of perception, version 2

172 Architecture History and Theory in Reverse

The history of space and the history of ideas are similar and related; and no doubt the established epistemes of 'space' and 'ideas' return to inflect the active processes of nomination and perception; but, all that being said, they are not identical. Like the familial relations among monarchies of medieval Europe, while their relationships are densely interwoven and difficult to tease apart, it would be a mistake to conflate the branches. As a child of two great lines, the histories of ideas and space, the history of physical language cannot be traced with certainty or in great detail. Even following the most careful reconstruction, the genealogy will not offer an explanation of the seemingly random appearances of meaning.

Where is the danger? From antiquity to the present, no method has been conceived to explain the history of physical language in a manner that is valuable beyond narrow specificities of time and place. Instead, we have histories. Attempts to trace a broader lineage run afoul of a base level contingency. Even studies of a single root form – the myriad treatises on the orders through time, for example – prove unhelpful. This led Hübsch to dismiss the orders and style completely. Call it the Babel contingency – the proliferation of histories of physical language all referencing their own unique and utterly contingent circumstances. Under the sway of Babel and subsequent Romantic digressions into naïve paternities, architecture is reduced to mere untranslatable matter. J-N-L. Durand saw past this and posited that architecture is an ensemble of forms that have been judged and named in advance – and in their presence, the possibility of a shared perception is born.

Notes

1 Increasing design "freedom" combined with a concomitant reduction in attention to meaning led John Ruskin to pine for "those days, I say, when there was something more to be anticipated and remembered in the first aspect of each successive halting-place, than a new arrangement of glass roofing and iron girder ..." See John Ruskin, *The Stones of Venice* (London: Folio Society, 2001), 123.

2 Jean-Nicolas-Louis Durand, *Précis of the Lectures on Architecture*, introduction by Antoine Picon, translation by David Britt (Los Angeles, CA: The Getty Research Institute, 2000), 201.

3 Political or religious freedom, the absence of an external authority that demands adherence, the freedom of any individual to participate or not, are freedoms of great – and hopefully self-evident – value. But protecting those freedoms is neither the same as nor in opposition to doing one's job. A politician who does not attend legislative votes or a preacher or rabbi who does not show up at the church or synagogue or temple is not practicing freedom so much as he or she is shirking responsibility. This is true likewise of an architect not engaged in the problems of shared physical language.

4 Biblical stories are an obvious and extreme example of this. Are these first-hand accounts, second hand descriptions, or oral traditions recorded long after the fact? Moving closer to the present does not necessarily improve our ability to distinguish. Consider Cook's accounts of Pacific islanders or Ruskin's observations of Venice; are these records of direct experiences, observations adjudicated through conversations with colleagues, or products of distant memories and reflections? It is almost always impossible to know.

5 These tendencies are not new to the discipline. Pevsner noted this in relation to the evolution of "Mannerism" and the "Baroque." See Nikolaus Pevsner, *An Outline of European Architecture*, Jubilee Edition (Baltimore, MD: Penguin, 1961), 383.

The *Précis* and the Paternity of Perception **173**

6 Even the roots of this bad faith are not new. That the related terms "creativity," "freedom," and "authenticity" are so often invoked to problematize a shared physical language and the value of architectural history is, in the end, simply another remnant of "seeing is forgetting the name of the thing one sees" thinking. Again, the assumption that *seeing* precedes or occurs in the absence of *saying* is problematic. To believe such is to imagine that we are real or complete or truly ourselves only when we are free of the "fictional," "disingenuous," and "foreign" element that is language and conceptual content. The consequences of this worldview are wide spread. It assumes a naïve flow of time and relation of mind and body; the disembodied observing mind is understood to respond just a little behind an unthinking observed body. Through these contortions of logic we are led to assume that all meaning and narrative content is an appliqué in relation to lived experience. The truth is undoubtedly more complicated. We are embedded in reciprocal webs, simultaneously observers and observed.

7 Durand, *Précis*, 88.

8 Ibid., 198.

9 Ibid., 131, 186 and 195.

10 See Chapter 14, "1440: The Smooth and the Striated," 474–500, in Gilles Deleuze and Félix Guattari, *A Thousand Plateaus: capitalism & schizophrenia*, translated by Brian Massumi (Minneapolis, MN: University of Minnesota Press, 1987). See also Chapter 12 of this book.

11 Durand, *Précis*, 111.

12 Ibid., 74.

13 Ibid., 127.

14 Elaine Scarry, *The Body in Pain* (New York: Oxford University Press, 1987), 233.

15 The psychologist Julian Jaynes claims: "Word changes are concept changes and concept changes are behavioral changes.... Without words like soul, liberty, or truth, the pageant of this human condition would have been filled with different roles, different climaxes." Julian Jaynes, *The Origins of Consciousness in the Breakdown of the Bicameral Mind* (Boston: Houghton Mifflin, 1976), 292. And Wilhelm von Humboldt wrote: "For however internal language may altogether be, it has at the same time an independent outer existence that exerts dominion against man himself." Wilhelm, Freiherr von Humboldt, *On Language: on the diversity of human language construction and its influence on the mental development of the human species*. Edited by Michael Losonsky and translated by Peter Heath. (Cambridge: Cambridge University Press, 1999), 28.

16 De Sade: "the blasphemy and the invitation…" Marquis de Sade's "The 120 Days of Sodom," in *The 120 Days of Sodom & Other Writings*, compiled and translated by Austryn Wainhouse and Richard Seaver, introductions by Simone de Beauvoir and Pierre Klossowski (New York: Grove Press, 1987), 518. James Joyce (via Stephen): "Near: far. Ineluctable modality of the visible." Joyce, *Ulysses* (New York: Vintage, 1990), 560.

17 Ruskin, *The Stones of Venice*, 150.

18 If the original equation is valid – "stimulus (sensation) plus order (ideation) equals Desire" – then all of the following are equally valid restatements:

> Conscious order (ideation) = known Desire – stimulus (sensation)
> Conscious order (ideation) – Desire = raw stimulus (sensation)
> Experienced Desire – raw stimulus = unconscious but established order

Although not math, and admittedly not really an equation, the analogical point is simple: as with any $x+y=z$ formula, the three variables of desire, ideation, and stimulus can be placed in any order; and, more importantly, it is relatively easy to solve for one missing variable.

19 Georges Bataille, *Eroticism: death & sensuality*, translated by Mary Dalwood (San Francisco, CA: City Lights, 1986). In particular, see Part Two, Chapters II and III, pp. 164–196.

20 This is the importance of Julian Jaynes' observation that "one of the essential properties of consciousness was the metaphor of time as a space that could be regionized such that

events and persons can be located therein, giving that sense of past, present, and future in which narratization is possible." Jaynes, *Origins of Consciousness*, 250.

21 Durand, *Précis*, 187.

22 De Sade, *Sodom*, 545.

23 This seeming clearly guided the thoughts of the early language theorists. For instance: "But if the question be considered in a purely conceptual fashion, we also assuredly do not go too far in making the general assumption, that every concept was originally designated by *one syllable* alone. In the invention of language, the concept is the *impression* made upon man by the *object*, either external or internal," Humboldt, *On Language*, 264.

24 "James Gibson calls attention to the at once startling and (once stated) wholly familiar fact that a person can literally 'feel' at the end of a walking stick the grass and stones that are three feet away from his hand, just as a person holding the handle of a scissors actually feels the 'cutting action' of the blades a few inches away." See Scarry, *The Body in Pain*, 248, as well as James J. Gibson's, *The Senses Considered as Perceptual Systems* (Boston: Houghton, 1966).

25 Durand, *Précis*, 108.

14

DE SADE VERSUS DESCARTES

Competing Conceptions of Language

For since nature seemed to cause me to lean towards many things from which reason repelled me, I did not believe that I should trust much to the teachings of nature.

(René Descartes, Meditations on First Philosophy*)*[1]

Why is it, Messieurs, the radiant creature inquired, that in this world there are men whose hearts have been so numbed, whose sentiments of honor and delicacy have been so deadened, that one sees them pleased and amused by what degraded and soils them? One is even led to suppose their joy can be mined nowhere save from the depths of opprobrium, that, for such men, delight cannot exist elsewhere save in what brings them into consort with dishonor and infamy. To what I am going now to recount to you, my Lords, to the various instances I shall lay before you in order to prove my assertion, do not reply, saying that 'tis physical sensation which is the foundation of these subsequent pleasures; I know, to be sure, physical sensation is involved herein, but be perfectly certain that it does not exist in some sort save thanks to the powerful support given it by moral sensation, and be sure as well that, were you to provide these individuals with the same physical sensation and to omit to join to it all that the moral may yield, you'd fail entirely to stir them.

(Marquis de Sade, The 120 Days of Sodom*)*[2]

A few years ago I had the pleasure of attending a lecture given by William Sharples, principal of SHoP Architects, New York. He began with a brief history of the firm's founding and the architectural currents then in vogue. There were at the time, he said, two options: one could be a "paper architect" (dealing primarily with concepts) or a "service architect" (making buildings for particular embodied uses).

176 Architecture History and Theory in Reverse

Within either of these realms, one had to choose between myriad '-isms' of style or content. According to Sharples, the problem with working under the typical models existing at the time of SHoP's founding was the inherent narrowness that follows and which, ultimately, requires a firm to redefine itself every decade or so if it is remain relevant or (what may amount to the same thing) "interesting."

Eschewing such easy classifications, Sharples and his partners opted for a Both/And response, merging conceptualization and physical making. There can be little doubt that the principals of SHoP have remained true to this unifying vision. There is honor in this approach and the resulting work is, more often than not, beautiful. In fact, there was nothing in the presentation deserving more than a mere quibbling "maybe you could have tried …" until the closing remarks.

As the last slide dimmed, Sharples announced that this form of practice – holistic integration of design, manufacturing, and construction – is the model for the future of the profession; he did not say "*a* model," he said "the." I wrote it down immediately. Arguably, an architect interested in Both/And thinking and abhorrent of narrowing or classifying agendas shouldn't talk like that. "But, hey," I told myself, "architects invited to lecture are expected to promote their process or solution as *the* process or solution." And, when speaking extemporaneously, we all use words we might replace if given time for reflection and the opportunity to edit. Nevertheless, alarm bells sounded that have just now quieted to the point that I understand what was really troubling in his use of "the": by and large, SHoP's practice has eliminated traditional concerns such as architectural language and architectural history itself as generative frameworks for form making (in fact, I suspect Sharples would cringe a little at the use of phrase "form making") in favor of concerns of *the* end – sustainability, constructability, sequencing, and costs. Is this it, I asked myself? Is "the" model for "the" future of architecture one that limits itself, almost exclusively, to a pragmatic hierarchy of specific ends over open-endedness? Of information over meaning? If so, it feels as if something is missing; something like trust in people to bridge gaps and resolve moments of uncertainty by importing or positing meaning for themselves; something like morals or character or authority have been discarded to foster a simplistic surface of completeness – though the terms "morals" and "character" and "authority" are too loaded to serve this purpose.

This contemporary anecdote may seem out-of-place in a backward narrative that has just looked at J-N-L. Durand and the *Précis*, and Hübsch and his famous question. And yet, the divide between concepts and use that Sharples and his colleagues have tried to bridge is a linguistic construct that witnessed its most extreme formulation in the two centuries prior to Hübsch and Durand's writings. On the side of concepts, René Descartes employed his *Meditations on First Philosophy* (1641) to free language and ideas from the shackles of matter and embodiment. This separation fostered not only bifurcations of mind and body, logic and emotion, or information and meaning.[3] Architecturally, it formed the wedge between space and place and asserted the primacy of the former's non-materiality.[4] On the side of use and embodied engagement, the Marquis de Sade wrote the equal and opposite response. His *The 120 Days of Sodom* (1785) is exemplary in this regard, providing a catalogue of perversions from which Cartesians, and in fact most of culture since, have fled into the purities of mind, logic and information. These two writers opened a gulf where a continuum once stood. Hübsch and Durand were close enough to its formation to straddle the two sides. Yet, as the rift grew, culture had to choose. And invariably it has clung to Descartes.

Immigrating to Space

That cities arose only after the development of agriculture is a popular myth. Jane Jacobs offered an analogy to explain its popularity. It was in cities, she argues, that research regarding electrical distribution and the actual technologies of the electrical grid were first developed and implemented. Over time cities evolved; they grew and pushed electrical production to the rural outskirts; and yet cities have come to rely on electricity to the point that, faced with a crisis that interrupts this steady stream of current, civic life devolves and chaos ensues. This reversal has altered our perspective. "If the memory of man did not run back to a time when the world had cities but no electricity," she concludes, "it would seem ... that use of electric power must have originated in the countryside and must have been a prerequisite to city life."[5] An analogous mistake has led us to believe that cities emerged from agriculture. And an analogous mistake has led us to believe that architecture begins with the positing of architectural space.

Our information age, the age of inconsequential meaning, celebrates *self* and its freedom from hierarchies, order, and the last vestiges of values accorded things. We are spatial now. The space race gave way to the space age which fractured into innumerable other spaces for innumerable Others. Cyber and virtual. Literary and polemical. Queer and gendered. There are spaces of tradition and identity and spaces that are blurred or hybridized. There are personal spaces and protest spaces: spaces to clear our heads and spaces in which to voice our dissent. Spaces are contested, memorialized, made sacred. And amid all of this physical absence, this literal nothingness – "So much nothing that you would not even be conscious that there was nothing there"[6] – spaces are claimed, nationalized, trespassed and fought over.

Given such a world, it is inappropriate – and not particularly useful – to shake one's head at the strangeness of it all. Nor will it suffice to argue that architecture might better serve communities and the sharing of values by giving up the incertitude of the void and returning to the language of matter.[7] We teach, write and think in an age in which not only the answer but the process of its discovery is presumed to be spatial. Talk of reestablishing 'physical language' can only appear as retrograde conservatism. Thus, as Jacobs called for an acknowledgment of the city's role in both the agricultural and electrical revolutions, it is important to understand that the evolution of our information-oriented, inherently spatial age has origins in earlier myth-oriented, non-spatial identities.

The problem can be summarized in a single question: How is it that space became the place of our thought to the point of seeming our native home?

178 Architecture History and Theory in Reverse

Admittedly, that single question contains two parts: immigration and naturalization, so to speak. But, at root, both parts find resolution in a single and relatively short answer. This answer begins with a well-known whipping boy; first name, René.

Descartes conceived body and mind – and, as extrapolated by others, spatial extension and thought – as dualistic co-identities connected in problematic ways, but wholly distinct in character, order, and appropriate methods (and relative certainty) of measurement. As a consequence of nearly four hundred years of subsequent deliberation based on those dualistic assumptions, the body–mind split was more or less reified as an ontological given. The only significant shift that has occurred since, and contrary to, Descartes is a recent and general tendency to double the bifurcation: the body, on one hand, is divided into objective "matter" and subjective "spatial extension" (together referred to as "the body in space"); the mind, on the other hand, is divided into repositories for received impersonal ideation or epistemes and internally generated personal narratives or stories. Subsequently, subjective components of both body and mind (personal space and narrative) are privileged over both objective matter and socially generated ideas/ epistemes. As a result, ideation and language (as non-spatial aspects of bifurcated humanity) are subordinate and must be conceived as appended to space in order to "have a voice" or attain "presence" sufficient for study.[8]

The preceding is a short answer to the question of how space became the place of thought. Yet it is incomplete insofar as it does not touch upon the assumptions inherited by Descartes and upon which he so easily separated mind from body. These can be divided into two types; those assumptions resulting from philosophy's deep legacy and those derived from Renaissance methodologies. The former, beginning in sixth century BC Greece and the separation of *psyche* (or soul) from *soma* (body), is beyond the scope of this work.[9] The sway of the Renaissance, however, is directly in the purview of a work on the evolution of western architectural language. Most writers of the Renaissance assumed that observed differences in order and measurement between two things are indicative of deeper ontological distinctions that ground the search for similitude and difference equally. This is arguably not the case. Comparisons of order and measurement only ostensibly allow for a finding of similitude or unity. In fact, such comparisons must presuppose difference from the start in order for differences to be observed. And, of course, perceptions of differences in order are always already intuitions of differences in measure.

What may seem like a semantic triviality turns out to be crucial to future conceptions of architecture. The traditional "order and measurement" assumption fosters a much more widespread and still-active corollary: observed – largely self-prophesized and self-fulfilling – differences between spatial extension and ideation impose their lineage of differences on the activities and products of each. The character of mental activity *per se* (an ideal design process, for example) is assumed to be of a different nature from mental work conducted in space (a specific design process in a particular space). It is this corollary of comparative thinking – which predates Descartes – that is truly the familial source of our sense of entitlement to a spatial inheritance.

This makes sense. In fact, it is so unproblematic that we might call it commonsense. But, as Jane Jacobs' analogy highlights, the seeming naturalness of the argument lulls us into easy conformity and highlights the depth of our indoctrination. One question might destroy this naturalness: from where does a space, any space, derive its character by which it becomes capable of influencing mental activity? Biologically, it is commonly accepted today that 'character' is not purely inherited from a progenitor. Philosophically, the character of a thing is the interaction of the thing's brute physical existence and the manner in which it is known – e.g. its configuration in the mental processes of a perceiver. Read more closely, the dualism of Descartes gives way to a tripartite condition in which matter and minds intersect in an always-charged (contextualized, mythologized) viscous sphere. Space is at best a resultant phenomenon of character and not the reverse.

This does not answer significant questions of where we could or should go from here. It does not help us deal with the spatial, post-meaning age. Big questions loom. What is thought or design thinking outside the strictures of spatial thinking? The seeming impenetrability of post-spatial thinking is a result of both the normal blind spots that every accepted historical framework imposes and our peculiar obsession with identity politics and spatialized difference. Unfortunately, identity through difference is merely the other side of similitude – neither very useful in the future we face. In order to make sense of these questions, we must become very uncomfortable with our inheritance.

The 120 Days of Sodom

> Vile. Repugnant.
> Unrewarding. Without aesthetic merit. Destructive of moral certitude.
> Disgusting.

Many today ask a question that critics have asked for decades – why read de Sade? – and, in preemptive response, mime the descriptions above as a litany of complaints justifying distance if not outright censorship.[10] Yet those descriptions along with that oft-repeated question belong to a constellation of descriptions and questions that should not be understood to cast doubt on the wisdom of reading de Sade but, instead, shed light onto his pivotal role in expanding language in the late Romantic period. There are better questions to ask regarding de Sade: Who was this person who catalogued and, at times, arguably, invented the sexual and homicidal atrocities recorded in *The 120 Days of Sodom*, thereby opening the frontier of modern literature? And – more important from the perspective of physical language – how did he overcome the subservience of signs to resemblance that tends to render the former as always and only markers for a non-present and, at times, non-existent presence? To borrow Elaine Scarry's language, how did de Sade achieve the greatest feat any artist can attempt, "the making real of the counterfactual," despite his use of flat characters, a near absent plot, and tortures extreme to the point of ridiculousness?[11] That we can ask such questions relative to *The 120 Days of Sodom*

180 Architecture History and Theory in Reverse

is a partial answer to the question, 'why read de Sade?'. Add to these the insights that might be gleaned on questions posed above – What is "post-spatial" design thinking? What is thought outside the strictures of spatial thinking? And, critically, how can such thought be communicative? – and the purpose of taking this short detour through de Sade seems less perverse and less a detour.

Consider first the breadth of content toward which the libertine's work was aimed. If *The 120 Days of Sodom's* flat characters and their horrific actions were nothing but rhetorical insults hurled at the contemporary mores of polite French society, as has been suggested by some critics, it would be easy to ask how this simplistic act does not reflect on its author and serve to diminish the lasting value of his oeuvre to later generations and other cultures. But the work is neither a collection of insults nor so narrowly aimed. The real target is the social sensibility of happiness promoted in and epitomized by Rousseau's contemporaneous writings. That our information age inherited the latter's worldview in the form of the social contract is perhaps the primary reason de Sade's work remains compelling; it is an equal and opposite path not taken – an ostensibly unwanted but nevertheless necessary Moriarty to our heroic Holmes … or, Satan to Savior.

De Sade has his four libertines debate an essential issue of the social contract toward the end of Part One of *The 120 Days*: "what need has man for sensibility? and is it or is it not useful to his happiness?"[12] These questions have architectural import. Space and spatial thinking in recent architectural discourse are presented as akin to pure sensibility; a form of animal hunting ground for the capture of experience. Already much discussed in the preceding pages, spatial thinking is a quasi-moral point of view cloaking the incertitude of the void – space as mere zone for all possible hunts – and indoctrinated into young designers as an intentional state, space can be good or bad; right or wrong; warm or cool; but neutrality or ambivalence is judged a failure. Due to the underlying framework of Descartes' primacy of self and Rousseau's social sensibility, information age spatial thinking is often a mix of Christian individualist morality and the Enlightenment's recasting of it in social terms; of the inner sensibility of the solipsistic space of "seeing is forgetting" with the altruistic hopefulness for democratic space attached to every community project.

De Sade's libertines simultaneously cast doubt on both levels of the social contract. In part, these characters are almost certainly the author's straightforward attempts at similitude, emulations of himself and his most vile desires as some critics assert.[13] But this is neither simple nor the extent of the action de Sade undertakes. Prescient of the impending multiplication of spaces in the West – starting with the Christian–Enlightenment bifurcation and sped along with their political recombination in the space of Rousseau's contract – de Sade redoubles the problems of the body, of sentience, of the direct interactions of bodies and the denial of interactions; this last problem being, perhaps, the most profound. As he has Durcet respond: "How can you be happy if you are able constantly to satisfy yourself? It is not in desire's consummation happiness consists, but in the desire itself, in hurdling the obstacles placed before what one wishes."[14] Desire's magnification is not couched in distance (in space) but in obstacles (in matter and adversaries). The world of de Sade is always and explicitly a material one – even if only imagined.[15]

Why does de Sade bother us so much? It is just a litany of degraded thoughts from a demented mind, right? Movements to burn or ban or, at the very least, shun the work make clear de Sade's success in making real the counterfactual. It is said that the magician's greatest trick is always, and only, the appearance of himself. The most stunning achievement of *The 120 Days* is, through its pages, one encounters its simultaneous and inherently contradictory presences as pure (and often impossible) fictions that are nevertheless insistently material (and believable) and these seem to stand as a true portrait of its author (as a record of his mind). That he achieves and simultaneously perpetuates these internally inconsistent conditions is worthy of note. How he does it, and how this effect is felt even in an information age society, is critical.

In language, whether physical or literary, technique matters. Linguists, philosophers, and psychologists have remarked on an *as-if* prerequisite for communication: the positing of a counterfactual identity for whom "we suspend our own identities," and, Jaynes argues, in "that brief second of dawdling identity is the nature of understanding language."[16] Consider this from *The 120 Days*: "Tis now your turn, I have done, and I would but beseech Messieurs to have the kindness to forgive me if I have perchance bored them in any wise, for there is an almost unavoidable monotony in the recital of such anecdotes;" De Sade has Duclos apologize for him from within the text, "all compounded, fitted into the same framework, they lose the luster that is theirs as independent happenings."[17] This is more than a mere rhetorical device. It is almost a form of antinomy; in effect, Duclos is saying: *I must be recounting to you a series of real happenings because, were these mere fictions, I would have recounted things far more life-like.* Truth, or the appearance of truth as a form of presence, accrues as layers of retellings accumulate. When we question the validity of any individual actor or speaker or thing, the meta-actor or speaker who retells or re-enacts the original scene rescues his or her or its facticity. If that narrator is suspect, aspects of her story are corroborated and elaborated by the next narrator. The most powerful affect of this technique is the strange vibration of truth that occurs in the text which forces the reader to oscillate between faithful attendance to the narrators within the text and belief in the existence of its author as a real and whole being outside the text. Only at first glance is *The 120 Days of Sodom* simply a listing of perversions of a disturbed but unquestionably real mind. At second glance, the book is a record of, and battle against, betrayals of identity the author himself suffered. De Sade's technique of retellings narrates a world into existence by prompting an oscillation between his identity, our identities, and an invented and formative one (the as-if) that floats in between.

The 'As-if' Prerequisite

Contemporary architectural discourse, if it is to reveal ideas that might re-engage the borders of literacy and foster a renewal of physical language, can be framed in two ways: (1) analysis of the physical representation of an idea or intended meaning (indication); or (2) analysis of the explicit and implicit meanings behind a representation (denotation and connotation). The difference may seem subtle at first; in fact, the inherent split contained within the second frame – the difference between denotative and connotative meanings – is easier to grasp and, as a result, more often discussed. Nevertheless, the differences between the forms of discourse identified here are significant, and in some ways more significant due to their subtlety. Studies of indication investigate things as carriers of ideas; studies of denotation and connotation focus on the ideas that things might represent or imply via semblance. Arguably, in architectural criticism of extant works, whether realized or theoretical, it makes little difference which frame one chooses; it matters only that some of each is practiced so that the profession does not forget that there are two approaches to the relationship of meanings and things. While sitting at drawing boards, however, facing computer monitors and sheets of cardboard – while sitting, in other words, at the precipice of a project's potential, the choice matters. In social terms, it may be the most important choice.

The potency of this choice has been mined for a few centuries in literature. Forget *The 120 Days of Sodom* as an extant artifact. Instead, imagine de Sade in the act of composition. Was his motive primarily (1) indication or (2) signification? In an absolute sense, it is an unanswerable question for it requires insights into the psyche of a man two centuries dead. And, in the absence of an absolute answer, even a provisional answer appears shrouded by inherent contradictions.[18] Yet, there are aspects of de Sade's intentions that are objective enough to study without plumbing the depths of his mind.

The Marquis is known to have held strong views on forms of government, hierarchies in society, and the oppressive tendencies of religions. That he wrote on the perversities of individual actions – both sexual and criminal – primarily as a way of engaging, exposing, and challenging those oppressive tendencies is evident. What is less clear, and perhaps for that reason more effective, is de Sade's tethering of physical representation (textual descriptions of horrific physical acts) to imaginary conditions of meaning (limitations on horrific physical acts as an impingement on existential freedom) while the actual context outside the novel (the contemporary French socio-economic system) is presented as merely a contingent reality. In other words, de Sade's essential beliefs enter the context of the novel only through Trojan rhetorical techniques involving grotesque but utterly physical imagery and imaginary moral systems that only pretend to justify the former. In the blatant and over-the-top combination of physicality and immorality, the cumulative weight of very different but equally offensive inequalities that de Sade perceives in society slip stealthily into the heart of the novel and, ideally, into the mind of the reader in that brief second of dawdling identity.

As a technician, then, de Sade was profoundly concerned with the ways in which matter (or material imagery) can be used to convey content that is wholly other than the representation suggests. Some might question whether the deeper content is successfully engaged or condemn de Sade for leaving us only *as-if* constructs as the meaning of his work.[19] Descartes would almost certainly have castigated such constructs as "confused modes of thought" produced by the "*apparent* intermingling of mind and body."[20] Descartes' denigration of the body and its value to thought would have rendered such as-if constructs abhorrent to him and, worse, all who have chosen his side of the divide. Fortunately, a few have chosen otherwise. De Sade prefigures the great post-Romantic stylists, authors like García-Marquéz and Rushdie, who hold strong beliefs and yet know that what matters more than meaning is the sensation of the representation itself, its *as-if* existence.

This pursuit of meaning via as-if constructs did not originate with literature or the Romantic period. Seven hundred years before de Sade, the builders of St. Mark's Basilica, Venice, practiced a similar technique. If it is pardonable to compare the austere simplicity of the standard Romanesque church with the moral rectitude of Rousseau, then St. Mark's is a de Sadian effusion of feints, starts, ostensible concealments of spatial relationships[21] that are, in fact, direct expressions of formal relationships that inspire awe – deception in the service of enriched experience, perhaps. A viscous proliferation of gold and mosaic surfaces and blendings of cultural references, East and West, palimpsested across time hides the physical church of St. Mark's in plain sight and proffers, instead, an impression that deeper and mysterious meanings are available to those willing to immerse themselves in the place. In this regard, Ruskin was the building's greatest devotee. He and others who have come under its sway have experienced the "pause of unknowingness," to borrow a phrase from Jaynes, which is crucial for the activation of consciousness.

Bastille to Venice, the above is a lost approach to architectural representation that grounds shared experience. Many criticisms of Modernity's highly prescribed forms of meaning were, no doubt, correct; and arguably there are reasons to fear the solipsism and puppetry of more recent phenomenological and sustainable agendas. And yet, the general sense of physical language, the impression that all this *might* mean something, is the content of a language of hope that, if there is purpose in the architectural profession, cannot be allowed to disappear.

Romantic Coda

De Sade's most brilliant discernment was the necessary play of life (experience, action, libertinage) across, and even against, a given episteme (accumulated codes, ethics, and honors).[22] All meaning and perception of quality arises, for de Sade, in the friction produced between messy action and purities of the mind. Architects cling a little too closely to Descartes instead – for whom the senses are useful only for detecting what is "beneficial or hurtful."[23] Cartesian episteme frame every architect's actions and each perceiving subject's experience. Against this datum, random sensations come to be seen as merely positive or negative, as perversions from the world as given. From such a perspective, too much, almost everything gets left out.

As pursued in the seventeenth and eighteenth centuries, the systemization of European architectural history in various treatises was such that, by arbitrarily

184 Architecture History and Theory in Reverse

eliminating strong identities and differences, the well-read inhabitant or experiencing subject arguably conceived each new work of architecture only as a deviation from the pure possibilities of an ideal type. The experiential remainder was termed "character" – understood more or less as a neutral term.[24] No doubt Pöppelmann's gate pavilion and Balthasar Neumann's Pilgrimage Church at Vierzehnheiligen stand in such strong relief from the stratum of fossilized works produced in the eighteenth century because these works flout the narrowing classifications of Cartesian thought. In these works, a Sadian quest for authorization and meaning is evident.

Thus, the criticism directed at William Sharples and SHoP, at the outset. THE model of integrated design-build feels like a loss when viewed in the context of an evolutionary and Sadian history. Against the backdrop of a truly Both-And perspective in which architecture is conceived as mind and body, concept and form, meaning and sensation, poetics and pragmatics, language that is both paratactic and conjunctive, and as an interior and an exterior irreducible to one another, any model which pretends to be THE model must be understood as a retrograde proposal. In Cartesian history, in seventeenth- and eighteenth-century architectural history as well as contemporary myths of the existence of any system that might serve as THE model of a profession, entropy goes unnoticed because it is perceived in such systems, good or bad, as simply the resulting "character." In THE integrated design-build model, whether of SHoP and of others, something is cast out of the process that, far from feeling like character, seems more like a yawning void, an absence. It is an absence of language; an absence of complex but competing concerns; an absence of non-end-oriented laws; or, if you prefer, an absence of content that is sharable without recourse to an understanding of how something is made or what it might do to or for the environment (or a client's pocketbook).

Notes

1 René Descartes, "Meditations on First Philosophy" (1641; Internet Encyclopedia of Philosophy, 1996), from *The Philosophical Works of Descartes* (Cambridge: Cambridge University Press, 1911), translated by Elizabeth S. Haldane, available at: http://selfpace. uconn.edu/class/percep/DescartesMeditations.pdf, 28

2 Marquis de Sade's "The 120 Days of Sodom," in *The 120 Days of Sodom & Other Writings*, compiled and translated by Austryn Wainhouse and Richard Seaver, introductions by Simone de Beauvoir and Pierre Klossowski (New York: Grove Press, 1987), 492.

3 Numerous writers in multiple fields have documented these separations and their outcomes. The seminal work, however, remains neurologist Antonio R. Damasio's *Descartes Error: emotion, reason, and the human brain* (New York: Avon Books, 1994). Damasio speculates that the, "Cartesian idea of a disembodied mind may well have been the source, by the middle of the twentieth century, for the metaphor of mind as software program," (p. 250) with all the attendant difficulties such a view poses.

4 Alberto Pérez-Gómez's *Attunement: architectural meaning after the crisis of modern science* (Cambridge, MA: MIT Press, 2016), offers one of the most recent and well-articulated versions of this argument.

5 Jane Jacobs, *The Economy of Cities* (New York: Vintage Books, 1970), 48.

De Sade versus Descartes   185

6 Jaynes is referring to literal blind spots in our visual field masked by the interaction, or lack thereof, of the brain's hemispheres. See Julian Jaynes, *The Origins of Consciousness in the Breakdown of the Bicameral Mind* (Boston: Houghton Mifflin, 1976), 114.

7 Like the terrified inhabitants of a fossil fuel world facing a post-petroleum future, it is doubtful that inhabitants of the spatial age can comprehend such a suggestion unless that community's identity is rooted in unusually strong connections to some fixed material identity; and there are surprisingly few Arcosantis.

8 If this seems a caricature, review conference themes from a variety of academic disciplines: non-personalized forms of thought now reside in space as immigrants, as trespassing aliens; the debates, when they occur, seldom focus on the appropriateness of these hierarchies or even the veracity of either split (mind v. body; objective v. subjective) but, instead, attempt to distinguish between those thoughts that inhabit space legally and those that should be deported from beloved spaces as potentially authoritarian or corrupting.

9 See Jaynes, *Origins of Consciousness*, Book II, Chapter 5, "The Intellectual Consciousness of Greece," particularly pp. 290–291. See also Indra Kagis McEwen's *Socrates' Ancestor: an essay on architectural beginnings* (Cambridge, MA: MIT Press, 1993), and the distinction between the live body and the dead, *chrōs* versus *soma*.

10 The French government considered destroying the manuscript as recently as 1955.

11 The phrase is borrowed from *The Body in Pain*; Scarry's analysis of this alchemic transformation in the rhetoric of liability trials is compelling; see 298–299. Elaine Scarry, *The Body in Pain: the making and unmaking of the world* (New York: Oxford University Press, 1987).

12 De Sade, *Sodom*, 544.

13 The suggestion that *The 120 Days* is nothing but a listing of de Sade's own wishes is derogatory only from within the dominant ethical sphere of the social contract or one of the myriad sub-spheres of moral and political space that have evolved since.

14 De Sade, *Sodom*, 361–362.

15 "It may be that the significance of de Sade lies in his terrible loquacity, in his forced outpouring of millions of words. In part, the genesis of sadism could be linguistic…" as George Steiner says, "[De Sade] verbalizes life to an extreme degree by carrying out on living beings the totality of his articulate fantasies." See George Steiner, *After Babel* (New York: Oxford University Press, 1975), 40. James Joyce stated this in a more literary fashion; see *Ulysses* (New York: Vintage, 1990), 701.

16 Jaynes, *Origins of Consciousness*, 97. See also: George Steiner, "Hypotheticals, 'imaginaries', conditionals, the syntax of counter-factuality and contingency may well be the generative centres of human speech," *After Babel*, 215; and Paul Ricoeur, "The symbol gives rise to thought," *Philosophie de la Volonté, Tome 2: Finitude to Culpabilité: La Symbolique du Mal* (Paris: Aubier, 1960), 323, quoted in Charles Taylor, *The Language Animal*, 299. Charles Taylor, *The Language Animal: the full shape of the human linguistic capacity* (Cambridge, MA: Belknap Press/Harvard University, 2016).

17 De Sade, *Sodom*, 568.

18 Even editors Wainhouse and Seaver note in their Foreword to *The 120 Days of Sodom* (xi) that:

> We alluded to the difficulty when we spoke of the two designs corresponding to two drives: to write in order to be read, and to write unreadably, in such a way as to preclude being read, and in answer to a very different but equally real purpose. To be known, and to be unknown; to divulge, and to conceal. To reintegrate society and broad daylight, and to hold to his cell, immuring himself in the night. Sade wanted both, and both at once.

19 If this seems a failure, however, a review of the myriad self-help and do-it-yourself books available today in which there is an explicit one-to-one correlation of representation to meaning makes clear we could do worse than de Sade.

186 Architecture History and Theory in Reverse

20 Descartes, *Meditations on First Philosophy*, 29. Italics added.
21 In this, even Pevsner is fooled by misdirection. See Nikolaus Pevsner, *An Outline of European Architecture*, Jubilee Edition (Baltimore, MD: Penguin, 1961), 117.
22 Umberto Eco quotes Benedetto Croce – "every true work of art has violated an established genre" – and rejoins him saying, "the very fact that Croce realizes it merely highlights the role played by his awareness of genre and his expectations and suspicions of it in generating his surprise and his positive judgment of taste." See Umberto Eco, *From the Tree to the Labyrinth: historical studies on the sign and interpretation*, translated by Anthony Oldcorn (Cambridge, MA: Harvard University Press, 2014), 539.
23 Descartes, *Meditations on First Philosophy*, 30.
24 This aspect of seventeenth- and eighteenth-century architectural history was rooted in a more general methodological approach to knowledge common in Europe at the time; but there is a difference: the approach pursued through the sciences was subtractive but only in its initial set selection. According to Foucault, after the first reductive act, the method led the fields of biology, linguistics, and economics to multiply identities and differences in order to create a tabular field of all possible entities and types. To its detriment, seventeenth- and eighteenth-century architectural history – and, as a consequence, the architectural experiences it underwrote – seldom took this step.

15
THE TENSE OF ABSTRACT NOUNS

We reach, finally, a Classical Age, at the birth of its second incarnation, and the publication of Leon Battista Alberti's *De Re Aedificatoria* (1486). Preceded by Vitruvius nearly 1500 years earlier and superseded by Andrea Palladio and his *I Quattro Libri dell'Architettura* less than 90 years later, it is easy to overlook Alberti's advocacy for architectural meaning. What distinguishes his thought from the conceptual migrations inspired by Descartes, the instrumentalities of Hübsch, and present-day infatuations with expressive and service-oriented architecture, is the shift from *Being* and nouns and presence as the media of shared meaning in the fifteenth century to *doing* and verbs and space as mechanisms of information transmission in the years that followed. And yet, this vast accumulation of time and texts hides as much as it reveals. Our enculturation obscures the value of naming to perception, abstract nouns to engagement, and the relations of grammar to time and image to tense. In order to understand architecture as it existed for Alberti as well as his contemporaries and predecessors, we must dismantle these information age blinkers.

Naming

> Plato also gives some useful advice: a grand name will lend a place great dignity and authority.
>
> *(Leon Battista Alberti,* On the Art of Building in Ten Books, *VI, 4)*[1]

From our vantage point, it appears that the need to act and the words necessary to describe those actions precede names. Nouns are the bastard results of the intense promiscuity of verbs. The indiscrete acts of verbs, to turn that sentence around, proliferate nouns. It is in this sense that art critic John Berger was correct in his now classic assessment, "Seeing comes before words." He missed only the subtle distinction between seeing as a purely physical reaction to light stimuli – that is, unconscious or semi-conscious vision (sensation) – and seeing as an intentional act aimed at recognizing, establishing or understanding – i.e. conscious looking (perception). His statement is undoubtedly true in the former sense but, given that he spends the remainder of *Ways of Seeing* analyzing "seeing" as perception, it is more than a little misleading.[2] A more apt expression might take the form: "sensation comes before naming which, in turn, precedes perception." Admittedly more cumbersome, this expanded statement allows designers and critics to shed a host of mysteries. Sensations are personal by definition, intensely private, and incapable of being shared even if one were inclined to try. Perceptions are collective. They are based on episteme that undergird naming, and, for that reason, are capable of being communicated.[3]

Berger lays out the real challenge to the establishment of physical language and the entailed potential for the "socialization of sentience"[4] four sentences after his opening salvo:

> The relation between what we see and what we know is never settled. Each evening we *see* the sun set. We *know* that the earth is turning away from it. Yet the knowledge, the explanation, never quite fits the sight.[5]

Written in the format of Figure 15.1, the conceptual dissonance between seeing and knowing that Berger describes is not mysterious: there is considerable cognitive activity separating the terms. Communicative experience clearly lies with the latter even if, by "communicative," nothing more is intended than the shared meaning of holding a loved one's hand and watching a sunset. Between sensation and meaningful experience we encounter another form of the Babel contingency – a translation gap between the personal and the social. Between our first fledgling judgments made in response to sensory input and the full-fledged experience of places and events accrued with maturity, the human faculty of naming serves as a lynchpin.

Naming is not a limitation or diminution of subjective consciousness – as *seeing is forgetting* and other modern rhetoric implies – but both its founding action and its resulting product. Naming is proof of consciousness (Figure 15.2). Obviously, this

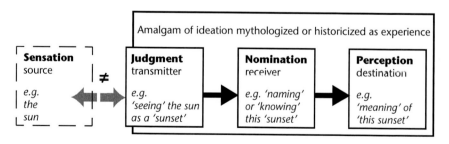

FIGURE 15.1   Seeing versus knowing

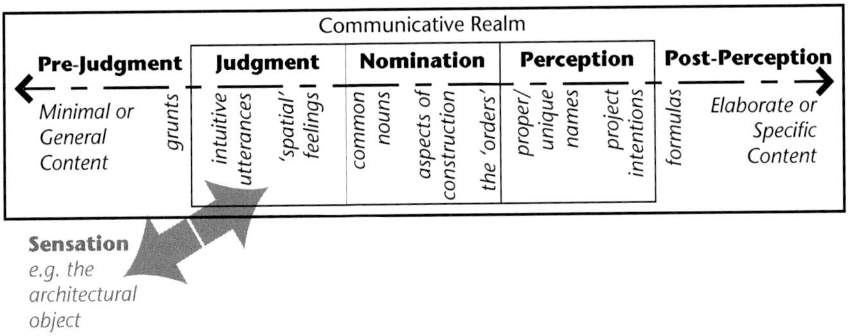

The Tense of Abstract Nouns **189**

FIGURE 15.2 Naming

activity takes many forms, from the (imagined) grunts of cavemen (meaning, perhaps, "pretty light") to common nouns ("sun") to proper or unique nouns designating particular examples of formed matter in context ("the Dublin sunset of 16 June 1904"). This vast range of specificity is crucial to our ability to dwell and can be plotted across the same continuum that separates seeing from perceiving.

The near synonymous character of heightened perception and sharpened communicative specificity should be clear: simply put, it is hard to perceive a generality.[6] We see, touch, taste, hear, and smell specific things. The identification of brute sensation, which is personal and private, even solipsistic, with a very general level of understanding is more difficult to understand at first blush. Our most intense and personal sensations, such as pain, certainly seem specific. But the change measured from left to right in Figure 15.2 is that of communicative potential. Of pain, one is able to say little, maybe nothing that truly conveys its content; in the very best of circumstances, one *locates* the feeling ("I hurt here") and, in the worst of times, is *reduced* to incommunicative grunts or moans. Love, by the way and to give it equal space here, does not fare much better in monologues or literature – we tend to stalk it, tangentially, circling a sensual center that our beloved can never exactly understand.

By contrast to the sensations of pain and love, perceptions gain clarity with specificity ("*this* is the reddest spring sunset I have ever seen"). Signification increases with the addition of representative values. At a glance, none of this is particularly controversial. Read carefully, however, the above entails an unexpected outcome: the addition of names does not increase the separation between seeing and knowing but instead acts to overcome the inaccessible contingencies of individuals. Naming does not limit meaningful experience but grounds its possibility. If I turn to my wife and say, "*This* is the reddest spring sunset I have ever seen over the Mississippi River," I am certainly not conveying a perfect correspondence to sensory input. She can look and take in the sensory content herself. What I have done instead is provide her with a framed image, a tether to my mind, into how I perceive the scene before me. Through this linkage, meaning – a sense of what is at stake – is created.

190 Architecture History and Theory in Reverse

We are now in a position to see fifteenth-century architecture – and communicative physical language in general – more clearly. Artifacts and the design processes that produce them are linguistic. This is not Enlightenment rhetoric but an acknowledgment that cultural artifacts and design processes are, along with the elaboration of written and spoken languages, acts of human differentiation aimed at increasing specificity. An act of judgment or informal classification is the source of names, artifacts, and processes.[7] Physical language is an amalgam of these judgmental traces, particularly the last two, but does not coincide perfectly with any one of them. It is in this sense that Leon Battista Alberti defined beauty as "the harmony and concord of all the parts achieved in such a manner that nothing could be added or taken away or altered except for the worse."[8] Artifacts are residual proper nouns; processes, such as designing or making, are gerunds in the retrospective view of history. Physical language lies in the territory between concrete nouns and gerunds, between names and records of actions. The best analog of physical language in grammatical language is the class of words known as abstract nouns.

Abstract Nouns

> I have told you that I desire to make my language Latin, and as clear as possible, so as to be easily understood. Words must therefore be invented, when those in current use are inadequate; it will be best to draw them from familiar things.

> *(Leon Battista Alberti,* On the Art of Building in Ten Books, *VI, 13)*

I beg some lenience[9] to begin this line of thought with a post-Romantic literary example that is not strictly an abstract noun: Stephen Dedalus' confounding phrase "*Black panther vampire.*" Why start here? Despite the fact that the phrase is constructed of well-known nouns – most people have an understanding of what a vampire is from television, films, and books; and even more know what a 'black panther' is, some from the aforementioned sources, some from direct experience – a quick tour through the *James Joyce Quarterly* and an even quicker spin through the blogosphere reveals myriad speculations on Joyce's intended meaning.[10] The goal is not to establish once and for all the meaning of this expression; quite the contrary. It is the simultaneous multiplicity of meanings and lack of authoritative, top-down information delivery that here are useful.

Propositions are to individual words what a given language is to its propositions; and a language is to one of its propositions what thought is to a given language or system of representation: a structure that clarifies what is at stake. Words elevate us above mere guttural expression because they are proto- or latent propositions. Each word points to a larger system in which it is classified as a word. Yet, understanding is not necessary. Words do not have to be final or authoritatively deciphered to be indicative of the existence of such a larger structure. *Black panther vampire* connects a group of scholars and lovers of literature, despite any one of them knowing precisely what it means. Words exist, in other words, as tokens or pledges in a system of exchange that sometimes relies on untested faith in the existence of collateral.

In this pseudo-economic structure, verbs are merely descriptors of the exchange. Nouns – proper, common, and abstract – and pronouns are the indispensable matter: most significant, perhaps, are "I" and "it" insofar as nothing has value unless "it" is believed to exist and "I" (or someone else) have enough interest to ponder or comment on it. For the purpose of social exchanges of meaning, however, abstract nouns are the currency. Simply put, a noun is abstract when it refers to ideas instead of persons, places, and things. "Democracy" and "justice" are oft-quoted examples. These nouns are far broader in scope than their common or proper kin. Here it is reasonable to place Joyce's cryptic phrase. *Black panther vampire* is variously conceived as referring to God, the creative process, sexual or artistic reproduction, the threat to any or all of the aforementioned, or directly to Bloom as God's representative in the text. The expression's meaning is latent, not fully formed, but suggestive. It is ethereal, not fixed, but nevertheless communicative. In this way, *black panther vampire* is a proper noun composed of common nouns that acts like an abstract noun.

For mere buildings to become meaningful components of a physical language they must undergo an analogous transformation: "the Robie House" – composed of roman bricks and deep raked joints, low pitched roofs and deep soffits, ornamental metal window grills and stone urns – is an exemplar of *Prairie Style Architecture* and an easy, if not wholly equivalent, example of the principle of amalgamation of common nouns in the service of the abstract. But the question, in both literature and architecture, is: how does this work? Clearly, words are adapted or adopted unchanged from one language to another just as design elements are borrowed, shared, and mutated across diverse styles but in no case does a word or an architectural element approach existence outside its language – even *the Word*, as variously conceived by the world's religions, exists within a given milieu. Matter tends to remain matter. Ideas, ephemera.

The relationship between words and the existences to which they refer is representative and all communication assumes a sign system even if, at root, we are forced to acknowledge that the sign system is arbitrary and, ultimately, groundless. Fine. But the power of a phrase like *black panther vampire* to inspire meaning does not rely upon the meaningfulness of its referents. This slant toward meaning in the transubstantiation of the abstract noun has prodded bloggers and scholars to attempt decipherment which, in turn, is less a result of a narrowing of referential specificity but instead signals a profound proliferation of references. It is similar to the evocative character of literary works by Salman Rushdie or Gabriel García Márquez which are less the result of *ex nihilo* invention than a dizzying multiplicity of references – multi-cultural in the best (that is, least postmodern[11]) sense of the word. Frank Lloyd Wright's genius was not so different. Neither was Alberti's.

Alberti privileged visualization of gods (and by extension other things that matter: ideas, philosophies) in the mind over the eyes (VII, 17). According to Alberti, the

192 Architecture History and Theory in Reverse

role of architecture is to prompt this mental visualization by embedding "some quality of philosophy" on walls and floors, by "patterning the pavement with musical and geometric lines and shapes" (VII, 10), and by appropriating patterns from silversmiths and quilters for the ornamentation of domes and vaults as the ancients did (VII, 11). That is to say, Alberti transubstantiated common and proper nouns in the service of abstract ideas in the mind of the visitor – a process Alexander Tzonis and Liane Lefaivre call "strangemaking" utilizing "syncretism" (the mixing of multiple canons) and "metastatement, a world of higher order visual statements."[12]

The analogy is simple. The act of design is the verb and the physical properties of resulting forms, materials, and borrowed elements are nouns laid out upon a malleable surface of context. The individual elements of a physical language thus resemble nouns in the way physical language as a whole resembles a grammar. This analogy can be pushed farther, however, toward provocative ends alluded to in Part I. Grammars introduce and record tense. Perhaps physical languages, too, operate in, and even construct, time.

Grammar Writes Time

Two hundred years after the publication of Alberti's *De Re Aedificatoria*, Gottfried Wilhelm Leibniz published his "Discourse on Metaphysics" (1686). Even at this early date, Leibniz understood our thoughts and perceptions are linked and mutually constitutive of time.[13] Thought and perception (that is, languaged sensation) evolve in intimate reciprocity.[14] It is commonly assumed that thought, so modified by and entwined with language, becomes divisible into rhetorical thought and grammatical thought: that is, stylistic, expressive, and bombastic forms of thinking versus those governed by rules and traditions of usage; creative thinking as opposed to logical ideation. This opposition, and the idea of multiple kinds of minds or mental processes in general, get a lot of print in self-help, pseudo-psychology, and even design literature.[15] Despite the print, serious psychological research has discovered no such dualism.[16] This split is but another post-Babel bifurcation. Language organizes thought to such an extent that the divisions and activities often attributed to thinking are mere polarizations, observer effects of seeing thought through language itself. To think and to know is to have gained fluency in a language that has been reified, or in an earlier language 'blessed,' as true. Every act of creative, stylistic, or bombastic thinking is either a self-conscious effort to supersede a known language – an attempt to mitigate the anxiety of influence – or an unintentional (automatic) mental process conducted in a vacuum of ignorance. And as ignorance by definition is insufficient to provide the conceptual consistency required for rudimentary communication, much less the establishment of a physical language, it is necessary to admit that design or creative 'thinking' in any of the arts (literary or physical) must be knowledge of a particular grammar or grammars combined with a self-conscious pretension of escape into a realm of free expression or else it is mere incommunicable noise.

In short, thinking is grammatical.

The Tense of Abstract Nouns   **193**

In this light, Foucault's notion that sciences, disciplines, and histories are well-made languages becomes tautological. It is equivalent to saying that sciences, disciplines, and histories are languages that are always already stamped as provisionally 'true' for the sake of communicative coherence. Of course. Such statements are necessary only to combat the fears of those who believe in the existence of two forms of thinking: if you believe that creative thinking *invents* and established ideation merely *perpetuates*, then it is possible to imagine that sciences, disciplines, and histories are dead or inert, fixed from the moment of their conception and incapable of change from within. Only under the sway of such beliefs is it necessary to extol Kuhn's "paradigm shifts" to account for changes in scientific, disciplinary or historical thinking. Without the creative-formal or rhetorical-logical or poetical-rational bifurcation, thought can be understood as simply evolving with grammar over time.

Herein lies the relation to time. From the emergence of the grammars of "sciences," "disciplines," and "histories" onward, time has been marked as mere datum for a succession of additions, revisions, and deletions to the dominant language. In science, it is the time of magic, the time of God/gods, the time of alchemy, of mechanics, gravity, relativity, quantum mechanics, and chaos. In western architecture, it is the time of caves, primitive huts, temples and basilicas, the Romanesque, the Gothic, the Renaissance and Mannerism, the Baroque, Modernism, Postmodernism, the spectacle of ethics, and the ethic of spectacles. As the dominant languages change, grammars evolve, various classifications of thinking, paradigms, are imagined into being, and time is dragged slowly into existence or awareness – which, following Berkeley's dictum, might be the same thing.

Paradigm shifts occur. Styles emerge. These become topics for disciplines as soon as they are named. Time trails behind this disciplinarity. Disciplines evolve as grammars do, faster than time, and much faster than the thoughts of noble savages or the willfully ignorant. What does this mean for physical language? In part, this suggests that the fear of being merely imitative, which inevitably arises when a designer begins to think about what conditions of form make a work communicative, is rooted in a misunderstanding of the relationship between time and the making of physical artifacts. To utilize an old cliché, the idea of architecture pursuing or attempting to capture its Zeitgeist is like a cart towing its horse. Physical language and its inexorable evolution create styles and histories and notions of appropriateness; the inverse, importantly, is not true.

Grammar writes time. Grammars have written time since the beginning of writing.[17] It is neither a difficult nor a particularly controversial idea and yet, when we look beyond its familiarity, it is possible to extract four far less obvious hypotheses: (1) Thoughts are exterior and posterior judgments resulting from attempts to mediate or connect with extant representations. (2) Languages are various exterior and posterior efforts to name and organize thoughts. (3) New representations are exterior and posterior effects of changes to or ambiguities in languages. (4) Time is merely the measure of accumulated moves; the floor across which this three-step dance takes place – a diagram of which is rather easy to draw (Figure 15.3).

194 Architecture History and Theory in Reverse

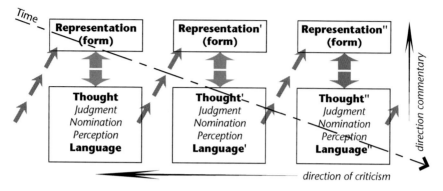

FIGURE 15.3 The time of language

In *The Order of Things*, Foucault appears to have grasped this schematic relation of time and grammar.[18] Yet Foucault failed to perceive how the actions undertaken through and sometimes for the sake of grammar write not just linear time but time with breadth and dimension. Evolution is not linear. The connection between language and representation is cyclical and proceeds by fits and starts as indicated in Figure 15.3. Seldom do grammatical actions unfurl perfectly parallel with or perpendicular to the ostensible flow of time. Criticism and commentary, for examples, differ in orientation toward the cycle of language. While both actions are effected in a generally backwards glance through time and bring the notion of 'past' and the possibility of 'history' into being, they operate at something like right angles to one another – criticism looks at preceding forms of language; commentary turns toward recent representations. Neither travels directly against the perceived flow of time; but it is also true that neither flows naïvely or unproblematically with it.

This complex relation to time has implications that Foucault failed to notice. These two 'imprisoning' grammatical actions he derides as resulting from the connection of language and representation – i.e. criticism and commentary – are axes, not vectors. That is to say, they are bi-directional, not mono-directional. To focus attention exclusively on the 'critical' or 'commentary' functions of grammar is to privilege the way in which language engages and creates the past. Yet each of these functions or actions is mirrored in equal and opposite trajectories, tracing the other ends of their axes, into a multi-dimensional future. Grammar does indeed write time. But grammatical time is not so much a line as a plane. And this plane is traversed by at least two axes: the axis of *criticism-speculation* and the axis of *commentary-imaginative description*. The first term of each pair is oriented toward the past; the second, literally, opens the expanse of the future. Ignoring this second function of grammar is problematic insofar as it spawns ideologies in which language – whether written, spoken or physical – is seen as inevitably limiting or backwards; by attending only to this backwards cast, language is and can only be representative.[19]

Arguably literature, philosophy, and theological texts are great or serious or revelatory to the extent that they work across, and thereby stretch, the fabric of time – past and present – critically, speculatively, descriptively and imaginatively. We should not await the breaking of the connection between language and representation or believe that representation is a modern invention any more than we should hope to forget the names of the things we see or imagine there was a time when people saw without naming: from the moment humans emitted a cry or grunt at the sight of an animal, whether from fear or hunger or curiosity or appreciation of beauty, people saw in the form of names. Instead, in the hope of creating a great or serious or revelatory physical language, it is necessary to increase the grammatical reach of time and, to this end, create works that look forward and back; appear poetic and rational: in literature, such techniques propel Rushdie and García-Márquez who each reference multiple traditions and yet embed these in inventive and incredibly provocative storylines; in architecture, Alberti's advocacy for "some quality of philosophy" is manifest in his façade for Santa Maria Novella (see Figure 15.4) and Ruskin's call for a re-imagination of Northern Gothic might be extended to twenty-first-century experiential equivalents of interiors like those of King's College Chapel in Cambridge – straightforward in plan and section; connected to types of somewhat known and generally accepted order; yet both summative and formative; otherworldly and suggestive. Unfortunately, MVRDV's Markthal is as close as we've come.

FIGURE 15.4 Santa Maria Novella, Florence, Leon Battista Alberti architect
Source: Photograph by Scott Penman.

Image and Tense

Arguably, grammar and time were once unified in works of architecture. Santa Maria Novella's nearly flat façade (1456–1470) aims higher than the now commonplace but prosaic "activating the space" in front of itself. Its patterning is suggestive of an embedded narrative, opening questions regarding origins and speculations on its content to present and future Florentines, "so that the mind may receive stimuli from every side" (VII, 10). King's College Chapel (1446–1515) is a powerful example of the breadth of time in its combination of "practical, matter-of-fact spirit with a sense of mystery and an almost oriental effusion of ornament."[20] From our twenty-first-century informational perspective, such expansive relations of grammar and time are difficult to tease apart, frame, and subject to analysis. MVRDV's Markthal, to return to the first example in this book, dabbles in historical market forms, makes reference to its purpose via a colorful mural, and speaks to modern technology via its structure and curtain wall systems. But the Markthal does not convey this rich mix effectively. This is due, in part, to the familiarity we have with such structures and with our own needs, attitudes, and habits of use. It is also a function of the frequency with which the Darwinian, non-teleological, non-goal-oriented aspects of architecture are derided if not altogether dismissed with a summative "in the eye of the beholder"-type evaluation. The Markthal is reduced to "Yeah, that's interesting."[21]

Of all the visual arts, only film retains its otherworldliness and prestige as worthy of mental effort. Film's privilege in this regard is almost certainly attributable to its tender age as a fine art, its reliance on narrative or storytelling, and its technological inaccessibility to the average would-be auteur. As the first and last of these reasons for critical transparency are changing and likely to be short-lived (film is growing old in comparison to various forms of interactive media and its once cumbersome and expensive technology is being democratized at an astonishing rate – think iPhone movies), it is film's use of narrative that promises to be most resistant to cognitive decline, because its lasting impact seems to have the least to do with 'newness,' and therefore to offer the most stable territory for analyzing the interplay of image, grammar, and time. The best filmic images support a complex and dynamic interplay of past, present, and future narratives by addressing all four quadrants of the field of meaningful grammars (see Figure 15.5): the past-sensory or "Commentary;" the past-conceptual or "Criticism;" the future-sensory or "Imaginative Description;" the future-conceptual or "Speculation." And, in this framework, Giuseppe Tornatore's *Cinema Paradiso* (1988) is an exemplar.

While the film makes use of the standard technique of flashback to operate at various timescales, it is the relative positioning of different characters – or individual characters seen at different times – that is exceptional. The film centers on the story of Salvatore Di Vita (Toto), from altar boy who has lost his father in the Second World War and thinks only of the cinema to his maturation as a successful film director in Rome, and his relationship with Alfredo, the local projectionist. While the fatherly Alfredo is presented as an apocryphal figure, Toto is at the mercy of at

The Tense of Abstract Nouns   **197**

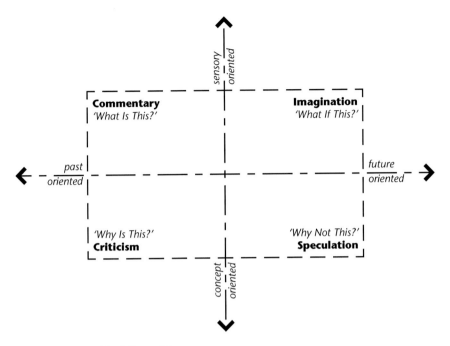

FIGURE 15.5 Field of all possible grammars

least four different relations to knowledge displayed across three stages of life: as a precocious boy of 6, as a hormonally driven adolescent, and as an introspective adult some thirty years later.

Although Toto is a sharp and even manipulative young boy, he is presented more often as prone to sensual attractions over deep concepts. He is primarily concerned with the present and its connection to an impending and largely unquestioned future – which is little more than an expansion of his present state. Thus, it makes sense to locate the young boy almost exclusively in the "Imaginative" quadrant. Yet, Toto's childhood is also his most complete temporal phase. There are moments when he occupies the "Speculative" quadrant – as is the case in his desire to become a projectionist, asking "Why not?" forms of questions. In asking such questions, however, more than the future is put into play. The apparent spontaneity, naiveté, and passive acquiescence to animal drives from which human curiosity seem to derive are revealed to be nothing of the sort. Every "why?" or "what?" is firmly rooted in a sign system inculcated from birth. These types of questions demonstrate belief in a previously established order, a past. Even when arguing his case to view deleted kissing scenes, young Toto cuts off one of Alfredo's rants not with logical argumentation but by parroting Alfredo's own, well-known quip. Such a broad temporal framework delimits an expandable but always bounded field of individual meaning.

In adolescence, Toto – as well as the film – stagnates. This seems intentional on director Tornatore's part. Toto marks off days in the closing months of his 1954

198 Architecture History and Theory in Reverse

calendar as he waits for Elena, the girl of his affections, to choose him. This counting of days is not an acknowledgment of a future or the past so much as a struggle to keep himself and the viewer centered in time. To root us in what would otherwise be a purely internal struggle. After Elena has acquiesced but has had to leave for the summer with her family – and as Kirk Douglas' *Ulysses* (1954) is mired in his struggle with the Cyclops on a large open air screen – Toto wishes for the interminable summer to end and the viewer, likewise, desires for this central passage without direction to draw to a close. Through such means and others, adolescence is portrayed as an odyssey lived at times sensually and at others conceptually but always slowly as it is tethered to the axis of the present.

It is only with adulthood that a complex and dynamic interplay of past, present, and future emerges. In the movie's most famous scene, Toto's solitary screening of a montage of redacted kisses spliced together by his now-deceased mentor, Alfredo's short film within the film reintroduces in the present memories of 'imaginative description' undertook in childhood and demands 'speculation' as to why Alfredo so vehemently refused to communicate with Toto over the last thirty years. The now archaic film countdown ("4, 3, 2, 1"), the marks and visual hiss of old celluloid, the closing "FINE," the amorous content's clear reminder of a time of repression in small Italian towns under Church censorship, and even the lingering memory that old celluloid burns are juxtaposed against the contemporary interior of Toto's screening room. These juxtapositions open avenues of "commentary" on old forms and perhaps "criticism" of ideas in the past. Tornatore's brilliance in evoking this interplay of tenses can be witnessed right up to the end, in the credits, when the adult Toto looks into the distance with the same look that his adolescent self first viewed Elena, suggesting that he has just rediscovered her; this moment at the end of the credits is thus both a return to an earlier point in the film and suggestive of another storyline beyond the time of the movie's setting.

In an information age, it is more difficult to analyze architecture in these terms. The difficulty dims, however, when we abandon information-oriented grammar's fascination with "how?" and ask instead questions of meaning: "what? why? what-if? and why not?" Every "what?" or "why?" is firmly rooted in a sign system inculcated from birth and demands that the inhabitant acknowledge a sensual and conceptual inheritance. Every "what-if?" and "why not?" challenges the same inhabitants to acknowledge meaning's potential to evolve. In principle, MVRDV's Markthal could be questioned in this way. And yet, its newness combined with our habituation to ask "how?" renders it opaque to meaning or what-is-at-stake questions. Its experiential potential is thus limited to an instrumentalized present concerned only with the next immediate present and the potential for commerce. At best, one *visits* or *tours* the Markthal.

Alberti's façade for Santa Maria Novella is altogether different. The façade does not often elicit questions of "how?" even from information age tourists. Instead, it seems to prompt "what? why? what-if? why not?" from locals and tourists, from students and professionals and lay people alike. Alberti's metastatements of the past and strangemakings of these to engage speculations of the future create abstract

The Tense of Abstract Nouns **199**

nouns tethered to past and future, the sensual and conceptual. Such broad temporal engagement delimits an expandable but always bounded field of individual meaning. For this reason, it is common to hear people say that they *pondered* or *contemplated* Santa Maria Novella. Some are *moved* or *touched* by it. Such descriptions of experiences with information age buildings are rare. But why? *Cinema Paradiso* and other narrative films gather emotive and communicative power by tethering images to multiple grammatical tenses. As with 'Film' and the physical 'Cinema' – like 'Humanities,' 'Sciences,' and 'Religions,' too – 'Architecture' is an ordered and imagistic grammar that constructs tense. And yet, these practices, particularly Film and Architecture, are not conceived as such in equal measure.

Sciences, Humanities, and Religions are projects pursued within existing episteme, and yet each holds as its intention the completion and demonstration of its own ordering as *the* meta-order. As such, Sciences, Humanities, and Religions accept and maintain the existence of 'other' orders as markers of a flawed context to which *IT* – M-theory, Postmodernism, Christianity – is the necessary (and for believers, final) correction. Film and architecture are not perceived by the general public as aspiring to such meta-ordering. Film operates through an explicit assumption on the part of its viewers that it constitutes a sub-ordering, a literal framing of narrow aspects of a much larger body of orders – those of genres such as science fiction or romance; tragedy or comedy. Perceptions of architecture differ from those of film primarily in that architecture is conceived as an art of degenerating order; that is, the general public tends to acknowledge the inherent order of, and is willing to assume an implied meaning in, the best works of architecture's classical tradition. The public's openmindedness ends with the breakdown of resemblance to known elements and rhetorical figures in contemporary practice. Architecture is understood, in other words, as temporally and formally disordered because it eschews reference. The filmic power of tense, on the contrary, resides nowhere as much as in the ordering that resemblance allows.

Notes

1 This and all subsequent references are taken from Alberti, *On the Art of Building in Ten Books*, translated by Joseph Rykwert, Neil Leach, and Robert Tavernor (Cambridge, MA: MIT Press, 1988).

2 See John Berger, *Ways of Seeing* (London: the BBC and Penguin Books, 1972), 7. The second line in the book – "The child looks and recognizes before it can speak" – contains at least two questionable word choices that reinforce this interpretation: first, it is impossible to understand the word "recognizes" without positing some sort of classificatory proto-naming system that allows the child to distinguish different groupings of photons; second, and related to the first, there is no evidence that the ability to "speak" is synonymous with or even emerges in tandem with the ability to name. As with dogs and other animals, it is probable that human children acquire the ability to identify objects by name before becoming capable of communicating via speech.

3 A host of linguists, philosophers, and psychologists since Humboldt have argued this position. See Theodor Adorno, *Aesthetic Theory*, translated, edited, and with an Introduction by Robert Hullot-Kentor (Minneapolis, MN: University of Minnesota, 1997), 104; Ernst Cassirer, *Language and Myth* (New York: Dover Publications, 1953), 24;

Julian Jaynes, *The Origin of Consciousness in the Breakdown of the Bicameral Mind* (Boston: Houghton Mifflin, 1976), 138; George Steiner, *After Babel: aspects of language and translation* (New York: Oxford University Press, 1975), 29 and 39; and Charles Taylor, *The Language Animal: the full shape of the human linguistic capacity* (Cambridge, MA: Belknap Press/Harvard University, 2016), 177–263.

4 Elaine Scarry's beautiful turn of phrase to describe Marx's attitude toward investment of the body in objects of production. Just before this description, she writes:

> What differentiates men and women from other creatures is neither natural acuity of our sentience nor the natural frailty of the organic tissue in which it resides but instead the fact that ours is, to a vastly greater degree than that of any other animal, objectified in language and material objects and is thus fundamentally transformed to be communicable and endlessly sharable ...
>
> Behind the surface of the face in the mirror is blood and bone and tissue but also friends, cities, grandmothers, novels, gods, numbers, and jokes; and it is likely to be the second group (the socialization of sentience) rather than the first (the privacy of sentience) that she at that moment 'senses' as the washcloth in the mirror moves back and forth over the illuminated surface of the skin.
>
> (Elaine Scarry, *The Body in Pain*,
> New York: Oxford University Press, 1987, 255–256)

5 Berger, *Ways of Seeing*, 7.

6 Or, as Rousseau notes: "General laws should always be distinguished from individual causes that may modify their effects." See Jean-Jacques Rousseau, *The Social Contract* (New York: Maestro, 2012), Book III, §8.

7 Umberto Eco, *From Tree to Labyrinth: historical studies on the sign and interpretation*, translated by Anthony Oldcorn (Cambridge, MA: Harvard University Press, 2014), 485.

8 Quoted in Nikolaus Pevsner, *An Outline of European Architecture*, Jubilee Edition (Baltimore, MD: Penguin, 1961), 314.

9 Lenience on two fronts: first, I am not a linguist but, despite my inclination to avoid the territory of linguistics altogether, I am forced to detour through grammatical or written language en route to a better understanding of physical language; second, abstract nouns are, tautologically, abstract, inaccessible to the senses, and therefore difficult to illuminate using concrete examples.

10 None of these speculations apparently are considered final or authoritative.

11 The postmodern practice of multiplying references is aimed not at constructing meaning but at demonstrating its frailty or ultimate absence.

12 Alexander Tzonis and Liane Lefaivre, *Classical Architecture: the poetics of order* (Cambridge, MA: MIT Press, 1987), 279–280. Or as Sir John Newenham Summerson said in 1963: "If the understanding of rule is one basic factor in the creation of great classical buildings, the defiance of rule is the other." See J.N. Summerson, *The Classical Language of Architecture* (Cambridge, MA: MIT Press, 1966), 20.

13 Gottfried Wilhelm Leibniz, "Discourse on Metaphysics," in *Discourse on Metaphysics: Correspondence with Arnauld, Monadology*, Introduction by Paul Janet, translated by George Montgomery (La Salle, IL: Open Court, 1993), 25.

14 It is reasonable to wonder why thought and language are not coalesced and treated as one process. The essential difference is one of lineage: infrastructures of thought are physiological and hereditary; systems of language are constructed between people and are socially transmitted. Genes versus memes, if you prefer. Thought and language are thus distinct in origin but intimately entwined. Conceived linearly, thought is a prerequisite to language; but, as with lovers of different nationalities, that one (thought) is a citizen by birth and the other (language) an immigrant does not make either primary or dominant in the relationship by necessity. The ordering that language forces upon thought as it unfurls no doubt feeds back and modifies thought and, in so doing, triggers the creation of new conceptual superstructures. Analogically, it is reasonable to assume

The Tense of Abstract Nouns **201**

that cross-border lovers will transform each other and acquire, as in all relationships, some of the characteristics essential or imagined to be essential to the beloved.

15 This current is strongest among architectural phenomenologists: Vesely and Pérez-Gómez, in particular. But one has only to pick up the nearest theoretical work to verify the prevalence of the "poetic" vs. "rational" paradigm.

16 Recent rhetoric regarding "embodied cognition" does not constitute contrary evidence for the simple reason that there is no such thing as disembodied cognition against which embodied cognition is an alternative.

17 Jaynes, *The Origin of Consciousness*, 176.

18 Michel Foucault, *The Order of Things* (New York: Vintage, 1984), 81: "until the connection between language and representation is broken, or at least transcended, in our culture, all secondary languages will be imprisoned within the alternative of criticism or commentary. And in their indecision they will proliferate ad infinitum."

19 Once, while discussing the merits of a work of literature, a colleague said to me, "I don't have time to read fiction, there are too many important books to read." For him, the important books were philosophical or political. Several years later, the same colleague forwarded an essay (from *Wired* magazine about the "New Aesthetic") which served notice that the aesthetic sensibilities of younger generations are not mired (much) in the aesthetic hang-ups of their elders. In very different ways, both his earlier quip and later enamorment with the New Aesthetic are assertions of faith in a near-absolute split between past and future. On the one hand, to not read fiction or literature is to admit a certain amount of skepticism regarding the value of imaginative or speculative work; it is to suggest that only discourses reflective of established epistemes deserve serious study. On the other hand, to be pleasantly surprised by the younger generation's lack of reverence for cultural norms that grounded one's own aesthetic principles is to believe that imaginative or speculative work is possible without a past; that ex-nihilo-noble-savage myths of creative endeavor deserve respect. These are extremes; and neither position makes sense – either of its own accord or in relation to the other. Nor does Foucault's. Nor does Rousseau's.

20 Pevsner, *Outline of European Architecture*, 252.

21 To be fair, most other visual arts are similarly opaque to the lay public. Modern dance suffers a reductive "to each his own" attitude and is seen as an act of such utter self-expression that its grammar and history are largely rendered invisible. And, painting and sculpture are condemned via an explicit verdict and implicit death sentence, "I could do *that*."

16

VITRUVIAN CYCLES 1

Representations Against Space

[T]he ancients held that what could not happen in the original would have no valid reason for existence in the copy. For in all their works they proceeded on definite principles of fitness and in ways derived from the truth of Nature. Thus they reached perfection, approving only those things which, if challenged, can be explained on grounds of the truth.

(Vitruvius, The Ten Books on Architecture, *IV, II, 5–6)*[1]

1. The Value of Resemblance

It is difficult to open Vitruvius' *De Architectura* (20–30 BCE) and not find oneself staring at a page of text that seems, at first blush, to be mere pattern book and, as one reads another page or twenty, more difficult still not to suspect that the author is interested in an unremitting perpetuation of the same. But this characterization of the author's intent is unfair, even if it is accurate regarding the book's effect. The rules espoused by Vitruvius are not limits imposed for the sake of sameness *per se.* Genera and taxis, criticism and speculation, grammar and time, image and tense: in all these relationships, the second terms take as their necessary prefiguring assumption a pattern of resemblance to things or categories of things – people, places, ideas or symbols – known and codified in the former. "Perceptual stays."[2] Arguably, stability of perception in the presence of a work of architecture, along with the architecture's communicative potential (if those are not the same), requires such grounding. If representation is not grounded in, structured by, and always in reference to an existing episteme or epistemes, it does not possess its obscure power to generate impressions of similarity or dissimilarity, of meaning or feeling. Without an episteme, there is no resemblance. Without resemblance, no communication.

That there exists a need to write the preceding sentences is an indication of an information age prejudice. Consider the rhetoric, fashionable at design conferences, aimed at protecting students from the burdens of historical reference; or, the presumption parroted at many design schools that future-oriented design acts ('imaginative description' and 'speculation') are inhibited by too much knowledge of the past (entanglements with 'commentary' and 'criticism'). Ignored is the relative nature of 'past' and 'future' as measured against the evolving present perfect progressive of the axis of the present as well as the unity within a grammatical field that is bisected by that axis (see Figure 15.5). At any given time within a given culture, representation and imagination are connected cyclically. Each "new" representation or juxtaposition of existing representations intended, ostensibly, as an imaginative leap toward the future alters the episteme(s) constitutive of and operative in the present. Every alteration of the dominant episteme(s) in the present fosters "new" representations of the past. This is why histories of the same events composed at different times differ so greatly. Historical commentary does not have to be arbitrary, but it is always relative.

Given the widespread dissemination of concepts derived from studies in artificial intelligence, it is common to conceive the human mind as a difference engine. There is no disputing the fact that the enumeration and even creation of differences are one of the brain's key functions. But, the brain is also a semblance engine – creating connections where, from another point of view or time, none would seem to exist. Understanding that both of these mental functions – positing differences and forming resemblances – involve imagination and representation exposes the "creative act-historical reference" dichotomy as nonexistent at its cognitive roots. As Umberto Eco succinctly put it, "in principle there is nothing that is constitutionally expression or content."[3]

Beyond the internal, cognitive linkages, representation and imagination are united within the field of meaningful grammars with the formation of episteme at all scales. "Human nature" is one such system, perhaps the meta-episteme. "Architecture" is another, smaller but perhaps important. High Gothic and Late Gothic, like Modernism and Postmodernism, are also epistemes, smaller still. To admit this scalar aspect of classification is not to reduce or limit the potential of architecture – whether understood as a whole or conceived only within the language of a particular style. Architecture at either scale is mutable, open to modification, addition and deletion, paraphrase, substitution, and permutation. Confusions regarding given representations, the endless but joyful play on resemblances experienced by some and the slow but inexorable slide toward fixed identities encountered by others, constitute nothing more or less than a catalogue of possible responses to an episteme's inherent openness. In England, for instance, Continental Europe's simple bifurcation of High and Late Gothic unfolds as a three-step progression from Early English to Decorated to Perpendicular.[4] Consider the Jesse Window, Dorchester, Oxfordshire (c. 1340); here stone mullions are carved explicitly in the form of trees and branches to which Gothic tracery already bore no small resemblance. Already suggestive of human figures, carved renditions of biblical and religious characters were added to this vegetal window pattern. The mullions are filled with stained glass in which religious figures are repeated and thus shown both in their physical condition (carved in stone) and spiritual quality (illuminated in glass). Such early blurring of subjective and objective aspects of form suggests that human imagination is not in such extraordinary need of protecting as we in an information age might think; judging by our recent works, however, the value of resemblance is.

2. Signs Are Not Spatial

Read. Read a few pages of any great book. Read the seemingly endless repetitions encountered in de Sade, in Joyce, in the Old Testament's record of births and retributions, and in Marx's factory and field journalism.[5] In all of these sources, the printed word enacts the "response" portion of the human call-and-response cycle. Great literature anticipates the human urge to sound its depths. It echoes before the call goes out. As a result, it makes it possible for even the relatively uninitiated to navigate its viscous surface.

That last phrase is not poetic – insofar, at least, as it should not be understood as a mere substitute for other expressions such as "to enter into the book's space." Literature is not spatial. Literature is volumetric. It has depth. Sometimes dense and blatantly resistant to exploration; other times, seemingly clear – its viscosity hidden from the casual reader. Literature, as an alluring, responsive and reiterative object, is oblivious to the openness of space. It has no need for, and would in fact dissipate in, open space. Alberto Pérez-Gómez is correct in his assertion that "the absence of this awareness [of space] characterizes a 'mythical world.'"[6] More generally, an absence of awareness of space characterizes any communicative world. Literature gains power to interact with humanity precisely because it does not feign to be a receptacle or passive field of operation for the human intellect; instead, it provides the everyday world with an equally substantial mythical companion. The power of great architecture, say, a Gothic cathedral, derives from the same privileging of viscous volumes over space. Architecture in an information age – obligated to being spatial as well as instrumentally informative – suffers from any comparison with the viscosity of literature or earlier meaning-imbued architectures. More simply, contemporary architecture suffers from the privileging of space over meaning.

The differences that have evolved between literary worlds and architectural volumes since Victor Hugo's time are profound. Literature, as a thing (manuscript) comprised of signs[7] (words) and organized around a perceivable framework of ideas (narrative), is capable of being pondered in a way that the literal absence at the heart of contemporary architecture is not. This is true, in part, because *the order of things* – our place in the world or the meaning embodied in matter – is impossible to analyze or discuss or even fully perceive without accepting a given sign system; and, as will be more fully discussed below, architectural space is incapable of carrying meaning. In its physicality, literature wins. It is capable of asserting both dominant and subordinate epistemes with which a reader must contend in order to engage its mythical world. The bonds of *idea* to *idea* that establish the dominant and subordinate epistemes also, thereby, establish the perceived order of things and, thereby, make possible the *conveyance* of meaning.

Subsequently, for any new idea to become a sign, it must conform to the dominant order or confront it so as to become a new subordinate order.

In the realms of literature, mythology and other communicative traditions, the content, function, and determination of any sign are the results of an order propped up by established episteme. Contemporary architectural space, because it is passive and eschews sign systems in favor of personal "expression," does not *convey* anything – not even the postmodernists' much-vaunted absence of hierarchy and order. Most contemporary architectural spaces are not so much anti-authoritarian as simply non-existent; they are literally non-things: nothing.

It is important to understand what makes the repetitions of Joyce and de Sade, Marx and the authors of Judeo-Christian texts, Cervantes and Kafka and Rushdie and others so powerful, so evocative, so moving even when we repudiate some of their specific content. Much of the affect or atmosphere resides in the way that literature undermines the presence versus representation dichotomy. Within a language, representation and presence are simultaneous and unified.[8] Literary representation in its essence is always parallel to itself; the order and the meaning of its signs are equivalent insofar as both are direct products of an earlier episteme that named, ordered, and gave meaning to things; but this earlier order – be it a literary, philosophic or scientific tradition or an evolutionary trace of a group's first intentional calls or marks – is not referenced by nor called forth in the later work. That is, a text is not an effort to acknowledge an earlier but now absent form. Each manuscript is a fully present manifestation embodying the genetics of its ancestors but nevertheless speaking in its own voice – an enactment of memory that does not require our constant rehearsal. Narratives hold our history and myths before us so that we can imagine new things without having to constantly remind ourselves that we stand on a ground of shared meaning. Architecture in our information age has, by and large, abdicated this responsibility and abandoned this territory in favor of advertising – or being – a brand. Architecture after Babel is an increasingly frantic and far-flung exodus.[9]

3. Only Signs Can Be Repeated

> There are certain elementary forms on which the general aspect of a temple depends.
>
> *(Vitruvius,* The Ten Books on Architecture, *III, ii, 1)*

> The cathedral was – besides being a strictly architectural monument of the spirit of its age – another *Summa*, another *Speculum*, an encyclopedia carved in stone.
>
> *(Nikolaus Pevsner,* An Outline of European Architecture*)*[10]

> In any kind of communicative interaction, it is clearly necessary to presuppose and infer the format of the individual encyclopedia of the persons speaking to us, otherwise we would attribute to them intentions (and knowledge) that they do not have.
>
> *(Umberto Eco, From the Tree to the Labyrinth)*[11]

206 Architecture History and Theory in Reverse

Literature – and, more importantly, literate architecture – allows active dissonance of commentaries for and against a given and well-known order by exposing the dominant to its own internal and submissive differences. This de Sadian revelation is significant insofar as, in the aftermath of this exposure, we witness the emergence of new subordinate orders and burgeoning dominant orders through which people are capable of narrating their own becoming.

Despite the praise directed toward literature in the preceding section, it does not fill a base or absolute need, strictly speaking. We could live in the barest sense without great fiction. Space, on the contrary, is necessary for inhabitation. Space, in the sense of a volume in which people and things exist and in which actions occur, is a prerequisite to architecture, literature, experience, existence itself. It marks an abandonment of logical thinking and critical observation, however, to assert that space is primary in architectural experience or – perhaps to say the same thing more directly – that space is experienced. The attendant experiential and design difficulties entailed by privileging the non-existent would be beyond the scope of the present discussion were it not for the dire consequences to physical language, communicability, and the possibility of shared meaning that space-centric thinking imposes on contemporary practice. Only signs can be repeated.

Listen to lectures by architects; read the views of architecture critics in books and journals; attend student design juries at practically any university. To do any of these things is to immerse oneself in something akin to a faith or cult of space. And in this pseudo-religious sphere, architectural space is not only placed on an altar as an absent but sacred object for humanity to strive toward, in these incantations architectural space is imagined to possess special powers that allows it to communicate with the hearts of men and women directly. While beliefs are important, personal, and should not be trod upon lightly, herein lie the problems with such a faith: (1) communication requires repetition – "iterability" it is called; (2) spaces in themselves are not repeatable; the capacity for repetition belongs only to things capable of being identified, recognized as "different" and "similar," and named; (3) as noted by Derrida, all things recognized are signs; and only signs are communicative.

Belief in the communicative power of non-signs – particularly architectural spaces – nevertheless flourishes like faith in myriad gods and goddesses, spooks and spectral figures, the world over. But even humanity's earliest encounters with such phantom figures were given names and locations (Apollo speaks from my left; Zeus from my right). As Pérez-Gómez has argued, architecture in the Classical era was more closely aligned with signs and literature than spatial configurations. Signs are marks, figures, gestures perceived as if imbued with intention.[12] And this originating cause, the mark of intention, makes the sign a non-self-sustaining figure because it is rooted less in a universal and more in the individual; as a result, signs have to be maintained by a system. The tendency to ascribe this function to absences – to non-signs, to spaces – derives from a misinterpretation of the power accorded pauses in music or meditative walks or the spaces between letters on a page of text. Silence, stillness, space only seem to

Vitruvian Cycles 1 **207**

acquire communicability in a context, in a place, a place and context which arguably does all the work (if this is unclear, consider the negative connotations of silence or stillness or blankness without their structuring contexts: the remains are deafness, immobility, and muteness). As when arguing with staunch believers in ghosts and UFOs, assertions against space as a communicative aspect of architecture are not well received. Nevertheless, for the skeptical and curious, this argument can take three forms:

1. *Certainty of relation*: the non-sign, being neither certain nor probable but instead mute or ambivalent, receives no Being from knowledge and is accorded no power within any episteme. Any knowledge perceived as connected with a non-sign is understood as applied, received from outside, provisional and endlessly malleable. The meaning often ascribed to the sanctuary "space" of Wright's Unity Temple, for example, is chameleon-like in its potential for varying attributions: it is linked to Wright's own mythos, to Mayan Temples, to the precepts of the Unitarian faith, to democracy itself. However, this jumble quickly resolves itself into a reasonably decipherable palimpsest of references if one looks at the signs, the physical elements of architecture and their relations, and not at the space. Unity Temple's sanctuary may very well record a multitude of different and even antagonistic metaphors within its surfaces and proportions and ornaments but it is possible, through those physically existent figures, to perceive and conceive a whole of parts in relation to one another. The non-sign, space, offers no such synthesis.

2. *Type of relation*: the non-sign is indistinct; its presence and re-presence are indistinguishable. To subject it to analysis or "decipherment" is not to decipher anything but instead is to add to the non-sign a series of figures or signifiers that are not inherent in the non-sign. This non-sign, because it is wholly other than a sign, is not measurable in time or "space" without transfiguration into a sign – or, in the case of architectural space, the framing of space within an architectural enclosure that is, as proxy, available to measurement. Perhaps this explains the utter failure of words, photographs, and even video (three types of sign systems) to convey the full sensation-ideation complex of experience found in great landscapes – the Grand Canyon, Montana's Big Sky Country, Oahu's eastern shore, Australia's outback – for each of these is a juxtaposition of signs and non-sign and thus always, in part, alien to language and, because alien to language, alien to the act of recording for future 'reading.'

3. *Origin of the relation*: it is impossible for the conscious products of human endeavor to exist as non-signs. Furthermore, there is reason to doubt that even (so-called) unconscious human products might be non-signs: trash heaps are clearly signs; so are rocks used as doorstops; sticks used as levers; and so on. Anything remembered, reflected upon, or known has – in that memory, reflection, or understanding – already undergone a transformation from non-sign to sign. But here, again, it is important to recognize that the *things*

208 Architecture History and Theory in Reverse

remembered, reflected upon or known about an "architectural space" are literally the enclosing or defining surfaces that constitute everything that is not space and the figures that occupy positions within.[13]

Picture the interiors of the Pantheon (see Figure 16.1), the Hagia Sophia, and Unity Temple. Different, right? Now, imagine each without the physical

FIGURE 16.1 Pantheon (interior), Rome
Source: Photograph by author.

manifestations of architecture. Imagine the great cathedrals of Europe without their surfaces of stone and glass. They are all the same. Nothing. Now, imagine only the actual materials and their particular distribution as surfaces; imagine the carved stone and cast concrete and leaded stained glass in their existing arrangement and proportion: what is embodied here? Everything. An encyclopedia of signs so great and projection of intention so suggestive that even the empty volume contained within acquires the character of a sign; it becomes a viscous atmosphere. And what has been lost by not conceiving of these great "spaces" as primarily spatial? Nothing. Literally.[14]

Notes

1 This and all subsequent references are taken from Vitruvius, *The Ten Books on Architecture*, translated by Morris Hicky Morgan (New York: Dover, 1960), here writing about the ancient's ornamentation and the correct expression of structural components of the orders in both original and copy.

2 According to Elaine Scarry:

> Our susceptibility to the prevailing description must in part be attributed to the instability of perception itself: the dissolution of one's own powers of description contributes to the seductiveness of any existing description …In turn, the instability of our descriptive powers results from the absence of appropriate interpretive categories that might act as "perceptual stays" in moments of emergency.
> (Scarry, *The Body in Pain*, New York: Oxford University Press, 1987, 279)

3 Umberto Eco, *From the Tree to the Labyrinth* (Cambridge, MA: Harvard University Press, 2014), 79.

4 Nikolaus Pevsner, *An Outline of European Architecture*, Jubilee Edition (Baltimore, MD: Penguin, 1961), 238.

5 As Elaine Scarry's analysis makes so clear. Note also Scarry's position in *The Body in Pain*, p. 283:

> The printing press, the institutionalized convention of written history, photographs, libraries, films, tape recordings, and Xerox machines are all materializations of the elusive embodied capacity for memory … They together make a relatively ahistorical creature into an historical one, one whose memory extends far back beyond the opening of its own individual lived experience, one who anticipates being itself remembered far beyond the close of its own individual lived experience, and one who accomplishes all this without each day devoting its awakened brain to rehearsals and recitations of all information it needs to keep available to itself.

6 See p. 13 in Alberto Pérez-Gómez, "The Space of Architecture: meaning as presence and representation," in Stephen Holl, Juhani Pallasmaa, and Alberto Pérez-Gómez, *Questions of Perception: phenomenology of architecture* (San Francisco: William Stout, 2006), 8–25.

7 I am here accepting St. Augustine's definition: "A sign is something which, over and above its sensible aspect, brings to mind something different from itself." Cited in Eco, *From the Tree to the Labyrinth*, 195.

8 Ibid., 21.

9 Some might object and argue that literature, thus understood, suffers the same potential for abuse by ideologues that seemingly plagued classical architecture for many centuries. A full rebuff to this position is not possible here; nevertheless, in short outline, it is

important to acknowledge that it is redundant to attempt to add an ideology to a dominant episteme or sign system, whether literary or architectural. Every dominant sign system is always already an ideology.

10 Pevsner, *Outline of European Architecture*, 170.

11 Eco, *From the Tree to the Labyrinth*, 73. He continues on the same page: "The fact that it is a Median Encyclopedia does not mean that all of its contents are shared by all members of a given culture, but rather that it is *shareable*."

12 The phrase "as if" is important. The correctness of this perception or attribution of intentions is unimportant to the emergence of signs. Hieroglyphs were understood to be signs long before the content could be deciphered and, more importantly, even if our present-day decodings are eventually revealed to have been erroneous and decipherment again becomes questionable, that will not alter our understanding of the hieroglyphs as signs.

13 The ancient Greek word "*peras*" fits. *Peras* means boundary and boundaries are required to provide order and order provides meaning.

14 Some friends have argued that this whole, *peras* and *apeiron* or the sum of matter and space, creates a "charged void" and it is this to which architects and theorists are referring when they casually use the word "space" (albeit with mystical overtones); and there is little reason to doubt that "space" is often used as a shorthand for the emergent experiential quality of the formal distribution of material surfaces. Unfortunately, as Jane Jacobs argued in relation to city economic development and the origins of agriculture, "the fallacy is to mistake the results ... for preconditions" (Jane Jacobs, *The Economy of Cities*, New York: Vintage, 1970), 48.

17

VITRUVIAN CYCLES 2

Physical Language and Shared Experience

In that gathering of men, at a time when utterance of sound was purely individual, from daily habits they fixed upon articulate words just as these had happened to come; then, from indicating by name things in common use, the result was that in this chance way they began to talk, and thus originated conversation with one another.

(Vitruvius, The Ten Books on Architecture, *II, I, 1)*

And since [early people] were of an imitative and teachable nature, they would point out to each other the results of their building, boasting of the novelties in it; and thus, with their natural gifts sharpened by emulation, their standards improved daily.

(Vitruvius, The Ten Books on Architecture, *II, I, 3)*

Then, taking courage and looking forward from the standpoint of higher ideas born of the multiplication of the arts, they gave up huts and began to build houses with foundations, having brick or stone walls, and roofs of timber and tiles; next, observation and application led them from fluctuating and indefinite conceptions to definite rules of symmetry.

(Vitruvius, The Ten Books on Architecture, *II, I, 7)*[1]

4. Four Hypotheses

In the preceding pages, I have attempted to communicate primarily about, and almost exclusively through, grammatical written language. There is no unified physical language alternative. Writing, literally "in other words," has acted as surrogate for its physical kin. This is justified. Narrations of Joyce and de Sade, biblical and Marxist traditions mined by Scarry, architectural history as conceived by Pevsner, the Social Contract of Rousseau, studies of translation by Steiner, and the analyses of literary figures like Kafka by philosophers like Deleuze and Guattari are so ubiquitous in academia as to form a nearly transparent currency that lends itself more readily to the complex bartering of intellectual exchange than do works of architecture. Words are easier to use and a more efficient means for transmitting ideas. But we have traced the exodus from Babel sufficiently to ask whether written and physical language are homologous, or at least sufficiently translatable, so that study of one is capable of providing real insights into the other.

Immediately, the observed disparity between the two forms of language suggests they exist as different kinds of skills. Physical language is further removed in communicative use and clarity than speaking is from writing. This is borne out in everyday experience. Almost all humans appear capable of learning how to extract meaning from some form of written language and, more importantly, readily believe there is communicative content awaiting extraction as reward for their efforts. With physical language, few learn to "read" perhaps because almost no one consciously assumes such divination to be possible. And of those who do, fewer still think it important.[2]

Any claim that physical language is on a par with written language in potential accessibility must be subjected to something like the scientific method. In this light, four hypotheses appear necessary: (1) physical language exists, as other forms of language do, on a continuum from primal human interaction with matter in light to sophisticated conveyances of content – historical, scientific, ritualistic, etc.; (2) objects of physical language operating on the primal and haptic end of the spectrum are, today, so transparent as to be linguistically invisible to self-conscious perception; in everyday language, almost everyone *gets 'it'* – e.g. the embedded content – so effortlessly that people are no longer aware that they are *getting* anything; (3) objects operating at the 'literary' or 'symbolic' end of the spectrum – paintings, sculptures, "architecture for architects" aka works of architecture – do not differ in kind from the objects of primal communication but, instead, are imbued with and perceived in multiple connections, like a rhizome, so that meaning is not prosaic or merely human or even other-than-human but arises as supra-human; and, finally, (4) this multiplication or layering of relatively transparent associations is misperceived as opacity, as intentional obfuscation, or, worst of all, a method for camouflaging an utter absence of meaning.

Hypothesis One

Physical language exists on a continuum from simple to complex forms of communication. Most philosophy and its appropriation into the jargon of the design disciplines segregate direct, felt, haptic experience from language; a residue of Descartes body–mind split. This tendency to see language as non-bodied and thus not fully human diminishes the breadth of languages and their mediation of self and other. This begs the question: Is it even other? Language in general, and physical language in particular, are neither arbiter nor go-between; it is not a supplementary translation. It is not a supplement of any kind. Physical language is enmeshed in acts of experience as their structuring matrix. To stand, to view, to move on an axis and up a monumental stair, temple or ziggurat, not only enlivens a cosmological or authority narrative, it is to acknowledge that we are bipedal and binocular, that we have a front, a back, and two sides, and that being vertical we share more with trees and stairs and walls than with the horizontal ground we trample. Unless we perambulate like zombies, humans' ability to orient in and to a world argues for an essential linguistic content in experience.[3]

Hypothesis Two

The extreme transparency of simple forms of physical language renders it conceptually invisible. As the structuring matrix of our engagement with the world, physical language is acquired evolutionarily. Pre-dating Darwin and deeply ingrained before humans learned to write, this acquisition allows us to coordinate our own movements and coordinate with others. As with other such evolutionary traits, such as bipedal locomotion or the handling of tools, a general understanding of the relationship between things and the human body is so ubiquitous that it is taken for granted and, thus, more or less conceptually invisible. The seemingly seamless interface we acquire for objects – such as our automobiles, musical instruments or drawing tools – hints at the communicative potential that resides in things. As with walking, holding a pencil, speaking or any other acquired ability, only when our basic understanding of physical language is compromised does it become conceptually present. Imagine the very real dangers inherent in not understanding heights or differences between hard and soft surfaces. Or, note the profound unease people experience when encountering someone who claims to receive communications from physical objects. Leaving aside the veracity of reports by shamans or schizophrenics,[4] this unease is a measure of just how engrained our expectation of physical object muteness is.

Hypothesis Three

The supra-human quality of complex forms of language. The tendency to differentiate is evident even when one views a single language. In its spoken form, for example, there is no shortage of people who would categorize the babbles of children, the stuttering of adolescents, and the oratory of statesmen as unique and easily distinguished. With a broader view, however, spoken utterances are all of a kind, even though diverse in deviations from established standards. With an even broader view in which all forms of language act as structuring matrices of engagement, the split between written and physical language reveals itself as a difference in degree, not kind. The close relationship of written and physical language especially in orienting words – left, right, up, down, forward, back – evinces the drive to communicate: to make things speak is to share. To say a thing is "imposing" or "heavy" simultaneously communicates phenomenological and formal content. The oratory of a statesman, the writing of Shakespeare, or the expressiveness of the statues of Bernini are all of a kind with our most basic drives. These allocutions differ from babbles, elementary school primers and the archetypal hut only in the techniques used to deliver content and degree of success.

While the observations in support of hypotheses two and three are rather elementary, together they shed light on two far more complex mysteries. The equivalence of written and physical language explains (1) a non-distinction between observation and relation, and (2) a dissociation caused by the constant reiteration of commentary. "Non-distinction" refers to a frequently encountered transparency between classifications organized by experience, mislabeled as "bodily," and those formed by conceptual or "linguistic" systems. Dissociation is the tendency – noted by formalists and phenomenologists alike – for repeated descriptions and analyses to have the seemingly paradoxical effect of reducing attention to the actual thing described. Both "non-distinction" and dissociation are relatively easy to understand once one accepts that written and physical languages differ only by degree. Commentary on a physical object *is perceived as* a diminishment of experience because it is redundant to the original engagement with that object's physical language: to see is not to forget the name of the thing one sees but to have already perceived its name; to annunciate the name after perception is therefore redundant.

Hypothesis Four

Complex forms are misperceived as opaque. Increases in the number of references made, types of content conveyed, and techniques of conveyance utilized are almost always accompanied by a concomitant decrease in the perceived transparency of the thing under observation, be it text, painting, sculpture or building. This inversion is fostered by the belief that interpretation is alien to things themselves and therefore is at best contingent if not utterly arbitrary. But this belief is false. Interpretations are not added to things; they frame us in anticipation of experience. Interpretation, like the related act of commentary, is self-perpetuating, not for its own sake and not for 'truth.' It is self-perpetuating because experience involves continual adjustment to changes of perspective. All deep emotions and meaningful relationships to which we return day after day, year after year, demand these re-framings and adjustments. Meaning, the what-is-at-stake in language, requires this work and is worth it. To class written or physical languages that require extended interpretation as "opaque" or "difficult" or "architecture for architects" is to blinker experience to everything that is profound. Arguably, these are the things we long to 'see' and share.

5. The Social Order

In Classical eras, physical language was more transparent than its written counterpart. That things were erotically charged and worthy of decipherment was a touchstone of pre-information age thinking.[5] Today, an oppressive, non-human opacity is decried wherever the chain of signification becomes longer or more difficult than media sound bites. This opacity, in no small part, results from a ubiquitous, if subconscious, misreading of the Social Contract: "All that destroys social unity is worthless; all institutions that set man in contradiction to himself are worthless."[6] Misread, the latter portion is an assertion of the primacy of conscientious subjects over the objective order of the former. No aspect of our information age has suffered this unfortunate misreading and arrogant presumption more than domains of physical language – *opaque works of art and architecture cannot possibly mean anything, and certainly not convey anything that is stable*, it might be said, *in contemporary Western societies that have finally embraced their heterogeneity*. While there is no question of the service Western societies have wrought humanity by championing individual liberties and the value of diversity, it is useful to acknowledge that a concomitant devaluation of communal values impacts the teaching, making, and reading of architecture. Architecture as a foundational societal text has given way to architecture as an expression of individual desires and mere entertainment. In the diminution of order as a potential tool of oppression, aspirations to meaning are surrendered to lesser ambitions, whether technological, formal or sensual.

What destroys the social order if not the presumption that physical diversification is a necessary outcome of humanity's diversity of opinions, ideas, hopes, dreams? This presumption is a product of earlier anti-authoritarian, anti-hierarchical, anti-order motives working behind the scenes of High Modernism and profoundly skeptical of the eye and visual order in general. This presumption, in turn, fuels a postmodern profession's self-sustaining circuit of meaninglessness that is not the result of natural entropy or an accident of time or even a necessary correction in the wake of discovering that the old orders were false assumptions all along. The self-perpetuating presumption of the rightness of – or, at least, acquiescence to – sprawling individuality and difference fuels this post-meaning (post-literacy, post-order) age. Among lesser consequences, this skepticism undermines the potential for resemblance (the similitude of physical language) to contribute to knowledge (the on-going accrual of social order).

Who are the twenty-first-century equivalents of Bishops Bernward, Aethelwold, and Benno, who drove the Romanesque toward new forms of surface articulation for the sake of greater unity and more profound expression? This question is not as traditionalist or as out of place as it may appear. What is needed is not a retracing of the doubts and misplaced notions of sense-equity-as-metaphor-for-social-equality (discussed in Chapter 4) that led to anti-authoritarian skepticism regarding vision and formal order. What is needed is a conscious revaluation of physical language and the relation of visual order to contemporary issues of meaning and language. At issue are the undreamt possibilities for forwarding communities and inventing new social ideas on the ground of shared place.

It is necessary to recall only two points to make clear we have not mined the depths of visual order's potential contribution to communication of shared meaning. First, resemblance and its chain of signification continue to function despite ongoing change in preferred forms of classification. In other words, many

216 Architecture History and Theory in Reverse

systems of knowledge based on vision that were established and tested prior to anti-authoritarian skepticism have remained in force. Traditional color and proportional theories are obvious examples of vision-based grammars, developed by diverse individuals codifying their subjective experiences into cohesive and thus communicable forms, that have retained their 'authority' – that is, have maintained their relative affect – despite the subtending of these traditions into alternative historical-political narratives. The optical adjustments, refinements and corrections of rigid classical orders, known since before Vitruvius' time, are another example.[7] Second, as knowledge accumulates through vision, the overall system of resemblances and its potential grows. The order of resemblance is an ever-expanding, rhizomatic order. Through resemblance, the potential for growth in both order and knowledge is infinite – or at least incomprehensibly vast. From an individual family's genealogy to an archaeology of human languages; from mapping the human genome to organizing the classes, phyla, and kingdoms of all living things; from the rib-vaults of the Romanesque Durham to the effusive tracery of the Gothic King's College Chapel to the mullions of the Jesse Window, resemblance connects large and small, general and specific, old and recent, here and there, in a chain of communicable significance. The value of this is not to be underestimated.

Rousseau's simplest assertion was arguably his most profound. "That which destroys social unity is worthless." And, we should add, that which forges social unity is priceless. Unfortunately, in Western architecture at least, the terms are flipped. Of course, we underestimate the value of resemblance. This is due, in part, to our general sense that resemblance is a product of interpretation. And interpretation is seen as a projective practice, an additive fiction. But interpretation is not added onto things; it frames us in anticipation of experience. Anticipation requires expectation; expectation requires familiarity. Thus, our general sense is backward. To interpret entails being conscious of a system of resemblances (and this is why biomorphism has failed to generate communicative architecture[8]). Furthermore, to intuit and to know, *to sense* and *to think*, are linked via resemblance. Even perception and logic, sensation and ideation, are conjoined in similitude and become translatable, otherwise there could be no suggestion of correspondence between emotions and ideas or sensations and concepts. Through resemblance, the two sides of these traditional (and misguided) schemas of bifurcation are connected – here, mind identifying itself as that body; there, body supporting the functioning of that mind. Orders of resemblance ground experience and meaning.

6. Cycles of Resemblance

Seeing, if understood as meaningful, is something more than looking, more than dispassionate observation, and more than private pleasure. Seeing, as a meaningful act, is never forgetting the name of the thing one sees. As the Buddhist monk, Thich Nhat Hanh, has said: "Every time we call something by its name, we make it more real, like saying the name of a friend."[9] For these reasons we tend to fall more deeply in love with people than with pets, with pets than with works of art or a house, and more deeply with artifice than mere lumps of unarranged and unadorned matter. Seeing is ontological.[10] We tend to be drawn to those things that activate conscious attention, particularly beings capable (or seemingly capable) of choice, of giving and receiving names, of carrying, asserting and questioning identities. Being-For-Itself, in twentieth-century existential parlance. Animate Qualities, in traditional fine art criticism. Regardless of the terms used, this strange power of the name is critical to meaningful sight. Without recognition of a name there is only what is: cold, inert matter; Being-In-Itself; inanimate stuff. Without names, things are neither similar nor different. A world without similitude is a world without signs. And a world without signs is a world without communication. Nirvana, some would call it; or Monastic. Or solipsistic.

Lonely would also fit.[11]

The ontological roots of desire, love, care, and concern are the philosophical equivalents of metaphor to literature[12] or of mirror neurons to neurology or memes to genetics – the perception of an idea, a concept, an action outside of ourselves that nevertheless mirrors a thought, a name, or an action lodged in our own record of experience and strikes a cognitive bell of resemblance.[13] Through this similitude, the person or thing observed is engendered with qualities of the person seeing, naming, touching, wanting. To see this way is to recognize *presence* as something more profound than mere inert existence and to recognize that the perception of presence (if this can be distinguished from presence *per se*) is diminished by the withdrawal of the name.

Architects who attempt to avoid the difficulties of physical language by recourse to sensual solipsism or technological instrumentality or banal formalism create artifacts that occupy space as incomplete presences and strike the visitor as bombastic, indecipherable or trite. As literary critic George Steiner notes:

> Western art is, more often than not, about preceding art; literature about literature. The word 'about' points to the crucial ontological dependence, to the fact that a previous work of body of work is, in some degree, the *raison d'être* of the work in hand.[14]

Without the incessant murmur of words, all architectural images, reflections, and appearances would be perplexing and deeply disturbing. Without resemblance, Classical, Gothic, Baroque or Modern temples become instead a series of mute and menacing forms.[15]

The stated purpose of the architecture undertaken at Babel was not to forget but to know. And, there is a reason that this myth resounds: people assume God destroyed Babel in order to preserve a veil between names and things, without which there would be pure identity in full presence; and, as a result, experiences of longing and desire, searching and hoping, would come to an end. *We would know too much.* Consciously appropriated or not, for some architects, this assumption fueled the ascendancy of "space" as the successor to identity and gave force to the notion that forgetting might be a prerequisite for seeing. But the assumption that

218 Architecture History and Theory in Reverse

full presence, the coalescence of names and things, is necessarily dead presence is false or, at least, premature; it is *precipitancy* on par with the biblical story.

Consider the distinction between an artist's signature on a canvas and the same signature on a contract. Even if the two signatures are materially and formally identical and both, arguably, stand for the absent artist and thereby convey legal and economic value, the signatures are ontologically of two kinds. The first type, the signature inscribed on a work of art, is a mark of prior presence at a work judged complete before the addition of the signature. We assume completion is a necessary pre-condition to the artist appending his or her name. In this light, the artwork is understood as having achieved full presence prior to the signature and, in terms of the quality of the work under consideration, the name of the artist is deemed irrelevant to experience the work's aesthetic and conceptual content. The second type, the signature on a contract, is different. Contracts are understood as being for, and legally requiring, the name of the artist. In other words, the contract has no purpose or meaning without the artist's mark. Only collectors and auctioneers conflate the two and conceive the signature on the work of art in contractual terms; and it is such people who demonstrate that the assumption that conceptual-perceptual co-presence denies experience is false.

When viewing a significant work of art, at most and at best, the signature of the artist allows excess content to be read into its surface. The name of the artist serves as hyper-content; the known facts and unknown mysteries of the artist's life become part of the work's invisible Being. Viewed this way, the work of art achieves a greater presence and comes closer to the experience of another human being, Being-For-Itself, by borrowing aspects of the artist's identity. When, on the contrary, we read the signature ("ah, Picasso!") and register only thoughts of the name's economic value, we cordon off the thing's presence as separable, discrete, and highly instrumental facts ("how rare is this? That sure is an ugly color but I bet I could sell it! Will anyone notice if I tuck it under my jacket?"). Separation of name and thing does not merely harm the work; the work in this case is lost. Our response to this potential loss cannot be to forget the scrawl in the lower right-hand corner but, instead, to mine the meaning of the whole – colors, forms, narrative content, and name – in order to experience something far more profound than any one aspect could deliver.

Architecture is not painting or sculpture. The problems of names and naming in architecture are not those of literal signatures. Yet one essential question is the same. It is not, how close can identity and matter come before the viewer's ability to intuit or interpret is infringed? It is, how far can one push the displacement of thing and name before resemblance, and thus significance, are lost? Religious architecture – particularly religious buildings built in other times, in foreign countries, under the sway of different traditions – suggests that this gap is pliable. The great Mosque at Córdoba (see Figure 17.1) predates my favorite churches in Europe by several centuries. It is structured differently; aisles of polychromatic stone arches; star-ribbed vaults. Its parts are recognizable, both the Islamic originals and Christian insertions. It is signed in numerous ways and loaded, perhaps

FIGURE 17.1 Mosque-Cathedral of Córdoba
Source: Photograph by Amber Ellett Penman.

overloaded, with narrative content. But to stand inside is to experience sensory input and conceptual content in such massive doses that our condition as tourists or immigrants, adherents or infidels, is irrelevant – the effect is total.

Contemporary western architects aspiring to impact individuals could do worse than Córdoba, and often do, because the privileging of information age innovations over Classical era identities blinkers us to the origins of identity and thus the origins of meaning itself.[16] Córdoba's Mosque and similarly regarded works of architecture are neither effective nor affective because something is missing or absent from the full sensory-conceptual array. Seeing them is not a forgetting but a profusion of qualities sensual and conceptual; physical and metaphysical. None of the experiences by which we judge our lives to have been well spent or joyful or filled with love or, in any other way, meaningful fit neatly into a narrowly bracketed view. Understood as forgetting, "seeing" cannot be understood as anything other than a reduction of the human animal to brute sensation – bipeds with binocular vision and hearing, oriented to the world with a front and back, a left and right, with a rudimentary awareness of above and below. To *see* Picasso's Harlequins, it is advisable not to forget the Harlequins in history or the Harlequins here in paint or the signature or the artist that signature represents. Seeing that gets recorded in the log of our lives as being meaningful involves sensing physical quantities (Vitruvian order and symmetry), perceiving physical qualities (Vitruvian arrangement and *eurythmia*) and conceiving embodied content (Vitruvian propriety and economy) in juxtaposition, holding these in the mind as related but with just enough differentiation that more meanings – from sensual to conceptual, individual to societal, synchronic to diachronic – can rush to fill the gaps from both sides. It is in the determination of this "just enough" that artists and architects spend the frustrating and rewarding hours of their careers.

In works resulting from a healthy pursuit of both the material conditions of the artifact (sensual and formal, qualitative and quantitative, aspects) understood synchronically (volumetrically in immediate presence) and its language (conceptual

220 Architecture History and Theory in Reverse

or narrative or symbolic content) understood diachronically (embedded in history), the gap of differences produced are not so great as to require conscious attention on the part of inhabitants or tourists. Pevsner's rapturous and surprisingly uncritical commentary on the Hagia Sophia – how its "concealed complexity [achieves] a magic scarcely ever surpassed"[17] – expresses the point of view of the trained observer confronted with such a meshing. With the disorder or near absence of information age architectural language, however, architects tend to cling to one side of this divide or the other; as a result, the balance between name and thing, or concept and percept, necessary to open a territory of meaning hospitable to shared experience is seldom achieved.

Notes

1 These and all following references are taken from Vitruvius, *The Ten Books on Architecture*, translated by Morris Hicky Morgan (New York: Dover, 1960).
2 At a recent review of careful and subtle student work, an architecture professor stated that he was "tired of seeing architecture for architects." I suspect such frustration is rooted in the sense that a deep chasm exists between elitists who believe architecture is potentially communicative and "the common man" who subscribes to architecture's banal instrumentality. But is this chasm real?
3 This notion is so central to Leibniz's "Metaphysics" that it comprises his entire thirty-fourth thesis. See Gottfried Wilhelm Leibniz, "Discourse on Metaphysics," in *Discourse on Metaphysics: Correspondence with Arnauld, Monadology*, Introduction by Paul Janet, translated by George Montgomery (La Salle, IL: Open Court, 1993), 57–58.
4 Nevertheless, it is unwise to dismiss all such reports as mysticism or hallucination. As Julian Jaynes noted in relation to schizophrenics, "the nervous system of a patient makes simple perceptual judgments of which the patient's 'self' is not aware. And these … may then be transposed into voices that seem prophetic" (Julian Jaynes, *The Origins of Consciousness in the Breakdown of the Bicameral Mind*, Boston: Houghton Mifflin, 1976), 90.
5 See Alexander Tzonis and Liane Lefaivre, *Classical Architecture: the poetics of order* (Cambridge, MA: MIT Press, 1986), 37.
6 Jean-Jacques Rousseau, *The Social Contract* (New York: Maestro, 2012), Book IV, §7.
7 Tzonis and Lefaivre, *Classical Architecture*, 87–88.
8 Biomorphism is often put forward as an appropriate technique of resemblance for our time. Unfortunately, my ability to use the word "technique" in the preceding sentence is one reason why biomorphism has failed to deliver meaningful forms. To date, its techniques have emulated the evolutionary processes of biological systems not their known or knowable order. The resulting works of architecture are not familiar enough to support a shared meaning.
9 Thich Nhat Hanh, *Peace Is Every Step: the path of mindfulness in everyday life*, Foreword by H.H. the Dalai Lama (New York: Bantam Books, 1992), 28.
10 Umberto Eco, *From the Tree to the Labyrinth* (Cambridge, MA: Harvard University Press, 2014), 348: "As far as human knowledge is concerned, not even existence, place, or moment are the proper object of the senses, but are predicated by a more complex discursive act."
11 Bill McKibben, *Deep Economy: the wealth of communities and the durable future* (New York: Holt, 2008), 96:

> We surrendered a fixed identity – a community, an extended family, deep and comforting roots – for, quite literally, the chance to "make something of ourselves." Now we create our own identities. We build from scratch the things our ancestors once took for granted. This liberation is exhilarating, and it is daunting; it is exciting, and it is lonely.

Vitruvian Cycles 2 **221**

12 See "From Metaphor to *Analogia Entis*," in Eco's *From Tree to Labyrinth*, 116–170.
13 Marco Iacoboni's *Mirroring People: the new science of how we connect with others* (New York: Farrar, Straus and Giroux, 2008), provides an accessible overview of mirror neuron research and connections to language and socially-constructed meaning. See also, Richard Dawkins, *The Selfish Gene* (Oxford: Oxford University Press, 1976).
14 George Steiner, *After Babel: aspects of language and translation* (New York: Oxford University Press, 1975), 461.
15 If there is doubt regarding these last points, read accounts of people blind from birth who suddenly have their sight restored. Moments of complete disconnect between sense perceptions, particularly vision, on the one hand, and knowledge of concepts and names, on the other, are seldom experiences of joy or wonder; these moments are more accurately described as disorienting and terrifying.
16 See Jaynes, *Origin of Consciousness*, 66. See also, Paul Ricoeur, *Time and Narrative*, vol. 2, translated by Kathleen McLaughlin and David Pellauer (Chicago: University of Chicago Press, 1985), particularly Chapter 2, "The Semiotic Constraints on Narrativity," pp. 29–60.
17 Nikolaus Pevsner, *An Outline of European Architecture*, Jubilee Edition (Baltimore, MD: Penguin, 1961), 40.

Now the whole world had one language and a common speech.

As men moved eastward, they found a plain in Shinar and settled there.

They said to each other, "Come, let's make bricks and bake them thoroughly." They used brick instead of stone, and tar instead of mortar.

Then they said, "Come, let us build ourselves a city, with a tower that reaches to the heavens, so that we may make a name for ourselves and not be scattered over the face of the whole earth."

But the Lord came down to see the city and the tower that the men were building.

The Lord said, "If as one people speaking the same language they have begun to do this, then nothing they plan to do will be impossible for them. Come, let us go down and confuse their language, so they will not understand each other."

So the Lord scattered them from there over all the earth, and they stopped building the city.

That is why it was called Babel – because there the Lord confused the language of the whole world. From there the Lord scattered them over the face of the whole earth.

(Genesis 11: 1–9)

PROLOGUE: BABEL...

Architecture begins at Babel. It is our discipline's origin story, but not because it represents the earliest work of architecture. The Babel story is the oldest and best-known record of architecture's ambition. Its finite quality makes it originary.[1] To look back across time, across the plain of Shinar, is not like looking at the intersection outside my office windows. There are very few 600 BCE buildings left to see – and none as they were. And while countless architects, master builders, and craftsmen shaped Babylon under Semiramis, Nitocris, and, most famously, Nebuchadnezzar II, those builders' names along with their ambitions are scattered and lost. This factual void represents the ultimate break in the assumed lineage of architectural practice. At Babel, backward history reaches a destination beyond which there is no trail.

The story focuses on the city's tower, probably evidenced in the ruins of the Etemenanki ziggurat. Etemenanki's age is unknown. Its master builder (or master builders) or architect (or architects) is unknown. It is important, however, to personify this unknown, for in so doing certain comparative questions become unavoidable. For instance, did this person suffer the uncanny attractions of seeking to invent while also grounding the work in traditions capable of being grasped by the public at large? Was he (and it would be a he) driven by both ethical responsibilities and a desire for spectacle or was one predominant? By the time of the construction of Córdoba's Mosque/Cathedral at least twelve centuries later, these bifurcations – newness v. tradition; ethics v. spectacle – are clearly evident; but it is unclear if they were part of design consciousness at Babylon. Did these bifurcations come into being with the earliest conceptions of architecture or are these evolutionary transformations that acquired their status as "natural" only much more recent?

While these are unanswerable questions, it is useful to consider what evidence would be necessary to formulate an answer. Short of finding some lost journal or

224 Prologue: Babel …

testament, the most basic information that would shed light on these questions would be to know whether an architectural media existed at the time of the tower's construction. In the presence of architectural media, there are traditions to follow or to overcome or both, traditions of responsibility, and traditions of exceeding mere responsibilities. Without this mediating ground, architecture is either independent of all other bodies of knowledge and bodies *per se* (therefore, free-floating and incommunicative) or merely a derivative subset of some other body of knowledge (religion, politics, philosophy, cultural studies, physiology) with no communicative potential or cultural role of its own.

Without evidence that a Babylonian architectural media once existed, these unanswerable questions must give way to others that, while also unanswerable, afford speculative response. Such questions include: To what extent were the master builder and his benefactor satisfied with evoking a sensation of enormity? Was the purpose to communicate? If so, was a general impression or an explicit content intended? Finally, was the purpose to convey information (i.e. to record or transmit a "name") or meaning (to render "ourselves" appreciable to the world)? Unanswerable, yes. But we can get a sense of the answers by inquiring into the nature of sense itself.

Does What We Say Always Reside in What We Sense (Even Though What We Sense Has No Necessary or Permanent Relation to What Is)?

"Sense" has two obvious but divergent connotations today. One is casually understood as physical; we receive qualities via our senses (sight, hearing, touch, taste, and smell). The other is understood, just as casually, as psychological; we intuit embedded content via linguistic relationships. Words formulated in response to the first sense of "sense"' are often informational (I saw, I heard, etc.) while the latter invokes words aimed at meaning (I understand this to suggest …). This is not always the case and meaning and information are not mutually exclusive terms. Still, it is reasonable to assert that "sense," in one form or another, drives all attempts at communication.

The impulse to build the Tower of Babel was rooted in sense at this most fundamental level. As origin story, it sets disciplinary precedent. Architecture is a record and the attempted communication of sense. Perhaps this was an architectural truism in civilizations predating the compartmentalization of sensation into discrete perceptual and conceptual kinds that marks the first measurable phase of entropy in western architectural language. In the twentieth century, perceptual and conceptual sensations subdivided into social, practical, and journalistic concerns; and, in the twenty-first century, these have given way to sociological, technological, and marketing tropes. Today, the idea of architecture as the communication of sense can seem naïve, at best. But this contemporary discomfort does not diminish the importance of the relation between maker and made, between sensory source and its transmission – particularly in western architecture's origin story.

Does Evoking a Proper Name Close Sensation, Stabilize and Kill It?

This question, aimed at Babel, is not a new postulation of "seeing is forgetting the name of the thing one sees," here in interrogative form.[2] All time is local. All sensation is local. To understand architecture's origin story, we must acknowledge underlying differences. Today there are a multitude of classical, romantic, modern, postmodern, professionalized, and anti-professional sensations and times. At the far end of our story, there were Babylonian sensations and times. Not necessarily simpler or better.[3] The Etemenanki ziggurat was built in a time other than, and with senses that should not be assumed equivalent to, our own. These differences are significant.

In our own time, it is possible to answer the question "does evoking a proper name close sensation, stabilize and kill it?" affirmatively insofar as we inhabit an episteme that accepts the division of interior from exterior as parallel to freedom vs. tyranny. Sensation *in me* is mine and thus meaningful. Sensation expressed *in the world* through a name is something potentially taken from me; its connection to me severed, it dies. Reading both Herodotus and the biblical account, it is unclear if 'interior' and 'exterior' held an analogous meaning. In Herodotus, interior and exterior are most evident in the division of individual precincts to the city as a whole or the city to the larger countryside and beyond. In Genesis, the terms are best applied, if at all, to the divinely ascribed limits to human endeavors. Yet, this latter form of interior-exterior bifurcation and the possibility that the tower's master builder could have contemplated its design at various scales and from distant perspectives – being within it, resting on its intermediate terraces, or standing on top and from there viewing an external world that is made either more distant or local by a turn of the head; or standing in lush gardens, miles removed from the city, and viewing it as an object that either draws the world together or repulses by turns of allegiance – are more compelling and writ larger than modern preoccupations with the individual and his or her mind-body or rational-poetic duality allows.

Architecture in an information age is the rendering of sense as *mine*, *yours*, or nothing at all. The archaeological evidence at the Etemenanki ziggurat suggests an architecture of *ours*, *theirs*, or everyone's insofar as it appears to eschew isolation and privatization of meaning in favor of an overt but rather straightforward *presencing* deemed essential to the day-to-day functioning of fertile crescent civilizations. This is not to suggest that information age moderns or non-Babylonian visitors in the time of Nebuchadnezzar II – or even the majority of Babylon's citizens – understood the Tower. *Architecture always runs the risk of being meaningless, and would be nothing without this risk.* Meaning demands this possibility.

The use of direct presence as an appeal to meaning was, however, without irony, which is a tactic that arises only when commonsense notions of reality are understood as distinct from Truth. In this way, it may be argued that the Tower was more akin to the *São Pedro* than the Pompidou: that is, more like a raft emphatically projecting its raftness than a building exterior masquerading as an interior; more of an objective fact than an appeal to an invisible truth made visible as a punchline.

226 Prologue: Babel ...

It would be easy to transcribe these statements on direct presence as an argument for gratuitous material expenditure and tautological obviousness – i.e. a big Tower will be understood as a big tower. This is true but trivial. What is most important in this architectural provision of "more than enough" is the mental space and time it dare not fill regarding ultimate meaning either for Babylonians then or generations that followed. Twentieth-century irony does not bypass meaning or prolong its decipherment; instead, it is merely another route; and often it is a short circuit that gets the reader to an intended meaning quickly without stopping for the thing itself. The Tower's imposing form was not relegated to such speedy enlightenment. It wowed; it filled viewers with awe; but it left its potential decipherment to subsequent hours of contemplation and in accordance with norms, rules, and systems of the time. If the Tower did more than this, if it told people what to think as political and religious treatises typically do, and as irony often does in prickly fashion, it would diminish its own potential as an object capable of serving as a backdrop to community.

Despite the Tower's non-ironical and slow-read design intent, it was a transmitter of information. This last phrase might seem contradictory to the preceding one. But the contradiction is only an apparent one. *Ulysses, The 120 Days of Sodom,* Fermi diagrams, codes produced by the Nazi Enigma machine and the scriptures of the Jewish Torah (despite the inappropriateness of the comparison) are all compilations of information that are difficult to decipher, at best. These artifacts are not intended to meet the subject halfway. The best transmitters of the "more" that I have argued is the goal of architecture are objects for the sake of objects; objects which leave the work of the subject to subjects. Architecture in the mold of the Tower of Babel is an essential solidity.

I doubt the Babylonians ever thought about the space formed by the Tower's presence in any way commensurate with today's use of "lived space" or "awareness of subjective space." Matter mattered, as did the relation between bits of formed matter at some distance; but these comments do not convey the profound difference that separates the two views of space. Here, I return to two earlier claims: (1) quality is a non-temporal measure against a change in, or expectation of, desire; every act of making quality, of seeking quality, and perceiving quality is an act taken in time against time; and (2) the transition of architecture from pre-information age spatialized time to information age lived space is a transition from time understood as subservient to space to time that is not believed to be spatial but is experienced as such. Perhaps at this point in the story, circa 600 BCE, these claims find a more comfortable expression: in pursuit of timelessness, time, seen as an inferior measure of life, must be battled with material qualities that express themselves as unchanging presences in space.

Can There Be Compatible Sensations? In Other Words, Can Sensations Be Shared?

This book implicitly balances two straightforward and yet contradictory themes: (1) history in general, and the history of architecture in particular, transmit no essential meaning from past to present; and (2) architecture is a deployment of materials, realized at the scale of real or imagined inhabitation, to transmit information. The contradiction is only apparent. Architecture-as-information distinguishes information from meaning and thus makes claims for architecture only as a signal, not as specific content or decipherment. The former theme, that architecture itself is meaningless, suggests that the receiver always constructs meaning in arrears from the information available – whether we are talking about deciphering architectural lessons in Babylonian ruins or perceiving the unity of a streetscape outside a modern office window.

Taken together, these themes frame western architecture's pursuit of language since the fall of Babel. One issue resides outside this boundary. If architecture is (or was once) the communication of sense by an architect or master builder, as suggested above, and if an inhabitant or visitor constructs meaning in arrears, is there any way of knowing whether a signal transmitted is received as intended when designer and perceiver are separated in time? How are we to understand the biblical charge – "Come, let us build us a city and a tower … and let us make a name, lest we be scattered abroad upon the face of the whole earth" – and the conditions by which this achievement could be measured?

I have argued that the dark, incomprehensible aspects of experience exposed by de Sade and the seemingly limitless expanse of these revealed in Joyce are synonymous with the experience of the search for meaning itself. Meaning is, in part, a measure of the duration and difficulty of a decipherment process through which a perceiver struggles to determine what is at stake; and, in part, it is an assumption or pledge, also on the part of a perceiver, that he or she has discovered a meaning through this process. This pledge, of course, does not necessarily match the designers' intentions; and, there was no way to know that the builders at Babel even took an oath to a particular meaning or set of meanings. The pledge is taken in backwards glance, I've said. Its entire content is drawn from the realm of the existing physical thing, present-day subjective judgments on the part of a perceiver, and any assumed or inherited understanding of the cultural context of the object under consideration known to that perceiver.

Babel's challenge, recast into this post-Romantic language, was to transmit its pledge to future visitors – namely, "wow, these Babylonians really made a name for themselves" – merely through an arrangement of bricks and tar. This transmission of a pledge of sense and its reception intact across time (without relying on a supplementary architectural treatise or other text[4]), requires moving beyond the limited experiential economics previously discussed. It requires stable sensations.

What Would a 'Stable' or 'Sharable' Sensation Be?

The seeming impenetrability of these questions is a result of both the normal blind spots imposed by every accepted historical framework and architecture's peculiar obsession with spatial and political identities at the expense of ideational differences.

228 Prologue: Babel …

As with all creative disciplines, architecture has to both acknowledge and assert a range of epistemes if it is to communicate subject-to-subject in a society, from those which are easy and comfortable to those which are less so. The roots of desires are found in this interaction.

The eruption of a unique condition in language – whether written or spoken or physical or, simply, a sense that lingers because it is a desire to which a category of response has yet to be identified – is conceivable only as figure against a backdrop which is striated and fossilized and, thus, known to a community of speakers and readers. A stable or shareable sensation can exist only as an Other within a commonly held ideational framework; and *otherness*, as present-day media makes abundantly clear, lasts only so long as the time it takes the general populace to embrace it as "familiar" or "non-threatening." This changes the terms somewhat, but clarifies the central theme: the ambition at Babel was to build a tower that maintained its otherness across time and cultures.

How is this achieved? De Sade narrated a world into existence that has retained its character as Other, even in the permissive atmosphere of modern western culture, by pairing conventions of polite society with the frighteningly off-putting. Harrowing complications in language trigger otherness. Otherness triggers desires. The ideational calls forth the sensual. This strategy is significant.[5]

Babel is a parable of ambition that resonates even today. Why? Literary worlds and great buildings hold our history and our myths before us so that we may imagine new things without having to constantly remind ourselves that we stand on an evolving ground. Most of these texts and images have been so woven into the striated fabric of language that they have lost their character as Other. Arguably literature, philosophy, and religious texts are great or serious or revelatory to the extent that they work across, and thereby stretch, the fabric of time – past and present – by critically, speculatively, descriptively and imaginatively asserting otherness. *Ulysses, The 120 Days of Sodom*, and the story of Babel are among the written works to have retained their otherness. In the case of Babel, the reason is rather clear: what better example of otherness than a biblical story in which God is so threatened by humanity's ambition that he must resort to violence, fragmentation, and sprawling exile in order to halt their creative assent?

If only a small percentage of western civilization's literary output remains alive, architecture fares much worse. The apparent stability of meaning of any building or pattern or motif is little more than an illusion perpetuated by the fact that our lives are so very short. When we take a broad view of architectural history, we see the aftermath of Babel: the proliferation of physical languages all referencing their own unique and utterly contingent circumstances, and often indecipherable to us today. Many aspects of Stonehenge or Machu Picchu serve as ready examples. And yet, the general sense that there IS a physical language there, the impression that all this *might* mean something, is the content of a language of hope. The dedication and joy one sees on the faces and hears in the voices of researchers at Stonehenge and Machu Picchu serve as evidence of both this assumption of meaning and its hope-inducing quality. This promise, if anything, is the only meaning of which architecture is capable of transmitting across time; and this, if nothing else, should both perpetuate and reward its ambition.

... a Contemporary Rejoinder

In our age, dismissive of if not hostile to direct presence, it is necessary to be strategic. To this end, there were four principal forms of otherness that prodded searches for meaning in earlier times, are maintained in the present in exemplary works of art, and could, even in information age architecture, trigger awareness so that shared meaning might take root. These forms – inconvenience, alienation, contrast, and antipathy – are unlikely to fit preconceptions of language appropriate to architecture. Therefore, I will briefly discuss each in turn, first outlining the term's most common associations, followed by an example of that form of otherness used in the visual arts, and ending with a note on the potential of each to provide a medium in which social values might grow.

Inconvenience

Inconvenience is a measure of literal distance or complication of path between two things sufficient to deny direct comparison. This measure of distance between places or objects is an active form of otherness. Inconvenience and the distinction of places are one and the same and correspond to the innate metaphor of spatialization of content in consciousness.

In many ways, this spatialization of content is the simplest and most straightforward form of otherness. Richard Serra's torqued steel sculptures operate by inconvenience, as does Siah Armajani's *Bridge over a tree*. In the work of both artists, there is a similarity to known experiences – in the case of Serra, references to mazes, labyrinths, and alleys; in Armajani, a combination of two readily nameable elements (bridge and tree) – but a profound dislocation in terms of path. Serra's work intentionally disorients; beginning, middle, end as well as notions such as closer and farther are rent from one another in favor of a magnification of the pervasive distance between observer and sky. Quite differently, Armajani's work undermines expectations of the simple relationship of here and there across a field by prompting us along an observable, graspable but utterly illogical path over a tree thereby subverting the function of "bridge," our relation to "tree," and the notion of traversing the ground. In both cases, the works are both conceptually and literally inconvenient. By comparison, John Portman's placement of a tree in the atrium of the Renaissance Center in Detroit is merely ironic.

Arguably, Serra and Armajani's works are architectural. The success of each artist suggests that the pursuit of an effective and ordered architectural language does not necessarily come at the price of simple one-to-one correlations of given object to accepted meaning. In such work, the territory between name and thing is cultivated when widened to the point that concept and percept are noticeably distinct. Through such distancing, the analogous spatializing of consciousness is redoubled – or perhaps I should say pre-doubled in the physical world so as to stretch the processing time of experience and open a gap in which alternative interpretations are afforded time to blossom as meaning.

Alienation

Alienation is a form of "inconvenience" that can be understood even at close range. While the actual physical separation of things might be small, their conceptual differences are such that the two things are seen as adjacent or layered but always juxtaposed as opposed to conjoined in meaning. In consciousness, alienation is the troubling non-coincidence of some bit of the world excerpted by our attention with some other bit of excerpted matter or ourselves or both despite their apparent proximity. A form of the uncanny used to artistic effect.

While popular as a technique of twentieth-century literature and cinema, the most widely known examples of visual alienation are the works of painter René Magritte. His most famous paintings, such as *La condition humaine* or *Ceci n'est pas une pipe (This is not a pipe)* clearly use alienation. In *La condition humaine*, we are presented with a painting of a window looking out at a beautiful landscape; however, a painting within the painting is situated between the viewer and a large portion of the view promised by the frame of that window. In *Ceci n'est pas une pipe*, on the contrary, we are clearly and simply shown a painted image of a pipe while underneath are scrawled the words of the title: "this is not a pipe." What is common to these works is a fictionalized promise (*there is a real landscape to be seen just behind this canvas* and *this is a pipe*) that is simultaneously denied in the body of the work and therefore acts to make us question the truth of all subsequent appearances: *what is it we are looking at?*

Truth or reality do not matter. What matters is that such works are triggers to existential questions. By definition, the act of questioning embeds the questioner in language regardless of whether he or she utters a sound or writes a word. A wordless question is still a question. More importantly, doubt more often than certainty drives us to communicate, to share our ideas and concerns with others, to build, imagine, and foster place. Though it sounds paradoxical, architectural alienation through a denial of final meaning prompts socialization.

Contrast

Contrast is the combination of inconvenience and alienation. It is weighed by an interested observer who acts as a fulcrum across which the physical separations of inconvenience and the classificatory destabilization of alienation are leveraged. Contrast is active and malleable in a way the previous two forms are not because consciousness attempts to narrativize contrast into diachronic plots of cause and effect, a series of reasons, and ultimately temporalized meaning.

Prologue: Babel ... **231**

Robert Irwin once created an installation in which he altered the color of every surface in a museum along the path to the gallery he was assigned. Every surface was modified except those in his space. To the white room at the culmination of this experience, he did nothing. The work of art, so to speak, arose as a result of the human perceptual apparatus; by fatiguing the eye through the obsessive presentation of one color, viewers were conditioned to 'see' his white gallery transform into the first color's complement within a few seconds of entering the blank white room. As with the work of Serra and Armajani, this work is already architectural in that it is both sensually and conceptually manipulated matter. It is also an exemplary work of contrast.

Seeing is not forgetting the name of the thing one sees but a prompt. In the case of contrast, to see is to be forced to ask questions due to a dissonance between a thing perceived and the name one wants to apply to it. Unlike the experience of alienation, contrast does not necessarily emerge as, or result in, an either/or construct but potentially, as in the case of the Irwin work just described, it prompts a both/ and narrativization (the experience of a color AND its complement; of path AND room) that forces recognition of the temporal basis of experience and meaning.[6]

Antipathy

Antipathy is an instance of otherness so strong and so insistent that it will not rest as merely one of the forms of distance. Antipathy has the dangerous power of expelling, of rendering things oppositional. It is contrast made personal, vicious, even harmful. The antipathy-sympathy pair gives rise to all known forms of difference as the poles toward which resemblance can move – here receding from, there advancing toward comfortable forms of appearance – and is mirrored in consciousness as the tendency to incitement or conciliation.

Several artworks might serve as compelling examples of antipathy: among these Andres Serrano's *Piss Christ* and William Christenberry's *Klan Room* could be counted as exemplars. And yet, Kara Walker's racially and sexually charged silhouette cut-outs are more evocative. Everything about these works is familiar, known, and instantly recognizable: from the technique of cut paper to the black figure on white ground to the stereotypical imagery of gender, race, and hierarchical power relations in slavery. Here resemblance is turned against everything one might wish to see in children's kindergarten silhouettes. The mundane quality of every square inch of surface, every millimeter of profile edge, is put in the service of inciting shock and horror at the violence of repression and abuse.

Architecturally, this is the hardest of the four forms of otherness to understand. Few willingly pursue antipathy. Eisenman attempted something like it with the Memorial to the Murdered Jews of Europe in Berlin (Chapter 4). And Libeskind at the Jewish Museum, also in Berlin. Moneo's Museum of Roman Antiquities in Merida, Spain. Some of the unbuilt projects of John Hejduk and Lebbeus Woods come to mind. But none of these achieve the simplicity of means or ease of recognition that Walker does with her paper cutouts. Nor do these architects come close to providing the same opening for communicable content. In this acknowledgment a simple fact is revealed: architects fear resemblance far too much to simply provide surfaces onto which the general public can – and are encouraged to – quickly append their own bodies of knowledge, common agreements, folk truths, etc. much less their hopes and dreams. The built evidence of our information age suggests that architects do not believe that transparent meaning can evoke or incite or cause people to think. But this is not true. Kara Walker's silhouettes are powerful in direct proportion to their commerce with a physical language almost everyone knows. Her work is not obscure but neither is it trite; it does not tell pleasing stories or convey cinematic fantasy but it also does not retract into the narrowness of personal obscure narrative.

There are a few examples that exist halfway between architecture and art. Works with the edge of Kara Walker and the physicality of architecture. These are labeled folk-art or self-taught artists' structures, often dismissively. My favorite is the late Reverend H.D. Dennis' Margaret's Grocery in Vicksburg, Mississippi. Concrete blocks. Red and white (and a little yellow) paint. A bus turned chapel. 2x4s, corrugated tin, and wooden lattice. Plastic beads, souvenir shop trinkets, and Christmas lights. Bible quotes. Bible quotes everywhere. Newspaper wallpaper. Institutionalized racism mixed with religious indoctrination mixed with commerce. A grocery store, church, art garden. There is even a tower to alert passersby to the horrors of our information age (see Figure 18.1). It is falling down. It is in ruins. And it is inspiring.[7]

Architects would do well to take note.

FIGURE 18.1 Margaret's Grocery, Vicksburg, Mississippi, Reverend H.D. Dennis
Source: Photograph by author.

Notes

1   Finite does not connote narrowness so much as denote limits without which communicative potential would be squandered in randomness; and it seems clear from the fragmentary observations of Herodotus and the archaeological evidence that Babylonian builders were not given to randomness. The Babylonians undertook extraordinary public works projects aimed at social and political control. See *The History of Herodotus*, edited and translated by George Rawlinson, vol. 1 (New York: Appleton and Company, 1885), 178–200; David Gordon Lyon's "Recent Excavations at Babylon," *Harvard Theological Review* 11(3) (Jl 1918): 307–321; and Robert Koldewey's, *The Excavations at Babylon*, translated by Agnes Sophia Griffith Johns (London: Macmillan and Co., 1914).

2   An ancient claim that the proper name closes vision is not translatable into modernity's "seeing is forgetting the name of the thing one sees" – though the two expressions appear similar. The entropy of western architectural language, its fragmentation over a vast expanse of time, rend the two expressions: to Babylonians, it is possibly a warning of dangers inherent in privileging one aspect of sensation (the conceptual or abstract) to the detriment of the other (the bodily or physical) as if these are not co-necessities of experience; to fans of Robert Irwin, Paul Valéry's famed modern quote is an implicit accusation in which the name is denigrated as extraneous "noise" in the transmission of otherwise pure and complete sensory information.

3   As no made thing can ever stand completely outside the classification systems of its times, the artifacts of Babel are not open to direct comparison to artifacts made under modernity. Any pretense of timelessness, if the artifact is judged in its final state as a transmitter of sense, must inevitably fail.

4   It is interesting to note that the goal attributed to the Babylonians in their building of the Tower (to make a name for themselves) is accomplished, not in brick and tar, but by the recording of its destruction in Genesis. In other words, and a bit ironically, it is the biblical record that renders the Babylonians and their Tower famous.

5   Did the design of the Tower utilize this strategy? From the limited physical evidence available, I would say "no." The Tower of Babel was not the first ziggurat; brick was the most common building material in Babylon; and other civil engineering works of extraordinary scale were documented by Herodotus and have been verified by modern archaeologists. If the Tower challenged any convention, it was merely height; and height, even radical height, is insufficient to provoke an experience of antipathy.

6   This potential to present multiple contents (white and colorful, yellow and magenta, places of rest and paths for movement) as a whole comprised of serialized contrasts is well known. In this information age, however, surprisingly little of this is consciously embodied – in fear, I suspect, that such provocations somehow infringe on viewers' free experience of space; yet, as Marx might have said, freedom does not really exist in space, but in the soil (or on surfaces) and across time.

7   See Stephen Young, "'All of world-kind have been right here': The Theology and Architecture of Rev. H.D. Dennis," *The Southern Quarterly*, 39(1–2) (Fall–Winter 2000/01), 100–111.

FURTHER READING

Chapter 1

Castells, Manuel. (1996) *The Rise of the Network Society*. Oxford: Blackwell.
——. (1997) *The Power of Identity*. Oxford: Blackwell.
——. (1998) *The End of the Millennium*. Oxford: Blackwell.
Groys, Boris. (2014) *On the New*. New York: Verso.
Harries, Karsten. (1997) *The Ethical Function of Architecture*. Cambridge, MA: MIT Press.
Said, Edward. (1994) *Culture and Imperialism*. New York: Vintage.
Vidler, Anthony. (2010) "Architecture's Expanded Field," in A. Krista Sykes (ed.), *Constructing a New Agenda: architectural theory, 1993–2009*. New York: Princeton Architectural Press.

Chapter 2

Appadurai, Arjun. (2005) *Modernity at Large: cultural dimensions of globalization*. Minneapolis, MN: University of Minnesota Press.
Gleick, James. (2012) *The Information: a history, a theory, a flood*. New York: Vintage.
Kołakowski, Leszek. (1997) *Modernity on Endless Trial*. Chicago: University of Chicago Press.
——. (2001) *Metaphysical Horror*. Chicago: University of Chicago Press.
Vidler, Anthony. (1992) *The Architectural Uncanny: essays in the modern unhomely*. Cambridge, MA: MIT Press. In particular, see "Architecture Dismembered," pp. 69–82.

Chapter 3

Jameson, Fredric. (1999) *Postmodernism, Or, the Cultural Logic of Late Capitalism*. Durham, NC: Duke University Press.
van Toorn, Roemer. (2005) "No More Dreams? The passion for reality in recent Dutch architecture … and its limitations," *Harvard Design Magazine* 21(Fall 2004/Winter 2005): 22–31.
Woods, Mary N. (1999) *From Craft to Profession: the practice of architecture in nineteenth-century America*. Berkeley, CA: University of California Press.

Chapter 4

Eisenman, Peter. (1996) "The End of the Classical: the end of the beginning, the end of the end," in Kate Nesbitt (ed.), *Theorizing a New Agenda for Architecture: an anthology of architectural theory, 1965–1995*. New York: Princeton Architectural Press.

——. (2007) *Written into the Void: selected writings, 1990–2004*. New Haven, CT: Yale University Press.

Holl, Steven, Pallasmaa, Juhani and Pérez-Gómez, Alberto. (2006) *Questions of Perception: phenomenology of architecture*. San Francisco: William Stout.

Pallasmaa, Juhani. (2012) *The Eyes of the Skin: architecture and the senses*, 3rd edn. New York: Wiley.

Zumthor, Peter. (2006) *Thinking Architecture*. 2nd edn. Basel: Birkhäuser.

Chapter 5

Derrida, Jacques. (1976) *Of Grammatology*. Translated by Gayatri Chakravorty Spivak. Baltimore, MD: Johns Hopkins University Press. In particular, see "The Hinge [La Brisure]," 65–73.

——. (1978) *Writing and Difference*. Translated by Alan Bass. Chicago: University of Chicago Press. In particular, see "Edmond Jabès and the Question of the Book," 64–78.

——. (1996) "Architecture Where Desire Can Live: Jacques Derrida interviewed by Eva Meye," in Kate Nesbitt (ed.). *Theorizing a New Agenda for Architecture: an anthology of architectural theory, 1965–1995*. New York: Princeton Architectural Press.

——. (2000) "Pointe de folie – Maintenant l'architecture," in K. Michael Hays (ed.). *Architecture Theory since 1968*. Cambridge MA: MIT Press.

Frascari, Marco. (1996) "The Tell-the-Tale Detail," in Kate Nesbitt (ed.), *Theorizing a New Agenda for Architecture: an anthology of architectural theory, 1965–1995*. New York: Princeton Architectural Press.

Tschumi, Bernard. (1994) *Architecture and Disjunction*. Cambridge, MA: MIT Press.

Venturi, Robert, Scott Brown, Denise, and Izenour, Steven (1977) *Learning from Las Vegas: the forgotten symbolism of architectural form*. Revised edn. Cambridge, MA: MIT Press.

Chapter 6

McLuhan, Marshall. (1994) *Understanding Media: the extensions of man*. Introduction by Lewis H. Lapham. Cambridge, MA: MIT Press.

Scarry, Elaine. (1987) *The Body in Pain: the making and unmaking of the world*. Oxford: Oxford University Press. In particular, see Chapter 2, "The Structure of War," pp. 60–157.

Shannon, Claude E. (1949) *The Mathematical Theory of Communication*. Introduction by Warren Weaver. Urbana, IL: University of Illinois Press.

Chapter 7

Burke, Kenneth. (1969) *A Grammar of Motives*. Berkeley, CA: University of California Press.

Doesburg, Theo van. (1975) "Towards a Plastic Architecture," in Ulrich Conrads (ed.), *Programs and Manifestoes on 20th-Century Aarchitecture*. Cambridge, MA: MIT Press, pp. 78–80.

McWhorter, John. (2003) *The Power of Babel: a natural history of language*. New York: Harper.

Steiner, George. (1975) *After Babel: aspects of language and translation*. London: Oxford University Press. For an excellent review of modernity's literary turn from direct writing, see pp. 176–190.

236 Further Reading

Wittgenstein, Ludwig. (1997) *Philosophical Investigations*. Translated by G.E.M. Anscombe. Malden, MA: Blackwell.
——. (2001) *Tractatus Logico-Philosophicus*, 2nd edn. New York: Routledge.

Chapter 8

Casey, Edward S. (1998) *The Fate of Place: a philosophical history*. Berkeley, CA: University of California Press.
Giedion, Sigfried. (1967) *Space, Time and Architecture: the growth of a new tradition*. Cambridge, MA: Harvard University Press. In particular, see "The Research into Space: Cubism," pp. 434–443.
Massey, Doreen. (2006) *For Space*. London: Sage.

Chapter 9

Bloom, Harold. (1995) *The Western Canon: the books and school of the ages*. New York: Riverhead. See Chapter 16, "Freud: A Shakespearean Reading," pp. 345–366.
Freud, Sigmund. ([1919] 1955) "The 'Uncanny,'" in *The Standard Edition of the Complete Psychological Works of Sigmund Freud*, 24 vols. London: Hogarth Press.
Ramachandran, V.S. and Blakeslee, Sandra. (1998) *Phantoms in the Brain*. New York: HarperCollins.
Vidler, Anthony. (1992) *The Architectural Uncanny: essays in the modern unhomely*. Cambridge, MA: MIT Press. In particular, see the "Introduction" and "Unhomely Houses," pp. 3–14 and 17–44, respectively.

Chapter 10

Harvey, David. (2000) *Spaces of Hope*. Berkeley, CA: University of California Press.
Kołakowski, Leszek. (2008) *Main Currents of Marxism: the founders, the golden age, the breakdown*. Translated by P.S. Falla. New York: W.W. Norton & Company.
Marx, Karl. (1990) *Capital: a critique of political economy, volume 1*. Introduction by Ernest Mandel, translated by Ben Fowkes. New York: Penguin Books. In particular, see "Part One: Commodities and Money," pp. 125–244.
Williams, Raymond. (1977) *Marxism and Literature*. New York: Oxford University Press.

Chapter 11

Birx, H. James. (1998) "Evolution and Materialism: Critical Reflections," in *Evolucionismo y Racionalismo*. Zaragosa, Spain: Institución Fernando el Católico, 39–47.
Darwin, Charles. (1998) *The Descent of Man*. Amherst, NY: Prometheus Books.
Dawkins, Richard. (2004) *The Ancestor's Tale: a pilgrimage to the dawn of evolution*. New York: Houghton Mifflin Company.
——. (2006) *The Selfish Gene*. 30th anniversary edn. Oxford: Oxford University Press.
Deacon, Terrence W. (2013) *Incomplete Nature: how mind emerged from matter*. New York: W. W. Norton & Company. For more on design and purpose, see pp. 110–128; for more on information and evolution, see pp. 407–430.
Dennett, Daniel C. (1995) *Darwin's Dangerous Idea: evolution and the meanings of life*. New York: Simon & Schuster.

Further Reading **237**

Chapter 12

Foucault, Michel. (1982) "The Subject and Power," first published in English in H.L. Dreyfus and P. Rabinow's (eds.) *Michel Foucault: Beyond Structuralism and Hermeneutics*. and reprinted in James D. Faubion's (ed.) *Michel Foucault: power, essential works of Foucault, 1954–1984*, vol. 3, Paul Rabinow, series ed. (New York: The New Press, (2000), 326–348.

——. (1994) *The Order of Things: an archaeology of the human sciences*. New York: Vintage.

____. (1995) *Discipline and Punish: the birth of the prison*. Translated by Alan Sheridan. New York: Vintage.

Frascari, Marco. (1991) *Monsters of Architecture*. Lanham, MD: Rowman & Littlefield.

Hübsch, Heinrich. (1992) "In What Style Should We Build?" In *In What Style Should We Build: the German debates on architectural style*. Introduction and translation by Wolfgang Herrmann. Santa Monica, CA: the Getty Center for the History of Art and the Humanities, pp. 63–101.

Humboldt, Wilhelm, Freiherr von. (1999) *On Language: on the diversity of human language construction and its influence on the mental development of the human species*. Edited by Michael Losonsky and translated by Peter Heath. Cambridge: Cambridge University Press.

Taylor, Charles. (2016) *The Language Animal: the full shape of the human linguistic capacity*. Cambridge, MA: Belknap Press/Harvard University Press. See Chapter 1, "Designative and Constitutive Views," and Chapter 4, "The Hobbes-Locke-Condillac Theory," pp. 3–50 and 103–128, respectively.

Chapter 13

Bataille, Georges. (1986) *Eroticism: death & sensuality*. Translated by Mary Dalwood. San Francisco, CA: City Lights. In particular, see Part Two, Chapter II and III, pp. 164–196.

Durand, Jean-Nicolas-Louis. (2000) *Précis of the Lectures on Architecture*. Introduction by Antoine Picon. Translated by David Britt. Los Angeles, CA: The Getty Research Institute.

Ruskin, John. (2003) *The Stones of Venice*. Edited by J.G. Links. Cambridge, MA: Da Capo Press.

Taylor, Charles. (2016) *The Language Animal: the full shape of the human linguistic capacity*. Cambridge, MA: Belknap Press/Harvard University Press. See Chapters 8 and 9, "How Narrative Makes Meaning" and "The Sapir-Whorf Hypothesis."

Chapter 14

Damasio, Antonio R. (1994) *Descartes' Error: emotion, reason, and the human brain*. New York: Avon Books.

De Sade, Marquis. (1966) *The 120 Days of Sodom & Other Writings*. Compiled and translated by Austryn Wainhouse and Richard Seaver. Introductions by Simone de Beauvoir and Pierre Klossowski. New York: Grove Press.

Descartes, René. ([1641] 1996) "Meditations on First Philosophy." Internet Encyclopedia of Philosophy. *The Philosophical Works of Descartes*. Cambridge University Press (1911). Translated by Elizabeth S. Haldane. http://selfpace.uconn.edu/class/percep/DescartesMeditations.pdf

Pérez-Gómez, Alberto. (2016) *Attunement: architectural meaning after the crisis of modern science*. Cambridge, MA: MIT Press.

Chapter 15

Alberti, Leon Battista. (1988) *On the Art of Building in Ten Books*. Translated by Joseph Rykwert, Neil Leach, and Robert Tavernor. Cambridge, MA: MIT Press.

238 Further Reading

Summerson, John. (1966) *The Classical Language of Architecture*. Cambridge, MA: MIT Press. See Chapter 2, "The Grammar of Antiquity," pp. 13–20.

Tzonis, Alexander and Lefaivre, Liane (1987) *Classical Architecture: the poetics of order.* Cambridge, MA: MIT Press. In particular, see Chapter 7, "Critical Classicism: the tragic function," pp. 273–287.

Chapters 16 and 17

Eco, Umberto. (2014) *From the Tree to the Labyrinth: historical studies on the sign and interpretation.* Translated by Anthony Oldcorn. Cambridge, MA: Harvard University Press.

Summerson, John. (1966) *The Classical Language of Architecture*. Cambridge, MA: MIT Press. See Chapter 1, "The Essentials of Classicism," pp. 7–13.

Tzonis, Alexander and Lefaivre, Liane (1987) *Classical Architecture: the poetics of order.* Cambridge, MA: MIT Press. In particular, see Chapters 1 and 2, "Taxis: the framework" and "The Genera: the elements," pp. 9–115.

Vitruvius. (1960) *The Ten Books on Architecture*. Translated by Morris Hicky Morgan. New York: Dover.

IMAGE CREDITS

0.1 The four-fold structure of language
1.0 Markthal ceiling
Source: Photograph by J. David Lewis.
1.1 Markthal, Rotterdam, MVRDV Architects
Source: Photograph by J. David Lewis.
1.2 Markthal, Rotterdam, MVRDV Architects
Source: Photograph by J. David Lewis.
2.1 Public Library, Seattle, OMA Architects
Source: Photograph by Scott Penman.
2.2 Public Library, Seattle, OMA Architects
Source: Photograph by Scott Penman.
2.3 The structure of communication
4.1 Museo di Castelvecchio (exterior), Verona, Carlo Scarpa architect
Source: Photograph by David C. Lewis.
4.2 Museo di Castelvecchio (detail), Verona, Carlo Scarpa architect
Source: Photograph by David C. Lewis.
4.3 Memorial to the Murdered Jews of Europe, Berlin, Eisenman Architects
Source: Photograph by Dennis Daniels.
4.4 Therme Vals, Graubünden, Peter Zumthor architect
Source: Photograph by Sully Clemmer.
5.1 Parc de la Villette, Paris, Tschumi Architects
Source: Photograph by Amber Ellett Penman.
5.2 Pompidou Centre (façade), Paris, Piano and Rogers Architects
Source: Photograph by Amber Ellet Penman.
5.3 Pompidou Centre (corner), Paris, Piano and Rogers Architects
Source: Photograph by Scott Penman.
6.1 Chicago Federal Center, Chicago, Ludwig Mies van der Rohe architect
Source: Photograph by David Buege.
6.2 Chicago Federal Center, Chicago, Ludwig Mies van der Rohe architect
Source: Photograph by David Buege.
6.3 Shannon's diagram of communication
Source: Claude Shannon, *The Mathematical Theory of Communication*. Copyright 1949, 1998
by the University of Illinois Press. Used with permission of the University of Illinois Press.

240 Image Credits

7.1 Casa Batlló, Barcelona, Antoni Gaudí architect
Source: Photograph by David C. Lewis.

8.1 (a) Section of Loos' Lido villa; (b) Theo van Doesburg's 1923 composition of horizontal and vertical planes
Source: Drawings by Ryan Fierro.

9.0 Pantheon Dome
Source: Photograph by author.

9.1 Saint John's Abbey Church, Collegeville, MN, Marcel Breuer architect
Source: Photograph by David Buege.

9.2 Het Schip, Amsterdam, Michel de Klerk architect
Source: Photograph by J. David Lewis.

9.3 Het Schip, Amsterdam, Michel de Klerk architect
Source: Photograph by J. David Lewis.

9.4 Het Schip (detail), Amsterdam, Michel de Klerk architect
Source: Photograph by J. David Lewis.

10.1 Strata of physical language (based on Foucault)

10.2 Piazza d'Italia, New Orleans, Charles Moore architect
Source: Photograph by Laura Smith Taylor.

10.3 Lincoln's Inn Fields home and museum, London, Sir John Soane architect
Source: Photograph by Acroterion. Wikimedia Commons. CC BY-SA 3.0. https://commons.wikimedia.org/wiki/File:Soane_museum_gallery.jpg Converted from color to black & white.

10.4 Gucci
Source: Photograph by David C. Lewis.

11.1 Value transmission, taking translation into account

11.2 Value transmission, maker's perspective

11.3 Value transmission, perceiver's perspective

12.1 Zwinger, Dresden, Matthaeus Daniel Pöppelmann architect
Source: Photograph by David M. Morris.

12.2 Zwinger (detail), Dresden, Matthaeus Daniel Pöppelmann architect
Source: Photograph by David M. Morris.

12.3 Flying buttress
Source: Photograph by David C. Lewis.

13.1 St. Mark's Basilica, Venice, Domenico I Contarini architect
Source: Photograph by David C. Lewis.

13.2 The birth of perception, version 1

13.3 The birth of perception, version 2

15.1 Seeing versus knowing

15.2 Naming

15.3 The time of language

15.4 Santa Maria Novella, Florence, Leon Battista Alberti architect
Source: Photograph by Scott Penman.

15.5 Field of all possible grammars

16.1 Pantheon (interior), Rome
Source: Photograph by author.

17.1 Mosque-Cathedral of Córdoba
Source: Photograph by Amber Ellett Penman.

18.1 Margaret's Grocery, Vicksburg, Mississippi, Reverend H.D. Dennis
Source: Photograph by author.

INDEX

Note: **bold** page numbers indicate figures; numbers in brackets preceded by *n* are chapter endnote numbers.

Aalto, Alvar 43, 44
advertising *see* marketing
aesthetics and ethics 157
agency, linguistic 147–150; and discipline 148–149; and interchangeability of ideas 147–148; and subjectivity 149–150
Alberti, Leon Battista 135, 137, 187, 190, 191–192, 195
Alexander, Christopher 57
alienation x, 229, 230, 231; of architects, from design process 28
Allen, Stan 32, 37(*n3*), 80
Ankgor Wat (Cambodia) 135
anti-discursive methodologies 48–50
anti-reductionism 55, 64(*n9*)
antipathy 231–232
Appadurai, Arjun 19
Aravena, Alejandro 122
archetypes 47, 152
architect: alienated from design process 28; and authorship 24–25, 29(*n8*), 130–131, 141; formalistic 42–43; as hero 63; and increasing complexity *see* complexity/complex systems; intentions of *see* intentions; as making subject 3; and media 7, 12, 13; "paper"/"shop" 175–176; professional, recent emergence of 31–32, 33, 34–36; self-promotion by 8
architectural discipline 31–37; and capitalism/professionalism 33–34; late

33; marketing of 34; and pairs of identity/intention 41–42; recent emergence of 31–33; repetition in 33
architectural discourse xv–xvii, xviii–xix, xxi(*n4*), 2, 10–11; and architecture history 26–28; and as-if prerequisite 182; and media 13, 15; and norms/rules/systems xv, 17–18(*n21*)
architectural education 17–18(*n21*), 21, 29(*n12*), 57, 162, 164
architectural experience 49, 55, 206
architectural language xiii–xiv, xvii–xviii, xx, 15–16, 71, 148, 164, 166–167; -commodities 124–125, 126–127, 132; and Augustine 84; entropy/disorder in 36, 42, 220; four assertions regarding 73; legibility of 118, 119; and polysemy 28; and senses/perception 169, 178; variations/monsters in 155–156, *see also* communication, architectural
architectural practice: and ethics 13–14; four new principles in 15
architectural theory 67, 89(*n11*), 130; and formed matter/value 140–141, **140**; of middle way 57; and other theoretical traditions 24–25
architectural tradition 1–3; newness in 15; pluralism/minor architecture in 2, 3(*n1*); rift in forms/intentions in 3

242 Index

architecture: of architecture 63(*n*1); end of 44–46; origins of 103
Architecture for Humanity 13, 80
architecture journals 7, 21
"Architecture Where Desire Can Live" (Derrida) 53, 64(*n*13)
Arendt, Hannah xviii, 77(*n*4)
Aristotle 13, 14, 71–73, 78(*n*13), 81, 136, 155
Armajani, Siah 229–230, 231
artifact 103–104
artificial intelligence 203
Arts and Crafts Movement 85, 124
artworks, signatures on 218
as-if prerequisite 114, 137, 181–183, 210(*n*12)
Augustine, St. 84, 209(*n*7)
authenticity x–xi, 48, 49, 126, 163, 165
authorship 24–25, 29(*n*8), 130–131, 141
avant-garde 163
Aztec architecture 135, 137

Babel xvii, 46, 50, 64(*n*13), 73, 80, 83, 85, 101–104, 140, 223, 228; and artifact 103–104; and deity 102; and humanity 102–103; and knowledge 217–218; and Modernism 103–104, 107–108(*n*9); and naming 225–226, 233(*n*4); otherness of 228; and personal-social gap 188; and sense/communication 224, 227
Babylonian architecture 135, 152–153, 223–224, 225, 227, 233(*n*1)
Baird, George 57
Barcelona (Spain) 68, 85, **86**, 89(*n*15)
Baroque 28, 162, 172(*n*5)
Bataille, Georges 169
Baudrillard, Jean 128–129
beauty 47, 163, 176
Beckett, Samuel 19, 70, 71, 115
becoming 44, 106, 108(*n*14), 160(*n*30); and smooth/striated history/space 156–157
behaviorism 134
being *see* ontology
being-for-itself 21, 22, 217, 218
belief 13, 16, 68, 96, 108(*n*12), 112, 138, 141, 206; as act of imagining 160(*n*18); and epistemes 150; and meaning 135; religious 105, 136–137, 138–139, 152
Benjamin, Walter 61
Berger, John 187–188, 199(*n*2)
Bess, Philip 13
Bible xvi–xvii, 11, 143, 172(*n*4), 203, 211, 232, *see also* Babel; Genesis; Torah
bifurcations 73–74, 150–152, 156–158, 160(*n*23), 223

BIG 14, 33, 80, 122
bioform/biomorphism 15, 216, 220(*n*8)
biology 41, 81, 179, 186(*n*24), *see also* evolution, theory of
"Birth of Venus, The" (Botticelli) 169
blogs/blogosphere 7, 10
Bloom, Harold 19
Body in Pain, The see Scarry, Elaine
body, the xvi, 12, 47, 68, 79(*n*24), 143, 145(*n*15), 180; and architecture 33; and civilization 37(*n*5); and epistemes 147; and mind 41, 43, 74; universal 58
Both/And thinking 176, 184, 231
Botticelli 169
branding 80, 205
Breuer, Marcel 116–117, **117**
Bridge over a tree (Armajani) 229–230

caesura 55–56
Cage, John 25, 29(*n*15)
Calatrava, Santiago 14
call-and-response 167, 204
Callistratus 141
Capgras syndrome 111–113
capital 122
Capital (Marx) 122, 123, 129, 134
capitalism 33–34
Cartesian dualism 176, 178, 179, 183, 185(*n*8)
Casa Battló, Barcelona (Gaudí) 85, **86**, 89(*n*15)
Casa del Balilla, Rome (Moretti) 42
Casa Milá, Barcelona (Gaudí) 85
Cassirer, Ernst xiv, 113, 129, 144(*n*3)
Ceci n'est pas une pipe (Magritte) 230
Center for Maximum Potential Building Systems 14
Cervantes, Miguel de 19, 205
Charterhouse, Granada, Sacristy of (Arévalo/Vasquez) 162
Chicago Federal Center 68, 69, **69**, 70, **71**
Chicago Fire (1871) 36
Chinese architecture 37(*n*6), 135, 152–153
Chomsky, Noam 81, 88(*n*4)
Chora 55, 64(*n*2), 96, 125
Christenberry, William 231
cinema *see* film
Cinema Paradiso (Tornatore) 196–198, 199
cities 177; planning 1–2, 20, 116
civilization 32–33
Classical age 32, 58, 103, 187, 214; Foucault on 148, 158–159(*n*6); and history-commodities 124; and naming/ perception 190
Classicism xviii, xx, 25, 43; end of 44–45

collage 59
Colquhoun, Alan 57, 65(*n*21)
commodities/commodification 9–10, 123–125; language- 123, 124–125, 126–127; pleasure 128–129; and solicitation 130–132; and value/use-value 129
communication 28, **28**, 113, 135; mathematics of 75–76, **75**
communication, architectural 80–81, 85, 202, 220(*n*2), 224; five elements of xiv–xv; and norms/rules/systems xv; and progress/becoming 106; and repetition 206; and shared meaning 215–216; and uncanny 116–117, 118, *see also* architectural language
Communitarianism 80
community 105–106, 108(*n*12), 164, 215, 220(*n*11), 226
complexity/complex systems 35–36, 39, 55, 57–58, 64(*n*9), 69, 115
Condillac, Étienne Bonnot de 151, 152
Congress for the New Urbanism 57, 82
consciousness 84, 87, 108(*n*15), 146, 173–174(*n*20), 183; and naming 188–189, **189**; spatializing of 230
contrast 230–231
Córdoba, Mosque-Cathedral of 218–219, **219**, 223
Crary, Jonathan 47
creativity 162–163, 164, 173(*n*6)
Croce, Benedetto xx, 186(*n*22)

Darwin, Charles 122, 126, 141; and Marx 134, 135
de Klerk, Michel 117
de Sade, Marquis 15, 18(*n*21), 74, 137, 184, 203, 205, 206, 211, 227; intentions of 182–183; and post-Romanticism 183, *see also 120 Days of Sodom*
De Stijl 76
Deacon, Terrence 75, 79(*n*21), 134
Debord, Guy 33
deconstructivism 29(*n*10), 52–56, 80
Decorated 203
Deleuze, Gilles 18, 18(*n*21), 19, 29(*n*14), 79(*n*19), 116; on desire 65(*n*22), 97(*n*6); on Kafka 65–66(*nn*22, 30), 212; on minor architecture 3(*n*1), 151; on progress/becoming 106, 160(*n*30); on smooth/striated history 156–157, 165
Dennis, Reverend H.D. 232, **232**
derealization 82
Derrida, Jacques 35, 50(*nn*4, 6), 52–56, 69, 113, 132(*n*9), 158(*n*1), 206; and caesura/

fissure 19, 28(*n*2), 37(*n*12), 53–54, 55–56; and culture 53, 55, 56; and imitation/mimesis 30(*n*19); and language games 50, 63, 82; and ontology 53–56; and skepticism 56
Descartes, René 176, 178, 179, 183, 187
design intelligence 24
designer *see* architect
Desire 17–18(*n*21), 45, 51(*n*11), 88, 97(*n*6), 166, 169, 180–181; and stimulus/order 167, 168, 173(*n*18)
deterritorialization/reterritorialization 19
Deutscher Werkbund 85, 88–89(*n*7)
diagrams 15, 29(*n*12), 54, 91, **92**
Disney Concert Hall, Los Angeles (Gehry) 9
Duany, Andres 26, 27
Durand, Jean-Nicolas-Louis 83, 135, 137, 161, 162, 169, 176, 177; and forms/proportions 171, **171**, 172; and impediments to shared physical language 164–166
Durham Cathedral 216
dwelling x, 55, 56

Early English 203
Eco, Umberto 186(*n*22), 200(*n*7), 203, 205, 209(*n*7), 210(*n*11), 220(*n*10)
"Edmond Jabès and the Question of the Book" (Derrida) 53, 64(*n*12)
Egyptian architecture 37(*n*6), 135, 152–153; and Las Vegas 58
Einstein, Albert 104, 162
Eisenman, Peter 42–43, 44–46, **46**, 56, 64(*n*12), 77(*n*11), 79(*n*24), 80, 231–232
Elizabethan style 148
emotivism 14, 80
Engels, Friedrich 134
epistemes xvi, 146–152, 160(*n*17), 161, 202, 203, 228; as *a priori/a posteriori* truth 150, 151, 158–159(*n*6); and agency *see* agency, linguistic; and authority 149; and creativity 163; and discipline/rank 148–149, 152; Foucault on 148; and language 146–147, 149, 188, 199; and truth/speculation 150–152; and value 149
Etemenanki ziggurat, Babylon 226
ethics 13–15, 17(*n*19); and aesthetics 157; of intentions *see* intentions, ethics of; of spectacles 14–15, 18(*n*22)
eugenics 134
evolution, theory of 134, 184, 194
existentialism 19, 21, 53, 126
experience 75, 78(*n*16)

244 Index

feelings and architecture xvii, 42, 48, 49
film 9, 33, 34, 67, 115, 116, 196–198; and
  meaningful grammars 196, **197**; and
  ordering 199
Fiske, Pliny 14
Fletcher, Banister 2, 27, 89(*n*15)
flying buttresses 156, **157**
Ford, Richard 138, 144(*n*7)
form/function dialectic 71, 73, 75, 76,
  79(*n*24)
formalism, architectural 5, 13, 36, 42–44,
  45–46, 47, 52, 165; and language 57, 80;
  and names 58; and ontology 54, 56
formed matter 85, 96, 117, 136, 159(*n*6); and
  quality 139, 140, 141; and value *see* value
Foster, Norman 14
Foucault, Michel xviii, 15, 17(*n*19), 45,
  114, 132(*n*10), 144(*n*5), 147, 159(*n*9),
  186(*n*24); on *a priori/a posteriori* truth
  148, 158–159(*n*6); on language/
  representation 29(*n*12), 56–57, 78(*n*16),
  114, 151, 193, 201(*n*18); on strata of
  physical language 124–125, **125**; on
  subjectivity 149; on time/grammar 194
Frampton, Kenneth 10, 11–12, 83
Frascari, Marco 60, 65(*n*29)
freedom 162–164, 165, 166–167, 172(*n*1),
  173(*n*6), 233(*n*6); and acting in good
  faith 163–164; political/religious 172(*n*3)
Freedom Tower, New York (Libeskind/
  Childs) 35–36
frequency 61, 63, 68, 70
Freud, Sigmund 112, 113, 114, 115, 117, 122
Fuller, Buckminster 81
functionalism 13, 81

Garciá Marquéz, Gabriel 183, 191, 195
garden city movement 116
Gaudí, Antoni 85, **86**
Gehry, Frank 9, 14, 16(*n*3), 20, 25, 27, 80,
  87; Santa Monica home of 33
Genesis 101, 102–103, 225, *see also* Babel
Gideon, Sigfried 83
Gilgamesh 138, 139, 155
Gleick, James 24
Gödel, Kurt 145(*n*10), 165
Goff, Bruce 85
Gombrich, Ernst 58
Gothic 151, 195, 203
Gould, Stephen Jay 81, 141
Graafland, Arie 11, 12
grammar: and film 196, **197**; and tense 199;
  and time 192–195, **194**, 196, 203
Greek architecture 32, 37(*n*6), 71–72, 96,
  98(*n*14), 151; and Las Vegas 58

Greek philosophy 72, 178, *see also* Aristotle
green architecture 53, 79(*n*24)
green spaces 35
Greenberg, Allan 27
Greenberg, Clement 19
Ground Zero Memorial (New York) 36
Guattari, Félix 18, 18(*n*21), 19, 29(*n*14),
  79(*n*19), 116; on desire 65(*n*22), 97(*n*6);
  on Kafka 65–66(*nn*22, 30), 212; on
  minor architecture 3(*n*1), 151; on
  progress/becoming 106, 160(*n*30); on
  smooth/striated history 156–157, 165
Guggenheim, Bilbao (Gehry) 9

Hacking, Ian 83
Hadid, Zaha 87
Hagia Sophia, Istanbul 208–209, 220
Harlequins (Picasso) 219
Harries, Karsten 15
Heidegger, Martin 41, 53, 55, 64(*n*14), 82,
  113, 116, 126
Hejduk, John 42, 231–232
Heraclitus 70, 71–72, 156
Herder, Johann Gottfried 170
Herodotus 225, 233(*nn*15)
Het Schip, Amsterdam (de Klerk) 117,
  118, **119**, **120**
heurism 72, 75, 78(*n*13)
hierarchies xv, 25, 37(*n*3)
hierarchy of needs 135
"Hinge, The" (Derrida) 53
Hirstein, William 112
history 1, 2, 10; architecture ix, xix, 26–28,
  45, 183–184, 186(*n*24), 226–227;
  backward xviii, xx, xxi, 223; of forms/
  intentions 3; and information age
  202–203; and perception 171–172, **171**;
  stratification of 123–125, **125**, 156–158
Hitchens, Christopher 10, 12, 16(*n*6),
  132(*n*17)
Hobbes, Thomas 151, 152
holistic design/construction 176
Holl, Steven xviii, 41, 43
Hollein, Hans 71
Hübsch, Heinrich 135, 137, 144, 155–156,
  172, 176, 177, 187; on bifurcation 151;
  on episteme/style 147, 149, 150, 161;
  on novelty/variation 8, 16(*n*2); on
  truth/rightness 152
Hugo, Victor xiii, 31, 33, 47, 73, 79(*n*24),
  103, 107, 204
Humboldt, Wilhelm von xiv, 65(*n*25), 80,
  146, 151, 156, 159(*n*15), 167, 170,
  174(*n*23)
Husserl, Edmund 41, 78(*n*13), 82

Index **245**

Huxtable, Ada Louise 10
Hymes, Dell 152

Ibsen, Henrik 130
ideational content xvii, xviii, 48, 49, 227;
and emotional content 50(*n*6);
incompleteness in 165, 166; and sensual
169, 228
identity 39–41, 179, 181, 220(*n*11)
Il Girasole, Rome (Moretti) 42
imagination 50(*n*4)
Incan architecture 135, 137
inconvenience 229–230
Industrial Age 11, 112, 122
Industrial Revolution 124
information age xviii, 46, 57, 81, 177, 198;
community in 105–106, 215; freedom
in 162, 163–164, 233(*n*6); function/
decoration in 147; information glut in
24; lack of historical reference in
202–203; late 7, 10, 12, 15, 25, 33; and
Marx 122–123; media/migrations
19–20; and misidentification/uncanny
112–113; rejection of order/shared
meaning in 161–162, 163, 164–166;
religion/faith in 103, 104; and sameness/
difference 26; space/spatial thinking in
177–178, 180, 204; *true/false* in 119;
uncanny in 114, 118
information theory and architecture xiii,
xiv–xviii, 14; and abandonment of
myths/metaphors xv–xvi; and direct/
indirect concerns xv; and five elements
of communication xiv–xv; and
mathematics of communication 75–76,
75; and noise interference 14
Ingels, Bjarke 14, 80
innovation, technological 8, 16(*n*2), 33, 35,
150, 164
intentions 77, 170–171; and as-if
prerequisite 181–183; and authorship
24–25, 29(*n*8); ethics of 20–22; and
motivations 29(*n*7); primacy of 24; and
sameness/difference 25–26
internet xiv, 8, 125–126
Irigaray, Luce 48
irony 52, 56–59, 80, 226, 229
irrationality 74
Irwin, Robert 25, 231, 233(*n*2)
Izenour, Steven 57–59

Jacobs, Jane 177, 179, 210(*n*14)
Jameson, Frederic 33
jangadas 60, 61
Japan 37(*n*6), 135

Jay, Martin 47
Jaynes, Julian 50(*n*5), 113–114, 160(*n*23),
173–174(*n*15); 220(*n*4); on consciousness
108(*n*15), 173–174(*n*20), 183, 185(*n*6)
Jencks, Charles 29(*n*10), 57
Jesse Window, Dorchester 203–204, 216
Jewish Museum, Berlin (Libeskind) 231
Jones, Inigo 159–160(*nn*10, 16)
Joyce, James 15, 18(*n*21), 63, 203, 205,
211, 227, *see also Ulysses*
Judeo-Christian tradition xvi–xvii, 105,
143, 205, *see also Bible*

Kafka, Franz 15, 18(*n*21), 25, 29(*n*14), 114,
205, 212
Kahn, Louis 43, 44
King's College Chapel, Cambridge 195, 196
Kipnis, Jeff 42–43
Klan Room (Christenberry) 231
knowing 217–218; three modes of 163,
172(*n*4)
Koolhaas, Rem xiii, 14, 16(*n*3), 57; and
Seattle Public Library 22, **22**, **23**, 62
Krier, Leon 26, 27
Kuhn, Thomas 193

La condition humaine (Magritte) 231
La Tourette (Le Corbusier) 11
labor 77(*n*4), 122, 124, 131
Lake Shore Drive apartments, Chicago
(van der Rohe) 68–69
landscape 15, 207; architecture 25, 135
language xiii–xxi, 15–16, 56–59, 65(*n*25),
106–107, 173(*n*15); abstract nouns
190–192; anti- 47; and bifurcation
150–152; as currency 190–191; and
desire 168–169; and epistemes *see*
epistemes; four-fold structure of xviii,
xix; games xix, 50, 52, 80–88, 139; and
image/tense 196–199; invention of/
early 174(*n*23); and materiality/organic
84–88; and media 11, 12; and
phenomenology xix, 43, 47; physical *see*
physical language; and public vs. private
81–84; and representation 195,
201(*n*18); stratification of 124–125, **125**;
and temples *see* temples/sacred buildings;
and thought 200–201(*n*14); and uncanny
118; written xiv, 2, 84, 200(*n*9),
211–212, *see also* communication;
grammar; names/naming; nouns
language-commodities 123, 124–125,
126–127, 132
Language/Nature/Desire 113, 115, 116,
124, **125**

246 Index

late information age xv, 15, 16, 36, 68; critics 15; and media 7, 10, 12
Latrobe, Benjamin 33
Le Corbusier 11, 48, 53, 104
Learning from Las Vegas (Venturi/Scott Brown/Izenour) 57–59, 67
Lefaivre, Liane 192
legibility 20, 57–58
Leibnitz, Gottfried Wilhelm 192, 220(*n*3)
Leibniz, Gottfried Wilhelm xiv
Letchworth, Hertfordshire 116, 118
Lévi-Strauss, Claude 47, 56–57, 65(*n*25)
libertines 73–74
Libeskind, Daniel 231–232
Lin, Maya 25, 45
Lincoln's Inn Fields home/museum, London (Soane) 126–128, **127**
linguistics 53, 72, 118, 186(*n*24)
literary criticism 41, 52
literature 79(*n*19), 87, 195, 201(*n*19); absence of space in 204; desire in 169; uncanny in 113–116
Locke, John 81, 151, 152
Longleat, Wiltshire 148
Luke, Timothy 11
Lynn, Greg 163

MacArthur Foundation 122
Machu Picchu (Peru) 135, 228–229
McKim, Charles Follen 33
McLuhan, Marshall 74
McMorrough, John 3(*n*2)
McWhorter, John 81, 89(*n*12)
Magritte, René 231
Mannerism 106, 172(*n*5)
Margaret's Grocery, Vicksburg (Dennis) 232, **232**
marketing 9, 13, 34
Markthal, Rotterdam (MVRDV) 8, **8**, **9**, 10, 195, 196, 198; ceiling **5**; mural 82
Marx, Karl 81, 122–123, 132(*nn*1, 10), 203, 205; and Darwin 134, 135; and historical strata 123, 124, 125; and process 124; and value/exchange of commodities 123, 129, 130, 132(*n*13), 133(*n*19)
Marxism 122, 211; and process 124
Maslow, Abraham 113, 135
Massey, Doreen 106
master builders 2, 35, 224
materialism/materiality 28, 41, 85, 87
mathematics 140, 150, 165, 173(*n*18)
Mayan architecture 135, 137, 152–153, 156
Mead, William Rutherford 33

meaning 33, 73–75, 82, 83–84, 106, 227, 228–229; and abstract nouns 187; and communication 75–76, 135; in information age 161–162; shared, rejection of 161–162, 163, 164; and uncanny 113, 114, 115, 119; and usefulness 135, 138; and value 136–138
meaning-message 74
meaninglessness 56, 74, 85, 215, 227
media xiii, xix, 10–16, 31, 41, 81; and architects/architecture 12, 21, 107; double narrative of 11; historical shallowness of 10–11; late xv, xxi(*n*4); news 10; proliferation of categories of 12; and teleology 11; as theater 7, *see also* marketing
Meier, Richard 16(*n*3)
Memorial to the Murdered Jews of Europe (Eisenman) 45, **46**, 231
Mencken, H.L. 134
Merleau-Ponty, Maurice 41, 113
metaphor xv–xvi, 47, 124, 136, 167, 173–174(*n*20), 215, 217
metaphysics, end of 45
Metro Station (Paris) 85
Michelangelo 19
minor architectures 2, 3(*n*1)
misquotes 57, 58
Mockbee, Samuel 14, 17(*n*20), 122
Modernism xviii, xx, 2, 20, 24, 28, 41, 63, 88, 203; and Babel 103–104; and language/vision 47, 48, 57, 107–108(*n*9), 113–114; and ontology 53; and systems of meaning 113; transition from Romanticism to 124, **125**, 126, 133(*n*18), 136; and uncanny 113–115, 116
modernity 19–36, 50, 85, 143, 183, 233(*nn*2, 3); and designer/designed 21–25; and ethics of intentions 20–21; and history 26–27; and information age media/migrations 19–20; and language/communication 85, 89(*n*17), 119; and sameness/difference 25–26
modernization 55–56
Moneo, Rafael 117, 231–232
monsters 155, 156, 158, 160(*n*30)
Montesquieu 150
Moore, Charles 126–128, **127**, 129
Moretti, Luigi 42
Murcutt, Glenn 14
Muschamp, Herbert 10
Museo di Castelvecchio (Scarpa) 39, **40**
Museum of Roman Antiquities, Merida (Moneo) 231

MVRDV Architects 7–8, **8**, **9**, 10, 14, 33, 80, 122, *see also* Markthal
Mycenae (Greece) 135, 137
myth xv–xvi, xviii, 17(*n*19), 83–84, 102, 104, 118, 163

names/naming 42–43, 58, 62–63, 67, 168; and Babel 102, 103, 225–226; and Classical age 187–190; and judging 170; as proof of consciousness 188–189, **189**; and works of art 218
natural selection *see* evolution, theory of
Neo-Platonists 53
neotraditionalism 13
Neumann, Johann Balthasar 184
New Babylon (Nieuwenhuys) 73
new pragmatism 24
New York Times 7, 90–91
Nietzsche, Friedrich 15, 18(*n*21), 53
Nietzschean aesthetics 13, 14
Nieuwenhuys, Constant 73
noise 75–76, 77, 233(*n*2)
North Wabash building, Chicago (van der Rohe) 67–68
nostalgia 48, 51(*n*18)
nouns 187; abstract 190–192

object-subject relations 128, 129
objectivity 141, 204
observer effects 165–166
OMA 14, 33, 80, 122
120 Days of Sodom (de Sade) 116, 169, 175, 179–181, 226; bifurcation in 74, 151; and Descartes 176–177, 183; difference/hyper-difference in 62, 131; identity in 181; and intention 182–183; otherness in 228; and social contract 180, 185(*n*13); and spatial/post-spatial thinking 180–181; and uncanny 116, 119
ontology 19, 21, 53–56, 72, 168, 178; and plenitude 70–71; of seeing 216–217; of signatures 218
orientalism of matter 87–88
Origin of Species (Darwin) 134
ornament 57, 61–62, 196; technology as 67, 68
Other/otherness xvii, 87, 141, 177, 228, 229–232, 233(*n*2); and alienation 230; and antipathy 231–232; and contrast 230–231; and inconvenience 229–230; and Self xviii, 20

palimpsests 124, 128, 129, 183, 207
Palladio, Andrea 187

Pallasmaa, Juhani 41, 46–50, 56; anti-discursive methodologies of 48–50
Pallasmaa/Holl/Zumthor 80
Pantheon **109**, 208–209, **208**
Parc de la Villette, Paris (Tschumi) 54, **54**, 59
Parker, Barry 116
Parmenides 72, 156
perception 95, 169–172, **171**, 202, 209(*n*2); and conception 44; direct/mediated 8; and intention 170–171; and language/ideation xvii–xviii, xix; and naming/judging 170, 187–189; and seeing 188; and time 192–193, **194**, *see also* seeing
Pérez-Gómez, Alberto 41, 184(*n*4), 201(*n*15), 204, 206
Perpendicular 203
Pevsner, Nikolaus 2, 83, 132(*n*7), 133(*n*18), 153, 159(*nn*10, 16), 172(*n*5), 205, 212, 220
phenomenology, architectural xvii, xviii, 11, 12, 36, 41–50, 165, 183; and anti-discursive methodologies 48–50; and language 57, 80, 82, 88; language-experience dichotomy in xix, 43; and names 58; and ontology 54, 56; and Pallasmaa 46–50
Phronesis 72–73
physical language xvii, 15, 57–59, 135–136, 159(*n*9), 211–212, 232; and abstract nouns 191, 192; accessibility of, four hypotheses on 212–214; and as-if prerequisite 181–182; and Babel 85, 107(*n*9–10); and community 106; five impediments to 164–166; as formed matter *see* formed matter; and freedom/creativity 162–163, 166–167, 173(*n*6); and grammar/time 193, 195; and historical strata 124–125, **125**; literacy 91, 96–97, 118; and need/comfort/pleasure 134–136; and other language systems 65(*n*25), 106; and perception **171**, 172, 188, 189–190; and postmodernism 126; and social order 214–216; and technique 181; and three modes of knowing 163; transparency of 213, 214; true principles of 166–167; and written language 212, 213–214, *see also* architectural language
physiognomic meaning 58
Piano, Renzo *see* Pompidou Centre
Piazza d'Italia, New Orleans (Moore) 126–128, **127**, 129
Pichler, Walter 78(*n*16)
Pilgrimage Church, Vierzehnheiligen (Neumann) 184

248 Index

Pinker, Steven 81
Piss Christ (Serrano) 231
pledge 136, 137–138, 141, 147, 150, 227
plenitude 70–71
poetics xviii, 10, 11–12, 43
poetry 56, 72
Pollack, Sydney 20
Pompidou Centre, Paris (Piano/Rogers)
    14, 52, 59–63, **60**, **61**, 67, 80; legacy of
    68; and *São Pedro* 60, 61, 62, 225
Pöppelmann, Mattheus Daniel 153–156,
    154, **155**, 184
Popper, Karl 134
Portman, John 229
positivism 72, 75, 78(*n*13), 134
post-Romanticism 124, 125–126, 128,
    130; and de Sade 183; and Joyce 116,
    190; and value 126, 129, 132, 136,
    143–144
postmodernism xviii, 20, 28, 29(*n*10), 203;
    and authorship 24, 130–131; and
    information 68, 70; and profession of
    architecture 31, 33, 36, 41; and
    relativism/meaninglessness 33, 82,
    200(*n*11), 205, 215; and value 68, 126,
    128–129
poverty/homelessness 13, 17(*n*19)
power relations 149, 159(*n*14)
Pragmatist tradition 29(*n*11)
presence 80, 217–218, 229
Price House (Bartlesville, Oklahoma) 86
printing xiii, 31, 45, 47, 51(*n*17), 107
production, episteme of 148–149
program, as unifying principle 15
progress and becoming 106, 160(*n*30)
Protestantism 105, 106
Pruitt-Igo 41
psychiatry/psychoanalysis 72, 111, 141, 152
psychology xix, 25, 41, 58, 108(*n*9), 118,
    203; gestalt 95; Jungian 152; and
    language 135, 173(*n*15); of perception
    170
public vs. private 81–84
publishing and architecture, co-evolution
    of xiii

quantity-quality, bifurcation of 73–74
quantum mechanics 95, 150, 165–166, 193
Quine, W.V. 140, 141

Rajchman, John 24, 29(*n*12)
recycling 85
relativity 91, 104
religion 85, 106, 166, *see also* Babel; Bible
Renaissance 28, 106, 178

Renaissance Center, Detroit (Portman) 229
repetition 33, 60, 61, 68, 76, 205–209
resemblance 83, 179, 199, 202–204,
    215–216; and biomorphism 216,
    220(*n*8); cycles of 216–219; subversion
    of 231; value of 202–204
reverse chronology xx
Rio de Janeiro (Brazil) 59–60
Rogers, Richard *see* Pompidou Centre
Roman architecture 32, 37(*n*6); and Las
    Vegas 58
Romanesque 215, 216
Romanticism xviii, xx, 53, 114, 119, 152,
    158, 165–169; and impediments to
    shared physical language 162–166;
    mind-nature connection in 167; and
    monsters 155, 156; and passion/order
    167–169; and perception 170; transition
    to Modernism from 124, **125**, 126,
    133(*n*18)
Rome (Italy) 42, 67
Rome, Open City (Rossellini) 67
Rorty, Richard 82
Rossellini, Roberto 67
Rousseau, Jean-Jacques 7, 30(*n*19), 47,
    50(*n*4), 81, 113, 200(*n*6); and social
    state/contract 132(*n*5), 135, 139,
    144(*n*3), 147, 160(*n*19), 180, 212, 215,
    216
Royal Crescent, Bath (Wood the Younger)
    137
Rural Studio 13, 14, 17(*n*19), 33
Rushdie, Salman 183, 191, 195, 205
Ruskin, John 100, 107, 137–138, 151, 156,
    172(*nn*1, 4), 195; and St. Mark's Basilica
    167–168, 183
Russian Ark (Sokurov) 9

Said, Edward 10, 12, 15, 17(*n*17)
St. Ignatius, Seattle xviii
St. John's Abbey Church, Collegeville
    (Breuer) 116–117, **117**
St. Mark's Basilica, Venice 167–168, **168**,
    183
sameness/difference 25–26
Santa Maria Novella, Florence (Alberti)
    195, **195**, 196, 198–199
São Pedro 60, 61, 62, 225
Sapir, Edward 163, 166
Sapir-Whorf hypothesis 166
Sartre, Jean-Paul 19, 53, 126
Scarpa, Carlo 39, **40**, 43, 44, 48, 117
Scarry, Elaine 37(*n*5), 82, 89(*n*10), 126,
    160(*n*18), 166, 179, 185(*n*11), 209(*nn*2,
    5); on authorship 143, 145(*n*15); on

form/function 79(*n*24); and Marx 200(*n*4), 211; on war 68, 78(*n*17)

Schiller, Friedrich 85

Schlegel, Friedrich 19

science x, 55, 64(*n*9), 72, 104, 134, 186(*n*24), 193; and art xviii, 35, 36; and epistemes 150, 151

Scott Brown, Denise 57–59

Scruton, Roger 85

Seagram Building (New York City) 67–68

Seattle Public Library 22, **22**, **23**, 62

seeing xvii, 47, 187–188, 216–217; and form/space 105; and knowing 188, **188**; and naming/forgetting xix, 12, 41, 49, 58, 170, 173(*n*6), 219, 233(*n*2); and perception 188

self-referential cycle 24–25

self-substantiation 143

sensation 43, 170, **171**, 175, 183, 184, 188, 225, **225**–229; and ideation 73, 157, 167–168, 173(*n*18); and naming 225–226; shared 226–229

sense 224, 233(*n*3)

Serra, Richard 229–230, 231

Serrano, Andres 231

Sesame Street 29(*n*11)

Shakespeare, William 19, 150

Shannon, Claude xiv, 14, 75–76, **75**, 77, 79(*n*21)

Sharples, William 175–176, 184

SHoP Architects 175–176, 184

signatures 218–219

signs xv, 13, 83, 132, 204–209, 209(*n*7); and ideologies 209–210(*n*9); and literature 179, 204, 205, 206; and repetition 205–209; and space 204–205

silence 25, 49

Siza, Álvaro 117

Skinner, B.F. 134

Soane, Sir John 126–128, **127**

social constructs/relations 123–124

social contract *see under* Rousseau, Jean-Jacques

social Darwinism 134

social justice 13, 33, 79(*n*24), 150

social media xiv, 125–126

social order 214–216

social transubstantiation 144(*n*3), 149, 191, 192

Sokurov, Alexander 9

SOM 33

Sontag, Susan 10

Sophia-Phronesis separation 72–73

space 104–107, 108(*n*12), 176, 177–179, 217; body in xvi, 178; and Cartesian dualism 178–179; and communication 205, 206–208; and de Sade 180–181; Einsteinian 104–105; and literature 204; mental 70–71, 226; and perception/language 124–125, **125**, 169–170, **171**, *see also* void

spacing 53–54, 55–56

Speaks, Michael 24

spectacle of ethics 14–15, 18(*n*22)

Steiner, George 25, 29(*n*17), 45, 89(*n*8), 101, 113, 145(*n*9), 185(*n*15), 212, 217

Stern, Robert A.M. 26, 27

Stonehenge 228–229

Strindberg, August 130

student protests (1968) 39

style 146, 147, 148, 156, 161, *see also* epistemes

subjectivity 46, 81, 122, 139, 149–150, 164–165, 204

suburbia 35

Sullivan, Louis 73

sustainable architecture 14, 164, 183

Sykes, A. Krista 2, 3(*n*2)

symbol/space, hierarchy of 57, 58–59, 62

Tati, Jacques 115

taxonomies 147–148, 151; and fossils 156; and monsters 155

Taylor, Charles 147

techne 78(*n*13), 151

technological determinism 52, 62–63

teleology xx, 2, 10–11, 14, 122

temples/sacred buildings 96, 98(*n*14), 152–156, 207, 217, 218–219; differences between 153–155, 208; effect of 219; similarities between 135, 136, 152–153, 156, 208–209

Terragni, Giuseppe 42

Therme Vals, Graubünden (Zumthor) 48, **48**

Thich Nhat Hanh 216

"This Will Kill That" (Hugo, *The Hunchback of Notre-Dame*) 37(*n*2), 47, 51(*n*17)

time 26–28; and grammar 192–195, **194**, 196, 203

Toledo Cathedral (Tomé) 162

Tomé, Narciso 162

Torah xvi–xvii, 166, 226

Tornatore, Giuseppe 196–198

tourism/tourists 9

traditionalism 26, 27

translation/transmission of value 29(*n*17), 138–143, **140**, **142**, **143**, 144

transubstantiation, social 144(*n*3), 149, 191, 192

'Truth' 63, 67
Tschumi, Bernard 16(*n*3), 54, **54**, 59, 82
Tzonis, Alexander 192

Ulysses (film, 1954) 198
Ulysses (Joyce) 10, 63, 66(*n*32), 115–116, 117, 129, 169, 226; "black panther vampire" in 190–191; otherness in 228
uncanny 112–120; in architecture 116–120, **117**, **118**, **119**, **120**; Freudian theory of 112; in literature 113–116; subversion of 115–116, 117
Unity Temple, Oak Park, Illinois (Wright) 207
unthinkable, ideal of 20, 21
Unwin, Raymond 116

Valéry, Paul 49, 233(*n*2)
value 68, 69–70, 76–77, 85–87; and authorship 141; and capitalism 122, 123; and epistemes 149; exchangeability of 136–137; as labor time 132(*n*1); and meaning 136–138; and post-Romanticism 126, 159(*n*6); simulacra 129; and solicitation 130–132; translatability/transmission of 29(*n*17), 138–143, **140**, **142**, **143**, 144
van de Velde, Henry 81
van der Rohe, Mies 37, 67–77, 80, 82; and fixed reference/closed loop 68–69, 70; form/function dialectic 71, 73, 75; and Shannon's communication theory 75–76, **75**, 77; and technology as ornament 67, 68; and value 69–70
van Doesburg, Theo 85, 86
Vasquez, F. Manuel 162
Venturi, Robert 57–59, 76, 82
Venturi Scott Brown 52, 56–59, 62, 80
verbs 187, 191, 192
Verona (Italy) 39
Vesely, Dalibor 10, 12, 17(*n*16), 201(*n*15)
Vico, Giambattista 170

Vidal, Gore 10
Vidler, Anthony 15, 33, 112
Vietnam Veteran's Memorial (Washington DC) 25
visual sense 47, 48
Vitruvian Man 85
Vitruvius 58, 132(*n*10), 135, 137, 187, 202, 205, 211
void 31, 32, 39, 88; and branding 80; charged 210(*n*14); communicative 41, *see also* space

Walker, Kara 231–232
war 68, 78(*n*17), 80
Weber, Max 20
Weisgerber, Leo 11
West, Rebecca 130
White, Stanford 33
Whorf, Benjamin Lee 56–57, 163, 166
window shopping/shopper 126, 128–129, **128**, 130, 131
Winter Palace (St Petersburg) 9
Wittgenstein, Ludwig 73, 82–84, 85, 89(*n*8), 113, 139; and usefulness of meaning 135, 138
Wood, John the Younger 137
Woods, Lebbeus 231–232
Woods, Mary N. 9
Word, the 82, 84, 103, 143, 191
World's Columbian Exposition (Chicago) 35
Wren, Christopher 144
Wright, Frank Lloyd 85, 191, 207

Xanadu Gallery (San Francisco) 85

Zeitgeist 163, 193
Zen Buddhism 29(*n*15); 43
Zumthor, Peter xviii, 10–11, 41; Therme Vals 48, **48**
Zwinger, Dresden (Pöppelmann) 153–156, **154**, **155**